MW01030279

JOHN of OLD,
JOHN of NEW

The Awakening of an Apostle

Sharon Prince

SHINING BRIGHTLY BOOKS
HOUSTON, TEXAS
2008

Shining Brightly Books
11010 Hanning Lane
Houston, TX 77041
713-896-9887 fax

ISBN# 0-9800061-1-2

www.JohnofNew.com

Production Team
Rita Mills of The Book Connection — Project Manager
www.BookConnectionOnline.com
Peggy Stautberg — Developmental Editing
Faye Walker — Line Editing
Vicki Mark — Cover Design

Ron Cooper — Cover Photo on Coast of Oregon December 1999
www.roncooperphotography.com

The paper used in this publication meets the requirements of the American National Standard for Permanence of Paper for Printed Library Materials Z39.48-1984.

Printed in the United States of America

To John, my spiritual brother—

Thank you for your unconditional love, friendship, and support.

Thank you for believing in me when I doubted myself and for giving me the courage to share our story with others.

Table of Contents

Acknowledgments

Thank you, Jeshua, for guiding me to find and to help awaken Your beloved friend and disciple, John, to his sacred mission. Thank You for speaking to me and through me for John and others, and for giving me this opportunity to serve You.

Thank you to my beloved angel friends and spiritual guides, whose unconditional love, and dedicated service to my life have blessed me many times over with divine guidance and protection.

I would like to thank my dear, dear friend John, who has encouraged, inspired, and awakened me to my higher purpose, and without whose love, friendship, and support, this story would not have come forth.

I would like to thank Randy for his patience and support of my spiritual work over the years.

I thank my mother, Barbara Prince, whose unconditional love and support and belief in me have given me the courage to be who I am and to share my spiritual gifts with others.

A very special thanks goes to Nick Bunick, for his courage to speak the truth and share his story, teachings, wisdom, and love with others, and for allowing us to quote him in our book.

I would like to also thank the following people who have courageously allowed us to use their real names, and whose professional support and spiritual gifts have blessed us tremendously: Judy Goodman, Carol Berman, Dr. Elizabeth Borg, and Michael Baumann.

Special thanks goes to my friend Brooke Parkhurst, for helping to edit the early incarnation of the manuscript; to Carol Nicotera-Ward, who blessed me with her many years of professional copy editing experience during the re-editing the first manuscript; and to the final editor, Peggy Stautberg, whose professionalism and support in this project has meant so much.

Extra special thanks goes to Rita Mills, for her belief, friendship and support of this project. Thank you for listening to the Higher Call to serve. Without you this book could not have gone forward.

I would like to thank my friends for supporting us and believing in us, including Kim Bunick DeNeffe and the former staff of The Great Tomorrow, Julia Hanson, and Peggy Keating. I would also like to thank John's readers, including "Sara," Atira, Jacquelyne Ellis, Kiara, Rita, the reader from the Renaissance faire, the reader at the Whole Life Expo in Ft. Lauderdale, and the others.

I owe a thank you to Dolores Cannon for allowing us to quote her and for giving us valuable feedback on this project.

Thank you to Ron Cooper for allowing me to use his beautiful photo for the cover of our book.

And last, but not least, thank you, my dear Rommy, for being my "lightning rod for divine guidance" when I needed you. I will miss our long walks together.

———•·•———

Story Behind the Cover Photo — By Ron Cooper

My wife Penny and I had been married 36 years when in February 1999, she was diagnosed with a stage four sarcoma. Her treatment included chemotherapy and a major surgery. On Thanksgiving morning, 1999, she died quietly beside me.

It was the darkest time of the year and one of the most difficult periods in my life.

After some discussion, my three adult children and my only grandchild decided not to spend Christmas alone, but to meet at the Oregon coast where we could share Christmas together and support each other.

Upon arrival the weather was typical for December on the Oregon coast, dark, wet, and stormy. The weather cleared near the end of the day and the sun began to shine through the clouds and my son took advantage of the break in the weather to walk on the beach. The black and grey that had filled the sky only a short time earlier, gave way to spectacular colors that reflected across the wet sand, creating a mirror-like reflection of the scene. I shot several frames before the display ended as abruptly as it began.

The remarkable sunset set a joyous tone for our Christmas together and I have always believed that it was a reminder from Penny that my profound sadness would end eventually and joy would return to our lives.

She was absolutely right.

Foreword

Sometimes our lives are suddenly changed; occasionally great things are required of us and in most cases, this story might not have been written. Let us assume that your life seems to be on track; things are going along well and you believe that you are doing the things you were meant to do. Out of nowhere, your thoughts, dreams and memories are filled with things you do not understand. Suddenly your life is no longer your own; you are on a journey that began thousands of years ago.

You are about to read a story about my friend, John Davis. I would describe him as a "man's man!" John is what I sometimes call a "gentle giant." He looks a little like an overgrown teddy bear, the kind of person you want to spend time with and introduce to your friends. John has a heart of gold and a depth of compassion that reaches into other people's pain. All of this is bundled up in a package that is sometimes transformed into a swashbuckling Renaissance kind of person.

Can you imagine how challenging it would be for anyone to venture into "reincarnation" and find themselves on a journey that began thousands of years ago? John's experience is something he had not counted on! It was hard for him to embrace what was happening. This book tells the story of how much a man must change in order to honor his destiny. You will learn of the challenges that John continues to face. What price would you be willing to pay, and just how far would your current belief system allow you to go? This has not been easy for John; you will feel the doubts and disbelief that he has encountered. Before you finish the book, I believe you will feel the gentle healing energy that is so much a part of John.

Would you be willing to share the story of your life and expose the wounds and disbeliefs of a spiritual journey? This has required a great deal of courage and determination from a man who faced his own demons. I am glad you have decided to read John's story, it will warm your heart and provide you with a wealth of information. This will not infringe on your belief system, but will take you on a life-altering journey.

John is not the first person, nor will he be the last, to go through such an experience; why then, are these books written? I know the author, Sharon Prince, well enough to say that this is not about finding her own fame. Within the confines of this story are many levels of spiritual awareness. John is an evolved, humble soul that came into his path a bit reluctantly. There are many spiritual coincidences that caused the paths of these two people to come together for *The Awakening of An Apostle*.

This book is a gift of hope for each of us! Your *path* will not necessarily be like John's, but I find great comfort in knowing that destiny brings us in touch with the people, places and things that compliment our own journey. Whatever your experience might be; no matter what this story will mean to you; do not be afraid to reach out beyond your level of understanding. Embrace your own unique adventure and perhaps a *messenger* such as Sharon, will tell your story one day. Walk with a good man who struggled with an issue of "reincarnation," something that would change his life forever. Feel his humility as he remembers walking with Christ. Look through John's eyes, and grow in spirit as he has.

—**Judy Goodman**

Introduction

Our work together began in the summer of 1997, when John and I met at the home of some mutual friends. Three weeks later, I would give John a reading that would change both of our lives and set us upon a journey that we never would have imagined possible. From the very beginning, we were guided to those people who would assist us and bless us with their support. We are grateful to the wonderful people who have enriched our lives; without them, this story would not be possible.

I was born with a gift that through the years I have learned to develop. What started out as warnings or premonitions later became more detailed messages for others and myself. I believe that every individual has the ability to receive his or her own divine guidance.

Some people say that I am a psychic reader, but I prefer to be called a spiritual reader. I receive information from a person's angels and spiritual guides that can enhance that individual's growth. I will be the first to tell you that I am not omnipotent. The purpose of my gift is not to predict lotto numbers. My readings are about spiritual growth and the big picture of an individual's life.

People often ask me how I know the things I do. It's hard to explain. It's something that has to be experienced to be understood. I receive information through intuition and psychic feeling (also known as claircognizance and clairsentience, respectively). Those are my strongest psychic centers. I have also used my third eye (clairvoyance) and psychic hearing (clairaudience) when doing readings. I truly endeavor to be as clear as I can be for a reading—to set aside my own ego and to trust what is coming through.

I first became aware that I had a gift at around the age of twelve when I started getting warnings and premonitions. As a teenager, I would pick up on information about people's personality characteristics and personal history only minutes after meeting them. These would be details that I would have no way of knowing unless I already knew the person very well.

By the time I reached college, my gift had become even more apparent. When asked, I could easily go around the room at a party and tell perfect strangers about their likes, dislikes, attitudes and talents. This would scare some people, but others were fascinated that I could know things about them without our ever having had a real conversation. When people started responding with strong reactions (both positive and negative) toward my gift, I realized I was definitely on to something. It was then that I also realized I needed to be responsible with my gift and use it only to help others.

This "knowingness," as I like to call it, has warned me of danger, reassured me when all was well, has instructed me in what to do during emergencies, and has given me insights and previews of future events in my own life, as well as the lives of family members and close friends. In my later teens and early twenties, I started getting information about future events, including visions, and was alerted when family members were in trouble or needed help. But it wasn't until I was going through a divorce from my first husband in my early thirties that I realized that I was what people call a "reader." The counselor I was seeing at the time was the person who first told me this; in fact, she asked me for a reading after we completed our work together.

My boyfriend who became my husband, a performer at the local Renaissance Festival, wanted me to work there, too. Knowing that I was an artist, he encouraged me to apply for a job as a face painter there. I contacted the woman who ran the concession for face painters and she informed me that she also supervised the massage therapists and readers. When I heard the word "reader" I knew that that was what I wanted to do. She set up an appointment with me for a reading in order to determine if she thought I was accurate enough to read for clients at the festival. Apparently she thought I was good because she hired me.

I was a little apprehensive, at first, to take the job because I had never done real readings for strangers before, but, with the support and encouragement of my mother and future husband, I went into it with a blind faith that I could do it. I ended up doing nearly 200 readings for complete strangers in seven weekends that year. People who had had readings from me at the festival asked me to give them private readings later, and recommended me to their friends. This is how I started doing readings, and I have been giving spiritual readings ever since—for sixteen years now.

How do I do it? I start with a brief meditation and invocation or prayer. Then I open myself up and let the guides and angels "speak" through me for my clients. The guides (as I call them collectively) usually start with a word or phrase, or sometimes a picture, which they then expound upon through intuitive thought impressions. I start speaking and the words just flow. I never know what I am going to say in advance, nor do I want my clients to give me their questions ahead of time. I want to be completely in the moment, receiving information as it comes. That way my ego and mind don't get involved and the information can come out purely.

The guides will usually deliver a personal message to my clients about what is currently happening in their lives, what issues they are dealing with, and how their circumstances are affecting them now. They may give my clients some advice or choices on how to handle a certain situation or problem, but they never tell them what they "must" do. After the initial message, I invite my clients to ask their guides any questions they may have. If my clients don't have any particular questions, then the guides will continue to give them information about their spiritual purpose here. Often the guides, in their initial message, will address the very issue the person wanted to know about in the first place.

The more open a client is, the easier it is for me to access information for him or her. I suggest that my clients meditate or say a prayer before their readings to open up the pathway between their guides and angels and mine. I tell my clients that they have the power to change any prognosis received during a reading that they do not like. Nothing is set in stone. Predictions are only based on the assumption that a person will continue on the same path without any major changes. I tell them that everything happening in their lives right now is the result of choices that they have made up to this point. If they don't like what is happening, they can simply change what they are doing or thinking and that will change the future outcome. It's that simple. We all have free will to determine our own future and we can call on our guidance to help us through any situation. I believe each of us has the ability to receive our own divine guidance if we are open to receiving it.

It is not my place to make decisions for others. My goal is to verify for others (even if it is at a subconscious level) what they already know within themselves to be true. In other words, the people I read for already know the answers to their own questions. I remind my clients that if something is said during the course of a reading which does not feel right to them, to either ignore it or set it aside to come back to later. Sometimes as an individual's perception changes, he or she is better able to process the information that had been received in a reading earlier.

I believe God speaks to each one of us every day, and that there is such a thing as personal revelation. Whether we receive this personal knowledge for ourselves or we give a reader permission to access it for us, our angels and guides are working on our behalf to make sure we are aware of our divine gift. It is our right as children of God to speak to our Creator whenever we want to and to receive answers to our questions. It is my belief that each of us is prepared, in our own ways, by our angels and spirit guides, to awaken to new levels of spiritual awareness, as we are ready for it.

It was no accident or chance happening that brought John and me into each other's lives. As I discovered later, John and I are from the same soul family (spiritual brothers and sisters who share a common goal or purpose), and our souls agreed, before we came into this life, to do this important spiritual work together. I believe that we all come here to do our own individual spiritual work—whatever that may be—and that we are guided to the people and situations we need to accomplish our spiritual goals. All of John's personal and spiritual experiences had prepared him, up to the point that we first met, for the influx of information we received in our readings and for the extraordinary experiences that followed. Everything in my personal and spiritual background had prepared me for being the messenger who would deliver the words that John received from Master Jesus and his angels.

My work with John has brought me to a new level of spiritual awareness. I am using clairaudience (or what might be called receiving channeled messages from spiritual beings) much more than I have ever done before. Because of this and the fact that I was given the incredible opportunity to speak for an Ascended Master such as Jesus, I went through moments of personal disbelief and doubt concerning my ability to receive and impart the messages clearly. I have also struggled with the issue of worthiness to do this work. Through it all, John has encouraged me to have faith in myself and in my ability to speak what was coming through me.

I share our story with you because, in my heart, I know that we have received messages from the Divine that are much bigger than either John or myself. These messages are for everyone. But it's not something that just we are experiencing. Anyone can ask for guidance from their angels, guides, and masters and receive answers. Anyone! I have learned that Jesus does not judge us, nor do our angels. We judge ourselves, and in so doing, we often cut ourselves off from our own divine guidance. We can communicate with God or Jesus or our angels anytime and anywhere, no matter how imperfect we may deem ourselves. I've found that the issue is not about our being worthy; it is about being open to this type of communication in the first place and having faith that we will receive it.

We do not need anyone to be a spiritual intermediary for us. We can go directly to God ourselves. We do not necessarily have to be in church to feel God's presence. We can speak to God anywhere! We can commune with God through nature and we can see God in our loving relationships with others. God truly dwells within each one of us! We have been conditioned to believe that we cannot be our own spiritual authorities, that we need someone else to tell us what is right for us. It is my conviction that we need to go within for our own answers. Within is where God dwells, not sitting up on a cloud somewhere outside of us. We have been taught not to trust our intuitions or inner knowingness. However, God communicates to all of us, everyday, through our thoughts and feelings.

It is wise for us to use discernment when considering the messages we are receiving. But it is also important to have an open mind. I have found that messages that teach love and bring out the best in us are from God. It is up to each of us to live our lives in the highest manner possible. Sometimes divine messages challenge us to grow, but the end result will always be for the higher good, and full of truth, if it comes from God.

Though many of the events spoken of in this book may seem incredible, they are true. I have endeavored to tell this story to the best of my ability with as much honesty and integrity as possible. The people in this story are real and most have agreed to let us use their real names. However, we have changed the names of a few people in order to protect their privacy. We are grateful to all our friends and others for the roles they played in bringing our story to you. When reading this book, remember that the divine plays a part in all our lives, every single day.

JOHN of OLD, JOHN of NEW

The Awakening of an Apostle

CHAPTER ONE

Old Friends Meet Again

It was a hot afternoon in Burlington, Ontario, August 1997. I heard voices coming from the balcony of the home of Ellen and Ian, some friends of ours who were hosting my husband, Randy, along with several other performers at the Ontario Renaissance festival in Canada. I went out to see with whom Susan, another house guest, was talking. I saw a big, attractive guy, with a neat brown ponytail and a striking dark beard sitting at the picnic table with a group of people. He had just arrived and was telling Susan about his recent divorce and the emotional upheaval he had been through. Everyone at the table seemed to know and like him. The first thing I thought was how familiar he looked—a lot like a fellow actor with whom I had worked back home in Houston, Texas. However, this man's personality and energy were very different.

I stood by Susan and looked over at him. When there was a break in the conversation, Susan said, "Sharon, I would like to introduce you to my friend, John Davis. John, this is Sharon Wothke. Her husband, Randy, plays with the Scottish band that is performing at the Renaissance festival." I offered my hand and John shook it. "Hi, how are ya?" he said in his deep, lilting voice. "I'm fine, thank you," I said, smiling back at him. Something about John felt so familiar, yet we had never met. "Why do I feel so comfortable with him?" I wondered. He felt like an old friend. The conversation turned light-hearted, and I heard him laugh. Again, there was that feeling of familiarity. John had a distinctive, warm laugh that just invited people into his space.

The next night, the den and kitchen area of Ellen and Ian's house was full of people eating, talking, and watching television. I started to walk over to where my husband was sitting. As I passed by the kitchen table, I noticed John leaning back in his chair watching the crowd of people. He was observing the area just above each person's head. When his eyes followed me, I saw that he was looking around and above me, but not directly at me.

At that moment, I realized what he was doing. "You're looking at my aura,[1] aren't you? You can see auras, can't you?" I said with delighted surprise. I thought it was pretty neat that someone there besides myself was tuned into spiritual energy. He seemed genuinely shocked that I knew what he had been up to. My assertion left him almost speechless.

"Maybe. Why do you say that?" he said with a mischievous chuckle.

"I know that's what you're doing, aren't you?" I insisted.

"Yeah," he admitted, "but how did you know?"

"I could tell by the way you were looking around me, but not at me."

"That's exactly what I was doing, but this is the first time anyone's ever caught me at it." We both laughed. "Not only that," I went on, "but you are a healer!" "I've been told that before," he responded, "but I don't know about that." John's eyes seemed to be able to look into a person's soul. There was definitely a spiritual bond between us. At that moment, the two of us became instant friends. I was excited to have found someone there that I could talk to about spiritual matters, and John was curious to know more about this person who was able to "read" him so well.

During the next week that John and I were both staying at Ellen and Ian's house, we talked a little about some of our individual spiritual experiences. I shared with John that I was a spiritual reader. He was curious about my intuitive ability for he had only had a tarot card reading before from a friend, a few years earlier. He also wanted to know more about this healing ability that he had been told he had. Although I didn't know it at the time, he wanted a reading from me; however, he wanted to test the waters, so he suggested to his friend, Kosha, another performer at the Renaissance festival, that she have a reading done with me first and give him feedback as to how she felt about it. Apparently her report was enthusiastic enough to persuade him to schedule an appointment with me a couple of weeks later when we were both in Maryland.

———•◦•———

I had retired from teaching earlier that summer to join my husband in traveling with the band full-time. I had been looking forward to participating at the Maryland Renaissance Festival,[2] where the band was scheduled to play two weeks after the Ontario faire. John's comedy sword fighting act was also contracted to do the Maryland Renaissance Festival, and I was looking forward to not only seeing the faire I had heard so many good things about but also getting to know my new friend, John, better.

2   Sharon Prince

As John's and my friendship developed during our stay in Maryland, we both felt we had known one another before. I do believe in the reincarnational cycle and that we all have the opportunity to experience various lifetimes as a way of coming to know God. I felt sure that we had a past life together. There are certain people—and I have met a few—whom we feel we have known all our lives, as soon as we meet them. I believe that many of these dear "old" friends are souls with whom we have incarnated before. When we see them again, there is an instant spiritual recognition.

A few days after arriving in Maryland, John scheduled his first reading. I didn't know John's personal history and had no idea what he wanted to know or ask about during his reading. We agreed to do the reading in his trailer, a place where he felt comfortable. He started by asking me very general questions having to do with his family and why he had had certain experiences with them. I could tell that he was testing me by not giving me any information at all about his family background. I tuned into John's energy field, and I told him, through spiritual guidance, that as a child he had felt unloved and unsupported. I could feel (though my eyes were closed as they always are for my readings) that this big guy was quietly crying. The sorrow was coming from deep within his soul. This sudden emotion surprised even him.

He was told he had chosen his family and those circumstances in order to experience what it was like to feel unwanted and that he had entered the body three months before birth in order to experience this. Our angels and guides explained to us that spirits enter their bodies at different times during the mother's pregnancy. Some surround their mothers and enter at the moment of conception, while others wait until closer to the moment of birth. We were told that it depended on the soul "doing" the entering and what it wished to experience.[3]

John's life experiences had allowed him to have compassion for others and gave him wisdom beyond his years. My words relieved him when I told him that these were his biological parents, who were doing the best they knew how to do, but that they were not his spiritual parents. For the first time, he had an intellectual understanding of why he did not have the family relationships and support he wanted. For the first time he realized that his parents were people who dealing with their own issues and who were not themselves perfect, and that it wasn't that he was unworthy of their love, after all. As John would later say: "My parents were in over their heads with six children, struggling to put food on the table. When you're the sixth child of seven children, you can easily get lost in the shuffle." He could now step out of his past, knowing that he was loved and watched over by beings who knew he was special and worthy of love.

We discussed many things in that first reading. John later told me how dumbstruck he was that I was able to pick up on all this information. Toward the end of the reading, I spontaneously said, "They're telling me you walked with Jesus."

John surprised himself by saying, "Yes, I did." Somehow when he heard it, he knew it was true.

I went on with the reading, almost forgetting about the information I had given him about that past life. Later, he asked me to elaborate on this for him. "I want to know more about this 'walking with Jesus' thing."

"Well, you know that that's a whole other reading in and of itself," I replied.

"All right, how about next week when we all go to Rehoboth Beach? There's a special place on Cape Henlopen where I want the reading to take place." (John had invited a group of people, including me, to join him for a couple of days at Rehoboth Beach, Delaware—his hometown. Cape Henlopen is just north of Rehoboth Beach near a historical town named Lewes.) "So will you do it?" he asked.

"Okay, but I don't want you to freak out if I tell you that you were an apostle or something!" I said half-jokingly. "I won't," he promised.

In the meantime, John went to the bookstore—a favorite pastime for him—and was browsing around when he came across the book *The Messengers* by Julia Ingram and G.W. Hardin, which told the story of Nick Bunick's spiritual awakening following a series of past-life regressions that uncovered his memories as the Apostle Paul. John had seen this book on several occasions in other bookstores. He repeatedly picked it up and put it down because the cover art reminded him of a romance novel. He would even try to read the jacket cover, but each time he looked at it, he put it down. This time when he picked it up, however, he opened it and was amazed at what he saw before him. There, on the first page he turned to, were the words "He Walked with the Master." Those were almost the same words that I had told him in the reading! This got his attention, and he knew immediately he had to buy it. When John saw me again, he showed me the book and briefly explained its premise to me. He told me he thought I should read it and didn't say much else about it. As it happened, I didn't end up reading the book until a year later.

After John had purchased *The Messengers,* but before the reading at

Rehoboth Beach the following week, something inexplicable happened. The faire was extraordinarily hot and people were wearing tank tops and shorts to stay as cool as possible. In fact, it was the kind of day during which most people were using their programs to fan themselves off, as sweat dripped from every pore.

During one of his shows, John noticed a man who looked as though he were in his thirties, sitting in the audience, who stood out from the rest. He had long, reddish brown hair, a neatly trimmed moustache and beard, and was wearing a long-sleeved tee shirt and blue jeans. John thought it odd that someone would be wearing clothing that warm on a day that was so hot. One might at least expect this gentleman to have rolled up his sleeves, or that his shirt would be wet with sweat. However, he was perfectly composed during the whole show; as far as John could tell, not so much as a bead of sweat formed on the gentleman's forehead.

As if being pulled by a magnet, John found himself looking out at this man every chance he could get. Each time their eyes locked, the man would look at John with an intensity that went right through his soul. Their eyes would meet again and again during the course of the show, and to John, it was as if there was no one else in the audience but him. "Could it be? How could it?" John asked himself. "He looks just like Christ." No matter what, he could not shake the feeling that this was not an ordinary audience member.

John and his partner Spencer were finishing up the show, which ends with John saying the line, "For God and for Country." John, who usually looks up into the sky when he says "God," found himself looking into the eyes of this young man again. The man smiled knowingly and nodded. Time seemed to stand still for a moment. There was a sense of recognition in John's heart that he could not explain.

As John and Spencer bowed to the audience, John once again turned to look at the man who had so captured his attention. He was gone. One would think that someone wearing long sleeves and pants would stand out in this crowd. Although the audience had just begun to leave, the gentleman was nowhere to be found. He had vanished.

———•—•———

The next Monday, the second week of September, a group of us traveled with John to his parents' home in Rehoboth Beach. John had gotten permission for us all to stay there while his parents were in Florida.

Rehoboth is a quaint, oceanside resort in southern Delaware. It had a relaxed atmosphere, perfect for having fun at the beach, which we all did the first day we got there. The next morning, John and I traveled to a remote place on the tip of Cape Henlopen. This is where John wanted to do the second reading, but it was windy and overcast that day, so we searched for the right spot that would protect us from the elements. We found a place between two sand dunes that created a horseshoe-shaped haven from the wind.

We settled down on the sand, sitting cross-legged and facing one another. I felt a powerful energy surround me, and I knew that it was the spirit of Christ. Immediately I burst into tears, for I felt unworthy to communicate for Him. John did his best to comfort me, but it took a while for me to regain my composure. After much reassurance from John, I was finally able to find the courage to speak the words that were already pouring into my mind. The intensity of the love energy that surrounded me was not to be denied. I knew that I was in the hands of the Master as I felt the great love he had for John.

John and I held hands as the Master spoke to him. **"John of old, John of new,"** He began. We both knew intuitively that He meant John the Apostle. **"I love you. I have always loved you. I will always love you. I am with you. I have always been with you. I will always be with you. You have come here to serve a great purpose. You have come to prepare my way. You were chosen for this mission by me."** I could hear John's breath over the wind as Master Jesus spoke to him through me. It was a truly amazing experience. I felt so embraced by His energy that I didn't have time to doubt or question it. I just let it flow through me as I observed what was happening. It seemed effortless, as if He were doing all the work. **"You will see me in the body that I possessed in Galilee, in this lifetime.**

"Do you want to you see me now?" Jesus asked. "Yes," John answered. **"Then close your eyes and see."** John closed his eyes. **"Can you see me?"** He asked. "No," John answered honestly. **"Focus and you will see,"** prompted the Master. John did what he was told and in his mind's eye he immediately found himself on a beach. He felt himself lying face-down in the sand. The sand was white and coarse. As he raised his face up out of the sand, he could see and feel the grains begin to fall away. He first saw a foot in front of him. As his eyes followed the body upward, he saw the face of Jesus. Many months later, during meditation, John would be able to pinpoint exactly when this scene had taken place in that previous life.[4]

Some time during the course of the reading, I began to recite some verses from the Bible, which was pretty amazing to me, since I am not familiar enough with the Bible to recite any scriptures. (Later that day, when we were at a local bookstore, we looked in a Bible and determined that the verses were from the Book of John.) Jesus used the phrase "**John of old, John of new**" several times during the reading and He also referred to John as "**Beloved John.**" Both of these phrases would be confirmed almost a year later, when John came across the writings of a famous "channel"[5] named Edgar Cayce.

Because John felt he had to play the role of comforter for me, it put him in a more intellectual position mentally, which enabled him to stay grounded and to keep his ego detached from the information coming through. However, he knew in his heart that the things that were spoken were true. As the reading came to an end, the wind started kicking sand into our faces. We opened our eyes and saw a storm suddenly coming in so we ran back to John's van. As soon as we got inside, it started raining.

After the reading, John dropped me off at his friends' Tim and Randi's house so I could do a reading for Randi. John had told her all about the first reading I had given him, and she was anxious to have her own reading done. While I stayed there to give Randi her reading, John went to the workplace of Tim, his oldest childhood friend, to tell him about what had just happened. He soon realized, after sharing his experience, that he had to be careful about deciding to whom and how he would tell his story. At first Tim thought John was joking. He could not understand the experience John had just had, and so he dismissed it. This made John wonder how anyone else could believe what had happened if his oldest friend in the world thought it incredible.

That afternoon, we all went back to the beach because the sun had come out again. John and the others were sitting on the beach talking. I had taken a walk along the shore to gather my thoughts. I felt completely buzzed with energy. I was walking toward them, about 200 feet away, looking for a good spot to sit and meditate. Unknown to me at the time, John was once again gazing at auras. As I was walking by the edge of the water, he watched me and noticed that my aura had a huge cord or column of light that went out of the top of my head straight upward into the sky, disappearing into the clouds. John now lovingly refers to this as "the umbilical cord to God," which always makes me laugh.

For the next two days, John had a very strange, new experience. He saw the world as a field of energy, and he felt at one with everything. His perspective had changed. For the first time, he realized that we are all connected as one and that what happens to one, on some level, happens to all.

This new awareness was quite a contrast to John's previous spiritual experiences, which had begun seven years prior to this.

I also felt very expanded during this time. I felt an increased spiritual vibration in and around me. Something profound had happened to both of us, and we knew our lives were about to change in a dramatic way. During the coming years, we were to share some incredible experiences. We had tapped into something bigger than both of us, something that seemed to be orchestrating our whole spiritual experience. As time went on, it became apparent to us that we needed to share our story with others as a confirmation that God works in all of our lives.

CHAPTER TWO

Growing Pains

John grew up in the small resort community of Rehoboth Beach, Delaware, the sixth of seven children and the product of what his parents jokingly called "the failed rhythm method." From an early age, John was aware that his birth had been unplanned. His parents were devout Catholics. His mother was a housewife; his father, a plumber. John felt lost in the shuffle and did not regard himself as one of his parents' favorites. This led to very low self-esteem, which manifested itself into a two-hundred sixty-five pound, fourteen-year-old who was a quiet, sensitive boy, talented in art and singing.

John had profound insight into people's personalities and in his interpersonal relationships with others, which he did not understand at the time. He saw the games that people played with one another, and he wanted no part of them. It was not that he felt he was better than anyone else, but that he saw life from a different perspective than those around him. He was different and his classmates knew it. Needless to say, he didn't fit in with the crowd. When he tried to play the games in order to fit in with others, he hated it, so he stopped. He decided it was better just to live for whom he truly was and not for what society or his family wanted him to be.

As a teen, this new-found self-awareness empowered him, but on many levels he was still a child struggling for acceptance. As the years passed, John became a man who was outgoing and funny and loved by everyone who knew him. One would never guess that he had been dubbed the "quietest kid in school." He was schooled in both art and architecture, and later, after studying acting and stage combat, he began performing as an actor at his local Renaissance festival. A few years later, he formed a comedy sword-fighting show with his acting partner, Spencer.

John met a young woman when he was in his early twenties: a beautiful, tall, dark, curly-haired woman named Jennifer. He described her brown eyes "as so deep, you could drown in them." She had a brutal honesty that captured him wholly. She was not a game player, and she gave him the support he needed. His time with Jennifer was a period of personal growth for John. At last, he felt unconditionally loved by someone. However, this was unfamiliar ground for John and his insecurities made him overly dependent on her.

After five years together, Jennifer decided to leave the relationship in order to establish her own independence and to empower herself. Though this was a crushing blow to the—in John's own words—"fat child" inside, it was also a time of personal awareness and growth for John. It was during this time of numbness that he married Lisa, a woman who was even more needy than himself. Lisa was a manic-depressive anorexic who had terrible mood swings and volatile behavior.

John became a strict vegetarian, exercised every day, and reduced his weight from 320 to 200 pounds. He worked as a landscape architect during the week, but on the weekends, he would fly out to do shows at various Renaissance festivals around the country. It was during one of these weekend trips that a spiritual awakening occurred.

John was performing at a Medieval faire in New Orleans. Unfortunately for everyone involved, there was a long cold spell that made the weather forty degrees colder than normal. At night the temperature was about thirty degrees. John was staying in his partner's tent, and one night, while lying there shivering in his sleeping bag, he got an idea. He remembered a television show in which some Buddhist monks had warmed their bodies by using the power of their minds. It was the perfect opportunity. Why not try it for himself? He had nothing to lose. John concentrated first on warming his feet and suddenly they got warm. Then he focused on bringing the warmth up his body through his legs, up to his stomach, and then to his chest. Although he tried and tried, he could not make the warm energy go any farther than his chest.

He heard a voice—almost a thought—say, "relax into it," so he did. What happened next was incredible. His arms, which were crossed over his chest, suddenly felt as if they were straight out to the sides of his body. He could feel the heat or energy flying out from his body in all directions. And though his eyes were closed, he saw a burst of brilliant white light. It scared the bejeebers out of him!

When he awoke the next morning, he told his partner, who practiced meditation, what had happened the night before. His response was perplexing to John. Spencer said, "You've awakened your kundalini."[6] "My kunda . . . what?" John queried.

"It's your bodily energy," Spencer knowingly replied. "Now that you've done that, you're going to have all kinds of cool things happen."

John was wary.

The following night, while John lay there again, he heard the tent door unzip and in walked Spencer. Normally this would not be strange, since it was his partner's tent. What was odd was that John watched Spencer step over him and then, inexplicably, suddenly John was looking down at his own face from the ceiling of the tent. All the while he heard a strange humming noise. This incident really scared him and he found himself quickly sputtering out what had just happened.

"I looked directly at my own face!" he exclaimed.

"Did you hear the humming noise?" Spencer asked. "Yes," John admitted, taken aback by Spencer's question.

"You were out of body.[7] It happens to me all the time," Spencer said casually.

John wanted to know how an ordinary person could go out of his body and why this had happened to him. Most important, he wanted to know if he could do it again. This strange new world fascinated him. Little did John know, but his spiritual journey had begun, and this was just the start of many extraordinary and wonderful experiences yet to come.

He returned home to his wife and tried to share what had happened. Although Lisa showed no interest in her husband's out-of-body experience, John knew that his experience was more powerful than she gave it credit. He determined that it did not matter what her thoughts on the subject were—he had to know more about this. From then on, he noticed that when he closed his eyes to go to sleep, he no longer saw the usual blackness. Now he was seeing colors—wonderful colors! He learned to manipulate these colors, moving them, spinning them, even making them bigger or smaller. He was now having unexpected kundalini experiences frequently. This was actually fun!

While pondering these experiences, John was in contact with his sister Patti and her husband, Mitch. Both of them had been on their own spiritual quests for some time. One night while John was speaking to Patti on the phone, she told him about a book that both she and Mitch had been reading that had been life-changing for them. After he hung up the phone, he immediately forgot the title.

A few weeks later, he decided to go to the bookstore to buy a new book. He thought about the one that his sister had recommended but could not remember the title. He figured that he would recognize the right book when he saw its title. At this point in his life, he had no idea that there was such a thing as "New Age" or metaphysical philosophy. He thought that the book he was looking for would be found in the religion section. As he perused the books in this section, he learned what the Crusades, the Inquisition, and the Salem Witch Trials were about. His eyes were really opened to the fact that there were so many religious thoughts and philosophies in conflict with one another.

As he stood there searching for the book, he heard a voice in his head, almost like a thought, say "turn around." He turned to face the opposite bookshelves, and there was only one book whose front cover was facing him. It had a simple green cover—John's favorite color—and he recognized the title as the one his sister had recommended: *The Celestine Prophecy* by James Redfield. It would be his introduction to metaphysical thought. He was fascinated by the "insights" and how true they rang for him in his own experiences. Through this book, he learned about auras and began to see his own energy and that of plant life around him. He also began to see other people's auras as well.

As his spiritual awareness continued to grow, his marriage came to an end. Eleven months after they wed, Lisa pursued an extramarital affair with one of John's friends. When they finally divorced a few months later, John felt a huge weight had been lifted off his shoulders. Although the experience, at one point, had been stressful enough to put him in the hospital, he later considered this experience to have been worthwhile, for it made him stronger.

After the divorce, John renewed his relationship with Jennifer once again. His love felt stronger this time, which he credited to a self-assurance that came from his burgeoning spirituality. He thought that this empowerment was due to his new confidence in himself, and he felt more whole and complete than he had ever felt before. However, as their relationship blossomed and grew stronger, his old fears surfaced again and made him run away. He had broken up with Jennifer a few months before I met him.

John continued on his spiritual quest, mindful of the energies in the universe. He discovered that he could control his out-of-body experiences, and he began to "play" with this new-found ability. One night, he went "out of body" to his friend Tim's house. He went to Tim's bedroom and saw him sleeping. Then he traveled to the house of another friend, Beau. He saw his friend sleeping and got an idea. "I wonder if I can enter his dreams?" thought John. So he did. He knew that he would have to say something outrageous to his friend so that he could verify that he had actually been in his friend's dream. He said, "Hey, Beau. Purple rhinoceros! Purple rhinoceros! Purple rhinoceros!"

The next day, while in Annapolis, Maryland, appearing at the Renaissance festival, John called his friend, Beau, in Rehoboth Beach, which is a good two-hour drive away. "I had the weirdest dream last night," Beau said. "You came into my dream and said 'purple rhinoceros' to me." John smiled knowingly but didn't say a thing to his friend. "He wouldn't have believed me if I told him!" thought John.

One night, soon after this, while John was attempting another out-of-body experience, his "astral" eyes opened[8] and he found himself in a room of pure white light. He saw a man and two women standing in front of him. The man looked at him and said, "You're not supposed to be here yet." He turned to the women and made a gesture, and to John's surprise, they tickled him back into his physical body. John sat up laughing. Not only had he entered another dimension, but he had discovered that God had a sense of humor!

During his stay in the Maryland Renaissance Festival campground in September of 1995, John met a man named Rhett, who was a follower of Native American ways. Nothing about this man's appearance or demeanor would suggest to John a person on a spiritual path. Rhett had a raspy voice, wild hair and a beard, and dressed like a biker. He also lived in a teepee, which was unusual, even in the world of Renaissance festivals.

At first, the two men had their prejudgments about one another, but once they overcame them, they discovered that they had much more in common than they had originally thought. They were both fascinated with energy. Rhett was a massage therapist and knew how to direct energy in his work with others. He introduced John to the concept of "energy balls."

"Hold out your hand," Rhett said. John did as he was asked. Rhett put his own hands out, as if he were holding a volleyball. He brought his hands over John's, and motioned as if he were dropping a ball inside them. Immediately, John felt a "ball" of energy hit his hands. He was amazed. Then Rhett showed him how it was done.

"It's just a matter of focus," Rhett instructed. "You focus on the energy between your hands and it collects." John created his own energy ball. Then Rhett created another energy ball and dropped this one into the energy ball inside John's hands. The force of the combined energies forced John's hands apart. "Wow!" John thought. "This is amazing!"

One day, Rhett decided to show John just what energy balls could do. As John was standing in the campground, he suddenly felt a rush of energy at the back of his head. He quickly turned around to find Rhett standing about two hundred and fifty feet away, laughing. He had thrown an energy ball and struck John in the back of the head!

This modern-day shaman fascinated him. As a child, John had had an affinity for Native American culture. Much to his mother's chagrin, he would build teepees in the backyard, using her favorite blankets as teepee covers. He would always play "Indians," not "Cowboys." In fact, his first acting experience was playing an Indian chief in his sixth-grade play. Soon after he had met Rhett, John learned the reason for his obsession.

As John was attempting to go out of his body one day—this had become routine by now—he experienced something different. As he closed his eyes to relax and focus, he saw a flashing blue light in his head. The light would circle by again and again, like the light on top of a police car. He tried several times to grab it and manipulate it like he had done with the colors he saw when he meditated, but this time he could not. The light kept passing by again and again.

As he focused on the color, he found that his consciousness could go through it. He "passed through it," and found himself somewhere else. For a second, he had full sensory awareness and a sense of knowing where he was, but as soon as he felt his senses taking hold, he lost them because of fear. Many times he tried to focus on his "senses," but each time he did, he felt the experience slipping away.

Finally, he made a last attempt. This time when he went through the blue light, he found himself sitting on a horse. "I could feel the sweat of the horse on the inside of my legs. The sun was hot on my back. As I breathed, I could feel the heat in my nostrils. I was an American Indian. I looked around and there were two others with me. Intuitively, I knew that these two were my best friends from childhood." John recognized his friends, Beau and Tim, from this lifetime. "I have maintained my friendship with these two and have always considered them like my brothers. Yet here they did not look like themselves. Instead, they were Indians."

It was at that moment, he understood that we reincarnate into this world many times over. He came away from that experience understanding about past lives. John's world was getting larger all the time. With his divorce behind him and a lull in his work schedule, he spent the winter at his parents' house in Delaware. It gave him time to think about all these new experiences.

In the following March of 1996, John started preparing to go to his next gig at the Georgia Renaissance Festival. There were still three weeks before the festival began and John needed somewhere to camp. During this time, he kept seeing pictures of griffins.[9]

For the next three weeks, it seemed that everywhere John turned, he saw pictures of griffins, signs with the word "Griffin" in them, or heard the word "griffin" spoken. He didn't understand why he was being bombarded with references to this legendary creature. As he was mapping out his route to Georgia, he discovered that the closest campsite to the festival was near Griffin, Georgia, at a state park called High Falls.

John already understood that the "coincidences" in our lives are not chance happenings and took this as a sign that this was the place where he should camp. He pulled into the park and began to back his travel trailer into a beautiful, shaded site. Just then, a handsome man in his thirties with a neatly trimmed beard and shoulder-length, light brown hair came walking up to him. He told John that the power was out on the site he was backing into and that he didn't want John to go to all the trouble of unhooking his trailer only to find this out later.

John thanked him and pulled into the next site. After unhooking and setting up his campsite, he went in search of this man who had helped him. He thought maybe he could recommend some activities to do in the area, but the man was nowhere to be found. John told me that he felt that this man was really an angel or spiritual messenger.

That night, a terrible storm blew through the area. (John found out later that a tornado had passed within ten miles of the campground.) It was a pretty rough night, as his trailer rocked back and forth from the force of the wind. The next morning he awoke and looked outside. There in the exact spot where he would have been sleeping had he parked his trailer at the site next to his was a huge tree that had fallen during the storm.

Suspecting that perhaps his "messenger" had actually been sent to warn him of danger, John decided to test the outlet on the site next to him. He took a lamp over and plugged it into the outlet. The lamp lit up with no problem whatsoever! It was obvious that there was nothing wrong with the power on the site. John suddenly realized that he had been saved from serious injury or death. But why? Apparently, he was meant to do something with his life, but he had no idea what it was.

————•◦•————

John finished out his season of festivals that year and the following January, in 1997, he did a show in the Florida Keys. This is where, for the first time, John met a group of people who shared his spiritual interests. His focus at this time was on researching the validity of past lives. He wanted to know as much as possible about this subject and was curious to know what past lives he had experienced himself.

He was offered a place to stay with some new friends, Rick and Donna, in southern Florida. While camping in his trailer in their backyard, he began to read the writings of hypno-regressionist[10] Brian Weiss. One night, while he was sitting by the pool in his friends' backyard, the conversation turned toward the topic of Dr. Weiss. Little did he know that Donna had done a hypnoregression with one of Dr. Weiss's colleagues. As she relayed her story, John became convinced that he, too, wanted a regression. However, it would not be until almost three years later that John would get his first past-life regression.

John made many new friends during this time; one of them, named Vasco, did not have a vehicle. His new friend needed a ride for a fight practice that he and John were to attend together. Vasco had given John extremely precise directions to his apartment. The final part of his directions were: "Turn right when you see the apartment complex sign; then turn right into the first driveway. You will see an apartment building with the letter 'H' on it. Go behind this building to the building with the letter 'I' on it. Park in front of the stairs. Come up the stairs and turn left. Apartment 209 is down on the right."

John followed his friend's directions to the letter and found himself in front of Apartment 209. He knocked on the door and then knocked again. There was no answer. On the way to his friend's house, he had received a page on his pager. Thinking that Vasco might have paged him to explain why he wasn't in his apartment, John drove to a convenience store across the street to check his voice mail. He soon discovered it was not Vasco, so he drove back to Apartment 209, hoping that he would be there.

As he parked at the base of the stairs and got out of his van, he saw an elderly woman in a nightgown walk out onto the balcony above. John estimated that she was about 85 years old and she was only about five feet tall. Now, if you can imagine this scene: here's John standing six feet one inch tall and weighing in at two hundred and sixty pounds. He is wearing cut-off jeans, an oil-stained tank top, his hair falling to the middle of his back. He was sure that he looked like a big, scary giant to this fragile, little woman.

However, she showed no signs of fear. Instead, she yelled down to him. "Did you find him?" Shocked at this knowing question, John responded, "I was looking for . . ." She answered, "Whoever lived in 209 moved out yesterday, but you might want to come up and knock again. They may still be inside, not finished moving." So he came up, expecting her to just leave after she gave him that information. However, she stayed right there. As he went to the apartment door again, little did he expect what was to happen next.

As they knocked on the door and peered into the windows of Apartment 209, she calmly said, "You were much healthier when you were a vegetarian." John knew that the universe had its messengers and here was one right now. In that moment, John suddenly realized that he was in the

16   Sharon Prince

presence of an angel! Over the next ten minutes, this tiny old lady told him that he needed to meditate more and explore his gift for healing. John knew that a woman of her age and generation would be unlikely to discuss such matters. She ended their conversation with, "I think you should meditate right now." He obediently complied with this small messenger of light's suggestion. "Yes, ma'am," he said and immediately went to his van, where he meditated for the next twenty minutes.

After meditating, he drove to the convenience store and paged his friend. "Where are you?" asked Vasco. "I've been waiting." John told him how he had been knocking on his door but there had been no answer. "Come back over, and I will meet you outside," Vasco said. John drove back over to the apartment and knocked, but there was no Vasco.

Then a thought came to him that he later attributed to the divine guidance that had come to him through his meditation. "I wonder if there is another sign for the apartment complex?" he thought.

So, he drove back to the main street, turned right, and drove down a half a block until he saw another sign. He turned right into the next driveway. There he saw another building with "H" on it, turned again and saw the building with the letter "I." Sure enough, there was Vasco standing outside. John shared with him what had happened. In all the years that his friend had lived there, no one else had ever made the mistake John did. Vasco had no idea that the directions to Apartment 209, in the complex next door, were exactly the same as the directions to his apartment! Funny how the universe sometimes puts us out of our way for reasons we later discover were for our own good. John had certainly been put out of his way to receive the messages that would set him on the next leg of his spiritual journey.

About a week later, John was watching an episode of *Unsolved Mysteries* on television and couldn't believe what he heard. The show told of a woman, who had recently gone through a divorce, trying to make ends meet so that she could feed her children. It was Thanksgiving Day, and all she had to give them were bologna sandwiches. She took her children to the park to have a picnic and to play. As she was going home, she felt bad that she could not afford a better Thanksgiving meal for her children.

As the woman was going to her apartment upstairs, a little old lady, about five feet tall and in her eighties, came out of the apartment below and said something like, "Honey, where have you been? I've been waiting for you." Surprised by this person she had never met, the woman found herself and her children being invited into the older woman's apartment. There was a huge Thanksgiving dinner spread out on the table. The woman and her hungry children gratefully ate the dinner and felt comfortable enough to stay for several hours visiting this elderly neighbor.

When the time came to leave, the elderly lady insisted that the woman take the leftovers. They packed all the food into plastic food containers and the woman and her children took them home. The next day she transferred all the food into her own bowls and washed out the containers to bring them back to the woman who had shown her so much kindness. To her utter amazement, when she got to her new friend's apartment, it was completely empty. In disbelief, she asked the apartment manager about the little old lady who had been living there. She was shocked when the apartment manager told her that the empty apartment had not been rented for months! The similarity of this apartment angel was not lost on John.

A short time after his encounter with the angel, John found himself floating aimlessly in Rick and Donna's pool. Something about encountering this divine little messenger had changed his perspective on life. As he looked up at the palm trees over-hanging the pool, he came to the sudden realization that he was still very much in love with Jennifer. He realized that his leaving her had been based in fear. He decided to call her to ask her to come on the road with him and travel to the various places where he was doing shows. In his heart, he just knew she would say yes. To his surprise, he discovered that she was preparing to go to Africa to serve in the Peace Corps for two years.

They talked for a long time, and he convinced her to come see him. They spent a wonderful week together before she left. They discussed the possibility of getting back together upon her return to see if they could make another go of their relationship. What he did not realize at the time is that he would need this two-year period alone to discover more about his spiritual nature and the mission he had come here to serve. So much was to happen in the next two years, that even John would not have believed it.

A month after Jennifer left, John came across the book *Conversations with God, Part 1* by Neale Donald Walsh and purchased it. He could not believe the revelations that came from this book. It really spoke to his sense of truth. This was also the time he started seeing the book *The Messengers* in the bookstores. He kept picking this book up and putting it down. He would not actually read the book until a month later, after I had given him his first reading, which alluded to his life as an apostle.

Sharon Prince

CHAPTER THREE

Wrestling with the Past

I am thankful that John kept an open mind to the messages that we have received from Spirit—whether from our angels or from Jesus. There were many times during the early years that I leaned on John's supportive friendship to get me through my own doubts and fears.

I would like to take you back, once again, to the beginning of our story, in order to share with you what John's impressions were of our first spiritual experiences together. He agreed to let me use his own words. I feel it is important for you to be able to see this part of the story through John's eyes.

In John's own words:

> My partner [Spencer] and I took our show to Canada, where we stayed at [his] girlfriend's [Ellen's and Ian's] house. It was in that house where I met the most influential person on my spiritual path. We were sharing the house with several other performers, many of whom were part of a Scottish bagpipe band.
>
> One evening, while sitting in the kitchen, the conversation was hot and heavy on the far side of the room. I sat in the corner as quiet as could be, watching people's auras, when [a] band member's wife stood up and walked directly over to me. She looked me in the eye and said, 'You are looking at my aura!' I was shocked. 'The energy from you is so strong. You are a healer,' her Texas accent belted forth.
>
> Well, in my mind, I had healed no one and did not know what she was talking about. Yet, intuitively I knew she was right. This woman astounded me as we became friends. Her gifts kept dumbfounding me. Now, I had met people who had claimed to be psychic before, but never one who truly demonstrated the gifts she had. She was giving readings for [love] offerings, as well as working for her husband's band. [Her husband is] a man I am fortunate to know as well. I would watch as people would get their readings from my new gifted friend and was impressed with how many said it was life-changing. Yet, I had not had one [myself].

I went on to Maryland, where I was pleased to see the band (who have also become very good friends since that time) camped across from me. This gave me the chance to get to know Sharon and her husband—a couple who love each other very much and are strong enough to walk different spiritual paths. Finally, I set up my reading. It started with her asking for something of mine that I usually carry with me at all times. I've forgotten what it was, but I filled the request. She then meditated with the object for a few minutes before speaking.

She slowly began to speak. She explained to me why I was the way I was. 'Your energy is very strong,' she said as her eyelids flickered. As she spoke for my spiritual parents she said all of the things my [biological] parents never said. 'We are proud of you. We love you. We are there for you. You have chosen this path and were meant to walk on it.' This last part, of course, my parents would never have said. Sharon explained to me [that] my path was chosen to experience the trauma of being unwanted so I would be strong enough for what was to come.

Her face erupted into a large smile as she uttered, 'They're telling me you walked with Jesus.' My reaction to that powerful statement is what shocked me. 'Yes, I did,' was my response. Somehow, deep inside, I knew the truth of the matter. I had [walked with Jesus].

Ever since I was very young, I had a fascination with the appearances of Mary [mother of Jesus], all over the world. For some reason, I had an attraction to the photos, articles, and newscasts about such events. I remember when I was a teen, my mother brought a Xerox copy of a photo a friend took at Medjugore, in which Mary had appeared [in the photograph]. I quickly told all my friends, who of course, thought I was being weird. Now I was finding out why I had had this interest in Mary all my life.[11]

Sharon finished her reading, which during the parent part reduced me to sobbing. We sat and discussed the reading, first of all to clarify, and second, to validate Sharon. During this post-reading conversation, Sharon began preparing me for the eventual news. She said, 'Now I don't want you to freak out if I tell you that you were an apostle or something.' She knew I had been [an apostle] but not anything more, like which one. I quickly asked for another reading to clarify this news. We arranged for another reading, as she denied my payment for the reading.

All that week I was chomping at the bit to know more. Later that week I went to Rehoboth alone, where I found a copy of *The Messengers* in a local department store. I had seen the book many times and passed it over because the cover art was far too 'frou frou' for me. This time, instead of being turned off by its cover art, I opened it. Normally, when I pick up a book, I read the back [cover] and the inner sleeve. This time, however, I opened the book to the center and was shocked to find a page with the title 'He Walked with the Master—The Manuscript.' I bought the book and devoured it.

The story of Paul the Apostle and his reincarnation as Nick Bunick was laid out before me. The thing that astounded me most was that many of the 'coincidences' that led Nick to this realization had paralleled my own [experiences] thus far. In *The Messengers*, Nick Bunick recalls a reading he got from [a reader named] Patty in which Nick tells her that he was feeling guilty because he didn't pray very often and he didn't meditate, but that another reader had told him that he thought 'in another realm, at another level.' Patty told him that he was absolutely right and added, 'Do you know who you communicate with?' 'I assume with my angels,' was Nick's reply. Patty smiled as she pointed to the ceiling, 'You're getting yours from the boss.' (p.116) In one of Sharon's readings for me, I asked about the guides and where she got her information.

Sharon told me that when she does a reading she speaks to the person's guides. I asked who my guides were and she said, 'You get yours from the top.' Patty would go on to tell Nick how he filled the room with light when he entered. Years before, I was told by a reader named Kiara [who casually told me that she could see that] I had a glowing ball of light around me. A reiki master,[12] Brooke, would later tell me the same thing.

A week later [after the first reading], Sharon and I had gone to a place in my hometown to have the [second] reading. We found a secluded place between two sand dunes. She was very upset, and I did not understand why. She explained to me that she had some issues with worthiness, and I tried to comfort her. We then held hands, and she began reciting what she heard in her head. It started with '**John of old, John of new.**' I realized at that miraculous moment, that Jesus was speaking through Sharon. He then proceeded to tell me, through Sharon, that He loved me and that He was always with me. I was then led into a memory of my face in the sand. As I raised my face up, I saw a foot in front of me. As I cast my eyes upward, I saw Him for the first time in this life. And though it was unbelievable to see Him, I was shocked by being able to feel His presence. The love that emanates from Him is amazing! Sharon then started reciting what sounded like scriptures. Since neither one of us was well versed in the Bible, after the reading, we went and looked it up in a Bible at the bookstore. It was found in the Book of John.

When you witness a person channeling, it's an interesting experience; but when that channel tells you you were an apostle and [she] channels Christ, that's a lot for your brain to process. Though I knew in my heart that it was true and that these events were real, this information was something that my ego and my intellect needed to wrestle with. Because if you start telling people that you were an apostle, people will think you are 'loopy,' especially my very Catholic-driven family. I soon discovered also, that some of my friends would not be able to see me in that light. And I became very judicious of who would be privy to this information.

After our trip to Rehoboth Beach, John and I returned to Maryland as changed people. We spent the next week trying to put everything into perspective. Who would believe what just happened? I wasn't sure if I even believed it! Either I was the biggest con artist in the world, or something truly profound had just happened!

That September, my husband, Randy, and I, along with the rest of the band, left the Maryland Renaissance Festival to do three weeks at another faire in Kansas before heading home to Texas to finish out the last half of our home faire. Regretfully, I had to leave my new friend behind in Maryland. I knew that I would see him again in February, when once again, my husband's band and John's sword-fighting show would be entertaining in the same area. We said our good-byes, but somehow we both knew that we would be a significant part of each other's lives from then on, much as if we were members of the same family. Later we would come to realize that we *were* members of the same family—the same *soul* family.[13]

John did not have his own phone with him during that time, so I had no way of reaching him except by leaving a message on his business voice mail. I left a couple of messages but didn't hear back from him. I felt very frustrated because I longed to talk to him again and share some more spiritual experiences. When a few weeks turned into two months, I began to wonder if I would ever hear from my friend again.

Finally, I had had enough of waiting for him to call me. I figured that because John and I had such a close spiritual connection, that I would try an experiment with telepathy. One day, a few weeks before Christmas, while I was walking around in my backyard in Houston, I sent out a message: "John Davis, I know you can hear me. Call me! Please?"

The next day I was delighted to hear from him. I said, "Did you get my message?"

He said, "What message?"

"I sent you a telepathic message to call me," I replied.

"You did?'" he asked. "Well, I must have gotten it because when I opened up my phonebook today, out dropped your business card with your home phone number written on the back. I had looked for it but couldn't find it. When I saw it, I thought, 'I should give Sharon a call.' So I did!"

We spent the next hour or so catching up. John had told me, before I left Maryland, that he was planning to travel with his friend, Gracie, to see a woman in Atlanta, Georgia, who was to receive a channeled message from Mother Mary on October 13, 1997. Since I hadn't heard from him I was anxious to know what had happened. He told me that while he and

Gracie were preparing to fly to Atlanta to see this channel, John received his first "appearance" of Mary the day before they left. He looked into the sky and saw her image clearly in the clouds. "You could see every detail perfectly, as if it were a painting," he said. He took this as a confirmation of her presence in his life. He would have two other appearances from Mary at other significant times in the months to come.

"Why didn't you call me sooner?" I asked.

"I needed some time to think things over," he admitted. "It's not every day that a person hears he's been an apostle, and from none other than Jesus Himself!"

"So, do you think it's true?"

"I have no doubts that it is absolutely true," he stated confidently.

"So what makes you so sure of that? What if I was wrong and have unintentionally misled you into thinking you're someone you were not? After all, I am human," I countered.

"Sharon, stop doubting yourself," he said. "You *know* it's true."

As real as the interaction with Jesus had been for both of us, it still seemed too incredible for me to believe, even though I knew I had felt His powerful yet gentle loving energy come through me. Who was I to be giving a personal message from Jesus to John? What if we were both wrong in concluding that Jesus had meant that John had been His apostle? What if John had been just an *ordinary* John—a John who had listened to Jesus speak but who had not been an actual apostle? I knew that either I was right on about this or I was deluding both of us. I shared my apprehensions with John, who again reassured me. He told me that after searching his own heart and mind, he had come to the conclusion that he had, in fact, been *the* John of old that Christ had spoken of. And what had affirmed this for him were the glimpses of his past that were now spontaneously springing to the surface of his awareness.

During that October, while in meditation, he had received another visual recall of Jesus. John remembered seeing Jesus for the first time, walking along the shoreline while he was standing on the beach. Jesus was walking with three or four other people past where all the boats had been pulled to shore. What had struck John most about this encounter was that he could "feel" Jesus' presence, even from fifteen to twenty feet away.

Although he was accepting it now, the information he was given about his past life had been so overwhelming, that after we parted ways, he had needed a "mental vacation" from it all. (Later, when I discovered my own past life from this same time period, I would go through a similar experience.) He had been trying to process the whole thing and come to terms with it. He told me he had shared his story with several people who had differing reactions. Most of his close friends believed him at once. Those with whom he was not as close questioned and challenged him about it. He was discovering that not everyone could see him in the "light" of being a reincarnated apostle, or even accept the idea of reincarnation in the first place. (Although, since that time, John and I have been guided to share this story with many people whom we would not have expected to accept it as well as they have.) I felt much better after our conversation. Our friendship had been renewed.

I met up with John a couple of months later in February 1998 at the Florida Renaissance Festival in Ft. Lauderdale, Florida, where Randy's band had been hired to play. Although John was not employed by the faire to do his regular sword-fighting show, he was hired as a stage-fight consultant. He and his partner were actually doing another faire about forty-five minutes north of where we were working. Although Randy and I were camping on the Florida Festival site, John decided to camp near us in our campground, so that he could be close enough for us to do some more spiritual work together. I knew John was serious about doing the work when I saw the nice campground he had given up to be near us and the sacrifice he was making to drive an extra forty-five minutes every weekend day to get to work.

It was in our humble campground where John received his second message from Jesus. Understandably, he had questions about how to use his healing ability to heal others. He wanted to be ready for this but didn't know how to start. Both of us now wish we had recorded this and the other sessions like it during which Jesus has spoken to John through me. What stood out the most in my mind from this session was Jesus' use of metaphor to describe John's spiritual talents. He told him that he could partake of the food on His table—that the food represented spiritual gifts and he could partake of anything he wanted to, he just needed to reach out and take it. John was being mentally prepared for his future work but was not given specifics yet. That would come in bits and pieces later.

John and I had only three weeks together in Florida, so it didn't seem we accomplished much at that time. However, looking back, it was more a time of bonding and time for John to settle into his new, growing role. He was already starting to get some information from his guides, but he resisted trusting his intuitions. At that point, he found it much easier to ask me questions than to go within for his own answers. However, as time went on, he would amaze me again and again with his spiritual insights, and I came to ask him for advice many times.

We soon parted ways although we stayed in closer contact by phone than we had before. John continued with his traveling work schedule, and Randy and I continued with ours until we met up again in northern Ohio in late June 1998. This would prove to be a time of transformation for me. It's John's habit to tell all his friends about my readings and how exceptional he feels they are and to recommend to them that they get a reading from me. True to history, he had four people lined up for readings when I got there. Little did I know how much in demand my gift would be that summer. I would end up giving eighteen readings in all.

One particular person I read for that summer, Danny, had given me a blue stone pendant carved into the shape of an arrowhead. He said that he knew that I was meant to have it after a reading I gave him and said that it represented my ability to point people in the right direction. I hung the arrow on the rear-view mirror of my car, but the next time I got into the car, it was gone.

I was disappointed and the next time I saw Danny, I told him that I had lost it. "Don't worry," he said. "It will show up again when you least expect it." And he was right. The arrow would show up again and again when I least expected it and serve as a confirmation that I was on the right path.

Most of the performers and vendors from the Medieval faire in Ohio were staying at a beautiful, wooded, private campsite that was also a wildlife preserve. One night at a camp party, John and I were talking about our experiences. I shared with him my fears of being a clear-enough channel for him, and that I hoped I didn't disappoint the people whom he had recommended to me for readings. He started to reassure me that I indeed had a gift, and when I tried to deny that I was worthy of it, he began to say things that I had never heard him say to me before. Although his words were loving, they were also strong, and he basically kicked me in the pants, so to speak. He does not remember what he said now, but I believe he was channeling information for me about my work and why I had come here to do this. It was the first "reading" that John had ever given me, and it was awesome! When one hears the truth, one knows it. John was speaking the truth, and this truth spoke to my heart. However, this would not be the last time he had to reassure me in my role as messenger for Jesus.

John is a great artist, and that summer, he was inspired to do a couple of acrylic paintings. One he did of a friend of ours and the other was of Jesus looking down from the cross, His face in shadow. His eyes were large and—something else I hadn't expected—they were blue. I had always assumed that since Jesus was Jewish, that He would have brown eyes. I had my doubts at first that John was remembering this scene from his past life accurately.

When I asked him if he really thought Jesus had blue eyes, he was positive of that. He said, "I remembered His grey-blue eyes, so tired, looking down at me from the cross."

"Wasn't He in a lot of pain, too?" I asked.

John shocked me with his answer. "Not really. I don't remember Him suffering that much. He just looked very tired. I remember looking into His eyes. They were full of love, and then suddenly His eyes became huge—much larger than His face. And that was all I could see, were His huge eyes and nothing else."

John's memory of Jesus having blue eyes and His not seeming to be in pain would be verified a year later in a book by Dolores Cannon called *They Walked with Jesus,* and another book she wrote called *Jesus and the Essenes.*[14]

One day, I received a message from my guides that there was a message for John. I went over to John's trailer to tell him that I felt that I should do a reading for him. He was not home, so I left a note on the door. "John, I'm being told that I need to give you a message. Let me know when a good time is to give you a reading. Love, Sharon." To this day, John jokes about his message from God: "John, God called. He wants you to call him right away!" So we scheduled our reading soon afterward, and John knew just the spot where he wanted to do it.

John had found a waterfall in the river by an old bridge near the campsite. We settled down on a rock ledge near the waterfall to do the reading. I had no idea going into it why I was being called to do this, but it soon became apparent, from the energy surrounding us, that it was going to be another channeled message from Jesus. This was the third time I had channeled Jesus for John, but it was the first time that I really discovered that Jesus had a sense of humor. How I wish I could remember now everything He said! John was discussing with Jesus the ability to manifest something, seemingly out of thin air. "Just think of the practical jokes you could play on someone!" To which the Master replied with humor, **"You know of only one."**

Jesus told John that he was connected to the "Sacred Heart" because of his big heart and that others would feel his love and receive healings from this love energy. He told John that he could heal others just by faith alone and that it was not so much a matter of him *learning* how to heal as it was a matter of him *remembering* how to heal. Jesus said, **"Heal the way I taught you—by calling on My name."** He cleverly made some points using humor, and while we were laughing so hard that tears were in our eyes, He would turn serious. Looking back on it, I believe He got us to laugh at ourselves first so that we would let our defenses down long enough to hear His message.

The reading then ended with me leading John back to his lifetime as John the Apostle. I asked John to remember a time when he saw Jesus do a healing. I asked him what he saw, and he remembered Jesus healing a lamb's broken leg. He said that a little girl was crying, and Jesus had healed the lamb in order to mend the girl's broken heart.

At the end of the reading, I was pondering what the Master had said, and I wondered what the "Sacred Heart" meant. A short time later, as Randy and I were taking a drive in the quaint Amish countryside, we passed a church called "The Sacred Heart Church." A thought entered my mind that I should go in there and ask them what the name meant, but we were busy at the time, and I forgot to do it later. However, the "coincidence" of seeing these words really hit home with me.

The faire in Ohio came to an end in late July. Randy and I had three weeks before the Maryland Renaissance Festival started. Just after we had left Ohio for Maryland, John got a reading from a fellow performer there named Melinda, who told him: "You were yourself in another lifetime! You were John! You walk in the Christ light and you work with Archangel Gabriel!" He had been in no hurry to leave Ohio because, for the first time in many years, John and his partner would not be doing the Maryland show.

Randy and I had traveled to Maryland to set up camp before flying to Scotland for a wonderful two-week trip. When we got back, there was a message on voice mail from John, who was staying at Spencer's parents' house in Virginia while doing landscaping for them. I could hear the excitement in John's voice: "Sharon, you won't believe what I've found! You need to read page thirty-two of Jess Stearn's *Edgar Cayce*[15] *on the Millennium!* Call me as soon as you get this message!"

When I called John from the camp phone to find out what all the excitement was about, I was not prepared for what I was to hear. He read the passage to me:

> As before, Jesus was to have his forerunner, said Cayce. John the
> Beloved of Christ, who always sat by His side. There is soon to come
> into the world a body that to many has been representative of a sect, a
> thought, of a philosophy, yet one beloved of all men in all places

where the university of God in the Earth has been proclaimed. There the oneness of the Father is known and is magnified in the activities of individuals who will proclaim the rising of the day of the Lord. Hence that one John, the Beloved in the Earth. His name shall again be John.

Cayce had predicted some twenty-five years before John was even born that John the Apostle would reincarnate before the millennium and that he would again be called "John." I nearly dropped the phone! Here was the first proof I had received that John really was who we thought he was.

My head started to spin. My next question was: "Why me and not someone else to deliver this message? There are many talented full-body trance channels who I am sure could do a better job than I can." John assured me that he would not have listened to anyone like that because he would not have trusted them the way he trusted me. I stumbled back to the motorhome in the darkness. What did this all mean? Was it really true? I was in a state of confusion and fear. I desperately wanted to be reassured about the accuracy of what we received. I decided to ask the "Big J.C." Himself. Who else better to answer the question? If I could channel Him for John, why not for myself? Would He really answer me? I was about to find the answer to this question in a big way.

CHAPTER FOUR

Conversations with Jesus

B ecause my husband and I stayed in so many campgrounds that require pets on a leash, we would walk our cat, Rommy, on a leash
every night. Rommy was the most intelligent cat we have ever had.
We had gotten him as a rescue kitten who nearly died at five weeks old. He
was a big, beautiful, black and white short-hair, an alpha male "watch-kitty,"
and he did not suffer fools gladly; but he also had an endearing, sweet, soft
side that he only showed to us. Randy and I would usually walk him together, but my husband was involved in a good book, so I went alone this
night. As it happened, I wouldn't be alone at all.

It had been a whole day since I had spoken to John about Edgar
Cayce's predictions and my mind was in a fog about what to make of Cayce's
confirmation that John the Apostle would reincarnate with the name John
again. You might think that would be enough to convince me, but I still
had doubts. In fact, I was deeply disturbed by the implications of such
evidence. It was as if I had suddenly realized that John was a part of a bigger,
divine plan and that I was being catapulted with him into this wide-open,
heavenly abyss from which there would be no turning back. What was my
role in this whole thing, and why would I, of all people, be the one to
awaken John the Apostle?

The campground at the Maryland Renaissance Festival is a small,
hilly area, nestled inside a grove of trees. A dirt path leads out of camp to
an open field. This is where the participants park during the weekends
when faire is going on. The festival had not started yet, so the field, for
the most part, was deserted. I felt a little nervous being out there all alone
with my cat in the darkness. But the questions that had plagued my mind
were now screaming out for answers. My inner tension had been building
up all day. I had been so confused and afraid because this whole thing was
starting to seem so real. The emotional pressure valve inside me finally
released, and I began to cry out loud. I wanted answers. No, I *needed*

answers. Although I was afraid of what I might "hear," I had to know the truth, once and for all.

"Jesus, please help me. I'm so afraid and confused. Please tell me. Is John Davis really the reincarnation of John the Apostle?" I asked plaintively.

Immediately, I felt this intense, loving energy surround me. It was up close and around my face. I knew who it was right away. There was no mistaking the now-familiar feeling.

"What do *you* think?" He asked.

"I don't know," I protested.

"What does your *heart* tell you?"

I could feel the panic rise in my throat. "I don't know!" I choked.

"Listen to your heart, beloved. It will always tell you the truth," was His gentle response.

It would have been so easy for Him to just answer my question outright. However, the Master wanted me to come to my own conclusions about it. I knew what the answer was. The fact that He was here with me now, communicating through telepathy, was pretty much a testimony in itself.

"Why me of all people to do this work?" I earnestly wanted to know.

"Why not?" was His response.

"Well, I'm sure there are a lot of channels who do full-body trance who could do a much better job than me," I objected.

He proceeded to explain why I had been chosen to do the work. He said it was because of the heart connection between John and myself. Our friendship made the channeling process seem fun and natural to us. **"If this had been presented to you as an enormously important task for which the world was waiting, it would have seemed too daunting."** He told me that John and I had worked together before this lifetime, which made our work together easier now. **"This heart connection is part of a greater heart,"** He said. **"You are part of an angelic presence known as the 'Sacred Heart.'"**

"What *is* the 'Sacred Heart?'" I asked Him. Immediately, my mind went back to the reading that I had given John in Ohio a month before.

"Look it up," He replied.

I was a little perturbed at that answer. Why didn't He just come out and tell me? I guess He wanted me to confirm it on my own. Maybe it would seem more real to me if I read it somewhere in a book. Was He teasing me or again teaching me to trust?

Feelings of guilt and unworthiness flooded my being. I had been told by a reader years before that I had had a chance to become an apostle in that lifetime but had turned the opportunity down. Now I was feeling the weight of that possible decision on me. "I don't really know who I was in that lifetime, but I feel like I let you down," I sobbed. **"You didn't let *me* down. You let *yourself* down,"** He stated simply. He was passing no judgment on me, for I felt His love. Obviously, there was some truth to what the reader had told me about this past-life because I could feel the sorrow welling up inside.

"I feel so unworthy to do this work!" I cried.

"It is not so much a matter of worthiness as it is a matter of preparedness," He responded.

Intuitively, I understood what He was trying to say. It's not that I'm not worthy to do it, but my feelings of unworthiness will get in the way of my being prepared. I needed to prepare myself. But how, when I felt this guilt inside that I could not explain? I knew I would have to face what I had done in that lifetime. It must have been horrible, I reasoned. Why else would I be feeling this way? Was I a Roman soldier who crucified Jesus? Or maybe it was not as bad as that. I must know more about this former lifetime. It seemed to be getting in the way of what I needed to do now.

As I was pondering who I had been, I suddenly heard a voice over my thoughts. **"You were meant to do this work with John. Why do you think we sent you to Patmos?"** A pang of truth raced through me. Of course! The only highlight in an emotionally painful trip I had taken to Greece in May 1993 with a group of women was two special days on the island of Patmos. I remember going into the cave where John had written Revelations. The spiritual energy was so intense in that sacred space that I was almost knocked unconscious when I tried to meditate in there. "Wow!" I thought. The connection I felt to that energy was now being confirmed five years later![16]

After my "conversation with Jesus in the parking lot," I walked back to the motorhome in a trancelike state. I barely was able to unhook Rommy's leash from his harness as we came inside. My husband noticed it immediately.

"Something just happened, didn't it?"

"Yes," I said faintly.

"Do you want to talk about it?" he gently asked. My logical, science-minded husband knew that now was not the time to bombard me with challenging questions.

"I just spoke to Jesus, but I can't talk about it now. I'll tell you later," I said as I crawled into bed in a stupor. The energy was still with me. Forget about a shower. I needed to rest! As I lay there staring at the ceiling in the dark, I prayed that I would receive more information about whom I had been during the time of Christ. I asked my angels to assist me while I dreamt that night.

Later on, I heard myself say it in my sleep: "I was Felix." I woke myself up in the middle of the night, bringing the information with me. "My name was Felix!" I exclaimed out loud. My husband stirred. My first thought was, "Felix? Where did *that* name come from?" Thinking what an odd name that was, I went back to sleep. When I awoke the next morning, I remembered the name I had been given. "Felix? I hate that name!" I thought. "It reminds me of Felix the Cat!" In my mind's eye I could see the black and white cartoon character from the '50s. "Was Felix even a name from that time period? I guess I will have to wait until I get home to look it up in my sister's book of baby names," I told myself.

The next morning I shared with Randy what had happened the night before. I was more intrigued now than ever. How accurate was the Felix information or did I just make up that name? How does this tie in with the lifetime of Jesus, and did this Felix character even know the Apostle John? It would be a few months before I would receive the answers to these questions. Meantime, my angels made sure that I was protected from hearing information that I was not ready to hear yet.

The Renaissance festival started that weekend, but the place seemed different without John. I suppose there was a higher purpose for our being separated. It was a time of great introspection for me and new insights. On one particular weekend, as I was picking up my sales basket, full of CDs and tapes for the band's next show, the arrow pendant that Danny had given me in Ohio mysteriously fell on my foot, from out of nowhere. "Perhaps it had gotten stuck in the weave of the basket," my husband said, but it was hard for me to believe that as many times as I had used my basket to do sales for the band that I had not seen it there before.

I smiled as I remembered Danny's words: "This arrow represents your pointing people in the right direction," he had said when he gave it to me. "Don't worry," he said when I lost it that summer in Ohio. "It will show up again when you least expect it." I stared at this little relic in disbelief. "Where have you been?" I asked, as I slipped it into my pouch for safekeeping. When I opened my pouch later, I could not find it. It had disappeared again! I would discover, a year later, that the arrow was not lost at all, but had just been waiting to make its next appearance.

I was lonely that season, for I missed my friend John. However, I did get to see him one time during the five weeks that we were in Maryland. John invited Randy and me to visit him a couple of weeks later in Rehoboth Beach, where he was staying in his trailer, which was parked in the backyard of his friend Beau's house. Randy and I stayed in Beau's spare

Sharon Prince

bedroom, where we were frequently visited by Beau's huge Labrador, Boudreaux. Beau's little house was not far from the beach. John asked for a reading almost as soon as I got there, so we headed for the beach.

John drove us down the street and through a neighborhood. He parked his truck on a street near the beach, and we walked past a few beach houses to an area where there were no people. After we settled down on the sand, I began my reading. It started out like a normal reading, but soon we had a visitor. Jesus took the opportunity to speak to John once again.

He told John that the two of them would meet again and that John would be ushering in His "second coming." He was told that he needed to prepare himself for the work ahead and He ended His message with a child-like poem. Part of it went like this:

We will meet again, just you and me,
walking hand in hand, by the sea.

As I suddenly realized that I was reciting a poem, I began to giggle. I was just repeating what I heard in my mind as I received it. I never expected that I would be reciting poetry for Jesus! So this Master has a sense of humor and is poetic as well. I was learning more and more about Him each time I channeled Him. I really liked Him as a person. He seemed so real and touchable, unlike the image I had had of this perfect being who preached all the time and who would not be accessible to the average person. What I found was He was this great being who was not only filled with love and compassion, but who used several different ways of communicating—and none of them was preachy.

Without warning me, John then asked about my past life during the time of Jesus. Immediately, my guides told him that "she's not ready to hear this yet." Perhaps believing that I was trying to block this information, he persisted with his questioning. I heard someone walking up, as again my guides refused to speak to him about it. Just then, I felt hot breath and a wet tongue on my knee. As I opened my eyes, I saw a friendly dog and its owner, a friend of John's. The reading was officially over now. I couldn't help but think that my angels had devised this clever little interruption for my own protection. I would need to be prepared, first, for the information that would come later.

When we got back to Beau's house after the reading, John insisted that I needed to have a past-life regression, so that I could release the past in order to continue my spiritual work. I argued that I could continue to give readings to people whether or not I had the regression done. John's keen perception was picking up on the great fear I had about taking a look at this particular lifetime. I had had one formal hypnoregression and about seventeen spontaneous ones, which had uncovered lifetimes that spanned the whole period of man's time on earth and the whole social spectrum. Why would I be afraid of this one in particular?

Although I did continue to give readings over the next year, John was right about one thing: in order to continue to do the work that was needed to put him in touch with *his* past life as John the Beloved and to prepare him for his future work, I would need to come to terms with my own past. The next year would be a gradual uncovering of this lifetime, which also intertwined with the life of the Apostle Paul and probably the other apostles, including John. This gradual awakening would also prepare me to hold a higher, more loving vibration in channeling Jesus for John, as well as for myself.

After John leaned on me, as is his way when he feels I am blocking or holding back on my spiritual work, he offered to let me borrow his hardbound copy of *The Messengers*. Up until this time I had not felt an urgency to read it, but now I did. The timing would be perfect for me to verify many things that had taken place since I had met John.

That night, after the reading, John had a vivid dream. In the dream, he was speaking to me, but instead of me having my own eyes, I had the eyes of Jesus, as John had seen them earlier in his spontaneous memories of Jesus while in Ohio. The next morning when he told me about this, I asked him what he thought it meant. His response was: "I think it means that you are really channeling Jesus." At the time, I thought the dream was only a symbolic one. I was still struggling with this worthiness issue. Only later did I come to realize that it was a personal confirmation from Jesus to John. I, on the other hand, would need quite a bit more convincing in the months to come.

The next day, John took Randy and me to all his favorite haunts, including the place where John and I had our first message from Jesus. It is a beautiful spot near the ocean that overlooks an old lighthouse in the water. That night John, Randy, Beau, and I went out to dinner at a local seafood restaurant. Since Randy had a gig in Baltimore, and John and I felt we still had some processing to do, I decided to spend an extra day in Rehoboth. John agreed to take me back to Maryland.

John and I spent the next day hanging out and discussing everything that had happened in the past year. Randi, the girlfriend of John's childhood friend, Tim, met John and me on the beach that afternoon. As we reminisced about the previous year's visit, I recalled a conversation that

John, Randi, and I had had at that very spot a year before. "You know I wrote down some revelations once," John had joked with us. "Who do you think held your pen?" Randi had retorted. John felt he had known Randi from that lifetime, and the reading I had given her the previous year had confirmed that, although I don't remember her guides giving us any specific details on it. I had told John of my trip to the Island of Patmos, when I visited the cave where John the Divine had written Revelations. That was the first time that he had heard about the cave, and since that time, he has wanted to go there. He knew in his heart that John the Apostle had also been John the Divine.

It was getting late, so we said good-bye to Randi and Tim and headed back to Maryland. On the way, John once again pressed the issue of remembering my past life. I was only too happy to remind him that he *himself* had not had a past-life regression, either! I felt that if he had the regression, it would verify for us the information we had received on our own. However, the things we had already received and would continue to receive in the near future would all be verified before either of us would have regressions done the following year.

As we drove home, I predicted that we would be not be spending as much time together the next year as we had in the past and that it was time for him to do readings for himself and not depend on me as much. He asked me why I did not want to read for him anymore. I told him that it wasn't so much that, but rather I was worried that I was becoming a crutch, preventing him from receiving answers to his own questions. He said he did not believe that he was using me as a crutch; however, I felt inside that this upcoming separation would provide an opportunity for him to grow in channeling his own divine guidance.

I said good-bye as John dropped me off at the campsite. It would be several months before I would see him again, but we would stay in close contact with one another. We knew we had a spiritual bond that could not be denied and that there was more spiritual work for us to do.

After arriving in Maryland, I immediately started reading *The Messengers* and could not put it down. I had no idea, when I started to read the book, how many parallels I would find in Nick Bunick's story to the conversations that John and I had had with Jesus in the previous year. I was so impressed with the similarities, in fact, that I kept a sticky note pad near my bed so that I could write notes to myself and stick them onto the pages that corresponded with our experiences. I wanted to be sure to document these "coincidences" so that I could share them the next time I spoke to John.

They were definitely confirmations of the information we had received.

When I read about Nick receiving confirmation from different readers that he had "walked with Jesus," it reminded me of the first reading I had done for John when I told him that his guides were telling me he had walked with Jesus. One reader had told Nick he had been the Apostle Paul and that he was returning to bring this healing energy from this former lifetime into the present time. This is the same reason that John had returned: to use the healing ability he had learned from Jesus to heal others now.

Later in the book, the main reader, named Sara, told Nick that he had the same personality and intellect that he had had as an apostle two thousand years ago—that he was basically the same person now as he was then. I was reminded of the reading Melinda had given John in Ohio: "You were yourself in another lifetime! You were John! You walk in the Christ light!"

I was struck by the subject of past lives in this book. When Nick recalls Paul's question to Christ about His having past lives, Jesus answered him by asking who he thought *he* was in a past life. This was the same type of response that I had gotten from Jesus when I asked him if John had lived a past life as John the Apostle: **"What do *you* think?"** He had asked me.

Paul indicated, later in the regression, that Jesus would be available as a spiritual guide whenever anyone needed Him after He left the physical plane. This would explain how Jesus could be speaking through me to John now. He was speaking to us because He was preparing John for his mission.

As I continued reading the book, I wanted with all my heart for John and Nick to meet. If they had both been apostles, I reasoned, surely they would recognize each other in this life. It seemed to me that they both had similar missions. It became apparent that I should start documenting some of the things that were happening to us. Perhaps I should write a letter to Nick, I reasoned, in hopes of "jogging his spiritual memory."

One night, as I picked up the book, I had the distinct feeling that I was skipping ahead in the story by a page or two, but I felt prompted to continue reading where I had started. This was so unlike me. I tend to be very meticulous about detail when doing anything of importance, such as reading this book for confirmations. I would later discover why I had been "guided" to skip those pages: they made reference to the past life I was not yet ready to hear about.

When I finally finished the book, I began to write a very long letter to Nick Bunick, spelling out the highlights concerning John's awakening in the last year. I had spent so much time on the ride home to Texas writing this rough draft letter on a note tablet, that my husband commented that Nick would never have time to read all of it. I agreed with him, but still I felt compelled to get everything down on paper. I firmly believed that the apostles had reincarnated during this time and would be reuniting with a message for the world. I felt I should do my part in bringing at least two of them back together, especially since our experiences seemed to be confirmed several times in *The Messengers*. John and I had felt so connected to this book and to Nick. It seemed only natural that we would share our story with him.

The first thing I did when I got home was to look up the "Sacred Heart" in a book I have called *Brewer's Dictionary of Phrase and Fable*. There it was! The book told of a religious sect that was formed in the seventeenth century when a French nun saw the "sacred heart of Jesus." Of course! It made perfect sense now. Jesus had been telling John that he was connected to Jesus's pure heart energy. What was hard for me to accept was that *I* might be connected to this energy as well. I felt, in my heart, that I was too judgmental to be connected to something as great and pure as the "sacred heart of Jesus." And yet, a part of me accepted this as a confirmation for both John and myself.

The next task was to find out the origin of the name "Felix," and if it could be a name from that time period. I looked in the baby names book my sister had given me years before and found that "Felix" meant "fortune" in Latin. I figured if the name were Latin, chances were that I had been Roman. Not good news as far as I was concerned. To my way of thinking, the Romans had been enemies of Jesus and His followers. I could only imagine what terrible things that lifetime would uncover. I wasn't ready to go there yet.

Randy's parents had given us their old computer during this time, so we now had access to word processing and would soon be getting an online connection to the Internet. I began to type the handwritten letter to Nick, but the rigors of settling back down in our home after several months on the road took precedence. I started to do temporary office work that fall to give us a financial cushion for the next four to five months.

I put finishing the letter to Nick on the back burner, so to speak. Besides, I reasoned, Nick probably receives thousands of letters every month and would be too busy to answer my letter anyway. In the meantime, John called to tell me he had a new cell phone. Now I could reach him anytime. He asked me about the letter and I told him I had been busy and had not finished it yet. He urged me to finish it and send it. "Okay, but why don't *you* send him a letter?" I countered, hoping to get off the hook. "You've already documented our story in your letter. I think *you* should send it," he said. "All right, I'll finish typing the letter and send it when I have time," I said.

Meanwhile, John and his friends, Gracie and Deane, went to the Edgar

Cayce Library in Virginia Beach that November of 1998. The Cayce library has complete records of everything Cayce had ever channeled and John and his friends spent a day and a half there. John found five different references Cayce had made to John the Beloved reincarnating in this life time for the purpose of being the "forerunner" for the second-coming of Jesus Christ.

The next two months would be a busy time for me. I was doing temp work and putting together photo albums as Christmas gifts. I was much too busy, I reasoned, to write a letter! My angels, however, had a different notion about this.

During this time, as I was doing some reception work for an oil company in Houston, a man walked into the lobby who looked just like the picture I had seen of Nick Bunick on the back cover of *The Messengers*. Oh, my God! What would Nick be doing in Houston? I couldn't help staring at this man. As he introduced himself to another receptionist, I hung on every word to make sure it wasn't him. It wasn't. Whew! I took in a deep breath. "Could my angels be trying to tell me something? Nah. Just coincidence," I told myself. Who was I trying to kid? There are no such coincidences!

A few days later I was driving home and saw a sign for a new business that reminded me of Nick's last name. "Bennick's" looked a lot like "Bunick" to me. Then John called me soon after that to ask if I had sent off the letter to Nick.

"That does it!" I thought. "I give up! I will finish the darned thing!" After all, I would soon be seeing John in Florida when I accompanied my husband and the band to a Highland Games in Orlando that next month, in January 1999. I couldn't face him without sending off the letter first. "I have to get this done, however inconvenient," I told myself.

I finished typing the letter to Nick on January 11, 1999, and put it in the mail. I included pictures of John, Randy, and myself taken that summer in Ohio. I didn't really expect to hear back from him very soon, if ever. After all, it was a serious time commitment to sit and read a cover letter and a detailed five-page story that spanned a year's time. I prayed that it would reach him and that he would read it, but it could easily get lost in the huge pile of letters he likely received each day. Imagine my surprise when a week and a half later, I received an envelope in the mail from The Great Tomorrow, Nick's nonprofit organization.

CHAPTER FIVE

Charging into the Unknown

"There's something in the mail for you from The Great Tomorrow," my husband said as he walked in the house with mail in hand.

"The Great Tomorrow?" I responded, surprised. I saw the white envelope that looked too large to be a letter. "Oh, it's probably the newsletter Nick Bunick's office publishes," I said, a little disappointed. I opened it up, and sure enough there was *The Messengers Newsletter* folded in half inside the envelope.

When I opened up the newsletter to read it, I discovered something I wasn't expecting. "There's a letter inside!"

"What?" my husband asked, looking up from his mail.

I could see "THE GREAT TOMORROW" at the top of the letterhead. "It's probably just a polite thank-you form letter that his office sends out," I said, assuming the worst. "Well, at least I tried."

The first paragraph read:

> Dear Sharon,
>
> Thank you for sharing your wonderful story regarding the channeling that you have done for John. Thank you for sharing your photographs and some of the experiences that you've had. I know that there are others like yourself who are committed to being messengers, who are also committed to help others understand their relationship to God as well as enhance their own spirituality.

"Oh, my God!' I exclaimed. "OH, MY GOD!" I looked at my husband in disbelief.

"What's the matter?" he asked.

"I can't believe it! He wrote me back! I mean he *actually* wrote me a letter himself!" I started to do a nervous little dance around the living room. "I can't . . . I can't read this!"

"Do you want me to read it for you?" Randy offered.

"Would you?" I pleaded.

"I will if you want me to," he chuckled.

"Yes!" I said, relieved. I felt like a high school student who had been waiting to receive acceptance into her favorite college.

Randy read me the two-page letter that Nick had written in response to my letter. It was obvious that he had taken the time to read every part of the long story I had written, for he responded to all the points I had made.

He agreed with me that all of us who had lived two thousand years ago are here again to usher in the new millennium. He said that he believed the new leadership of the world would not be political or commercial or academic or religious, but would be a spiritual leadership. He expressed hope that everyone would raise their consciousness and embrace universal love and universal compassion, and elect people in positions of power who would do the same.

He shared his personal belief that some spirits and entities that lived in the past are still in the spirit world, and that it is possible for more than one person on earth to have a spiritual connection to them and receive channeled information from them. He also believed that there are persons living now whose spirit and soul had indeed lived two thousand years ago. However, what was most important to Nick was what each of us was doing now, not who we had been before. He felt we were all messengers and that it was up to each of us to help bring in the new millennium.

Although he could not verify John's past life as John the Apostle, he seemed open to that possibility. He thanked me for sharing my story and gave me permission to share his letter with John. He closed by sending us love and blessings as we continued on our journeys.

"Wow. I've just received a letter from a successful business person, a spiritual leader, and a former apostle," I thought. "This is significant." And yet there was something so warm and personable about him that came through the letter. And dare I say it? Something familiar about his energy.

A couple of days later, I wrote back to Nick to thank him for taking the time to respond to my letter. I thanked him for the forethought he had given to his response because I knew he was a busy man. I told him I agreed that it was not important who we were in a past life, but who we are now. I also thanked him for having the courage to share his story with others and, along those same lines, told him that I had heard from John that Nick had an excellent new book called *In God's Truth*, which I was sure to purchase and read soon.

I closed my letter by sharing with Nick that I had read his letter to John, who was impressed that he had written back. I acknowledged John as the one who had introduced me to Nick's work—something for which I was grateful. I told him I supported his cause, and although my frequent traveling with my husband precluded my starting a Messengers study group in Houston, I offered to help his organization in any way I could. As I sealed up the letter, I said a prayer that my angels would make sure that Nick would read it.

Less than two weeks later, I heard from Nick again! He said he had been sitting at his desk staring at a large pile of letters on a Friday afternoon and had placed his hand in the middle of the pile and found my "very kind and loving letter." He said that he felt it was no accident that he had been led to answer my letter even though there were many others who had written to him earlier whom he had not yet answered. When I read this, I let out a little yelp. "Thank you, angels!" I cried.

He went on to thank me for understanding the comments he had made and not being offended by his statement that it is the present that is important, not the past. He said he knew there would come a time in the future when we would have the opportunity to meet in person.

I chuckled to myself when I saw that he had forgotten to sign his own letter. He must have typed it himself, I thought. If his secretary had typed it, she would have caught the signature as well as some minor typos. I liked this guy! He seemed like a real hands-on type of person.

"Wow! Another letter from Nick! I wonder when this will end?" I asked myself. Randy and I had hooked up to the Internet when we received our computer, but since we were having problems with our modem during my correspondence with Nick, I had written him a regular letter instead of sending an e-mail. At last, we had fixed the problem and were back online again, so I decided to follow up Nick's second letter with an e-mail letter this time.

I had seen Nick's symposium schedule in *The Messengers Newsletter* and couldn't help but notice that seven of his ten symposia were in cities where either Randy's band was performing or where we would be traveling later that year. However, not one of the dates in our schedules coincided with one another. I decided to list both of our schedules side-by-side in the e-mail so he could see how we would keep missing one another, sometimes by as little as a week. "I think our angels do so many wonderful things for us," I wrote, "but sometimes I wonder if they have a laugh on us once in a while! Look at our schedules…the angels must be snickering over this!"

I told him that I knew in my heart that he and John would meet one another someday. Why else would all this be happening in the way that it was? I also made reference to a beautiful and powerful prayer Nick had received from Spirit that was printed in the newsletter. He had asked people everywhere to join him in saying this prayer at 4:44 p.m. on April 4, 1999.[17] I told him that I had sent several copies of the April 4 Prayer to some friends on my mailing list and to a couple of metaphysical centers in Houston. I had also gotten the idea that night to use the Internet to send out copies of the letter to my friends via e-mail. I ended the letter by telling him that I intended to be an "itinerant preacher" on the Renaissance circuit as a way of spreading the word of *The Messengers* since I could not conduct a regular study group.

About a week later, I got a response. He liked my concept of sharing spiritual consciousness over the Web through e-mails. He said that his organization, in Portland, Oregon, was making plans for their own April 4 Prayer activity at a local Unity Church and that he had no way of knowing for sure whether they would have two hundred people or two thousand show up for it. He hoped that one day the number of people saying the prayer would grow large enough to fill up a huge athletic stadium.

He ended by saying he felt sure he and John and I would get to spend some quality time together some day since, as he said, "I only have another thirty years before I have to call for time out." He expressed his own and his staff's gratitude for the opportunity to bring people together who were on the same spiritual journey and stated that everyone's growth was being enhanced by the opportunity to help one another. He closed by saying that he was in the "lull before the storm" as his speaking engagements were about to begin in a couple of weeks.

"How cool that Nick remembered who I was and e-mailed me back," I told my husband. It looked like Nick and I were starting to become pen pals. I e-mailed him back with a touching poem my friend Janet in Ohio had forwarded to me.[18] I suggested that he might want to include it in one of his newsletters. I was so touched that Nick was taking the time to write me back in the middle of his busy schedule that I made sure I acknowledged him for it.

As I continued to write the letter, a thought popped into my head which I included in the e-mail as I was typing. The weekend of the prayer, which fell on Easter Sunday, was one of the few weekends that year that I was not working with my husband's band. I could use this time, while I was there, to pay a visit to my friend Lauren, who was now living with her parents in Portland. Because I could not attend any of the symposia, I reasoned, I could take the opportunity to participate in Nick's local prayer ceremony and have the chance to hear him speak and, possibly, meet him in person. I closed by asking him to e-mail me with more information about the ceremony because I was seriously considering joining them for it.

It seemed like a wild, fleeting thought. What had possessed me to ask that? Was I crazy for wanting to fly up there? And *why* was I wanting to fly up there anyway? It was time to have a conversation with my angels.

The next afternoon, as I was enjoying the outdoors, I asked my angels why I felt compelled to go to Portland to meet Nick and to join his April 4 prayer ceremony. I could easily say the prayer from where I was in Texas and still contribute to the energy being sent forth. My angels told me that I should go to Portland and that doing so would change my life *forever*. Now that was a scary thought! I wondered if they meant that I would have to go through a painful process first. Surely the change would be for my own good, but why would my physical presence be needed there?

I have learned not to argue with my angels. It does no good because they have the habit of pestering me until I listen to them. They are very persistent and "loud" when they have something important to say. "Okay," I sighed. "I will go to Portland. I don't know *why* I'm being guided to go there, but if you say I should go then I will." I feared, however, that I might be going crazy. I could only recall one other time in my life when I was asked to take such a big leap of faith and to risk money I really didn't have to spend to follow a blind, intuitive prompting such as this.[19]

I called John to tell him that I was planning to go to Portland. John, being the spur-of-the-moment kind of guy he is, thought it was a wonderful idea and was considering flying up there himself. We could both drag Lauren to this thing, and she would probably love it. And, most important, my dream would come true: John and Nick would finally have the opportunity to meet one another! This plan was starting to seem a little more rational, now.

I e-mailed Nick to tell him of my plans to travel to Portland, and that John was thinking about joining me. John had been having 444 experiences[20] ever since Nick and I had started corresponding, and I told Nick about how the previous two nights John had been awakened at exactly 4:44 a.m. I told him that I was starting to feel like the odd man out because I had not received any 444 experiences yet. "It seems my thing is the 11:11 experience," I told him.[21]

Then my e-mail letter took another direction. When John and I had been discussing the possibility of meeting for the April 4 Prayer, a hunch about my past life came up that I wanted to share with Nick:

You know, I said something to John that triggered almost a memory in me. I can't be sure at this point, but since I am playing the role of go-between for the two of you now, it makes me wonder if I had played that role back then. You said that Paul was disdainful of the other apostles in the beginning. Is it possible I could have been a mediator/communicator for the two of you? It's just a thought. Did Paul know someone named Felix back then? The night I had my conversation with Jesus in the parking lot in Maryland, I said a prayer before going to bed asking for more information about who I might have been back then. I woke up in the middle of the night saying 'Felix.'

I emphasized that I didn't want to go off on a tangent about it because it was, after all, conjecture at this point.

I told Nick that it would be very nice to be able to spend some time with him when I arrived in Portland, but even if we could not get together, I would still be very happy to spend some time with my friend Lauren. I ended by expressing that my sincerest wish from the beginning was to bring him and John back together again in this life and that I hoped they could finally meet one another at the prayer meeting.

When I sent off the e-mail, it was already the end of February, and I wasn't sure if I would hear back from Nick in a timely manner as I knew he was already busy getting ready for his speaking tour in March. Because of this—and the fact that John and I wanted to buy the lowest-priced advance-purchase tickets in enough time for the Easter holiday—I decided to e-mail The Great Tomorrow asking for more information about the time and location of the April 4 Prayer.

A couple of days later I received a kind e-mail from The Great Tomorrow staff saying they would be "honored" if I could join them. I was informed that the event would include speakers, such as Doreen Virtue—author of *Divine Guidance: How to Have a Dialogue with God and Your Guardian Angels*—and some local musicians. What impressed me most was that there was no charge for attending the prayer ceremony. This only confirmed my belief that Nick was conducting this prayer from the sincerest part of himself and that he believed that it should be free and available to anyone who wished to participate.

Fifteen minutes after this e-mail was sent to me, a second e-mail arrived from Nick's office. This time it was from Kim Bunick, Nick's daughter. I had been sending e-mails to Nick on Kim's e-mail address because that was the only address that I had for him; however, I was pleasantly surprised when suddenly I found myself corresponding with her. She thanked me for sending the poem and said that their staff would love to put it in the newsletter. Thus began my friendship with Kim, which would prove not only rewarding, but helpful in the future.

I called my friend Lauren to see if it would be all right if I stayed with her from April 1-5. She said she would be honored to host me during my visit. So it was all set. I took a deep breath and called the airlines to purchase a nonrefundable ticket to Portland for the Easter holiday. "This better be worth it," I told myself as I charged the ticket to my credit card. "Nonrefundable ticket" kept bouncing around in my head. "I can't back out now!" I told myself.

It was during this time that I started to lose hair by the fistful every day. I couldn't understand why I would be so stressed out about going to Portland. Maybe I was nervous about meeting Nick or maybe it was the thought of having to pay the bill for my airline ticket. Surely I wouldn't be *that* nervous to meet Nick. He seemed like a nice enough person from the tone of his letters. And it wouldn't be the first time I had charged a significant amount of money to my credit card. It just didn't make sense to me.

The funny part of this is that my extremely money-conscious husband did not even bat an eyelash when I told him that my angels were sending me to Portland, and we would have to pay for it on credit. In his eyes, using the credit card instead of cash was synonymous with committing a sin. This was so unlike him! Now I *knew* my angels were the guiding force behind this trip! Nonetheless, I was still very scared.

John called me in March to say that because of his financial situation, he would not be flying up to Portland, after all. Because Nick was scheduled to speak two weeks after the April 4 Prayer at a symposium in Ft. Lauderdale—the same city where John was staying—John decided to attend this meeting instead. I e-mailed Kim and informed her of John's change of plans and also shared with her that John had had four 444 experiences on four consecutive days and asked her to pass this information along to Nick. "Tell Nick to be looking for a big bear of a guy at the symposium in Ft. Lauderdale," I wrote.

It was during this time that John decided to e-mail Nick himself and share his story. He told me he felt the timing was right for contacting Nick, especially since they would be meeting one another the next month. In his e-mail letter to Nick, John outlined the highlights of his spiritual experiences, which had begun seven years prior. He realized how amazing some of his experiences might seem to others, so he felt compelled to reassure Nick that he had never used drugs in his life and that there was no history of mental illness in his family. When I read the copy he sent to me, I had to laugh to myself because I didn't feel John needed to reassure Nick of anything. I felt that Nick would believe all of John's experiences. After all, Nick was no stranger to these types of experiences himself. John ended by thanking Nick for having patience with his "over-long message" and for sharing with the world his message of love from Jesus.

John was excited about the possibility of his meeting Nick and also for my opportunity to meet him as well. "Wow!" I thought. "Both John and I will finally be meeting the person who was the subject of a book that has had such a significant impact on our lives."

The only disappointing part was that we would not be meeting him at the same time. If we were, then we could share that experience together. "Perhaps there is a reason for this," I pondered. I would find out later why I was being sent to Portland alone, but at the moment I had no clue. I was deeply grateful that John and Nick would at last be meeting one another. "If only I could be a fly on the wall and see this myself," I told John. "Don't worry. You'll hear all about it. *Believe* me!" he reassured.

Also during this time, I contacted a woman named Brenda who was about to start a Messengers study group in the Houston area to see if I could join her group. I thought it would be nice to meet people who had the same interests as me and eventually to share the experiences John and I had had with others who knew about Nick and his story. Brenda, who had a friendly, bubbly personality, and I hit it off on the phone and arranged to meet for dinner. I learned that she had met with Nick on several occasions and that they were actually good friends. The timing of this was not lost on me!

We met for dinner at a local restaurant and a long conversation followed. I shared with her my experiences with John and how I had channeled Jesus for him. She was fascinated with our story. As the conversation went on, I asked her to join me on the trip to Portland. She said she would have to check her children's school holiday schedule and clear it with her husband first, but she would love to come. Brenda invited me to her house the next day to give her a reading and to talk some more. She said that she would try to call Nick and tell him of our plans to come to Portland for the April 4 Prayer.

When I came over the next day, Brenda tried calling Nick and Atira, one of Nick's angel readers, but neither one was home, so she left messages instead. I gave Brenda a reading and we spent the whole day talking. She shared with me her own spiritual experiences and how she and Nick met and became friends.

The next day I received an e-mail from Brenda saying both Nick and Atira had returned her phone calls. Atira said she was looking forward to meeting me at the April 4 Prayer and would be looking for me. Nick had apparently already gotten the message that I was coming to Portland but was surprised when Brenda told him she was planning to join me for the trip. When I read her e-mail, I intuitively felt that, in the end, she would not be able to accompany me. As it would turn out, her plans were later canceled due to a terminal illness in her family, which only emphasized to me that I needed to make the trip alone. However, I knew that Brenda's call could help recommend me to Nick, in case he might be thinking I was a wild-eyed groupie.

During this time, John had asked me to give him a long-distance reading. I was busy working and was too tired at the end of the day to do much of anything, but when he dropped another hint, I resolved that no matter how tired I was, I would give him a reading on the evening of Tuesday, March 9, 1999. I asked him to meditate and pray at a certain time from his place in Florida while I did his reading from my home in Texas. I was hoping that his sending me energy, while I tuned into it, would allow me to have a stronger connection to him.

John had e-mailed me his questions earlier that day, so after meditating and praying, I began to answer the questions in the order in which he had written them. His first question was: "I feel as if I am not fulfilling my purpose. What am I to do and how do I achieve what I am here to do?" The Master Himself came in to answer this first question.

> Beloved John, you know what you have come here to do. You have always known it is to prepare My way. You may not know it, but you were chosen for this mission by Me, for the pureness of your heart. This great heart of yours is used to heal others' pain. You have always known that you would one day have all the answers to these questions. Time and time again you have asked, but you will not listen for the answers in your own heart and mind. You need to trust your own wisdom and communion with Me. For it has always been a supreme sacrifice for you to know Me. You must listen to your own guidance and trust it.
>
> Perhaps this reading will confirm what you already know to be true. You must let go of your fears and doubts—release the old and crippled ways that no longer serve you. To follow My path is one of sacrifice and love. When you put the needs of others before your own self-interests—when serving God is your first and only concern—then you will be ready for the mission you have come here to serve. Many times you have asked and many times you have been told that the pathway to God is through your own door.

The rest of the reading, which concerned John's future work and relationships, came through Spirit. When I was finished, I tried to call John but couldn't get through, so I started typing the reading into an e-mail message for him. While I was typing, he called to ask me how the reading had gone. I told him that the first part was a channeled message from "the big guy Himself." John just laughed and said, "In the beginning, when you had me meditate, I prayed that Jesus would come through and speak to you."

"Are you serious? That's exactly what happened! I didn't know that you had asked for that, but when He came through, I wondered if you had."

"How's that for a confirmation?" he asked.

"Oh my goodness. Yes. I would say so!" I sputtered.

As I read the reading to him over the phone, he asked me to reread certain parts, such as the channeled message from Jesus. I knew he would want a hard copy of it, so when we got off the phone, I finished typing the reading and sent it to him that night. I had prefaced it by saying I hoped that I had been in tune enough during the reading since I had been so tired.

The next day he e-mailed back. "I thank you from the bottom of my heart for the reading. You were able to verify a lot of the thoughts that I [had] already had," he wrote. He responded to all the salient points in the reading and ended with a reading of his own.

> So you see, my friend, your reading was perfect. It is time for you to trust your guidance. Step up to the front of the wagon train and lead some of these troubled souls. You are so afraid that your ego will get in the way. Don't you see your fear is slowing you down. I say slowing you down because you are always moving forward. There are people in this world who are jealous of your gifts, and still others who would use your gift for their own purposes. You know who they are when you meet them.
>
> The reason you get so down when things don't go as you expect is because you have a pure soul and you see things from a higher perspective. When people are not as evolved in their thinking as you are, it is disheartening for you. Using words from the reading you gave me, 'you have to protect yourself from the negativity of others.' You are absolutely the most connected person I have ever met. Anything you put your mind to you can accomplish. This includes the work you will be doing [with Nick in the future.] You will be having your own 444 experiences very soon. My experiences are a foreshadowing of yours.
>
> Every day I thank God for your friendship and am proud of all the work you are doing.

I appreciated very much that John was staying in touch with me by phone and e-mail during this time. He was helping me to deal with this feeling of foreboding I was having about the trip. Though I knew it wasn't the flying part that was causing me to be nervous, I just couldn't figure out why my anxiety was increasing the closer the time came for me to leave.

In mid-March, I accompanied my husband and the band while they performed on a week-long Caribbean cruise. I was hoping that the cruise would help me relax, but underneath the surface, I continued to feel anxious and I continued to lose hair. Luckily, my hair is naturally thick or I might have gone bald!

When I got back from the cruise, I found that Lauren had left me a voice mail message. "Sharon," she said, "I have gotten this incredible offer to accompany my Irish dance class on an all-expenses-paid trip to Ireland for the World Irish Dance Championships. The problem is that the trip is scheduled during the same time that you are due to come to Portland."

When I called her back, she was relieved when I insisted that she take advantage of this once-in-a-lifetime offer. I, in turn, was relieved when she said that it was okay with her parents that I stay at their house during my visit, and I would have the use of her car. Now if I had had any doubts that this was meant to be a solo journey, those doubts were over. There would be nothing to distract me from the purpose of my trip, whatever that was!

Although it was obvious that my angels had helped to arrange everything that I would need in Portland, I have to admit I felt very alone in my journey. I was going to a strange city, staying at the home of strangers, not knowing a soul there or what I was going to do with myself for the three days before Easter Sunday. I needed to lean on John to get me through this, and as usual, my friend was there for me.

Dear Sharon,

I know that things are very scary for you right now. Everything is moving so fast! That, I believe, is how things happen when you are coming to a point of life change. I know in my heart that you will be reading for Nick and that you are embarking on a new and exciting time in your life.

It is in this time of change that you must remain composed and alert. Your guides will be speaking to you clearer and more often. This, I believe, is a time of Renaissance for you and for the world. With Nick's guides helping you, I believe you will find a new path to follow. They will raise you to a new understanding of spiritualism and faith.

In the times you have read for me, you have channeled Jesus. In the times to come you will not only channel His thoughts but His essence (for lack of a better word). This is a gift to you from Him. It is a gift you must accept with open arms as the things you will be passing on will be for all.

I know this responsibility scares you. At times like that you must realize that we are all part of God, and you are only the means through which He is communicating. You are worthy as you are a part of Him. Who is to say that God is not worthy? Certainly not me or you. There is no worthy or not worthy. It just is. This means that there is no reason to be worried about what will be channeled through you.

In my heart, I know that you will do fine and that you are coming to a place you were always headed. It is the age of enlightenment, and you are getting positioned where you need to be for the world to evolve. I would say to you, 'God be with you.' We know, however, that He is always with you.

Just felt I needed to say this again.

Love.................John

This e-mail was the beginning of several powerful channeled readings from John that spring. John was finally doing the channeling I knew he was capable of. Although he has no memory of writing these e-mails, we were both inspired when we went back and read them again a few months later.

On March 21, I sent an e-mail message to The Great Tomorrow staff telling them that I would be flying to Portland alone. I asked if someone there could recommend some people in Portland who had the same interests I did and with whom I could connect when I got there. The next day I received an e-mail from Kim, who suggested that I might want to call Jacquelyne Ellis—an angel reader—or Peggy Keating, who was a Messengers study group leader in the Portland area. I called both the phone numbers listed, but neither person was home, so I had to leave messages for each.

Peggy returned my call first. She graciously offered to let me join her study group and to show me around the Portland area. This connection would prove useful in putting me in touch with some wonderful people there. Later that evening, Aron Fox, Jacquelyne's husband, called me back. He was under the impression that I had called to schedule a reading, but when I told him that I had really just called with the intention of hooking up with the people in their study group, he said that they had decided not to start a group after all because they were anticipating a move to Montana that summer.

A thought crossed my mind that perhaps I was being connected to Jacquelyne because I was meant to have a reading from her. When I inquired about this, I was told that the soonest she could meet with me was in late April. I told him that that would be too late as I would only be in Portland during the first week of April. Oh well, I thought. It would have been nice to have a reading while I was there. Perhaps Jacquelyne could have told me why I was making this trip in the first place. Aron must have sensed my disappointment. "Well, occasionally people call to cancel their appointments. I could put your name on a waiting list," he offered. A waiting list! This lady must be booked solid that people would have to request being put on a waiting list!

"All right," I said, not expecting much. "Go ahead and put me on the list. You can call me at this number up to March 31." Although I realized that there seemed to be little hope of getting in to see Jacquelyne, I had a gut feeling that my angels might work to get me a reading after all. "If it is meant to be," I told myself, "then there will be an opening." On the night of March 31, as if on cue, I received a call from Aron.

"Sharon? This is Aron, Jacquelyne Ellis's husband. We've had a cancellation on Friday morning, April 2. I remembered that you asked me to put you on the waiting list. Are you still interested in making an appointment for a reading?"

Was I still *interested?* "Yes!" I exclaimed.

"Someone must be pulling some strings for you," he said. I had to smile. The timing was just too perfect to be an accident. I thanked my angels for coming through for me yet again.

CHAPTER SIX

Portal in Portland

T he next day, I was on the plane heading for Portland. I settled back in my seat and looked out the window. What on earth could have possessed me to make this trip? Something had told me I should document my trip, so I brought a journal with an angel on the cover, which I now pulled out to record some of my thoughts:

> I asked my guides last week why they are sending me [to Portland], besides the fact that I am attending a prayer ceremony on Easter Sunday led by author Nick Bunick. They answered with a question: 'Do you really want to know?' That shut me up. I guess I really didn't want to know because I was afraid of hearing the answer. It's fear of the unknown and the fact that my guides have prompted me to come and told me that my life was about to change. Change is scary, especially when you don't consciously know what to expect. . . .
>
> Not long after I started [to read] the book, *The Messengers*, I began to feel connected to Nick Bunick. His words, spirit, and personality seemed familiar to me. His memory of the life of Paul and Jeshua (as Jesus was called then) was fascinating and somehow felt familiar. I suspect that I knew Nick and John in that past life. I feel like I might have been a go-between or a communicator for them. I know I will someday have the opportunity to relive that experience, but I don't know when. A part of me feels very guilty for something I did or didn't do concerning Christ, and I need to put it behind me. I have feared this, but I know I must come to terms with it.

As I continued to write the highlights of the experiences John and I had had over the previous year and a half, I noted that John had become my closest spiritual friend. In a way, I felt that I was taking a part of him with me to Portland. Although I was making this trip for my own spiritual reasons, I knew in my heart that John would benefit from it as well.

I arrived in Portland and took a cab to Lauren's parents' house. That night, after settling in, I drove to Peggy's house in West Linn, a suburb not far from where Nick lives on Lake Oswego, for the Messengers study group meeting. I shared my story of John with Peggy, who got chills when I mentioned he had been John the Apostle. She had been told by a reader a couple of days before that she would be meeting John the Apostle, and here I was telling her that John had almost made the trip to Portland! Maybe they would have another opportunity to meet in the future, I thought.

I met some wonderful people there, including a sweet woman in her late sixties named Margaret. She and I made plans to get together on Saturday to tour around the Willamette River countryside. She also invited me to join the rest of the Messengers study group at a special Easter Brunch before the April 4 Prayer Ceremony and to sit with their group that Sunday. Again, my angels had helped connect me with just the right people.

The next morning I prepared to drive to Jacquelyne's house for my reading. She was warm and welcoming, and I felt immediately comfortable with her. She recorded the session on cassette tape as she spent the next hour speaking to my angels. I had come there seeking answers to three major questions. The first question I asked concerned why I had been told by my angels that I should actually be present in Portland during the April 4 Prayer. The second question had to do with verifying if John had really been John the Apostle. (At that point in time, I had been the only reader—besides Melinda, who had made a reference to it in Ohio—who had told this to John, and I was anxious to receive verification of this information from someone else.) The third question concerned my past life during the time of Christ and why I was feeling so guilty about it.

Jacquelyne began to answer my first question by telling me that the connections I was making with the people in Portland would be lifelong friendships and would prove to be valuable networking for me in the future. Then her words took me by surprise:

"You could have joined with this prayer anywhere, but having you physically here amplifies it tremendously," she said. "Now this is what you do for us. You being here physically amplifies—now Gabriel's doing the horn thing—amplifies this energy…and sends it out…poof! If you weren't here physically, we would lose a lot of juice. Your being here somehow magnifies the concentrated energy that will happen in this church on Sunday. It magnifies it and catapults it out into and through the country in a way that if you weren't here physically wouldn't happen as easily.…I don't know why…[but] it's real clear that you pack an extra powder and you being here physically really makes a big difference." (That Sunday, *I* would be the one feeling very honored to be able to join my energy with the energy from all the wonderful people who had gathered in that church to pray with Nick.)

When I asked what the angels had to say about John's having been John the Apostle, I thought at first that Jacquelyne would not be able to access that information.

"This is where it gets a little complicated for me," she said. "Some of this is over my head…whew…sailing right over. They're showing me that from the angels' point of view, ultimately, it doesn't matter [whether] or not he walked in that body as that man or not…"

She went on to explain that some energies of great beings, such as Mary Magdalene and the Apostle Paul, became archetypal energies. Because they had a huge message to deliver and a commitment to carry a particular energy, especially during this millennial era, they had to split off or be divided in order to help awaken the planet. Therefore, there are many people who feel connected to them and carry the energies and memories of those great people although they were not the *original* embodiment of those people themselves.

"So," she continued, "they say that ultimately it doesn't matter whether he wore those sandals or not, but then they are going to go a little deeper and let me see whether or not this one is truly an incarnation of this being. They say definitely he carries the energy. Let me go a little further here."

As she paused to make a deeper connection, I held my breath. Would I finally get a confirmation that John had actually lived as John the Apostle? It was apparent to me that Jacquelyne was a gifted reader, and I felt I could trust her answer. I believed that she had integrity and that she wouldn't just tell me what I wanted to hear.

"Well," she said at last, "he certainly carries more than a token trace of this energy. *I would be willing to say that he was the man.*" Her words hit me like a wave. "If he was not the man, then he carries a significant amount of this energy, more than just a fleck or two that would be enough to awaken him to himself. He carries quite a bit more than that.

"They're showing that when these energies split off—when Paul split off, when Mary split off, and when Mother Mary split off into billions of little pieces to be shed and shared with all these different people—this one didn't splinter into little fragments. This one divided into what looks like three parts. He was one third of that energy. This looks like it is enough to say that it was him."

I wondered why John's energy had not split off in so many directions like the others. There had to be a reason for it, I pondered. Perhaps it was necessary that his energy and memories remain concentrated because of his mission to usher in the second coming of Christ. Then Jacquelyne elaborated on what John had come here to do:

> He carries the energy. He carries the frequency. He carries the message, and, because of this, he carries the responsibility to bear that message. There's a big responsibility that goes with that. He can't just blend into the crowd and be one of the guys anymore. This is a call to stand up. It's a call to stand out. It's a call to speak in a bigger way than he would have normally done by himself . . . he needs to find some way of taking this message out now to the public and not just holding this in. This is real important. This is a big responsibility. They're showing that he has been anointed and sent into service.

I was relieved to finally hear another reader, one whom I respected, confirm John's past life, or at least the possibility that he had been the original, physical incarnation of John the Beloved. I now felt that I could have more faith in what I had received. I knew John would be pleased to receive this confirmation, as well.

I began the third question by giving Jacquelyne some background information about John's discovery of Edgar Cayce's prophecy of the reincarnation of John the Apostle and how my wanting to confirm that information had led to my conversation with Jesus in the parking lot. "I'm just wondering," I went on. "I feel like I might be a connection to Nick and John…like somehow I might have been a go-between, because Paul had kind of kept himself separate from the other apostles." I told her how I had prayed for more guidance the night of my conversation with Jesus and had gotten the name Felix. "So," I concluded, "I have no idea if that is true or not…but I'm wondering if they feel, at this time, that they can share any information about that with me."

"You would be served by doing a regression, but I don't see that you need a regression about this particular lifetime because the information's coming up. It's being revealed…it is coming to the surface, bit by bit," she reassured me.

"I really get strongly that what you got from Jesus was absolutely correct," Jacquelyne said, referring to my feeling of guilt from that past life. "He never felt let down by you. He never felt like you didn't do something you should have. He says, '**You showed up to the meeting and you decided it wasn't for you.**' And He says that, '**what you needed to do was show up and you did that.**' Your [spiritual] role, usually, [has been] to sit on the side or to sit in the middle. You're often the one who holds the doorway between this and that...You're usually the one that sits in the middle so you can see both sides. Your job was to expose yourself to what was happening, to know what it was, and then you would be able to tell the truth [about it]."

Jacquelyne elaborated on my role as go-between in that lifetime. "There was this faction [who were the followers of Christ] that said, 'Oh, this is what's happening—this is what it's all about,' and then this [other] group [who were against Jesus], said, 'They don't know what they are talking about. They're all delusional, and this is madness, and this is crazy and dangerous.' You stood in the middle. You camped with these folks and you camped with these folks. You knew what the truth was. So you were able to be that discerner who stood in the middle, not choosing a camp.

"Some of your friends were very much against this Jesus guy. Some of the people you knew thought that this was absolute madness and that these followers were a little kooky in the head. Or . . . worse, were going to be very dangerous and were going to cause all kinds of things to come upon your people. So you needed to know what they [the followers of Jesus] were thinking so you...could tell the truth, so you could say, 'Hey, this is [what's really] going on.' If you had joined [with them], you wouldn't have known what they were doing...[or] thinking. You would have been too close here, and you wouldn't have been trusted by this side either. You needed to stay on the outside in order to know both sides.

"So, this was absolutely on purpose . . . [Jesus] knew these would and these wouldn't [join up with Him] and these would turn away from Him and say that He was full of it. **"And this one that was you,"** He says, **"would not join with me, would not walk with me, but would stay in fellowship with me, but would do so . . . on the sidelines."** And many people who knew you wouldn't have known how dear the message was to you. Because you didn't show it. You became the master of the poker face. You would often have to be in the midst of the enemy . . . taking it all in, interacting and knowing the truth.

"It's a very tremendous commitment, not to Jesus, but to the greater order—to God. Your commitment was to the bigger plan, and that was holding that pyramid of energy between the two. So, absolutely you did the right thing. He says, **"You let yourself down because you kept looking back** [during that life] **wondering if you had made the right decision."** You absolutely made the right decision. You'll get more of this in the weeks and months to come," she concluded.

For the first time, I was feeling like maybe this Felix character, whoever he was, was not such a bad guy after all. Maybe there *was* a higher purpose for this role of the go-between. The reading not only implied that I had known the followers (or apostles) of Jesus, but also had been intimately acquainted with their beliefs and had secretly supported them. If I had played the role of communicator between Paul and John in that previous lifetime, it would certainly explain the link I had with them now. Jacquelyne was right. There was more information to come, but for now this was as much as I could handle. I left the reading with a lot to think about.

The next day, Margaret, whom I had met at the Messengers meeting, and I went touring the beautiful Willamette countryside. Later that day, she introduced me to her lovely daughter, Ann. As Margaret and I said our good-byes that evening, we made plans to go to the April 4 Prayer Ceremony together with Ann and another lady from the study group. "Ann and I will pick you up in the morning for Stan and Lea's Easter brunch," she said, "But let's not stay too long. I want us to be at the church early enough to get a good seat."

"I'll be ready and wearing my angel dress," I told her. I remembered how John had teased me about my telling Kim and Nick that I was planning to wear my white "angel" dress so that they would be able to recognize me in the crowd. It was a dress that I wore when I gave special readings. In spite of John's ribbing, I felt the energy of the dress would be perfect for the prayer.

That night I had trouble sleeping. "I can't believe I'm still losing hair," I told myself. "This is ridiculous! I can't wait for this whole thing to be over." I got up early to get organized and dressed. I had found a picture on Lauren's bulletin board of John and his partner Spencer taken at the faire in Ohio, where Lauren and I first met. I decided to borrow it in order to remind Nick what John looked like. I put the picture, along with a twenty-dollar bill to buy my own copy of *The Messengers,* inside an envelope that I put in the pocket of my raincoat.

Margaret and Ann came by the next morning to pick me up, and we headed to Stan and Lea's house for a wonderful brunch with about twenty other people. Afterward, we drove to the Unity Church on Stark Street, arriving about an hour early.

I felt strongly that, for energy reasons, I should sit in a particular seat that was centrally located and close to the podium. This seat, which had previously been occupied, suddenly opened up, and I claimed it. The lady who had been sitting there said she had been guided to sit somewhere else. As I sat there in that special spot, Stan's wife, Lea, joined me.

While Lea and I were waiting, a woman from our Messengers group came up to us and told us that Nick Bunick and Doreen Virtue were downstairs in the basement, waiting to go on. I took this as a cue from my angels. The time had come for me to meet Nick. I invited Lea to join me. As we saved our seats with our coats, we both brought our cameras, and I brought my envelope—with John's picture and my book money inside—and headed for the basement.

Lea and I descended the stairs with nervous anticipation. As if on cue, Nick was walking to the center of the room just as we entered. I let Lea introduce herself first. I couldn't believe I was standing so close to this very special person whom I had seen only in the pictures on the covers of his books. Yep, he looked just like his picture. "I wonder if he will remember me?" I thought, as I waited for my turn. He exuded a warmth as he spoke to Lea, and his dark eyes sparkled as he glanced my way. Our eyes locked for a second or two.

"Oh, here it comes!" I said to myself as he hugged Lea and walked toward me. "Hi, Nick. I'm Sharon Wothke from Houston," I said. I extended my arm for a handshake, but Nick gave me a hug instead. Before I could remind him that we had been corresponding and that I had written to him about John, he did one better. He surprised me by remembering something I had almost forgotten.

"Oh, yes," he responded in his distinct Bostonian accent "You're the one that sent that beautiful poem to our newsletter." So he *did* read all the e-mails I had sent him! "So good to meet you."

"Thank you," I chirped. "It's so good to finally meet you."

"How *is* John?" he asked.

"He's doing great," I said, my head still swimming.

"I responded to his e-mail a couple of days ago. Did he tell you?" he inquired.

Did he *tell* me? Heck, John sent me a copy of the whole darned thing!

"Yes, he did." I said, trying to remain cool. "We stay in pretty close touch with each other. In fact, I brought a picture of him with me. Would you like to see?" I said, as I slid the picture half way out of the envelope. Nick held the envelope to get a good look at the picture. "I thought it might help you to remember what he looks like when you see him in couple of weeks."

He smiled as he looked at the picture. "That's right. John said he would be attending the symposium in Ft. Lauderdale," he responded. "Thank you, Sharon," he said as he gave me a big hug. "I look forward to meeting him."

Damn, this guy was good! He didn't miss *anything*, did he? I couldn't believe with all the people that wrote to Nick and all the people with whom he interacted each time he did a symposium that he would remember John and me. I was flattered.

"Would you like to meet Doreen Virtue?" he asked, surprising both Lea and me.

"Sure. That would be great," we said, as we walked toward an attractive blonde woman in a light purple dress who was sitting at a table and talking to Lea's husband Stan. Doreen smiled a warm, genuine smile as she stood up to greet us. Tall and slim, she towered over me in height as I introduced myself and shook her hand. I apologized for interrupting their preparation time, but she graciously assured me that there was no need to worry.

As Lea and I said our good-byes and headed back toward the stairs, I realized that I had forgotten to ask Nick and Doreen if they would pose for pictures with us. I hated to impose on them again, but I knew this would be my only chance to capture this special moment with a photograph as a keepsake for John and me. They were so nice about posing for us. Our business was done, so we thanked them again and headed back upstairs to wait for the ceremony to begin.

"Wow!" What an opportunity. The moment had been perfect. No one else was in the basement vying for Nick's attention, and as an extra bonus I got to meet Doreen Virtue. Life was feeling pretty good at that moment, and I was sure my angels had sent the messenger who told me they were there in the first place. I was riding high because Nick had recognized me and I had had a few precious moments to speak with him. I felt something click into place when we met, but I didn't know what that something was. One thing was certain, though: he was a very sweet, approachable person.

Lea and I took our seats, and Stan joined us soon after. The sanctuary was now filled to capacity, including the balcony area. There was some last-minute hustle and bustle as people found their seats, but the sanctuary became quiet as Nick took the podium. He slipped the microphone out of its holder and slowly walked back and forth across the stage as he addressed the audience.

Nick introduced himself and gave us an outline of who would be speaking and the order of events that would take place over the next three hours. He thanked us for coming and asked all those who had traveled from out-of-state to attend the prayer service to stand up. I noticed that there were quite a few of us. Maybe as many as forty of us stood up and were applauded by the rest of the audience. As I sat back down in my seat, my heart suddenly leapt as Nick unexpectedly pointed me out to the crowd.

"My friend, Sharon, came all the way from Houston to be with us today," he said.

I found myself in a shy, half-crouching stand, as I turned to acknowledge the audience's applause. Then, in almost the same breath, he introduced his angel readers Jacquelyne[22] and Atira,[23] who both stood up and acknowledged the audience's applause as well. He introduced the two Unity ministers who would speak and made an attempt to introduce his daughter, Kim, and the rest of his staff, but they were downstairs in the basement setting up the complimentary refreshments for the intermission. Talk about being included with fine company! I felt very honored.

Both ministers spoke, as well as Doreen, who moved us with her true-life stories and good humor. After a song from a very gifted singer, the audience moved toward the basement for a break and refreshments. I noticed that immediately, several people had lined up to speak to Nick and to have him sign their books. Books! That reminded me that I needed to buy my *own* copy of Nick's book from the church bookstore so that I could have him sign mine, as well.

I searched and searched for my envelope. Not only did I want to get a book with the money, but I was concerned that I had taken a picture that belonged to Lauren, which was now missing. I finally gave up looking and went downstairs to grab a bite to eat. I ran into my new friends from the study group and asked them to be on the lookout for my envelope. I also ran into Atira, who had been looking for me, and we had a brief, pleasant conversation. However, my mind was on finding that envelope, and I couldn't rest until I did.

As I was turning to go back upstairs, I was stopped by a lady, who said, "There you are! You're Nick's…aaaahh…Nick's…" She finally gave up. "*Who* are you?"

"I'm Sharon from Houston," I laughed. Nick's introduction had given me some momentary notoriety! Apparently, she must have thought that I was one of Nick's readers.

I remembered how intimidated I had felt when John said he believed that I would eventually be doing readings for Nick. Even Brenda had come up with that idea. "No chance of that now!" I said to myself. "No, siree. I will be on a plane back to Houston tomorrow. Now I can stop being so nervous about this whole thing." Reading for Nick, I reasoned, would not be the same as reading for John. At this point, I was happy just to be "Sharon from Houston."

The intermission was almost over, so I headed back upstairs to make one more search for the envelope. As I approached my seat, I saw that Nick was still standing there talking to a group of people and signing books. Though he had tried, he had never been able to leave the sanctuary. I felt bad for him because I knew from my association with my husband's band how dry one's mouth can get when one has to talk to a great many people and there's no time for a break before one has to go on stage again. I hurried downstairs to get him some water before he went on.

As I approached him with the cup of cold water, he looked genuinely grateful. "Thank you, Sharon, " he said as he took the cup from me and kissed my cheek. "I will take this up to the podium with me." He squeezed in a couple more people before going on. In the meantime, someone behind me asked me about "my" angel scribe website. Apparently, she, too had confused me as being one of Nick's readers. I started to get tickled with this mistaken identity. No, I didn't have a spiritual website, but that's a great idea, I thought.

Nick approached the podium, took a few sips of the water I had given him and paused briefly before addressing us again. He began preparing us for the big moment by asking us to meditate silently. I visualized sending him as much love and light energy as I could. I wanted to make sure that enough energy was being sent from the prayer to spread throughout the world. After the meditation, we all stood up with Nick and recited the prayer together.

> Dear God,
> We acknowledge that You are our Creator, our Father and our Mother, and we love You and are grateful for the gifts You have given unto us. We are honored that You have given unto us immortality by anointing us with Your Spirit.
> Jeshua, we acknowledge You as our Father's Beloved Son, our brother and our spiritual guide. We love You and are grateful for the example that You have provided us through your life while on earth.
> Our loving angel guides, we acknowledge that You are the messengers of God, who watch over us, protecting us and inspiring us. We ask You our dear Lord, Jeshua, and our angels in Your unbounded mercy that You forgive us, who are Your loving children, for our past failures to think, see, act according to Your will. We repent for every word and every deed that has given pain to others.
> We ask You with all our heart and all our strength, in total humility, to cleanse our spirits and our souls with Your love and Your light. We humbly ask that You accept our commitment to live our lives from this moment on in accordance to Your laws, embracing universal love, universal compassion, and living in truth.
> We thank You, Lord, for healing all of our spiritual wounds, and we shall always remain faithful in our commitment to You, from this moment on.
> *Amen.*

Sharon Prince

The energy in the room was so powerful, I felt like a part of me went outside of my body and was looking down on myself from above. Maybe this sensation was me connecting to my higher self. Nick led everyone in a spiritual healing by asking us to imagine different times when we hurt others and to forgive ourselves for it. It was like a guided visualization. The healing was very powerful. I felt something shift inside me.

Soon afterward, I would discover that the constant hoarseness that I had suffered over the past two years of speaking loudly over bagpipes every weekend in order to do sales for my husband's band was gone! My voice was clear as a bell and I could even sing again! This was significant for me. John wouldn't believe it, I thought. He had only known me with a hoarse voice. He had teased me by saying that he always knew when I was coming because his voice would suddenly go hoarse like mine. "What is it with this laryngitis thing?" he would ask me. "It must be some past life we had together!" We would both laugh about it. Whatever the cause of this hoarseness, it was now gone.

The ceremony ended and I was the first to greet Nick on stage. "That was great!" I said. He smiled and gave me a hug. By now I had figured out that he had probably taken the envelope with John's picture, thinking that it was a gift. In all the excitement of meeting him, I didn't even notice he had slipped it inside his inner coat pocket. When I sheepishly asked him for it back, he produced it from its hiding place.

I immediately went to the bookstore and found one small paperback version of *The Messengers* on the shelf. As I walked out of the bookstore, I met Kim, Nick's sweet, beautiful daughter, in the reception area. I gave her two copies of my husband's band's newest CD, one for her and one for Nick, as a way of thanking them for the information and help during my preparation for the trip. I decided to venture back into the sanctuary one more time to have Nick sign my book and to say good-bye.

As I approached the crowd gathered around Nick, I noticed that the people from the study group I had attended were speaking to him. I stood beside him and a woman from the group, waiting for my opportunity. Nancy, who is a clairvoyant reader, was telling Nick about the angels she had seen during the prayer, when she noticed me standing there. Suddenly her conversation focused on me.

"The angels told me that Sharon is an integral part of this prayer today—an *integral* part," she emphasized. I felt bashful as Nick suddenly looked over at me and smiled. "This is my opportunity," I thought.

"I'm sorry to interrupt," I said. "Nick, I left a present for you with Kim."

"Thank you, Sharon," he said as he kissed my cheek. What a sweet man, I thought.

"Could I get you to sign my book, please?" I asked as I handed him the book and a pen. Just then a man began speaking with him.

As I looked over his shoulder, he wrote in an endearing, childlike scrawl: "Sharon, God bless you. Nick Bunick," inside the front cover. "Thank you so much," I said as I took the book and gently slipped the pen out of his hand, which he held idly in the air as he listened intently to the man speaking. "Oh, the price of fame!" I mused.

"Good-bye. It was a privilege meeting you," I said. Thinking he had not heard me, I started to walk away.

"Bye, Sharon. Thank you for coming," he said over his shoulder. I attempted a farewell wave, but the crowd had already swallowed him up again. As Margaret and Ann and I walked out to the parking lot, we happened to run into Doreen Virtue and her husband, who were also leaving at the same time. We chatted for a moment and then everyone said good-bye.

When I got back to Lauren's parents' house, I called Randy to tell him about my day. Then I called John to share the highlights of my meeting with Nick and go over the details of my reading from Jacquelyne a couple of days earlier. He immediately noticed the difference in my voice, which we both laughed at. He thought the reading was a wonderful confirmation and couldn't wait to hear the tape, which I promised to copy and send him as soon as I got home.

"What a day this has been!" I told myself as I got ready for bed. I was so grateful for the few uninterrupted minutes that I got to spend with this special man whose story had meant so much to John and me. Though meeting Nick was the highlight of my trip, it would soon have more significance to me than I could have ever imagined. I was about to find out just what our connection really was during that lifetime with Christ.

CHAPTER SEVEN

Go Between

The next day Lauren's mom drove me to the airport. Soon I was on the plane, headed back to Houston. I was in an introspective mood the whole way back.

As I rested my head on the edge of the airplane seat and looked out the window at the last rays of sunset, I intuitively felt that this trip was just the beginning of many things to come. I had made some important connections in Portland, not the least of which was the one with Nick Bunick.

I was still losing quite a bit of hair and had no idea why, especially since the trip was now over. Jacquelyne had said that I was bringing in a huge influx of spiritual energy that would fully integrate within three weeks of the reading. I just hoped I would have some hair left by then!

The next day, after a conversation with John on the phone, I sat at my computer and typed a follow-up letter to Nick. I thanked him for the opportunity to meet him and told him what a privilege it had been to join him and such a special group of people for the April 4 Prayer. I shared with him the highlights of my reading from Jacquelyne and quoted everything she had said about John's past life as John the Apostle. Still not knowing who I had been, I briefly shared the general information given to me about my own past life during that time.

I ended by saying, "I am so excited that you and John will finally be able to meet. ...P.S. John says 'hello' and to help you recognize him (and he's making fun of me telling you I would be wearing my white angel dress to the prayer) he will be going naked and wearing a feather on his head." I sure hoped Nick would have a sense of humor about this, I thought as I typed that last line and sent it off to him with a copy going to John.

Since I had not yet had the opportunity to duplicate the tape of Jacquelyne's reading, the e-mail to Nick—which contained an exact transcript of everything Jacquelyne had said about John—proved to be a valuable resource to John. Again and again, he pored over her words.

"I find it wonderful that we have had such a straightforward verification of the John the Apostle fact," he wrote in an e-mail to me a couple of days later. "I think we are on a wonderful pathway. In the letter Nick sent to me, he said that the veil between the spirit world and the physical [world] is getting thinner. I think this is true."

Then my friend put things into perspective:

> There are times when we are talking that you afford me some undue respect for a life that I do not remember. I am John C. Davis. I may, at a different time, have been John, son of Zebedee, Fisherman, Evangelist, Apostle, Beloved. Yet you are farther down the spiritual path than I [am]. I am not as gifted as you are . . . As for now it is I who should be giving you my respect, and I do as your friend . . .
>
> You do need to prepare yourself for what is to come. Many great things. Anything I find myself involved in, I intend to drag you along . . . Maybe we can write a book that chronicles your spiritual awakening and mine and then show how they have intertwined…I think people want to hear that they are not alone on the path…I think it's time to not be "one of the guys anymore" and I think we should do it together . . . .
>
> By the way, I am looking for a good feather to wear to meet Nick.

John's words were encouraging, and this wasn't the first time writing a book had been mentioned; however, I found myself strangely wanting to distance myself from any talk of spiritual matters. The tension that had been building up during the weeks before my trip to Portland was still very much with me. I found this feeling of continuing anxiety one of the oddest things that I had ever experienced. It made absolutely no sense to me.

Then I received an e-mail from John a couple of days later that finally explained what my unconscious mind must have known all along. "Hey Soul Sister," he said, referring to Jacquelyne's statement that we were from the same soul family. "I was just reading my book called, *Who's Who in the Bible* and guess what? There is a large mention of Felix [in it]." John then quoted the book to me.

In disbelief, I read about "Governor Felix," who had been the Roman Procurator of Judea between AD 52-58. The Apostle Paul had been brought before him in Caesarea to be tried on the charges that he had been stirring up antagonism against the Jewish faith by allowing Gentiles into the temple. The book recounted the details given in the New Testament in Acts: 21-24. Felix put Paul under house arrest for two years, though the conditions had apparently been comfortable. It was during this time that

Paul and Felix had regular conversations with one another, and those conversations centered on Christ's teachings.

The book went on to say that even though it seemed as if Paul's arrest did little to benefit those in his ministry, it was the first stage of the legal proceedings that ultimately led to Paul's being sent to Rome, where he was free to share the gospel of Jesus Christ. The author contends that it was all a part of God's overall plan, as evidenced in Acts 21:11; 27:24.

"Well, my dear," John wrote. "How about them apples! A connection to Paul letting him speak and keeping him safely under house arrest where he could learn of Christianity privately, and all of it known by God and planned. How about that! Felix with a connection to Paul. I could see how you could be upset by it, but it was God's doing, so you didn't let him down. You let yourself down. Live and learn."

I sat there staring at the print-out I had made of the e-mail. I was utterly speechless. I couldn't remember reading anything about this in *The Messengers*. How could I have missed something so important? Surely, it was mentioned in Nick's regression as Paul.

I got out the copy my *The Messengers* and searched for the accounting of Felix. I found it toward the back of the book. Then an insight hit me. I remembered the one night, when I was reading the book, that I had the feeling I had skipped a page or two. And there it was mentioned, plain as day! I believe, now, that I was guided not to read that part of the book because I was not yet ready, and because Jacquelyne's reading would be necessary to prepare me first to hear the eventual news.

Also, I reasoned, if I had known this before I had met Nick, a part of me that remembered being Felix would have feared this, and I might have felt uncomfortable coming face to face with this person who had been Paul. In other words, I might have missed the opportunity to meet Nick in this life and make a connection to him as the person he is now. I believe this gradual unfolding of information had happened in a manner that was best for me.

I e-mailed John to talk about it. I was truly disturbed by this news however positively the book or John had tried to present it. "I read the part [in the Bible] where Felix left Paul in prison as a 'favor to the Jews,' and it just broke my heart," I wrote. "I feel that I loved and respected him so much . . . how could I betray him that way? Maybe I didn't know what to do with him and releasing him meant certain death at the hands of those angry Jews. Maybe I was just saving face and knew that my successor (Festus) would do what I felt I could not, which was send him to Rome. Was I being selfish because I didn't want him to leave? I must admit I am in a very somber mood right now. Do you think Nick will still like me if he knows who I was? I'm sure he can forgive me now because what is past is past, but how did Paul feel [about Felix at that time] and will that memory subconsciously influence the way Nick relates to me now? I know I should let go of any worry about it, but I just want him to know how sorry I am, that's all."

I ended the e-mail on a dry note. "Take care, my friend. And if you have any more revelations, keep them to yourself! I'm about at the point of shopping for wigs!"

John's reply came quickly. "There is no way that Nick will hold anything against you that was of God's devising. The things that were done all those years ago were between Felix and Paul, not Sharon and Nick. I am sure this is the way he feels. I am also sure he is grateful for any awakening that will verify what he is learning about that time and that life. Just as I am grateful for all the information that has come to me through you. So, just let go of any guilt you feel over this thing and relax. Besides, what Felix did in that life was to save Paul's life—a pretty noble deed, if you ask me."

He ended his e-mail on a humorous note. "Just for you," he wrote, "I will keep my spiritual revelations simple. That way you can keep your beehive intact." Then he apologetically asked me to expound on some spiritual insights I had given him and ended it with "your friend and greatest fan, John the Beloved (he he he)."

John tried to convince me that I needed to share what I had learned with Nick in a phone conversation that followed our e-mails. I told him that it would probably be a long time before I was ready to do that. As for answering questions requiring me to tap into my spiritual awareness, I told him that I would be on "spiritual vacation" until further notice.

After my conversation with John, I was in a stupor for the rest of the afternoon and evening. I wrestled with this information from my past life. "I was right about one thing," I noted wryly. "I was definitely Roman!"

I resolved not to say anything to Nick. Besides, hadn't he said that it's not who we were in a past life that is important, but who we are now? What purpose could it serve, anyway? No, there was no reason to mention this. "Besides," I told myself. "He probably doesn't even care one way or the other." But try as I might, I couldn't let go of it.

As if by divine timing, I received an e-mail from Nick the next day. It was April 14, 1999:

Dear Sharon,

    I truly did enjoy meeting with you at our 444 function on April 4th. There was so much sacred space created in that sanctuary, and I know that your energy was a tremendous contribution. Everyone who met you told me how much they truly enjoyed your participation as well as getting to know you personally. I am glad you had a chance to hook up with Jackie and those other people.

    The reading which you received was quite interesting. Thank you for sharing it with me. Tell John I'll be looking for him. I'll recognize him by his lack of clothing and his feather.

    God bless you as you continue to stand in His light.

Sincerely,
Nick Bunick

His reference to the lack of clothing and the feather made me laugh. "Good. He has a sense of humor and doesn't think we're weird," I said to myself. His letter was so complimentary and gracious that I just couldn't bring myself to write him about the Felix stuff. I sent a copy to John, as I did all the e-mails I received from Nick. Although I had received the letter around noon, it was nearly eight o'clock that night before I finally responded to it. After hours of deliberation, I could stand it no longer. Come what may, I *had* to tell him. I had to get the burden of guilt off my chest.

After thanking Nick for his kind words, I told him how I had felt an increased vibration in my aura since the prayer ceremony. I emphasized the seriousness of the commitment I had made by saying the prayer and that I felt I was being given a "second chance" (alluding to my Felix lifetime) to actively serve God. I also told him that Jacquelyne said I was at the beginning of my work and that it would take place in a far-reaching manner, such as writing a book. (Of course, the book John and I were considering writing together had come to mind immediately.)

Then I went for it. I started by making a reference to the e-mail I had sent him that February in which I had asked him if he remembered having a friend named Felix during his lifetime as Paul. I had told him how I had received a "slight twinge of memory" during a conversation I had with John "that made me wonder if I had been some [sort of] go-between" for him and John and maybe the other apostles. I recounted how I had received the name Felix and told him what a struggle I was having in sharing this information with him now.

I ended by saying, "I hope you and John have a little time to talk when you meet in Florida…I know he would love the chance to talk with you about some of his recent experiences. He has had a real opening lately, and Jacquelyne's reading has had a lot to do with his coming to terms with this past life as John and his present mission in this life." At the end of the e-mail, I attached a copy of the information John had sent about Felix.

Then, taking a deep breath, I pushed the button on the computer that irretrievably sent the e-mail off to Nick. "There it goes," I thought. "I'll probably never hear from him again. He probably has all kinds of horrible memories of this Felix guy." But I had done what my conscience had bid me to do, and surely that could not be a bad thing, if, even in the end, it meant losing Nick's friendship. I breathed a huge sigh of relief. From that moment on, all the anxiety that I had been feeling for the weeks preceding and following the trip to Portland was suddenly over, and so was my hair loss!

The next day John responded to the copy of the e-mail I had sent Nick. "I'm proud of you! To give him the opportunity to remember you is a great gift. I am sure that it was the right thing to do. I know that I kind of pushed you to do it. After all, isn't that what friends are for?"

Although the intense anxiety of the previous weeks was over, I was left feeling numb. "I really need to take a mental vacation from all of this, John!" I told him during one of our phone conversations. He was anxious to share his angelic 444 experiences, which were increasing at a phenomenal rate, and he wanted me to share my insights of what I thought would happen when he met Nick. "I don't know, John!" I begged off when he asked. "Remember? I'm on vacation!"

A couple of days later, on April 16, he sent a message to tell me that his friend Gracie had had a dream about what would happen when he met Nick at the Whole Life Expo:

> Gracie just called me all excited. She had a dream last night . . .
> that Nick Bunick was giving a speech and I walked into the back of
> the room. Just then, he stopped, said "John!" and hugged me. The
> thing that she thought was so cool was that three hundred people in
> the room knew that something spectacular was going on.

He ended the e-mail with a message he had channeled for himself that I believe came from the Master:

> This is a message to you, my son, that all that is happening is
> preordained. You will meet an old friend and the bond will be
> undeniable. You follow the path of righteousness, the path of truth.

What you know in your heart will come to pass. My arrival will herald the beginning of a new dawn. A dawn of peace, of love and togetherness. We are one. You know this. You have always known this. This [feeling of recognition] will confirm a lot for you and him. I will show you the way. Trust in me and all will be known. I am glad that you finally are listening. I have missed you (our conversation) very much. (The clock now reads 4:44.)

Well isn't that interesting? Wasn't expecting that! Wow! Don't freak out. You are on vacation. We are in a wonderful time. How lucky we are to be here when the world becomes enlightened. I am once again going to assimilate this. Whew!

———•—•———

At last the day arrived for John to meet Nick. John sent me an e-mail the next day, telling me all about how he and a friend of his had gone to the Expo together and what had happened when he finally met Nick. As he sent it off, he looked down at the computer clock—whose time was incorrect—and it read 4:44!

"Shizuko and I pulled into the parking lot around 11:15," John recounted. "The building was full and we had to keep driving up the floors. Finally, we found a spot and I parked. As we went inside, she saw a sign and said, 'Look, 4th floor, Row D (the fourth letter). All we need is one more.' As I turned around, I saw another sign that said *4th Floor, Row D, Terrace 4.* That was wild!"

John went on to tell me how they walked around the convention center browsing all the booths and how he enjoyed all the wonderful energy there. Then they walked down the last row, where all the readers were located. They stopped at one spot where a reader had her angel cards spread out on the table. John and Shizuko each picked up a card. As the reader started interpreting Shizuko's card, John read his. Then the reader looked at John, so he gave her his card. She started to interpret it, but suddenly stopped.

"They are telling me to tell you that you are a gifted healer. I see you healing with the laying on of hands within the next year. Right now," she continued, "your heart is wide open. Your third eye is opening, but not like most. Yours is opening interdimensionally. You are a conduit for the healing energy."

This insight amazed John and his friend, who both knew John was meant to be a healer. It convinced Shizuko that this was the person she wanted to have her first reading from. After walking a bit more, they decided to go back and have their readings done. Shizuko went first. Then John had his.

"I see you doing a lot of traveling," the reader told him. John described to her what he did for a living: traveling all over the country while performing on the Renaissance circuit. "But that is not what you will be doing. You will be writing a book," she insisted, "and then you will be traveling with spiritual shows like this, speaking. That *will* happen," she emphasized.

Talk about your verifications! She told John that he would one day have such a gift for healing that he would be able to look into someone's eyes and they would be healed.

During the entire reading, she kept telling him what an honor it was to be able to read for him. At one point, she began to cry. "It's such a privilege to be in your presence," she explained. John responded by telling her it was a privilege to be in her presence, as well. Then she said that she didn't feel worthy to read for him. ("Sound familiar?" he teased me.)

She went on to tell him that his partnership with Spencer would eventually end and that the two of them would soon be going in opposite directions. (The same thing had come up in the reading I had done for him in March.) She said that, down the road, she saw Spencer eventually doing spiritual work.

She gave John a time frame of one to two years for his book/healing/symposium work and said she had no doubt that she would be reading his book and that she would be seeing him on the circuit. John was struck by her choice of the word "circuit." He found it ironic that he would be leaving one circuit for another.

After attending a free lecture from a woman who is a channel, they went to listen to Doreen Virtue. John really enjoyed her workshop and her sense of humor. She gave angel readings to different people around the room, and though his hand was held high, she never called on him. It didn't bother him, though, for he felt that the people she picked really needed the guidance more than he did.

John's friend chose to do something else while John went alone to see Nick. John rushed toward the room where Nick would be speaking and got in line. As he was waiting, he heard some voices coming from behind him. Just as he turned around, he saw Nick talking to a group of people. At that precise moment, Nick glanced over at John and then did a double take. The recognition between the two was instant. "John!" Nick exclaimed, as he threw his arms open wide to give

John a big hug. This gesture fulfilled a major part of Gracie's dream. Although it did not take place inside the room, Nick's recognition of John was just as she had seen it.

They spoke to one another briefly before the symposium began. "I forgot the feather," John dead-panned. "Well, at least you remembered the clothes!" Nick retorted. They both laughed. Then Nick continued down the line greeting people as he walked into the room.

"His lecture was what I expected from the information in his books," John said. "During the lecture, I had a shocking moment. While watching him speak, I was looking at his aura. It was weird. It was like he had a hunch-back. Imagine my surprise when the hunch separated and I saw the shape of an angel. I should send this off to 'Ripley's Believe It or Not,'" he quipped.

After the lecture, John wanted to thank Nick for his words—both spoken and written, but people were rushing up to talk to him, so John waited his turn. When Nick finally got to John he said, "John, walk with me."

As the two of them exited the room together, Nick led the way to the bookstore, where he was scheduled to sign books. All the time they were walking, people kept rushing up to Nick. (I knew exactly how John felt!) He realized that having an in-depth conversation with Nick was out of the question. Eventually, the two of them got onto the escalator, which led down to the bookstore.

It would be the only time John would have to speak with Nick uninterrupted. As they stood on the same step, side by side, John finally had a chance to tell him how much his writings had meant to him. As soon as the escalator ride was over, though, the crowd rushed toward Nick once more as he and John walked into the bookstore.

"People were rushing him all the way, and I realized that he was so busy that there was no way to talk with him much more. So, I told him it was a pleasure meeting him, and he told me to be in touch." As John said good-bye to Nick, he noticed that Nick seemed a little disappointed that they hadn't had more of an opportunity to speak with one another.

Even as John left, though, something told him that this would not be the last time the two of them would meet. He thought it was wonderful that Nick was trying to touch as many people's lives as possible. And he knew in his heart that he, too, would soon be doing this same type of work.

That night, when John got home, he e-mailed Nick with a thank-you letter. Here are some excerpts:

> I am writing to thank you for the time you were able to spare for me on the eighteenth. I realized that you were extremely busy that day and I really admire [the] loving way you present [yourself] to all who approach you . . . .
>
> When Sharon first informed me that I "walked with Jesus," I did know, intuitively, that I had. However, as you well know, to say that to the world is a difficult thing, let alone allow your own ego to wrestle with it. Your books gave me the courage to speak out to friends and family.

He went on to share with Nick the reading he had gotten from the reader at the Whole Life Expo that day and how she had told him that he had a big responsibility to fulfill in this lifetime.

> I then asked [the reader] about the things I had been told in [Sharon's reading] that I would be seeing Jesus face to face in this lifetime in the body He possessed in Galilee. She said, 'Oh yes, this is true' and that, as before, I would be doing His work. All this, [I knew] in my heart was true. I only needed verification to trust my intuitions . . . .
>
> . . . let me say that it was indeed an honor and privilege to meet you...and [I] hope that we are able to see each other again in the near future. As before, you are a great teacher. God bless.

The next day, I sent Nick a follow-up e-mail myself. I told Nick how much John's meeting him had meant to him and that John had been bombarded by 444 experiences lately. I joked that I was starting to become jealous! I also said that these experiences, along with his experience at the Expo, had inspired him to listen to his own guidance and to start receiving channeled messages for himself. "I know that he is meant to do something special," I concluded, "just as you are doing something special, just as all of us will be playing our parts—some in more noticeable ways than others!" I attached a copy of John's 444s at the end of the e-mail and sent it off. I honestly didn't expect to hear back from Nick, but I had wanted to share John's experiences anyway.

Three days after I had told Nick that I was wondering if I would ever have any 444's, I had my first 444 experience. I was typing in an e-mail to a friend as my husband was watching television. Just then, a commercial came on and he asked me to hurry in to see it. As I entered the living room, the company's phone number flashed onto the screen. It was 444-4444!

I was so excited to finally have had a bona fide 444 experience, I just had to call John to let him know.

"John! Guess what?" I exclaimed.

"What?"

"I just had my first 444 experience!"

"Oh, yeah?"

"Can you believe it? I was typing an e-mail to a friend to tell her I was planning to share the experiences of my trip to Portland with her spiritual group when this ad came on TV. Can you believe their phone number was 444-4444? Isn't that wild?"

John laughed. "Well, you know, I prayed last night that the angels would send you a 444 experience."

"You did?" I asked, totally amazed.

"Yeah, and that won't be the last one, either. You're going to have a whole bunch of them!" he assured me.

I wasn't as convinced about that as John was. At first, I thought that maybe I had just gotten lucky, but the timing of it made me consider that it was more than a chance happening. Just after I had sent off that e-mail, I brought up another e-mail sent to me. In the address line, I could see that the e-mail had also been sent to Atira. I searched for the business card she had given me when I met her in Portland, and sure enough it was her address. Both e-mails had a connection to my trip to Portland—the first one in regard to sharing my trip with others and the second one sent to someone I had met there.

This is the way it would happen for all my future 444 experiences. They would always seem to coincide with some spiritual decision I had made, or a spiritual experience I had just had, or some comment I had made of a spiritual nature, or some action I had taken in furthering my spiritual growth. These 444s never seemed to be isolated incidents. They would serve as confirmations that I was on the right path, doing the right thing and that what I had received from my own spiritual guidance was true.

Five days later, I had my second—and the biggest—444 experience. From then on I had no doubts that these 444 experiences were really manifestations of the angels' presence in our lives. I had been asked by my friend Dinah to help out at her place of business while a co-worker recovered from surgery. I enjoyed working with Dinah, and we would go across the street to have lunch at a home-style restaurant and to visit.

One day, as Dinah and I were having lunch, I felt compelled to share my experience of reading *The Messengers* with her, and I shared with her the story of meeting Nick Bunick earlier that month. I told her about my recent 444 experience and explained that seeing three fours was the manifestation of the power of God's love and that it was a way that our angels were making their presence known in our lives.

Later that afternoon, as I was doing data entry on the computer, I overheard Dinah giving instructions to Lucy, a co-worker, on how to post billings for their clients. She said, as she looked over Lucy's shoulder, "the C.O.D. number is 444."

"Four-forty-four! That's interesting," I said. I wanted to ask them more about it, but I waited several seconds for them to finish their discussion before I interrupted. I looked down at my watch while I was waiting, and it said 4:44! When I asked about the billing they were working on, Dinah said that the total sales amount had been $444.00; the state tax had been $4.44 and the local tax had been $4.44. Then she looked at the computer clock and she noticed that it read 4:45.

I clarified the situation immediately. "But when you first said the C.O.D. was number 444 about a minute ago, it was 4:44 by my watch, which meant that it was actually 4:44 on the computer clock, too!" I explained. I couldn't believe it. Five sets of 444! At last, I felt like an official member of the 444 "Club"!

The next day, when I called John on his cell phone to share my big 444 breakthrough, he told me that he was walking through the local mall and that he had just stopped because he saw something he couldn't believe. It was a poster promoting a baseball team featuring a picture of a baseball player. On the player's jersey was the name Angel and under it was the number 4! Then below that were the prices and product numbers of the baseball videos being sold. There were 6 fours in those two columns of numbers. I couldn't believe he was having a 444 while I was telling him about mine!

Both John and I have continued to have so many 444 experiences that we could write a book on that subject alone. In fact, all the friends with whom we have shared *The Messengers*, or who had just begun reading the *The Messengers* when we happened to mention it to them, were also having 444s. One friend of mine, Iris, had even tuned into the picture of the angel that artist Stanley Martucci had painted, which was used on the cover of *The Messengers*, and painted that same angel for her art class without knowing the connection at all, for she had never seen the cover of the book.

From late April through mid-June, I was traveling to the Dallas area every weekend to work with my husband's band as they performed at a local Renaissance festival there. The second weekend in May, I received a message from my angels. As I was walking by myself to the campsite where our motorhome was parked, I felt the presence of my angels surrounding me. I could feel a vibrating energy around my head, hovering above and slightly behind me. I had felt their presence before and knew they were probably going to impart some information to me. Sure enough, they did.

"What should I know at this time?" I asked.

"Observe what's going on and document *everything,*" was their response, which came in the form of thoughts that I could practically hear inside my head.

I had already started to document the e-mails and letters that I had sent and received from Nick and John. I wanted to track the progress of spiritual growth in John's and my life and record our story so we could refer back to it. Now, I felt they were reminding me of this record because it would be important in our future.

I entered my motorhome and sat down on the couch to take off my shoes. I heard a soft "meow." Rommy jumped up in my lap, rubbed his head against mine. It had been a long, hot day, and I was looking forward to a shower and some dinner. Just as I was unlacing my shoes, they spoke to me again.

"Nick will be in contact with you soon," they informed me.

"Okay," I concurred. I had learned to just say "okay" whenever they spoke to me. No matter how exciting or unbelievable the information they imparted, it was much easier for me—and them—if I just went along as if the information were true. That way I saved myself from going through the denial or the freaking out that would otherwise accompany such enlightenments. In other words, I was learning to trust them.

The next week I was writing in my journal the documentation that my angels had guided me to write.

> John Davis and I have decided to write a book together about our spiritual experiences these last two years. We both realize that we are still experiencing the material we are writing about. [We] want to call it John of Old, John of New, [because these are the first words that Jesus ever spoke to John.] I've been collecting documentation for the book for the past month and a half. I've also started a time line from which we will write the book.
>
> John and I have stayed in close contact by phone and e-mail these past few months. He has been a big emotional and spiritual support for me. It is very scary to think that my name will be on a book that tells everyone that I had a conversation with Jesus in the parking lot. However, I think about my friend John telling everyone

that he was John the Apostle, and I don't feel so alone. We both face people thinking we are crazy and embarrassing our families.

I have considered backing out of writing the book or using an alias or nom de plume. When I was having these thoughts is when I was visited by my angels who told me to observe and document everything and that Nick would be in contact with me soon. All I know is that we are definitely moving in a direction with this and it feels like it has a life of its own!

John said that Gracie had a dream about John having a meeting with Nick and another man in a nice restaurant. . . . Perhaps this has something to do with the book. Gracie has prophetic dreams and she's had this dream twice [now].

Within eleven days of my receiving the message from my angels that Nick would be in contact soon, I received an e-mail from him. The angels had been right . . . again!

Dear Sharon,

I am truly sorry that it has taken me so long to respond, but I am truly busy traveling, giving talks around the country, and [with] other matters related to my spiritual journey.

As I am sure you know by now, John and I did have a short conversation in Fort Lauderdale. I enjoyed his energy, and even [in] the short time that we spent together, I could see what a loving, kind soul that he is.

As for the name Felix, there was a Felix who was head of the Judaic government in the Province of Samara and who met with Paul a number of times in reference to the accusations that were brought against him.

In reading your letter again, I see that we are talking about the same Felix. Paul met with him many, many times when Paul was under house arrest in Caesarea, before Felix arranged to have him shipped to Rome because Paul wanted to be judged by Romans as opposed to his accusers. Actually, Paul was never really tried, for the Romans would not have cared what Paul did when he was in Jerusalem, regarding his going into the sacred temple with non-Jews who had accepted Jeshua.

Well, it sounds like you have a lot of spiritual food on your plate. As always my friend, I send you my love and blessings,

Nick Bunick

That second to last sentence, in its own understated way, told me that Nick was seriously regarding what I had told him. He didn't come right out and say it, but I could feel that he was beginning to receive a confirmation on this himself. At least, the possibility that I had been Felix was now in his awareness.

The next day, I sent a message back. I told Nick that I completely understood about how busy he was. One only needed to be in his presence at a gathering where he was speaking to know this. I informed him that my husband and I were about to begin a long summer tour and that I had just purchased a laptop computer so that I could keep up with e-mails on the road and so that John and I could start writing the book, tentatively titled, *John of Old, John of New*. "I know I am plagiarizing the title," I joked with Nick, referring to the first words Jesus spoke to John when I channeled Him in Rehoboth Beach, "but I don't think the 'Big J.C.'—as John and I affectionately call him—will mind."

I shared with Nick my angelic encounter in the campsite of the Renaissance faire a couple of weeks earlier and thanked him for responding to the information about my alleged lifetime as Governor Felix. "It won't seem real until I get a regression on it nor will I be convinced otherwise," I had told him. I mentioned that the reading Jacquelyne had given me had assured me that I had made the right choice for me not to serve as an apostle of Christ and that the stress of remembering that lifetime resolved only when I had written him an e-mail about it.

"It was that very day that I stopped losing the hair I had been losing before I went up to meet you in Portland. On a soul level," I said, "that was a big one for me! It fascinates me how John's and my journey seems to be perfectly orchestrated. We are receiving so many signposts along the way that seem to say, 'Keep going—you're on the right path.' Meeting you seemed right on cue," I told him.

I thanked him for the spiritual healing he'd conducted at the April 4 Prayer and that my life had changed as a result. I ended by saying that I knew how busy he was and that I did not expect him to write back. However, I assured him that if he did want to stay in touch, that would be great by me, but that I would certainly understand if he didn't. "I have to admit," I teased, "I've gotten spoiled. I guess it started with all that letter-writing you were doing with me almost two thousand years ago!" And, on a more serious note, I ended by saying, "Thanks for the confirmation about Felix and Paul being friends. I knew in my heart that this was so. Perhaps Felix never told Paul this, but he loved and respected him so very much."

About this time, my friend Brenda from Houston had officially started her Messengers study group, and she sent me an e-mail informing me of this. Unfortunately, by the time the group was scheduled for its first meeting, I would already be on the road. I sent Brenda a message regretfully informing her of this and brought her up to date on my Felix lifetime.

"I started to recover some emotional memories from that lifetime last night," I admitted, "and it is my belief that not only did Felix love and respect Paul but they became very close during those two years of house arrest. It is also my feeling that Paul tried to get Felix to join him in spreading the gospel of Jesus, but Felix, [perhaps] because of social position or whatever, declined."

As I wrapped up my letter, I pondered where all this uncovering of past lives would lead John and me. "I know Nick and I have a heart connection. What our relationship will be in this lifetime remains to be seen; however, I am fairly confident that we will stay in touch, at least by e-mail." Although I didn't say it, it was my belief that my making this connection to Nick first was somehow going to be instrumental in connecting Nick to John and the other reincarnated apostles. Why this was so, I could not say for sure, but I knew in my heart that there was work to be done, and my relationship to Nick would be the foundation for that work.

CHAPTER EIGHT

Bridge from Past to Future

As summer of 1999 approached, John wanted another reading to confirm his past life and to clarify some other issues concerning the direction his life was taking, so he asked me who I would recommend. Because I was corresponding with Kim Bunick on a regular basis now, I felt comfortable in asking her to recommend another reader for John. Her first recommendation was Sara, who was the best reader who had ever read for her. She e-mailed me Sara's number, and I passed it along to John.

Several days later, on May 24, I followed up Kim's e-mail with a thank-you note:

> I gave [Sara's] number to John. He is so excited about getting a reading from her. He didn't want to tell her anything about why he wanted a reading, so he wouldn't prejudice the reading. He wants to see what she will pick up on her own.
>
> He's scheduled for June 3 and is counting the days! I'm sure she will knock his socks off. She told him that she wasn't going to be doing readings anymore—something about expanding her work to reach a wider audience. He feels very fortunate to be one of the last people that gets a reading from her.

June 3 finally came. Just before the reading, John had another vision of Mary. This time, however, it was different. He glanced upward to see her standing on a cloud instead of seeing her as a painting in the clouds. She was a glowing being who looked down upon him lovingly and reassuringly. I had decided to touch base with John just before the reading to lend him some moral support. That's when he told me about his Mary vision. I could hear the excited anticipation in his voice. We could sense that something big was about to happen: we kept the conversation brief, so he could prepare himself mentally and spiritually for the reading. With humor, I noted that John, who was usually calm, cool, and collected, seemed a bit nervous.

"I'll meditate during your reading and then call you afterward," I promised.

"Thanks. Well, I better get off the phone. I'll talk to you soon," he said quickly, as his words drifted off with his thoughts.

As I hung up the phone, I couldn't help but wonder what Sara would have to say about John's past life. I knew John was hoping she would be able to give him more information about this as well as give him some clarity on the expected changes in his career.

I was scheduled for a dance class and was hoping to be able to talk to John before the class started. However, when I tried to call him after his reading, he didn't answer his phone. I tried two more times, but nothing. "That's odd," I thought. "They either got started late or they are running overtime for some reason."

It was time for my class, so I gave up trying to reach John. It would be several hours before I was able to call him again. After dance class, I tried to use a pay phone, but it was busy and then everyone in our class went to an outdoor restaurant. While I waited for my food to come, I tried to reach John again on a nearby pay phone—this time successfully. For the next twenty minutes, our conversation had me jumping up and down with excitement as John related the highlights of the reading to me. Although he had gotten some great information from Sara about our work together and changes in his career, she seemed unable, or perhaps unwilling, to talk directly about his past life as John the Apostle. However, she did confirm it indirectly several times.

"There is a crossover situation in your career and it involves a person with an 'H' name," she had told him. Spencer's last name started with an "H," so John thought, immediately, that she was referring to his partner. But then Sara implied that John would be leaving their partnership and doing something new.

"I see you using humor and talking to men in business suits," she said. John explained that he was already a comedic actor on the Renaissance circuit, but she said that this was a different type of audience and a different type of message. "This new direction has to do with fluidity of expression. I see you getting people to laugh at society's skewed perspectives on life. You will be getting people to understand spiritual concepts through comedy. This is your forté. Your approach to spiritual work has been too serious. It's time to lighten up.

"In the past week and a half, you've gotten clarity on your direction," she went on. "You will be leaving those people behind who can't see you in your new role, including your business partner. Your spiritual work involves showing humor in speech and writing. This humor will be subtle instead of in-your-face. You will be leaving vaudeville for a more commentary style. You will be using a dry sense of humor and digging deeper for your material."

Sara was right about John's change of heart concerning his career. Only a week or two before, John told me that he had decided to eventually leave the Renaissance circuit altogether. His interest in stage combat was waning, and he felt that he was ready to move on. He still had some interest in directing, but once he got that out of his system—he had been hired to direct two faires in Florida that next year—he would be ready to move into his spiritual work full-time.

As I later listened to Sara's words on tape, my thoughts went to the reading I had given John a couple of months previously, in March:

> You will be moving on with your life. You will find you're addressing other concerns having to do with spirituality. A moment of truth will come next year when you must make a decision to go on with things as they are or to form a new partnership. Directing will be more a part of your life, but so will your spiritual work. This chasm will eventually make you decide what it is that you really want to do with your life. You may find that what you thought was important is not.

Sara continued the reading on that note. "You are ready for something new, something different. I see someone who's very tall, with angular bone structure, going through new doors and pulling you through into a new direction, such as TV or film. (John thought of his tall, angular friend, Brian, who was also a performer on the Renaissance circuit, and who was planning to do some film work in California the next year.)

John then tried to direct the focus of the reading onto his past life by asking Sara if she could give him any information that would confirm his past life from biblical times. She said he was focusing too much on the past and that he needed to concentrate on the present. He restated the question by specifically asking her about his past life as John the Apostle. She said that her angels were slamming the door shut on that topic. Changing the subject, John followed this by stating that Nick's book had given both him and me a frame of reference for our own experiences.

"It's a precarious situation to focus on the past," she maintained. "You need to integrate and move forward. The past pulls on you. You need to focus in this dimension. You are coming into full empowerment, and you do this by going within instead of listening to others. Part of the door-way on August 11th this year is becoming more aware from within. Others around you are still learning to focus on the heart. They are wasting your time and are projecting onto you their own stuff. Be available to move forward with that. You are very sensitive. Be aware of what you feel in your heart. Be aware of Spirit around you. The people around you look down on you. Your awareness is tried and true and has helped you get stronger. Those people who do not support you will be leaving you."

She continued. "In the next three months, you become very strong inside. Everything comes together at once: a stronger love and an integration of past spiritual awareness. People will either integrate or will be leaving you. Your love will be more strong, more gentle, more powerful. You are an innocent, loving spirit. A holy alignment will take place in the next three months. You've waited your whole life for this. *Your purpose is healing through word and through presence [emphasis mine].*"

She went on to tell him that this alignment included being handed certain qualities and virtues on a silver platter. Immediately, John was reminded of the second reading I had given him in Florida when Jesus had bade him to partake of any of the food (i.e., spiritual gifts) on His table. At the time, I told John I had received a visual image of Jesus standing behind a long table with a silver platter full of fruit at one end. **"These [spiritual gifts] are yours for the taking,"** He had told John. **"All you need to do is reach and partake of anything you want."**

Sara then gave some insight into John's childhood. She said the people in his life had made him feel wrong for being so open. He had had extraordinary experiences, such as visitations from one of his spiritual guides when he was small, but no one believed him. They laughed when he wanted to talk about his spiritual experiences and his so-called imaginary friend. John told me that he was amazed that Sara had picked up on his guide, whom as a child he had called "Jimmy Garden."

She went on to say that on some level his family could sense his greatness and was afraid of it. They thought that John's concepts, understanding, and spirit were too big. "Their intention was to diminish you 'cause they could not comprehend the bigness of you. So you physically overcompensated for this," Sara said, referring to John's weight as a child, which she had no way of knowing on her own. She went on to explain that the structure of religion and the identity that others had projected onto him had become less and less important to him as he grew older. John had become strong through these painful childhood experiences and learned to accept himself, whether or not others accepted him. He had learned to use humor to take the intensity off this issue, and through humor he would now be able to show others a different perspective on life.

Sara said that John was learning to open up and trust his intuitions once again. "No matter who anyone says they are or *were*, or who they will become, you will be walking your own path, not in the shadow of *anyone* else! You are to be guided strictly by your heart and knowingness," she stressed. "You are a *communicator*. This is what you are here for!" she pronounced. "You have an ability to ask questions that make people laugh and think in a different way. I see you being the 'entertainment' at the Expo. You will be live, in the moment. If you are not too serious, you can get more done."

The topic of our book came up without John having to ask anything about it. "You will write a book; the material will come through you. I see you writing a screenplay and little comedy plays of a spiritual theme." When he told her that he and I were planning on writing a book together, she said that we would be writing two books together. The first one, she said, would be told more from my perspective, and the second one would be told more from his perspective. "The third book will be all yours," she told John.

John then asked if it were true that I had been Governor Felix during the time of Christ. "Yes, and she's still driving from some of those decisions she made then. I see her getting some soul therapy and making some decisions to co-create from that lifetime. Those things are still serving her now." She said that I was not held to the past and that I would be fully integrating it, and that by doing so, I would become empowered and "in the flow." She admitted that I was already in the flow, but that two major, pivotal decisions from that lifetime were affecting me now.

She then focused on John's current relationship with Jennifer. She said that their relationship had needed time to mature and that when she returned they would be taking up where they left off. Sara likened it to getting on and off a train. Jennifer would simply be "getting on the train" with John, and they would continue the journey together.

John asked about some prophetic visions he had had of the future. Most of the visions were true, she offered, but the one that had scared him was not. In one of the visions John had seen a huge, dark cloud looming in the sky, which had given him a feeling of dread. She explained that he had been with someone who was fearful that day, and it had influenced the dark cloud that he had seen in his vision. Sara then encouraged him to protect himself against other people's negative energy by creating a gold funnel so he could spin out energies that were not his own.

The topic then turned to the angels who worked with him every day. She said that his life was protected because his heart was in the right place. "Whereever you are," she declared, "you are definitely protected. The ground you walk on is *holy*. The angels want to be where you are!" she laughed.

Sara then described some of John's angels and guides. "[One of your angels] has never been mortal. He deals with the collective conscious, the masses, the big picture," she said. "These energies [he brings] are pretty new, and you feel a dizzy, out-of-body feeling when they are around." It was true. John had lately been having short, dizzy spells for no apparent reason.

"[Another angel] works with your healing abilities," she informed. She told him that all he needed to do in order to heal others was "just be," and that his very presence had a healing effect on others. "The only limitations of this is where someone can't get to you," she explained. "Everything that you write or say is healing, and people don't have to physically touch you to be healed. The people who can't travel to be with you can still be healed from a distance," she explained. "[This angel] is helping you with this shift in your healing abilities."

Sara then confirmed John's close connections to Archangel Gabriel and Mother Mary. "Mary comes and goes," she said, confirming John's recent visions of Mary in the clouds. "She permeates your energy from the yin—or female energy—point of view."

The last question John asked about was the Edgar Cayce reading, which mentioned that John the Apostle would be known as John again in this life. Sara confirmed this at once. "This reading [by Cayce] gave you verification," she agreed. "You will meet Christ in your pineal gland or third eye," she said, as she wrapped up the reading.

In the reading I had given John in Rehoboth Beach the previous summer, Jesus had told him that they would be meeting again, face to face, in this life. This was the same reading in which I had recited the poem for Him. John had also asked me during the reading what he could expect while visiting the Edgar Cayce library in Virginia Beach that October. I had told him that there was a personal message waiting for him there.

While at the Cayce Library, John discovered five references Cayce had made to John the Apostle, or John the Beloved. Cayce, who was said to have actually channeled John the Beloved himself, referred to the modern day incarnation of John as "John Penial." John believes that "Penial" could be a misspelling of the word *pineal* or pineal gland, which is associated with the functioning of the third eye. John concluded that Cayce had actually been referring to John's connection with the third eye, or pineal gland, not that his last name would actually be "Penial."

Another Cayce reading alluded to the fact that John and Jesus would be meeting one another again in a place called "Penial." John believes that this key word, hidden in the text of the reading, was really the personal message that he had come to the library to receive. So, John believed he had actually sent this channeled message to his future self by using the code word "penial or pineal" as a way to remind him of how he would once again behold Christ.

When John finished giving me the details of the reading, I found myself a little breathless. Sara had made references to both the book that John and I were planning to write together, as well as to a future book, which meant that our stories would get published. She saw John meeting Jesus again and seeing Him with his third eye, which tied in with what Jesus had told him during our reading in Rehoboth. She saw John doing the spiritual expo circuit, which the reader at the Florida expo and I had each predicted; and she confirmed my Felix lifetime, which shed some light on my motivation for writing this book.

Though Sara did not directly focus on John's past life, she had indirectly confirmed it by addressing the relationships John had to Christ and to Mary and by referring to the Cayce reading as a "verification" for John. Her reading served as a signpost that John and I were headed in the right direction with our work. We would be seeing each other in less than a month, and we knew that we would need to use our time together wisely. We were blessed with the opportunity to get some serious spiritual work accomplished in the two and a half months that we were able to spend together.

While John was still in Georgia, he had another encounter with the divine. On June 1, 1999, there was a power outage at the campsite where he was staying. Something told John to go outside. He went out to the middle of the road and felt a rush of energy. His hands felt hot and were buzzing with energy. When John asked if it were Jesus' energy he was feeling, he again felt the surge of energy.

Every time he returned to his trailer, he felt guided to go back to the road. This happened three times. The third time it happened, he met his friend, Spydr, in the road, and was compelled to tell him the whole John the Apostle story. Surprisingly, his friend accepted it. When he returned to his trailer again, he noticed that his digital clock read 11:11. Pretty unusual, since after a power outage most electronic clocks reset themselves to 12:00!

Shortly afterward, John met another of his friends at a social gathering.

She was going through a divorce and having a rough time. At that moment, John felt inspired to share his story with her. Her response was, "I can one hundred percent believe that. You've always had something special about you."

During this time, my husband and I finished out the faire near Dallas and made preparations for the band's four-and-one-half months summer/ early fall tour. Our first gig was a Highland Games in Montana, so Randy and I, along with one of the band members, decided to treat the trip up there as a vacation. We spent two glorious weeks sightseeing through Texas, Colorado, Wyoming, and Montana. While we were on the road, I sent an e-mail to Nick updating him on John's reading and my new insights on Felix:

> It is my feeling that Felix was fascinated by what Paul had to say. He totally believed in the gospel of Jesus and was eager to discuss the various aspects of it with him. It [is also] my feeling that Paul tried his best to get Felix to preach the gospel of Christ to others, but for whatever reasons—probably social station…and fear of embarrassing himself and his family—he chose not to come out of his hiding place on that important issue. I think for Felix, the regret came from looking back the rest of his life and feeling like he had not done what he was supposed to do.
>
> This confirms what Jacquelyne said about it, but until I had the emotional memory of this, it didn't seem real. Now it does. It especially seems so now because John Davis had a reading from Sara, and she confirmed my lifetime as Felix as well as confirming John's lifetime as John the Apostle. She recommended that I have a regression on it, but…I have to admit this will not be an easy thing for me to do. [However,] I know I can do it as I have rarely backed down on doing my spiritual work even when I knew it would be difficult.
>
> The night I remembered Felix's emotions, I received the message that you had gotten your own confirmation about it . . . .

I sent the e-mail off from Montana just before we left. It was so good to have a computer that could travel with us. We continued on our journey, which led us through the Black Hills of South Dakota, Minnesota, Wisconsin, and Illinois on our way to the faire near Cleveland, Ohio. This is where John and I would meet up again in late June.

During this same period, John finished the faire in Georgia and flew to Europe to reunite with Jennifer, who had just finished her two-year work program teaching English with the Peace Corps in Cameroon, Africa. I was praying that their reunion would be a blissful one. As I sardonically noted in my journal, "I hope that [their trip] goes all right for them. If not, it will be hell trying to write the book with John this summer!"

As I found out later, they spent two wonderful, romantic weeks in France and Italy. Ironically enough, a leg of their trip took them to the beautiful coastline of Italy by way of train! Sara's metaphor of Jennifer getting on the train with John, so they could continue their life's journey had been so appropriate. They were able to resume their relationship as if absolutely no time had passed between them at all.

I was looking forward to Ohio with some apprehension. I was of course elated to see John again, but I was also anxious since this would be the first time that Jennifer and I would meet. I was looking forward to meeting this special person whom John had talked about many times over the past two years; however, I was a bit concerned what she would think of me. How was she going to take the idea of her boyfriend having a close female friend, and one that had been instrumental in guiding him down a spiritual path which, at that point, was somewhat foreign to her?

Jennifer and I finally met the third weekend of the Ohio faire. John had needed help in the costume booth that he co-owned with Patti and Mitch—his sister and brother-in-law—so when Jennifer returned from her extended stay in Europe, he asked her to work for him. He had gone to pick her up at her mother's house in Akron, and they both came to the campground late Friday night.

The next morning, I nervously went over to John's booth to introduce myself to her. She seemed pleased to meet me. She and John, who came to visit her every chance he could, made a cute couple. They seemed happy together, and I was delighted for them.

Before Jennifer had arrived, John had shared with me his secret plans to propose to her. The how, when, and where of those plans would soon change, as John grew anxious to start their new life together. It was funny, but I felt like I almost knew her. I had heard her name mentioned so many times in the past two years as John had waited patiently and faithfully for her return from Africa. Although many beautiful, talented women had sought him out during that time, for John there was only one woman, and that was Jennifer. I had admired his resolve because he could have dated nearly anyone he wanted.

During the next week John and I got to spend some quality time together working on the manuscript for the book. Jennifer had left to tie up loose ends and visit her family, and Randy and his band had gone to Toronto, Canada, to rehearse a show they were doing the following month. We both agreed that I should write the book from my perspective with John acting as consultant. Together, we compiled the details of our first meeting and the readings that followed. Also, John shared his journal writings with me, which included his previous spiritual experiences.

In late June, John asked me for a reading. He wanted more details about our "book" getting published and whether Nick Bunick would be involved in some way. He also asked who should do our past-life regressions. John's regression would obviously be important as a final verification of our story. My regression would help me come to terms with my past-life issues of worthiness, so that I could move to the next level of my spiritual work with John.

During the reading, the angels told us that the manuscript for the book would take at least five months to write and it would get published within a year of its submission. I told John that this seemed almost impossible since we were virtually unknown. We were also told that Nick could help us make connections to the right people in the publishing world. That expectation seemed a little ambitious to me since I wasn't even sure that he would want to read our manuscript.

When John asked the angels about who we should have do our regressions, we were told that there was someone in or around the Michigan area who would be able to do this. I am not good at geography, so after the reading I had to get out the atlas to see how far Michigan was from northeastern Ohio. "Isn't this terrible, John," I remember saying. "I don't even know where Michigan is or if we can drive it in a day," I said, as I looked up the state map for Michigan. Much to my surprise, Detroit, Michigan, was only a four-hour drive away. "If this person is in Detroit, John, then we could get there and be back the same day."

A few days later, I was led to the people who connected me to the therapist who would do my past-life regression. As I was walking past the jewelry booth of my friend Connie, she called out to me, "You know Rio and I are going to Michigan this week to visit friends. Her friends had a musical act that performed at this faire.

"Oh, really?" I said in amazement. "That's very interesting, because I was told during a reading I did for John that someone in Michigan would be doing a past-life regression for me. Do you think they would know anyone who could do that sort of thing?"

"I don't know," she said. "You could ask them."

When I asked her friends, they referred me to Judy, the violinist for their musical group. Judy said that someone had given her the name and number of a therapist near Ann Arbor, Michigan, who came highly recom-

Sharon Prince

mended, but that she wasn't sure if she could even find the number as it had been several years since she was given the number. She asked me to call her later, and, if she could find it, she would give it to me.

Judy finally called my voice mail and left a message with the phone number of Dr. Elizabeth Borg, a therapist in Canton, Ohio. She had found the number, which someone had given her ten years ago, written on a piece of paper and placed in a plastic baggie lying on her bookshelf. She told me that she usually lost things like that right away, but that it had "magically appeared" just when she had given up hope of ever finding it.

I tried to set up an appointment with Dr. Borg, but had to leave a message. After several attempts, I was finally able to reach her on the Friday before our last week in Ohio. I had only one week left to do the regression before Randy and I left for Maryland. Although it seemed unlikely that I would be able to get in to see her on such short notice, I knew in my heart that there would be an opening, just as I knew when I called her that morning that she would answer the phone.

And I was right. Not only did she answer the phone herself, but after looking at her appointment book, discovered she had an opening on Tuesday morning due to an unexpected cancellation. I gratefully made my appointment and thanked my angels for again helping me to get in to see someone who had a very busy schedule.

In the time between the last reading I had done for John and waiting for my appointment with Dr. Borg, I gave another reading to John and a friend of his, Gregory. John asked if he should schedule his own appointment with the same person I was going to see for my regression, but the angels told him that this person was meant for me, not him. They said that there was someone else out there who would be doing his past-life regression. Though they offered no specific information as to who that would be, I felt it would probably be someone in Maryland. During the reading, which was partially a past-life reading, we were told that Gregory had also walked with Jesus and had been like a brother to John in that life; another link to the past that I found fascinating.

It was during this time that I decided to have another talk with my angels. I wanted verification of the information that I had given John in the previous reading. They confirmed that I had indeed received everything correctly. When I asked them how Nick Bunick would like the manuscript, they said that he would love the book and feel connected to it. "We'll see," I said, somewhat disbelievingly. That afternoon, as a confirmation, I received a very unusual 444 experience.

Randy and I were expecting Lauren, our friend from Portland, and her boyfriend Jim over for dinner that night. They had come to Ohio to do some Irish step dancing with the band, and it was the day before Lauren's birthday. Randy was outside doing some work on the motorhome, when he told me he'd found two four-leaf clovers growing in a tiny clump under the rig. As I searched for them, he said, "Wouldn't it be neat if there was another one growing there as well?" I said, "You mean like a 444 thing?"

"Yeah," he said, surprising me.

I looked and found one perfect four-leaf clover and one shriveled up one. Upon further investigation, I found a third one! This one was also shriveled up, but it didn't matter. There were three, four-leaf clovers! I was so excited that I picked all three. As I got up to show Randy, I dropped the one good clover into a much larger patch of clover. "Oh, no!" I cried. "I was going to give that one to Lauren as a birthday surprise!"

Randy helped me search in the much larger area of clover, but they were all the normal, three-leafed kind. I was about to give up, but I decided to ask my angels for a favor. "Angels, if you don't mind, could you *please* help me find the good four-leaf clover that I dropped? I really want to give it to Lauren." I searched some more, but to no avail. The clover was gone.

Then I looked down one last time, and there, growing among all those normal clover leafs, was one perfect four-leaf clover! "Look, Randy!" I exclaimed. "My angels helped me find another one! What are the chances that I would find *another* four-leaf clover!" Not a single other clover in the small clump had four leaves nor could we find any others in the larger patch. I took it as a sign that I was right about the information that I had received earlier. "What a clever and unusual 444 confirmation!" I thought. I have to give my angels credit for creativity!

This extraordinary 444 experience preceded several more. It seemed that everyone was talking about the presence of angels that summer. John was having 444s and several of the people with whom we had shared the book *The Messengers* were having them as well. Even Jennifer, who doubted that the 444 experiences were real, had her own 444 experience when she woke up in the middle of the night. Just as she was thinking how silly all this fuss was about 444s, she looked at the alarm clock next to her bed. It read 4:44!

I continued to work on the manuscript for *John of Old, John of New* with John helping to fill in the details. I had taken several funny mental snapshots of John sitting and lying in various positions on the couch in the motorhome as we worked on the book. John was a doer, and I knew it had been hard for him to sit there hour after hour as we pieced our story together.

One minute he was playing with the buckle on his sandal, the next minute he was stretched out with his fists resting on his forehead. Yet, through it all, he supported my efforts and patiently assisted me in every way he could.

When I had completed the first three chapters, we decided to share what I had written with a couple of our friends and with Jennifer and her mom, in order to get some feedback. What encouraged me most was that each person I shared the manuscript with said they couldn't wait to read more in order to see what happened next.

As I stated before, John's and my biggest regret while writing this story was that we had not recorded our readings together, especially the messages from Jesus. If only we could convey to the reader the great wisdom, love, and humor that came through the words that the Master had spoken through me! We were determined that from then on, we would record every reading. Already, we were planning our annual reading at Rehoboth Beach and agreed that we would most definitely record the session!

One piece of information that John had received was how he could heal others. **"You may heal others by calling on my name,"** Jesus had told John in a reading I did for him in Ohio. John had healed his friend Brooke's son, Nigel, who had been very ill and running a high fever for a few days, by calling on the name of Jesus. Soon after John worked on him, Nigel's temperature broke and he was fine. When John and Jennifer were at her mother's house in Akron, Ohio, he healed a painful crick in Jennifer's shoulder by calling on the name of Jesus. In fact, the healing was instantaneous, which really surprised her because it would normally take a couple of days to get over.

As I prepared for my trip to Michigan on Tuesday, I packed my tape recorder so that I could record and transcribe the regression for my own personal use afterward. I thought that John would be able to accompany me on my trip to see Dr. Borg, but as it turned out, my appointment fell on a day that he had scheduled to spend with Jennifer. I certainly couldn't blame him for wanting to spend some special time with the woman he loved, and, since Randy would be leaving again for Canada the day before my regression, this was another journey that I was meant to make alone. Much like my trip to Portland, I had to trust that everything would go as the angels had planned. After all, weren't they the ones who had led me to Dr. Borg in the first place?

I got up very early to make the four-hour trip to Canton, a suburb on the west side of Detroit. I had the feeling that something might go wrong with my usually dependable car, so I prayed that I would arrive safely and on time, and return safely, as well. I believe that anything we ask for in faith, which is in accordance with our higher good, we shall receive. I arrived at Dr. Borg's office an hour early without incident. It gave me time to meditate and pray before the regression.

I met Dr. Borg, a calm, logical, yet compassionate, woman, a few minutes before the regression began. Elizabeth Borg, a slender woman, with shoulder-length blonde hair, in her early fifties, had been in practice for about twenty years. She interviewed me, asking me some questions about my personal history and what issues I wanted to address in my past-life regression. Instead of hypnoregression, she used a sound technique known as EDMS, which bilaterally stimulates both hemispheres of the brain by sending an alternating tone to each ear through a headset.

After some relaxation and visualization exercises, Dr. Borg was successful in regressing me. This bilateral stimulation technique brought me to a deep state of relaxation and allowed me to access information from my subconscious mind and bring it to my conscious mind. It also allowed Dr. Borg to simultaneously access my past awareness as Felix and my present awareness as Sharon, and to move back and forth from one to the other. In this way, Felix could receive the soul therapy he needed—which would ultimately benefit me as well—and those two aspects of myself—Felix and Sharon—could interface with one another to co-create a new spiritual awareness for both.

The regression started with a memory from my childhood, which Dr. Borg said was a surface memory for the much older, past-life memory. When asked to go back to the earlier memory, I found myself as the ruler of a region. I knew that I had gone back to the time just after Christ, when my soul was Felix, the Roman governor of Judea. We were able to uncover vivid emotional memories, which started with the heartbreaking farewell between Felix and the Apostle Paul as Paul was leaving for Rome. The guilt and regret of that lifetime was intense, but Dr. Borg was able to create a therapeutic environment for Felix to come to terms with his guilt.

The whole session lasted an hour and a half, but I felt that a significant healing of the past had occurred in that short time. I now feel that I am able to more fully access my spiritual awareness, unhindered by the deep feelings of guilt and remorse that Felix had brought upon himself, and which had been subconsciously influencing and limiting my present spiritual work.

Felix's choice not to speak out on Paul's behalf nor openly share the gospel of Jesus with others had centered on his very real fear of being imprisoned or killed for it. He was deeply afraid of ridicule and the demise of the career he had worked so hard to achieve. And he feared for the safety and well-being of his family because of the retribution that would certainly result from his opposing the Roman social and political system to which he belonged.

With the help of Dr. Borg, Felix was given the chance to express his truth and make the decision to share that truth with others in subtle, covert ways. He used his influence to get messages from Paul in Rome back to the other apostles in Judea and vice-versa. Hence, my connection to John and the other apostles was confirmed. I now share with you excerpts from that past-life regression in hopes that it will shed some light on how the past can influence our present decisions and also how we can creatively heal our past and integrate it with our awareness now:

Felix: (in reference to Paul) He has helped me so much. And I feel a oneness with God that I had not felt before. I feel a connectedness. And even though he's leaving, he's leaving something behind. I feel that I have . . . at least a part of the truth. I realize that it's watching over me. For my own selfish reasons . . . I'm not wanting to let [him] go. I'm afraid to let go. I know he still loves me. He doesn't blame me. He actually thanks me for giving him this opportunity . . . [for] taking him all this way . . . [i.e., keeping him safe and sending him to Rome in order to get a fair trial].

I was just angry [at myself] that I didn't have the courage to speak out on his behalf, to say that I knew that what he was saying was true. And I know that I am living my life with this burden on my shoulders.

Dr. Borg: Do you want to take the burden off? Are you willing to actually make a choice to let go of it? 'Cause it's your choice at this point. You know . . . that you both learned that there's no one to blame . . . Tell me, what do you get out of keeping that burden, Ruler? What's the secondary gain?

Felix: I'm paying penance . . .

Dr. Borg: When have you paid enough penance? . . . What does this [issue of feeling unworthy] absolve you of?

Felix: Making ready decisions for my higher good. Because I'm not feeling worthy, I don't have to take the responsibility . . . that I'm here to do.

Dr. Borg then challenged Felix to let go of these feelings of guilt and unworthiness; by doing so he would have to take the responsibility of being a more benevolent and enlightened ruler. Felix wanted to walk through the "doorway of light," but his fear got in the way. She challenged him to have the courage to walk through the door. She told him that courage is "an energy that is available to anyone" and that he can call it to himself.

Dr. Borg asked Felix what color this courage was and where he wanted to store it. He told her it is the color blue, and indicated that he needed to bring it into his throat, which would become the doorway through which the light energy could enter his chakra—or energy—system and anchor or connect him to the earth, and at the same time connect him to his higher self and to God. I was able to interface with Felix energetically and release the tension that his memory was holding in my body:

Felix: It's like it has to do with wisdom and being able to walk with that wisdom, to be able to integrate it into my body so that I can feel at peace with it. The mantra that keeps coming up is 'knowledge is power.' Now I know that the connection is [that] I have this knowledge, but because I'm not using it, I haven't come into the power of that knowledge. I haven't acquired it yet.

Then Dr. Borg brought Felix into the future, into my current lifetime, and allowed us to connect with one another consciously in order to share our resources and knowledge and to make him aware that in this period of time, it is safer for one to speak one's truth:

Dr. Borg: What resource [from Sharon] or way of incarnating this into your daily life would you most choose, Ruler?

Felix: Just having more courage to speak the truth...like Sharon has done.

Dr. Borg: It is easier to speak the truth in our time...because we have more freedom of speech. In your time, there's more suppression . . . there're more rules. It's much more confined in your time, Ruler. So . . . what's a realistic [and creative way of how you can speak the truth] within those limitations, in a way that preserves you and everyone around you, but still is a way to help whenever you can?

Felix: I'm passing the knowledge on [in a subtle way]. It's important for me to be there. I can get the word from [Paul] to the others. I can pass that word on. I do see myself [doing that]. I'm the mouthpiece. I'm the voice for someone who could not be there himself and still get this [message] out .

Dr. Borg: Good. How does that feel . . . in your throat and chest, Ruler? How does that help . . . the disturbance there?

Felix: Well, I feel like I'm doing some good. I feel like I can release my guilt because I'm allowing this flow to go through me. Maybe I can't actually speak it myself, but I'm passing it on, so that vicariously I'm speaking it. I'm speaking it by allowing this message to go forward, because I'm protecting . . . [and] . . . delivering the message. It's safe with me. I have the connections to get that message out. I'm the carrier . . . the messenger for the truth.

Dr. Borg then gave Felix the opportunity to really speak from the heart, and I was surprised by his hidden passion for wanting to help others know the truth about Jesus and God. His words moved me in a way I had not expected, and they shed light on the drive I was now experiencing to get this message out today. The following is Felix speaking to those who are against Jesus and His followers:

> You don't understand. There's no need to be afraid. We can walk with this light in our daily lives. We don't have to persecute one another. There's an inner wisdom in all of us. If we would just [have] the courage to reach that part of ourselves that knows the truth: that we can be at peace with ourselves. We don't have to struggle [with] a day-to-day existence. [Jesus] was teaching us to love ourselves and to reach that love part of ourselves that is connected to God. This is our bridge. This is our awareness. We shut this doorway off out of ignorance and fear. We shut this off and this is what makes us struggle in our day-to-day lives. If we could just find the courage to bring this oneness into our lives, we wouldn't have to struggle so much. We would know the answers. We would be at peace with ourselves.
>
> All of these things that you say are well and good, but why not give another message a chance? Why not hear? Why not open your hearts and your minds to something [new] . . . ? Why do you feel so threatened by this? Why is it that you judge something that you do not understand? This person you have ridiculed and this person that you are speaking out against so strongly meant you no harm. Why do you feel so threatened by this . . . inner wisdom and peace?
>
> Are you so threatened by this light that you cannot feel it in your beings?
>
> This person was about love . . . This person was not about punishment and negativity. These [are] things that you are ridiculing . . . [because] you're feeling trapped by your expectations. These expectations have been placed on you by others. There're no expectations here. There is only oneness in God, in love and peacefulness. Don't turn your back on something that is so right and true. Have the courage to at least listen and entertain in yourself the possibility that there's another way.

Felix then released the anger he felt toward the "fools [who] think they know all the answers." With the help of Dr. Borg, he was able to release his anger and sadness and to forgive and feel compassion for those people who were living in fear and ignorance of Christ's teachings. She asked Felix if he could now walk through the doorway of light, taking with him the knowledge and resources and understanding that he had acquired, realizing and having compassion for the limitations that his culture and time had placed upon him.

As the part of me who had been Felix released the past, I chose to walk through the doorway. I could feel the numbness that was in my hands and feet throughout most of my regression begin to increase, and I started to feel a kundalini-like energy begin to rise up through my body, sending a strong vibration to my throat chakra and ending in a peaceful, euphoric feeling in my head. Finally, I released the energy through my crown chakra, located at the top of my head, and it connected to a higher energy, which I believe was my higher self. Like a self-guided visualization, I could see myself being lifted up by the angels to where Jesus was waiting for me. I looked into His loving face, and He welcomed me. My body and spirit felt so light, as if I were floating.

Dr. Borg then brought my awareness to the present time, asking me to bring the new-found wisdom, peace, and resources that I had acquired in the regression into my present life so that I could move forward with this new understanding of applied spirituality. She asked me to ground myself in the room, which was not easy, and gave me the suggestion that I would remember the regression and would feel good.

"Now I'm at another level with that knowledge-is-power [thing]," I told her. "Now knowledge is *wisdom*," I said, laughing in recognition of this sudden insight.

Dr. Borg laughed in surprise, as well. "Yes! Hmmmm! Nice."

"I don't have to be afraid of the wisdom," I continued.

"It is another time and space. You're here now. And there are great opportunities to express yourself more than [in] any other time, probably, in history," she corroborated.

"What a wonderful thing," I said with new awareness.

I gave Dr. Borg an appreciative hug and stumbled out of her office. I could barely feel my feet touch the ground as I walked to my car. Thank goodness I had thought to bring something to eat and drink! After twenty minutes of sitting in my car, sipping juice, and eating snacks, I felt grounded enough to drive my car. I made it safely back to Ohio, but as soon as I parked the car, the battery died. It would have to be replaced altogether. My angels had brought me safely home just as I had asked them to do.

CHAPTER NINE

Confirmations

We were fast approaching the last weekend of the faire in Ohio, trying to tie things up and get ready for our trip to Maryland the next week, where Randy's band would again be performing at the same festival as John and his acting partner, Spencer. The memories and emotions of Governor Felix were still fresh within me, and I needed time to process and heal from what I had uncovered from my past life. There was a lot to process, and I had only just begun. I received an e-mail from John, who was still away with Jennifer. As if on cue, there was also a channeled message from the Master. His words were like balm for the wounds of my past.

July 26, 1999 [John's message]

Hey Girl,

I know that we are embarking on a powerful journey together. I just felt that I should first apologize for not going to Michigan with you; but I am sure it is for the best! Jen and I [are] going to come back to the campground on Tuesday and stay through Wednesday . . . and then I will work with you on the book on Thursday and Friday . . .

[Here's the channeled part:]

Sharon, many fears are dwelling inside you at this time, and we are helping to alleviate this for you. When your sacred mission is complete, and you are ready for this, you will have a full realization of your potential. This realization will empower you more than anything you have ever experienced. You will trust your inner knowingness and will act upon its guidance. This will lead you to the most rewarding time in your life . . . Now is your time, and you will be aware of this as the days go on. Heavy is the burden of the past. You and John on many occasions have allowed yourselves to dwell there. Though it is important to know, it is more important to live each present moment fully; to hold on to what cannot be undone is a futile effort that is being the burden on the camel's back.

What straw is yet to come that will topple the camel and upend the load? Forgive yourself, for you have done no wrong. Cut the cords of discontent, and find yourself. When you are fully realized, you will see that there is no forgiveness needed, as it is an earthly concept. We are always loving and not of a condemning nature. Love, and you have discovered what we are.[24]

John and Jennifer returned to the campground on Tuesday, having had a great time at Sandusky, Ohio. Jennifer left on Thursday, and John and I had just a little bit of time to work on the book before the weekend. Then, on Saturday, Jennifer returned with her entire family. It was a whole new world for them, this strange land of Renaissance and Medieval faires. I am not sure that they were keen on their daughter being a part of it, at least not as a lifestyle!

The last weekend of the faire ended with a big finale that took place during the pub sing. My friend Lauren, from Portland, had brought her new dance partner and boyfriend to the faire, and the day ended with a big Irish dance and music finale, led by my husband's band at the pub stage. Before we knew it, Randy and I were heading to Maryland. We took the opportunity, before the next show started, to spend a week and a half visiting Randy's parents. I hated spending this time away from John as I felt the precious time we had available to work together slipping away. However, I knew that this was the one time each year that Randy and I had to visit with his parents, who live in the beautiful Smoky Mountains of North Carolina. It was in the embrace of those mountains that I was to have another significant experience with the Master.

I had brought our laptop computer with us so that I could continue to work on the book, but it seemed more like a time for research than it did for writing. John had loaned me his book by Dolores Cannon called *They Walked with Jesus,* which I took the opportunity to read while I was away.

As I read the book, I found some accounts of John the Apostle, as told by a person named Anna, who remembers being Naomi, a niece of Jesus. In July, when John first read the book, he came across a passage that made us both laugh as he read it aloud to me. The following is an excerpt of the dialogue between Anna, who was Naomi, and Dolores Cannon:[25]

Anna: There seems to be a man called John. And this man . . . I've seen John a lot . . .

Dolores: . . . What does John look like? You said he's about the same age [as Jesus]?

Anna: Yes. He looks similar, except he has the dark eyes of many of the people around this area. And he's not as kind looking. [John found this especially amusing!] He's a bit huskier, too.

Anna's remembrance of John of Old was similar to John now: he is, again, a large man with brown eyes. The book also contained an accounting of the role that John took while traveling with Jesus and the other apostles.

Delores: Does John have any particular duties?

Anna: He seems to be very close to Jesus, and he seems to try to be the other eyes and ears for him. He keeps things connected, so people who need to see him get to see him, and to be sure [Jesus] gets to the gatherings. John organises [sic] many of the activities or meetings.

Delores: You mean he goes ahead of the group and sets things up?

Anna: Sometimes he does that, depending on the type of journey. But once we get to a location, he seems to keep our schedule organised [sic], making sure things get done, and bringing to the attention of the Nazarene anything he needs to know.

I was impressed by how much Jesus must have trusted John and how close they must have been that He would give him so much responsibility. In fact, according to the book, Jesus and the other apostles had the Last Supper at John's father's house in Jeruselum. No wonder Jesus has such a strong, personal connection to John, I thought. And that is probably why He wishes to renew this bond with him now, so that John may awaken to the work that he is to bring forth in preparation for the Second Coming.

As I continued to read the book, it became a teaching tool for me and a confirmation of some experiences that I would have later. As I wrote in my journal:

> It occurred to me why I was being guided to read They Walked with Jesus right now, in the middle of trying to write the book. It is because it is helping me work through my issues from the Felix lifetime, so that I can clear out the leftover karma in order to be clear to do the next level of work for John in channeling Christ . . . . I feel strongly enough about doing the right thing by Jesus—not for His sake, but for my own . . . He is definitely coming again, but it will happen in each of our hearts first. The Second Coming is happening now, one messenger at a time.

The first night we arrived at Randy's parents' house, August 5, I received a call from John. He was excited to share some news with me. He had been trying to reach Atira, the reader whom I had met at the April 4 Prayer in Portland, to set up a phone appointment. She had finally called him back. He related the phone call to me.

In a very routine manner she had begun setting up an appointment for a phone reading. "Hi, this is Atira. You left a message for me?" she inquired.

"Yes. I'd like to get a reading from you," John replied.

"That's great. Well, let me tell you about how I do readings. I don't do them the way most readers do them. I delve into people's past lives and tell them what issues are still affecting them now."

"It's funny that you should mention past lives," John remarked. "I have been told by five different readers that I was John the Apostle in a past life."

"Oh, my God!" Atira yelled in disbelief. *"You're* the one we've been looking for!"

"Oh, yeah?" John said, laughing at Atira's reaction.

"Oh, my God! I can't wait to tell the others. My angels told me that I would be hearing from you in a week's time, and it's been about a week!" One of Atira's friends, "Jason," who was a known author of spiritual books, had also been looking for John for about two years, and she couldn't wait to share the news with him and another friend of hers, named Michael Baumann, who is the reincarnation of the Apostle Philip.

Atira checked her schedule. The soonest that she could give John a reading was August 17, the day after he was scheduled to get a reading from Jacquelyne, the reader who had read for me in Portland. Atira seemed anxious to do the reading as soon as possible but was booked up until then. She told John that if she got a cancellation before then that she would call him. He was intrigued to find out that two people, whom he had never met, had been looking for him.

"Wow, John! This is hot news!" I said, astonished.

"Pretty cool, huh?"

Cool was an understatement. If I had had any doubts that we were being shown the way and being connected to just the right people to bring this message out, those doubts had now been laid to rest. First we were connected to Nick, and now this friend of Atira's, Jason, the author of a well-known spiritual book: the universe had gotten just a little smaller.

Later I learned that, as if by divine timing, Michael Baumann had called Atira right after she had hung up the phone with John. "Michael! You're never going to believe who I just talked to! I think I found the 'John' we're looking for!"

"Really?" Michael said, surprised.

"This guy called me to set up a phone appointment. I only talked to him for about a minute when I started to pick up that he was definitely someone biblical. I know that this is going to be a very important reading, Michael. I wanted to keep talking with him, but I cut it off so that I could save it for the reading, when I could really get into it," she explained.

"So when is the reading?" Michael asked

"In about a week or two," Atira replied, "but I'm going to try to move it up if possible."

"Well, let me know as soon as you get a feeling for him," Michael said.

"I don't think the reading is going to change my opinion at all," she asserted. "*This* is our John."

Michael Baumann was already pondering the possibility of meeting John. The previous year, Michael had had the privilege of meeting Nick through his new friend, Atira, at a symposium that Nick gave in Seattle. Later, Atira introduced Michael to her friend, Jason, the author of a best-selling book. Now it looked as though Atira was putting him in touch with yet another apostle.

Michael, I later learned, is a brilliant software developer in his "real life." He's average in height and weight, with fine, short brown hair which is perfectly coiffed. Michael is calm, level-headed, modest and very reserved. His manner and comments are usually understated and his humor is dry, but his eyes will sparkle when he is being funny or mischievous. He does have a wicked sense of humor on occasion, but he will only let you see this after he gets to know you well.

It was hard to believe that all this excitement had taken place since Randy and I had left Maryland earlier that day. John promised to call me if he heard anything more. With the synchronicities in our lives happening at a faster pace than ever before, I knew we needed to be spiritually ready for what was about to transpire.

Three days later, when I found myself alone, I went out onto the balcony of my in-laws' house to pray and meditate. I was trying to develop a closer personal relationship with Jesus so that I could channel Him more clearly for John. I wanted to be as prepared as possible to do my annual reading for John in Rehoboth Beach, which my angels had told me was going to be a more powerful connection to the Master than ever before.

I said a prayer for a closer connection to Jesus. Then I felt His presence come to me, as He had done before—His energy was most intense around my head and face. Communicating to me through telepathy, He asked me to put my palms face up, while I sat in a chair. He told me to focus on my heart. I felt this intense energy coming into my palms as I felt Him place his "hands" on top of my hands, palm-to-palm. I could not see Him, but there was no mistaking His strong, loving energy, which completely surrounded me. At one point, he even placed his hands on my temples. His presence was up close and personal, as it had been before in Maryland, and His communication, which I heard inside my mind, was very clear.

This intensity not withstanding, I was having trouble concentrating as I fought off the distraction of chattering squirrels and itchy spots on my body. Each time my mind wandered, He very patiently had me refocus my energy. **"Focus on your heart,"** I heard Him say several times. His presence was very real and very powerful. With His help, I was able to meditate more deeply than I had ever done before. As I noted in my journal that day:

> I think He wants me to feel His love energy more strongly, so that I can impart this to John . . . I feel, for the first time, that I was truly able to clear my mind. He then placed His 'hands' on my temples. I assumed this was to adjust my clairaudience [psychic hearing] to be able to channel better. When we finished [about forty minutes later], I felt different. Even Randy asked me if I were all right. He always seems to know when something significant has happened, which is a wonderful verification that something really has happened to me, and that it's not just my imagination.

I felt very peaceful and reenergized after the meditation/spiritual attunement with Jesus, but I wondered why He had sent me energy through my palms when it was my heart where He asked me to focus. I didn't think the palms and heart had anything to do with one another.

As I continued to read Dolores Cannon's book *They Walked with Jesus*, I discovered the connection between the center of the palms and the heart center or heart chakra. I read the past life memories of Naomi. According to her memories, Jesus was healing lepers in a lepers community, and Naomi was observing how he was able to ease the pain of one man.

Anna: And you can tell that this man...his face is at ease . . . the pain seems to be much less. And the Nazarene, the other day...he lifted my hand, and with a finger he drew a circle in my palms (she went through these motions). And he said, 'This, too, is the heart. The centre [sic] of your palms. In the centre [sic] is another heart chakra'. And that's why there is so much power in the healing of these hands, because of that energy coming straight through . . .

Delores: Did he mean your hands, or his own?

Anna: I think he meant everyone's hands. He took my hand...and he took the other one, and he said, 'These, too, are heart centres [sic].' (She went through the motions of drawing circles on the center of her palms.)

When I read these words for the first time, my heart felt as if it had stopped for a moment. The Master must have known that I was about to read that part of the book and took the opportunity to share with me the experience of meditating with Him, knowing that my reading this passage later would be a confirmation that our interaction had been real. I felt great emotion well up in my heart and throat. This wasn't a joke. For the first time, I believed that I could call on Him to help me anytime and that if I were sincere enough, He would come and talk to me.

A couple of days after my encounter with Jesus, Randy and I traveled to Glenville, North Carolina, to spend the day with a business associate who has a home there. Joyce's husband had passed away a few years ago, leaving her some lovely property in the mountains. She gave us a tour of the place. Behind the main house is a waterfall that flows into a beautiful, wooded creek. "This is a perfect place to meditate," I thought, and, so I left Randy and Joyce in the sunroom to chat while I hiked back to the waterfall.

As I sat by the waterfall and meditated, I again received a personal message from the Master. He told me that John and I would soon have another communication from Him and that it would be an awakening. When I asked Him where we would receive this message, He said Rehoboth Beach.[26] I asked Him if it needed to be the same spot at Cape Henlopen where we received the original communication from Him. He told me that we could receive the message anywhere; however, this was a place that had special significance for both of us, and the energy of the original reading was still at that spot.

I asked Him what kind of awakening we should expect, and He said that we would both feel more of His presence. I assumed He meant that we would feel His presence in a more powerful way, energetically speaking. Perhaps this meant that I would be a clearer channel, as well. It occurred to me that I needed to continue to develop a strong, more personal relationship with Him, so that I would feel more comfortable about channeling His messages and His love to John, and possibly to others in the future.

As our visit to North Carolina came to an end, we said good-bye to Randy's parents and made our way back to Maryland. During the drive, I continued to read *They Walked with Jesus* and gained more insights about my Felix lifetime. I learned of the danger one might encounter by going against the political and social systems in operation during the time of Jesus. First, it was extremely dangerous for an ordinary Jew to defy the Roman government, much less a Roman judge or ruler of the region. If that were allowed to happen, then the ordinary citizen would feel that he could rebel, and the government would lose control over the populace. It was extraordinary that Felix would seek Paul out in order to discuss the Gospel of Jesus with him. Even more extraordinary was the fact that he actually believed in it!

I also received two little "signs" on the way back. The first was a hand-printed sign that had been nailed to a post. It read: John: 3:16, "For God so loved the world that he gave his only Son, that whoever believes in him shall not perish but have eternal life." Then about forty-five minutes later, another sign came into view. This was a bigger sign, which read: John 17:3 "Now this is eternal life: that they may know you, the only true God, and Jesus Christ, whom you have sent."

When Randy and I got back to the Maryland camp on August 11, 1999, I was still mulling over the reasons why Felix felt he could not share the Gospel with others and was wrestling with my own misgivings about telling people, through the book, that I had actually had conversations with Jesus. Randy parked the car and I got out to walk Rommy, our cat. Deep in thought, I asked Jesus, "Do you think people are really ready to hear the message that *anyone* can talk to You and that they will receive an answer?"

Bam! He was right there. **"Yes, they are,"** He said with his intense, loving energy.

"I would ask you how you know this, but I suppose that would be a dumb question," I responded.

"Not really. This is what is missing in people's lives today: knowing that they can go within for this personal communication with me. They want a stronger connection to me, but it is not something that will come from outside of them, but from within them."

He said it in such an eloquent manner, that I exclaimed, "You have such a way with words!"

To which He replied with humor, **"That's what I have been told."**

Wow! Another communication with the Master! I ran inside to write down our conversation. I was feeling so connected to Him that I was ready to channel Him for John, right then and there. However, John was on his way out just as we were coming in. He had already made plans to spend a week with Jennifer in Rehoboth Beach, the place where John and I were originally planning to have a special 11:11 reading on August 11, 1999.[27] We spoke briefly and I agreed to take care of his dog, Odin, while he was away.

When I finished Dolores Cannon's book the day after we arrived, I noted in my journal some insights I had gained from it:

> August 12, 1999
>
> At the end of the book, when Naomi tells the regressionist that she is visited by Jesus several times after He is gone, it reminded me of my [encounters with Jesus.] Why would Jesus want to talk to an ordinary human being like myself? Or to anyone for that matter? The answer I got was: because in His eyes we are precious souls and He will reach out to anyone who reaches out to Him. He will not come unbidden. Like our angels, He must be invited into our lives. Most people do not trust their inner voice, so they do not think it is possible to talk to Him and receive answers. But they are wrong about that.
>
> When I asked Jesus why He should care about me when I probably never met Him in that lifetime, He assured me that He did care about me and that He loved me very much. He has been earnestly trying to get me to allow myself to feel His loving, healing energy. I am trying to open myself fully to this, but I thought about it last night: What if I allowed myself to experience such a pure love energy more intense than anything I had ever felt before? Surely I would crumble and my human form would no longer exist! '**Not quite that severe**,' I heard Him say with loving humor. '**Allow yourself to feel me and let me work in your life.**'

Randy was soon on his way to Canada for a week of rehearsals for the show the band was doing near Toronto with our Canadian friends that next weekend. "A whole week alone! I should get plenty of work done on the book while everyone is away," I thought to myself. Little did I know that I would be spending the entire week transcribing the Felix regression tape.

I can't think of many things more tedious than transcribing, word for word, twenty-one pages of emotionally charged dialogue. But, painstaking as it was, it was absolutely necessary in my own healing process. By the end of the week, I had not accomplished much in the way of writing the book, but I realized how beneficial it had been in helping me to understand why I felt compelled to do this work with John. Although I didn't recall it at the time,

Sara had said in her reading for John that I would be getting soul therapy for this past life, which I had done, and I had definitely co-created with my past in order to clear the way for bringing this work forward in the future.

I have to admit, all I wanted to do was get through that tape as quickly as possible, so that I could get back to working on the book. Even though I was going to a great amount of trouble to transcribe the tape, I was aware that it was entirely possible that Nick would have no interest whatsoever in reading it, although it might provide some insight, however small, into his own past. Mostly, I wanted to help Felix reach through time and be able to express himself in regards to Paul in a way that he had not been able to before. I finally determined that it made no difference whether Nick accepted my story or not, though I hoped that he would. I was doing this for my own growth and healing. Once I sent the transcript off to him, I could release the past. The opportunity to finally release the guilt I had been carrying with me for almost two thousand years was just too good to pass up this time!

Later in the week, as I was nearing the end of transcribing the regression—backing the tape up over and over again to catch all the nuances—my tape recorder started to significantly slow down for no apparent reason. I had charged up the recorder's rechargeable batteries the night before and had not been at my task long when this occurred. Annoyed by this unexpected interruption in my work, I took out the batteries and placed them back in the charger, so they could recharge, and went over to John's trailer to pay a visit to Odin, his big male Rottweiler, whom John had raised from a five-week-old pup.

Odin fiercely and loyally guarded the trailer when John was away. He could look ferocious and intimidating, but once he knew that you were John's friend, he was a big old teddy bear. A faithful gatekeeper, he did not let just anyone pass through; but he knew and trusted me, and was usually glad to see me when I came in. Earlier that morning I had turned the television on for him so that the sound of human voices would comfort him while he was there alone.

I came in and sat down on the sofa, and as usual, Odin sat at my feet. "Good, boy, O. Whatcha doin?" I gave him a hug and rubbed him on his head. There was a movie on about teenagers coming of age. It was not something I would normally watch, but I had some time to kill and Odin seemed to appreciate my company, so I stayed for a few minutes. I had come in at the tail-end of the movie, during a scene which showed all the teenagers gathering at the local diner the morning after the big prom.

I decided I had watched enough and was about to get up and leave when something prompted me to stay a bit longer. A couple of minutes later, the camera panned over to one of the tables at the diner. I couldn't believe my eyes! There, sitting on the table, was a cardboard cutout of Felix the Cat! "Wow!" I laughed. "That's exactly who I thought of when I first received the name Felix a year ago! I guess this is my angels' clever way of telling me that I am on the right track!"

I went back to the motorhome and tested the batteries, which had only been recharging for a few minutes—not long enough to have really made a difference. Sure enough, when I placed them back into the tape recorder, they worked perfectly! I finished transcribing the regression that day and had some time left over to work on the book.

The next day, on August 16, while John and Jennifer were still in Rehoboth Beach, John had his first reading from Jacquelyne. She again confirmed his life as John the Apostle. She told him that two others were carrying the energy and memories of John, but that John was the actual physical reincarnation of the Beloved Disciple. There is another person, she said, who was carrying the energy of John, but he was not yet willing to "come out."

Although Jacquelyne sent the tape off the next day, it would take about two and a half weeks for it to arrive. In the meantime, John would have a reading from Atira, and a "regular" reading from me. I was thrilled when I finally had the opportunity to listen to the tape Jacquelyne made, for it confirmed the publication of the book, his new career as a spiritual speaker, and his overall purpose for coming here.

A crowd of guides and angels gathered around when Jacquelyne asked for those beings most connected and purposeful in John's spiritual work. Although his guides said that he didn't really need them because of his direct connection to God, they wanted to "hang out" with him anyway, while he was conscious and awake. Not only had they worked with him a number of years and now wanted to observe the fruits of their labors, they just really enjoyed his company.

One of John's guides, who was a male energy, said his purpose was to help John "dig further, to go beyond the surface or beyond what's apparent." He said that substance and meaning in relationships was important to John.

Jacquelyne: Anytime you're listening to somebody talk, and you have a feeling that they're hiding something, or they're only telling you a certain amount [of the truth—that] they're not revealing everything, he says you can call on him. Just ask him to help you bring to the surface [the answers to these questions:] 'What am I missing? Reveal what's under the surface. Bring…to my awareness what else is here . . .' You can do this in regards to yourself, as well . . .

John was then introduced to a female guide, who said that she was a part of John's soul family and thought of John as a brother. Jacquelyne said that her energy had to do with expansion and expression in motion. She was the one to call on when John was ready to take on a new adventure, a new piece of work, or a new project.

Jacquelyne: If you're wanting to know, 'How should I get my work out there?' Or, if you're already in the process of getting out there and you want to know how to be . . . more creative or how to reach more people, she would be the one to call on. She really works a lot with your throat chakra, in just helping you get out there—express yourself out in the world.

And she says that one of the things that drew her to you was your sense of adventure. You're not satisfied just to sit on the fence and watch life happen . . . . You want to participate . . . You are a doer . . . . You're somebody who puts action behind your dream, and she really likes that about you. And she says that the two of you . . . have . . . in common this sense for the adventure and this risk-taking—a boldness, a why-not-try-it kind of attitude.

His female guide advised John to keep moving—that he would figure things out as he got to where he was going. She said that she wanted to be the one who helped him know when to plot a course of action and stick to it, and when to play it by ear. Both methods worked, she said, but the trick was knowing which method to employ and when. To help him, she would give him a signal or sign as to which would work best, depending on the situation.

This guide also said that John had grown more in the last four or five years than his angels or guides had expected him to and that his level of commitment to spiritual growth and to waking up was *very* strong. All this was very exciting to her.

Jacquelyne told John that there were four other guides that worked with him at all times as well as a personal angel, and that Archangel Gabriel was also working with him.

Jacquelyne: The only time I've seen Gabriel show up is if somebody has . . . an outward mission or like some kind of work to achieve that is going to affect or going to influence a number of people's lives. It's like a bigger work. It's more than just a personal thing.

John: My friend Sharon and I are writing a book together right now about all the things that have happened in the past seven years. I'm curious about that book and will it be published . . . I spoke to [Atira] who completely . . . freaked out when I talked to her, and she was telling me [how her author friend, Jason] has been looking for John the Apostle for a while now. I didn't know if there was a connection there or not, or whether . . . he will be involved in the rewriting of the book or something like that. I'm just curious about that.

Jacquelyne: Well, first off, part of the reason Gabriel is here is because of getting your work out. He says this story needs to be told. He says, 'Absolutely, it will be published. Absolutely it will be out there.' And . . . he gets a little bit possessive almost. It's like when we look at having somebody rewrite this, it's like 'Uh uh! Fine to get somebody else's input and ideas, but it is not really to be rewritten by anybody.' He says, 'If you wanted to run this by somebody and get their suggestions, fine. If somebody wants to put in a little piece in their own words at the ending or beginning, that's fine, but this needs to come out the way that it comes out from your memory and your awareness.' And so he says to...'hold it as a private thing before it goes public.' He says, 'This is personal, and it needs to really reflect your energy.' So absolutely it's going to be published. He just keeps saying, 'It needs to be told—the story needs to be told.'

John told Jacquelyne that he had been doing more channeling lately. He explained how he would be typing an e-mail to me and suddenly someone else, such as the Master, would come through and type out a message to me. He felt that this was starting to happen more frequently.

John: I've had a weird sense that I'll probably be [writing] books [which include] channeled writings . . .

Jacquelyne: Yeah, that's going to happen more and more. [Your female guide] says that this is one of the things that she was really nudged to open up within you. She says, 'Not only . . . do you first need to tell your personal story because that has to get out of you . . . [it's] taking up room in a room that we need to empty first. We need to tell your story first. And then, once those words are clear, then we will be able to download all kinds of information that we want you to put out. One of the things that makes you an important messenger is that you have a way of putting into words and making explainable and practical, concepts that in most people's heads would come out very airy fairy [and] very lacking in substance. You have an ability to travel...in the past...and in the future. You have an ability to visit various dimensions simultaneously and to be articulate enough and bright enough to put that down—to describe it in the only ways that a human can relate [to it] and without totally demeaning the information. Most people would dilute the information too much in order to bring it down. You don't do that. You help it to keep its form or its resonance. You bring it down in such a way that the average human [can] understand it [and] receive it.'

I knew John had always had this gift for channeling divine guidance, for I had seen him do it for me in moments when I wanted to doubt myself or was wondering if I were doing the right thing. In fact, even before

John was consciously aware he had this ability, he had received messages of inspiration for others. John had shared with me about a couple of his early channeling experiences which I'd recorded in my journal:

Before John met me, he knew a performer named Jeff, who was a severe alcoholic. Jeff came to John, one day, with a desire to kill himself. He felt he had nothing to offer the world. He was single with no family but his sister, who was a pediatric surgeon. He had come to the conclusion that if he killed himself, he could donate his heart to his sister, whose heart was failing. He believed he could do more good for the world if he ended his life. Because he felt he could confide in John, he had come over to discuss it with him.

When he asked for John's advice, a feeling came over John and he spoke more eloquently, and with a clearer logic, than he had ever done before. He explained to Jeff that during this time of enlightenment he had much to offer the world. He also told him that his heart was probably no good because of all his drinking, which would make him an unsuitable donor anyway. Jeff thanked him for his insights and left.

Later that afternoon, as John was lying down, he heard a conversation outside his trailer. Jeff was talking to a young woman who had recently broken up with her boyfriend. John had also been trying to help her. "Jeff, how are you doing?" she asked. "You seemed like you were upset earlier." To which Jeff replied, "Yes, but I talked to John and sometimes talking to John is like talking to God." When John heard this, he took it to mean that he had been channeling something from a higher place.

Sometime later, a very good friend of John's named Laura, who was a horse trainer, was distressed over losing her boyfriend, who was a jouster at the faire. She and John had become close enough friends that each knew when the other was upset, even when they were a long distance from one another. One day, this happened when Laura was in California and John was in Maryland.

John sensed that Laura was upset and that he needed to call her, so he did. When she told him that her life had gotten off-track and she wasn't sure she was on the correct path, he felt inspired to write her a letter the next day. He explained to her that she was always on the correct path, and that sometimes the path is rocky and sometimes the path is smooth; sometimes it's uphill and sometimes it's downhill. When one experiences the uneasiness of the rocky, uphill climb, one should know that just around the corner is the smooth, downhill path. And when one experiences the rocky sections of the path, that is what makes one strong and able to enjoy better the walk on the smoother part of the path.

When Laura got the letter, she said that it was the most inspirational letter that she had ever received or read and that John was obviously connected to some higher source. John didn't consciously know it yet, but he was tapping into a source greater and higher than his ego self. He was channeling information for his friends that came from his own divine nature.

Jacquelyne said that John's guides saw him as a very important messenger and that they definitely had plans for him to do more channeling. They wanted him to be focused on that. His guides and angels said that this would be his next piece of work; his next career. Jacquelyne made her point once again. "[This is] absolutely why Gabriel's here. I don't see him except with people who have a mission of communication—something that has to be expressed. And this is what he is talking about. It's going to touch a lot of people."

As I listened to the tape, I felt honored that we were getting assistance from an archangel. Learning of Gabriel's involvement not only validated our recent spiritual experiences but affirmed that the message behind those experiences was one that needed to be shared with others.

Jacquelyne said that she had met a lot of "wanna be's" who, although they may have been famous in a past life, were now resting on their laurels. Their stories were stories of the past, which had no real relevance to what was happening now. This was not the case with John's past life. She said he was somebody with a wonderful story to tell that still had value and meaning today.

She told John that by April 20, he needed to be "landed" somewhere because his angels and guides were about to unload massive volumes of material and that this would last until July 2 or 3. She said that he would be accessing both his past and future at the same time, and with this tremendous amount of spiritual energy being brought into his being, he needed to ask for it to be in harmony with his physical body.

When John asked her about getting a past-life regression, she said that it was unnecessary because bits and pieces of detail were coming in, and he was remembering the core events and turning points of that life anyway; however, the regression could be useful for making his past-life memory more rounded and Jesus more accessible to him.

<hr />

A few hours later, Atira gave John a reading, and as usual, John's spiritual support team showed up in numbers. At first, Atira did not remember with whom she was speaking because she does so many phone readings each day and had forgotten that John was the person she had been anxious to speak with. She began the reading with telling John that she saw him going through a lot of transition about what he would be doing for a living. She saw him speaking in front of groups, especially businessmen in three-piece suits. Like Sara, she saw John teaching seminars and delivering his message with humor. Atira said that John would be teaching people how to step into their power and how to use those skills in the workplace.

Atira's insight into John's past was remarkable. Although John didn't remember much about his childhood, Atira was able to pick up on the different challenges he had faced while growing up. By the time John was eighteen years old, Atira said that his life had been full of indecision, change, and feeling like he had not lived up to other people's expectations, especially his father's. That is when he decided to do his own thing and not worry about what other people thought because he couldn't seem to please anyone anyway.

Atira also saw the two significant female relationships in his life. She picked up on the relationship he had with his first wife, Lisa. She said that because of John's own experience of low self-esteem, he found himself trying to rescue Lisa, who was an emotionally disturbed woman. Atira said it had been like "trying to put bandaids on somebody…who…needed open-heart surgery."

After having given John insights into his family background, she gave him the opportunity to ask some questions. At that point, it didn't take long for Atira to realize with whom she was talking.

John: I'm in . . . like you said . . . a major transition. I'm writing a book with my friend Sharon right now, about my spiritual awakening over the past seven years. And I've had a lot of good insights from various people about it, in fact, readers included.

Atira: Okay, stop. Stop right there. You are . . . God, you're the one that everyone's been looking for. Oh dear, now I get why the three-piece suiters! Because, yeah, you are who you think you are. Oooh! Oooh! Oooh! [John laughs.] And, uh . . . oh, man, I can't even go back here! Okay, that's why you don't remember so much of your childhood. Because, a lot of things . . . a lot of this has been coming in for years for you.

John: Right.

Atira: You already know, pretty much beyond a shadow of a doubt who you are.

John: I know exactly who I am.

Atira: I get it, because now you'll be lecturing. Um, the book you're writing with Sharon is just the tip of the iceberg . . . . I believe the apostles will come together. Not all of them, but I think a lot of them are…going to come together, and out of that will come a book. That will [also] be a lecture tour. And that's why the three-piece suiters. Linear-thinking men are . . . needing to hear a message. One of the things Nick's book [*The Messengers*] did . . . for people was, it took a very successful, powerful, linear-thinking businessman [who] had an extraordinary experience and had the courage to write it down. So it opened the door for a lot of men to start in search of their spirituality. And here again is what you can do, too. You're the flip side of him. In other words, he's the very wealthy entrepreneur business-man and you're a person [who] more or less has followed [his] dream. And I'm not saying that you're not successful, but you certainly haven't done it in the mundane way. So you're a little bit more footloose and fancy-free kind of example of this…

John: Absolutely.

Atira then shifted gears and went back into John's childhood once again. Apparently, John had a significant experience as a young child, which he had completely forgotten about.

Atira: It seems to be. . .like a near-death, but not near-death. . .

John: You mean a long time ago?

Atira: Yeah, when you were young. It's like the experience of Fatima. It's beyond an out-of-body. It's beyond a near-death.[28] It totally is a spiritual experience that was real . . . . It is being expanded enough to see into biblical times but also to be on the other side at the same time . . . . And that is what set the tone for . . . knowing what you know now. And you had many, many other tweaks . . . of reassurance about this. I am just like a human telephone that is telling you one more time that you're right on and that those are very real experiences.

John: You're about the fifteenth person that's told me that.

Atira: So it's time, and I think what my job to do is to connect you to the other [apostles] now . . . you don't need confirmation. You know you are going where you are going.

Atira admitted to John that she didn't know how she knew the apostles in the past because the one regression she had done had taken her to ancient Egypt, not to Jerusalem in Christ's lifetime. She joked that perhaps she had cleared the table at the Last Supper or something.

Atira: I have no sense of who I may have been . . . but I do believe you are who you believe you are, okay?

John: Well, thank you. I know it, too . . . . and I've known it since my first reading. As soon as I was told, I knew it was true.

Atira: I'm not sure why all of [the apostles] are coming together. I certainly do not think it's gloom and doom and fear.

John: I don't think so either.

Atira: I think it's that the world is taking a new step into their belief system and their understanding of religion and that's why I think you are coming together.

It was Atira's belief that one of the gifts that John the Beloved had retained related to the statement that Jesus made about "greater works than I have done you will do." For some reason, she felt that was an important statement for John because it related to John's having done more teaching than Jesus did in that lifetime.

John told Atira that he needed to clear away all of "the stuff that's been put on us by the human mind and on spiritualism in general." He saw the need for creating a spiritual temple for himself because he needed to "take [spiritualism] back to what was, as opposed to what it's become."

Atira: The other thing I have to tell you is that I have run into another person who [carries] the essence of John the Beloved. The only way I can explain it is that I believe that sometimes we fracture our energies.[29]

John: Right.

Atira: And I think that there are people who have been in that energy with John or with Philip, or whoever, who retain that essence, who may have been disciples of those particular people. Because I have met one other person that I really feel has a lot of that energy, but [he] is choosing not to carry it forth. In other words, [he] will not become public or admit to it.

This led John into sharing what Jacquelyne Ellis had said about John the Beloved's energy splitting into three people—himself and two others—but that he was the actual physical manifestation of John. Atira agreed with this. She said that although Jacquelyne and she had only met about three times in public and had never read for one another, they had often gotten the same information for the same clients they had both read for, even so far as getting the same names for their clients' guides.

Sharon Prince

When the reading was finished, Atira said that she would call back later that evening to give John more information, which she did. She told him that her friends, Jason, the author, and Michael Baumann, who had been the Apostle Philip, would be calling him soon. A few hours later, John would receive the expected phone call from Michael.

———•—•———

Michael started out by introducing himself. "I'm a friend of Atira's," Michael said.

"Yes!" John responded.

"She gave me your name today. My name is Michael."

"Hi Michael. She said you're the one who was Philip?"

"That's what some say," Michael responded modestly.

John knew the timing of this was no accident; that there was a higher purpose for the two of them connecting at this time. "Yeah. She told me how you called her after the first time I called her."

"Coincidence how these things sometimes happen," Michael quipped.

"I don't know if I believe in coincidences," John said, laughing.

"Not in the last few years," Michael observed. "They've been coming like dominoes."

"They sure have," John agreed. "It's been a crazy last seven years for me."

"I guess she told you that we have been searching . . . for . . . John," Michael explained.

"I don't know anything more, except she said that Jason has been looking for John. I don't know why." [Jason, had said that the real John the Apostle, when asked, would have no clue as to what his purpose was or what he would be doing in the future.]

"Well, there's something the four of us need to do together," Michael said. He would fill John in later about the details. Michael was known to hold onto information until the right moment for it to be revealed.

This statement made John curious. "Okay."

"So what area are you located in?" Michael queried, changing the subject for a moment.

"I travel around quite a bit, but I would call Delaware my home state."

"I'm in St. Louis, in the center."

Then Michael went back to the subject of their work together. After some discussion on this topic, John shared his recent experiences.

"I read once that Edgar Cayce said that John would reincarnate into someone named John. And if you read the Cayce writings, it says Penial is where Jesus and John first met face to face," John revealed.

"Interesting," Michael remarked.

Then John made a reference to the first reading I did for him at Rehoboth Beach. "On a reading I had, I told the reader that I thought it was the pineal gland, or the third eye, where John would see Jesus. And she said, 'I think you're right.' And since then, I've had three or four spontaneous regressions where I've talked to Jesus in my third eye."

"I know there are one or two [men] that have taken on the name of 'Penial' just to try to be the next John," Michael offered. "Uhmm. What is your connection to Mary?" Michael knew that John the Beloved had had a close relationship to Mary.

"Well, I've actually seen her three times," John recalled. "The first time I saw her was when a lady was having visions in Georgia. I decided to fly down from Annapolis to see this. I was leaving the campground, and I just kinda said, 'What am I doing?' Then I looked up in the sky, and there was Mary praying, looking down at me. And I said, 'Okay, I've gotta go.' So I went, and I felt this very amazing energy."

"No doubt it was something that has influenced you to make other choices," Michael acknowledged.

"Oh my gosh yes, for sure!" John responded. "And then, I started to doubt it a little, maybe it was just my imagination, and then I saw it again. This really blew my mind. I've seen her [three] times, and each time it's pretty profound. What's your story? I'd love to hear it."

Like John, Michael's story had also begun seven years ago. "Well," Michael began, "I started talking to people in 1992 and have [had] a lot of readings [done] since then. I've found that most psychics are not always privy to biblical information. About three years ago, I walked by a psychic at a conference, and she literally pulled me in. She gave me a serious look and said, 'I know who you are.' And she then told me exactly what I needed to start doing. She told me to get over this doubt about who I think I am and get on with using this Light that travels with me."

"Interesting," John said. He was already noticing the similarities in their stories.

Michael continued. "And then in Sedona, I had a very similar thing happen to me. I was in a shop out there where they had a lot of readers. I was on my way out when I encountered a lady whom I noticed had her picture on the wall, as a reader. I walked out of the shop, and something made me turn around and go back in for a reading with her. It took about two minutes for this lady to tell me that I was Philip. She proceeded to fill me in on my relationship to all sorts of people from that time. And then there have been a number of others that have told me the same thing. So finally, I suppose we accept it a little bit."

John understood exactly how Michael felt. "It takes a lot to convince you of something like this, doesn't it?"

"Absolutely," Michael agreed.

The two men discussed their schedules and when they might run into each other. Michael was fascinated with the Renaissance era and knew he would enjoy visiting a festival where John was working. Michael told John that he was considering coming to see him in Georgia, John's next faire after Maryland.

As their conversation drew to a close, both men had felt a natural rapport, as if they had known one another for years. It had been an uplifting and confirming experience for both, and they were looking forward to the time when they would be able to meet face to face.

The next day, John returned from Rehoboth Beach with Jennifer, who was sporting a beautiful 1920s diamond engagement ring. Much to everyone's surprise, including John's, he had proposed to her a lot earlier than he had planned. I was happy for both of them. Their paths had brought them back together again and this time they were determined to make it work.

The future would hold many changes for them both, especially John, who would be discovering more about his past life and what his present life mission entailed. Some of the things we received from Spirit about what John was here to do were nothing less than astounding.

CHAPTER TEN

All in Divine Order

S ummer drew to a close, but our story grew with intensity. New people would be coming into our lives, including the person who would be responsible for doing John's past life regression, and new revelations would emerge from the next two readings I did for John. I wrapped up the work I had done on my past life and sent the transcript of the Felix regression to Nick along with a copy of the tape and a letter.

> August 18, 1999
> This may or may not be of interest to you. However, I feel that my soul
> owes this to Felix so that he may have completion with Paul . . . .
> Through this regression, I have learned how our lifetimes are connected
> with one another and how we sometimes unconsciously bring in issues
> from other lifetimes that still need to be worked through . . . .

In the letter, I assured Nick that before my angels gave me the name Felix (in the fall of 1998), I had never read the account in the New Testament of Paul being taken before Felix to be tried, nor had I read *The Messengers* yet, so I was certain that this information was not coming from my subconscious memory in this lifetime or from wishful thinking. I told him that I felt certain that if he listened to the tape, that it would touch something inside of him, and that the part of him that remembered being Paul would finally understand what had been going on behind Felix's poker face as the two men were saying good-bye for the last time.

I sent an e-mail to Kim Bunick telling her that I was sending a copy of the regression to Nick through her so that I would be assured of him getting it. I also updated her on Jacquelyne's and Atira's readings for John as well as the connections he had made to Atira's author friend, Jason, and to Michael Baumann.

August 18, 1999

I hope I'm not imposing on our friendship to ask you for these favors, but I feel it is important that Nick knows what is going on on this end. We all have this past-life connection during the time of Jesus in common, and I feel that it will play a major part in our present life mission, as well.

A few days later she e-mailed me back:

August 23, 1999

Dear Sharon,

Wow! A lot is happening right now for you . . . . I will pass on this info to my Dad. I LOVE hearing from you, so don't feel like you are imposing . . . . Keep in touch!

Love, Kim

This was followed up with another message to Kim, which gave her more updates about the things that had happened in the short time since I had last e-mailed her. I thanked her for passing on the information to Nick and told her that she was welcome to listen to the tape I had made:

August 23, 1999

I have to admit, the whole thing is pretty astounding. What started out [two years ago] as an ordinary reading for John and his picking up *The Messengers* a couple of days later, has made a huge circle, with many connections [to] other things and people. We are all connected and it's freaking me out!! I have an important reading to give John from Jeshua. I just hope I am up for the task . . . . Thanks a thousand times for delivering the "goods" to your dad . . . .

She replied the same day:

August 23, 1999

Dear Sharon,

I just love hearing about the wonderful things that are happening with you and all around me. It is so beautiful: all the "coincidences" and wonderful community gathering and becoming stronger. I am really interested in listening to the regression. I am really fascinated by your visits with Jeshua as well and can't wait to read about what messages you were given. Good luck with the book and all your great work!

Love, Kim

With perfect timing, I received an e-mail the next day from my friend Brenda in Houston:

August 24, 1999

Atira told me she finally had a session with John, and he is definitely John the Beloved—how exciting! She also told me she gave the information to connect with [another apostle] . . . . can't wait to hear the outcome! Things are definitely moving right along. When will you be back in town? We would love for you to share your experiences with our Messengers group. Atira will be visiting here the first week of October. What did John think of his reading? I hope all is well on the road. I look forward to seeing you again soon!!!

To which I replied:

August 25, 1999

Tell Atira she was right about John having a near-death experience at the age of five. John had dinner with his father and brother and his brother told him about it tonight. [His brother had said that John had become very ill with a high fever and his family wondered if he were going to make it. Then suddenly he recovered as if nothing had happened.] John has no memory of it at all.[30] I am back on the book, and John and I plan to go to Rehoboth Beach tomorrow (weather permitting) for a special message . . . . Jeshua has come to me about three times recently to give me instructions, answer my questions, and to prepare me for the reading. John and I have felt anxious but don't know why, like something big is going to happen.

Brenda responded with:

Can't wait for you to do the reading. This is so exciting! Where is all this leading to?

John and I continued to have 444 experiences at a steady rate. Early that day we had gone to the local office-supply store to buy a new ink cartridge for my computer printer and some more computer paper, so I could print out what I had written of the book. We had found a box of paper that seemed like a good bargain, but just as we were walking to the register to pay for it, we passed by some computer paper on sale. The price was $4.44 a ream and was a "buy two—get one free" special. We just laughed. Of course, we put the box back and bought this newly discovered paper that been brought to our attention as a confirmation from our angels!

The next day John and I went onto the Internet to look up therapists who did past-life regressions. He found a local Ph.D. and called her to set up an appointment. It didn't take long for us to find that we did not have a good feeling about her doing the regression for John. She told him that she would use hypnosis to delve into his past life as a method of therapy for his present life. When John told her that he was simply trying to recall his past life, she persisted that he had unresolved issues from this one and that is why he was seeking hypnosis in the first place. He felt very uncomfortable with the way she kept pressing him on this issue. (John ended up finding another therapist later.)

John was clear about why he wanted to be regressed: it was because he wanted to verify—through a professional with credentials—that he had actually been John the Beloved Disciple, and he also wanted to uncover the mystery of his near-death experience as a child. After some discussion, we were both of the opinion that hypnosis was the best way for him to truly remember his past life. Personally, I had had incredible success with a past-life regression I did under hypnosis eight years before this, which uncovered facts I would have had no way of knowing on my own, but which were verified after much research a year later. I knew there was nothing as real as actually seeing and reliving your past life, as if you were watching a movie inside your head. I remember the vivid colors and the minute details of my past life memory even now.

Later that day, John and I headed for the local beach for a "regular reading." We were still planning on having our annual Rehoboth Beach reading the next couple of weeks, but John was anxious to know what the angels had to say about his connection to these new people in his life. A part of me was having trouble believing how quickly all these things were happening. When I told John that I had asked my angels for a sign that I would be able to accurately channel for him, he teased me.

"She wants a sign! She wants a sign!" he called out to the heavens in a nasal tone of voice. As we traveled to our destination, there was not a single 444 along the way. When we pulled up to the beach parking lot, we were still searching for a sign. There was a Jeep with a license plate that read 555 parked in front of us. "There you go, Sharon," he said. "Five-five-five! That's one better than a 444!" We both laughed, which seemed to let off a little pressure.

The beach was very hot that day, and though I had brought my favorite straw hat, it didn't do much to help keep me cool. We sat there an hour and twenty minutes—dripping sweat—all to do a reading near the water! I teased John later about his putting me through my paces. "I only go this long for you, John. Nobody else gets this much from me! Nobody!" This just made him laugh. "You know you had better!" he teased me back.

The reading had revealed John's relationship to Michael Baumann. Apparently John the Beloved and Philip had been the best of friends in that lifetime. Philip had been quiet and observant just like Michael is now. Like John and Nick, it seemed as though Michael had reincarnated with basically the same personality he had had as an apostle.

I found it interesting to later discover that John was the only apostle to mention Philip in any of the books of the New Testament. "See, John," I said. "You were looking out for your buddy back then and making sure that people would know and remember him, even though he was the quiet one."

In contrast, John the Beloved apparently had a strong personality. I read a passage in a book that said how Jesus had dubbed John and his brother James "The Sons of Thunder." The story imparts that one day Jesus and his disciples had been kicked out of the village where Jesus was to speak. John and James were infuriated by the disrespectful way in which Jesus had been treated and pleaded with Him to call down lightning out of the sky, so it would strike the village and burn it to the ground. It was hard for me to imagine John saying something like that now. For the most part, he is a very even-tempered, laid-back person. However, he assured me that when he was younger he had more of a temper.

The reading had also revealed a little more about John's "Fatima" or near-death experience. We were told that during this time, John had been visited by Jesus, who explained to John what his purpose for coming here was. He was told that though his childhood would be difficult, he needed to hang in there for the work he would be doing in the future, which involved ushering in the Second Coming and other sacred duties. John said later that the reading had been pretty powerful.

After my reading with John, I returned to the campground, and opened the drawer of the cabinet in our rig where Randy and I kept our pens and paraphernalia, and I got a surprise. There in plain sight was the arrow pendant that Danny had given to me the previous summer! I had cleaned out that drawer before we went on the road three months earlier and had even turned it upside-down to shake out all the dust, before I wiped it with a rag and reorganized all its contents. Now, Randy and I had been in that drawer many times since I had cleaned it, and neither of us had seen it in there. It looked as if the angels had given me the sign I was looking for. I was heading in the right direction.

A couple of days later, John went to see a past-life regression therapist named Carol Berman. She was much more amenable to the idea of John exploring his past life simply for the purpose of remembering it and perhaps unravelling some of its mystery. The purpose of their first session was so they could get to know one another and feel comfortable working together. As if to confirm that he was seeing the right person, John would receive a few signs that day.

On the way to the regression, he had called Jennifer on his cell phone. When he looked down at the phone's timer, it indicated that he had talked to her for 4 minutes and 44 seconds. When he took the exit to Dr. Berman's house, he looked down at the clock, which read 4:44! When he arrived at her house, he went into the room where the regression was to take place, and it reminded him of a lodge where he had stayed at in Ohio— a place in which he had felt very comfortable. John found Dr. Berman very easy to talk to and liked her a great deal. He scheduled his regression with her for the following Wednesday, September 15.

Time was running out for us to do our annual reading at Rehoboth Beach, as John only had two more weeks left in Maryland. I hadn't felt as connected as I did when I had come back from North Carolina, so I had put off doing the reading until I felt ready. I was hoping that if I waited long enough that the feeling would return. John thought I was stalling, and perhaps I was. I have to admit I was a little nervous about doing a good job, especially since I knew I would be channeling Jesus "in a big way." I had built up the reading so much in my mind that I was almost expecting the clouds to open up and Jesus to descend before us upon a ray of light.

In spite of not feeling ready, I agreed to do the reading on Tuesday, September 14. I woke up in pain that morning and wasn't feeling particularly connected. I wondered how on earth I could channel when all I could think of was how uncomfortable I was feeling. We got up early for the two-hour drive to Rehoboth Beach. On the way, we stopped at John's favorite bagel shop for breakfast. When we got the bill, the total was $11.11.

I knew this 11:11 was a message for me. John and I had originally planned to do the Rehoboth Beach reading on August 11, the day when the earth was to receive a huge influx of awakening spiritual energy. Much to my disappointment, the trip that Randy and I took to North Carolina had preempted that. However, it was the day when I had received a message from Jesus, telling me that people were ready to hear that they could have close, personal communication with Him. This 11:11 sign indicated to me that this was a good day to do the reading after all.

We arrived at Cape Henlopen and settled into our now-familiar spot inside the horseshoe-shaped sand dune. I thought that I would receive this huge flux of energy when we got there, but I was not feeling energetic at all. I prayed that I would be able to receive the information that John and I had come here for.

The reading was a combination of direct channeling and intuitive interpretation. The following are excerpts from the reading:

Jesus: There's a third wisdom that is coming to you now. This has been planned since the beginning of time. This wisdom will be made known to the world and will be coming forth very soon. You are a planner, the organizer, and now a distributor of this information. You, and others like you, will be doing this important work together. Trusting what's inside of you is very important right now. This innate wisdom will be coming forth by the bucketful! [Sharon can feel His humor.] You are wise to plan and prepare for this influx of information that will be coming to you. You have known all along that this has been the plan. You are now ready to bring it forth. Treat this wisdom with gentleness, and impart it with gentleness and kindness . . . It's not something that needs to be forced or hurried in any way. It will be arriving in its own time. This wisdom that you feel inside of your soul . . . it's very important, John, for you to listen to this. You are connected to a higher energy a light far beyond your understanding at this time. But you've seen glimpses of it. What you are bringing forth is part of a divine plan.

There is a sacred tomb, deep within the earth, which shelters a storehouse of knowledge of this planet—where she has come from and where she is going. The shackles are about to be released. It's a pouring forth of knowledge to those who will listen and hear—an awakening for the planet. Deep within the recesses of your memory banks is a knowledge of this. You could be channeling this important information for the world to understand. I've entrusted to you these sacred records. They're inside the very veins inside your body, in the blood, in the cells. In the memory banks of the cells in your body is a storehouse of knowledge. There's going to be a physical unlocking of this energy.

John: When?

Sharon: Right when you said "when," I got springtime.

Jesus: It is an activation—an energy activation for you. You do not need physical tablets or disks to read. This is not necessary. They are already stored inside of the cells, like memory chips inside of your body. And being in contact with this energy will awaken them, like a computer program coming alive after sleeping for many thousands of years. You've been implanted with some of this knowledge. An activation inside of you will awaken this knowledge. This is not something to alarm you with. Think of it as a 'spiritual implant.' [Said with humor] But this knowledge in the wrong hands would be very dangerous. For there are those who would wish to use it for their own purposes. But we entrust this to you because of your pureness of heart, because of your pureness of soul, and because the love energy that you carry will be the right energy to bring this forth. I could see in you this great wisdom, oh these many, many years ago. You bear forth this knowledge now and the same energy and the same love. There is a spiritual entunement[31] that's very important.

John: Meaning what?

Jesus: Meaning, prepare yourself for this spiritual entunement because, when it arrives, it will arrive in a very strong manner.

John: How do I prepare myself?

Jesus: By going within and listening to the inner voice—the inner guidance—that tells you what you need to be doing in your daily life. By checking in each and every day. And being totally guided as to what you need to do: when, where, how, and why.

John asked about the new people in his life, including Michael.

Jesus: Michael [is a part of this process] more than you would expect. Michael and you have a very strong etheric connection—a pathway of communication the two of you are already engaged in out-of-body. You carry a similar energy. The others are supporting the work that you and Michael will be doing together.

Sharon: I feel the energy around me John. I just don't know what to do with it.

John: Hmmm. Uhmm, Jesus, I ask you to come in and help Sharon....And I also ask that you come in and give a physical sign so we both know we are on the correct path. And I ask that in the name of Jesus.

Sharon: I hear the words that "we've been here before."

John: Been where before?

Sharon: In this place, in this space?

John: Then come be with us now.
(Long pause. Adjustment of sitting and recorder.)

Sharon: You don't have to do anything, John. (chuckling) You don't have to send me energy.

John: I'm not.

Sharon: (chortles loudly) Really?!

John: No.

Sharon: Really? It's coming through my hands! I'm hearing these words...

Jesus: "**Many times you have asked, and many times you have been told...**"

John: What have I been told?

Jesus: **That the pathway to God is through your own door. Open this door wide. Let the love-light flood in. What do you see in your mind's eye?**

John: I see red...red now. (chuckles)

Sharon: I see, like a...doorway. And Jesus is standing in the doorway, and there's light behind Him, like He's opened the door and now He's standing in the doorway. He's inviting you in. And I see Him. I'm watching Him put His hand over your heart. Something to do, I think, with the Sacred Heart. You carry this energy inside of you. There was something that's been transferred. Some energy that He transferred to you before He left the physical plane. It's like His heart is also an interdimensional doorway. This is how He enters and leaves. If He manifests physically, it's through this doorway. It's almost like the Sacred Heart has a door that opens up. I don't know anything about what it looks like . . . . [but] it's like there's a key or something, and . . . it's like . . . to open the door, you have to . . . there's a key. I guess it's maybe an activation, an opening up . . . [or] turning. I'm feeling like there was some . . . exchange that happened before He left. That He gave you something energy-wise. It's like the two of you are connected through this interdimensional doorway of this Sacred Heart. That you have a truer connection than anyone else. You have the strongest connection to Him, you might say, in this manner. Of the apostles, He chose you for this...you know, [to receive] this energy. It's almost like this storehouse of knowledge . . . it's in this little 'sacred heart', like in this chamber inside the Sacred Heart.

I'm just wondering if you have any memories of His saying anything or touching you or there's an understanding, like you're looking into each others' eyes and there's a moment when you feel energy flooding into your being before He left the physical plane? I'm just asking if you ever heard . . .

John: Uhmm hmm! On the cross.

Sharon: That's what I was getting, too. Uhmm, before He left . . . He wanted, I guess, to send . . . to leave a part of Himself here . . . (John: Uhmm hmm.) . . . in the physical, and so He gave you something. It was like a gift, I guess you might say. An understatement! He gave you some . . . like a love connection, love energy, and you still carry that within . . . your being. It's like you're coming to the forefront of this plan. That's why you've been called the "forerunner." Because, like in times past, you ran before the others (laughing with insight) to set the path for Jesus to physically walk. Now you're spiritually setting that path for him to walk. You're bringing an awareness to others. It's like you're preparing the way, so that when He does arrive, the door will be open [for] hearing the message—that it won't be such a far-fetched idea to actually physically speak to Jesus and to receive answers.

John: Will He be here in the body he possessed in Galilee?

Sharon: Well, this is the body that most people know Him [by] . . . they identify with this. Because we're human, because we become attached to physical things, it would be easier for people to hear His message if He looked the way He did [then]. So I'm thinking that He most likely would choose that, if He does physically manifest, that He will choose that way to come.

John: [So] will He physically manifest?

Sharon: This has been a debate for some time with people, as to whether He will physically manifest or whether He will just manifest in people's hearts. I think that when there's enough energy in people's hearts to let Him in spiritually, then the physical manifestation will just be like a natural occurrence, afterwards. Do you see what I am trying to say?

John: Uh huh.

Sharon: And so . . . it's a preparation on a heart level, first, which will be preparing people to see the physical manifestation. That He will come and speak as He has before. It's like, to groups of people, here and there, and that people would hear of this. And some people will say that it's not true, and other people will say that they knew it would happen and they believe it. And other people won't know what to think. It's like He will be manifesting in different parts, all over the world, to those people who are ready to listen.

John: And when would something like this be occurring? Soon or hundreds of years from now?

Sharon: No. This is in this time period. This is what you are here to prepare people for. You will be able to impart this love energy that opens the key to people's hearts and [that] opens this doorway in their hearts that will accept this love energy from Jesus, so that they will be connected, just as He connected with you.

John: So I am, I am the forerunner of that?

Sharon: Uh huh. Yeah.

John: Whoah!

Sharon: I see you being the spokesperson. Well, there will be many spokespersons . . . you know, there will be more than one spokesperson of the group, but it's like, you're leading the way.

John: Leading the way…

Sharon: For the other apostles. It's like a forum, where everyone will bring different parts of the story to the table. You'll be sort of the one that holds it all together. You know, you'll be the one who will speak. Many times you will be speaking for the group. The way has been prepared. Like through your writing. The first stage is taking place now. That's the project that we're working on [referring to the book]. The second stage is coming after that. Actually, [it] will be overlapping the first stage. By the springtime, you will have so much information coming to you that you will literally need to stop in your tracks and to let this information pour forth and to write it down—to record it. I see Jacquelyne [Ellis] being correct about April being a time where [the spiritual guides are] going to just unload tons of stuff—tons of information. A little blue flash, thank you. [My spiritual confirmation is seeing a flash of blue light.] So maybe . . . if you do something . . . that will activate you in March, that by April you will be needing, very seriously, to catalog it all.

John: Then, hmmm, what do I do to prepare for March? What do I need to do between now and then? What will I be doing between now and then? (Both laugh) That's a better question.

Sharon: You need to center your energy on the present and what you need for that particular day.

John: What day?

Sharon: Any day.

John: Uhmm hmmm.

Sharon: Like when you meditate. If you meditate in the morning, to receive—ask for knowledge. Ask for empowerment. Ask for guidance for that particular day, to focus on each step as it comes.

John: Uhmm hmmm.

Sharon: So your energy needs to be in the present, so you can manifest the future. The future is made through the present. You know, the present moments of now create the future. So the energy needs to be here right now, so you can create what it is that you desire in the future.

John: So how will I make the rent this winter until March?

Sharon: They are saying "a less than desirable plan." They're saying it's possible that you will take an alternate course in what you had originally planned. The circumstances will be less than desirable. You may take an alternate course as a way to . . .

John: What alternate course could that be?

Sharon: From other sources of income, other than what you had originally planned.

Maybe in conjunction with what you are doing. Or maybe instead of . . . you're still in the . . . uhmm . . .

John: Transition?

Sharon: Right. You're in the process of deciding, because you have, of course, the free will to make that choice. Uhmmm, you'll be deciding at that time what the best course is for you. You may find that you will make that decision based on what will support your spiritual work, not necessarily what brings in the most money.

John: That's my problem. I don't see what I can do. I would rather do something towards my spiritual work . . . I don't see what I can do.

Sharon: It will be something that will allow you to work on your spiritual work while you're trying to make a living.

John: I'm still doing [comedy sword fighting], I'm assuming.

Sharon: (laughing) For a wee bit longer!

Jesus: Soon enough there will be a time when the worries and cares of the world will be set aside. Your first and foremost thought will be channeling the information and knowledge that's being imparted to you, and this will flow effortlessly and freely. It's a direct connection that you have to these storehouses of knowledge—these sacred records. It's time for people to be activated. Those that have the right spiritual nature will understand these things. Some people are still asleep—are still dormant in their spiritual awakening, and this will be the catalyst for that awakening. The books that pour forth from you...you will be in amazement—in wonderment—of where this is coming from, because you will know, beyond a shadow of a doubt, that it is not coming from your storehouses of personal knowledge. These sacred truths will be coming from a much higher source.

Sharon: . . . keys of awareness.

John: What's that?

Sharon: Oh, I just got [those] words: keys of awareness. It's like you're . . . you're bringing in keys of awareness. Like keys to awaken awareness in others.

John: Is it a title of a book?

Sharon: (laughing) Oh, that's good! Yeah, that sounds good. Why not? Let it . . . I'm kind of going in and out here . . . part of it is channeling, part of it is just coming in intuitively. It's like . . . you're explaining simple truths, but when people read it, when they hear it, they feel it inside of their beings that they just know it's true. And it will be like an "ah ha" kind of experience for people. It's like they're going, "Oh, yeah. I knew that!" You know?

Jesus: The truth will be spoken so plainly that people can't deny it.

Sharon: (elaborating) It's like saying "the sky is blue," "the moon is full" or "the sand is grainy." I would say something that most people will not be able to dispute.

John: And this information will start coming through in April?

Sharon: It's already starting. It's being set up right now. It will be coming through in increments. It will come at first slowly, but as you get closer to that point of activation—once that key hole has been turned, it will . . . (excitedly) I see this . . . huge light . . . wheeewh! . . . . like you're looking down at something. And it's like you've opened something up then . . . wheeeewh! All this light! It's like it's almost a circle of light that projects out in all directions, like a huge . . . like a circular radius. I mean, like a cone-shaped [light coming] out of this base and pouring forth. It's, uh . . . you know, like the Ark of the Covenant . . . in Indiana Jones and the Lost Ark? (John: Uhmm hmmm.) You know how the light comes out of the ark? (John: Uhmm hmmm.) That's sort of like . . . it's like a Pandora's Box, but it's in a good way. Wheeewh! You know. It's like an incredible amount of energy and light coming out of there.

John: And what happens to me when that happens?

Sharon: (laughing) Uh, hmmm. Don't you just want to kind of find out? Do you really want to know in advance?

John: I want to know in advance.

Sharon: Could you want to be surprised?

John: No.

Sharon: (laughing)

John: (laughing) That's not my ride, you know better than that!

Sharon: An increase in vibration. A complete opening of a doorway. Incredible! Like an instant knowing. Like any information you need—bam!—it's there . . . .

John: Now, I'm supposed to meet Michael in a few weeks. Is it going to happen?

Sharon: It's going to be an instant . . . well, you probably feel the connection anyway, to him. It's like . . . someone you can trust is what you are feeling now. But when you physically see each other, it's just going to be like an understanding. "Aahh!" you know? (John: Hmmm.) It's going to be in the eyes. You're going to look at each other, and it's going to be like "ding! ding! ding!" you know. (John: Hmmm.) There's a light coming out and going zzzzhhhh! (laughing)

John: So is Nick Bunick involved in any of this?

Sharon: . . . he'll be assisting, I think, from the sidelines. He'll be watching with . . . interest to see what happens. I think he will [eventually] combine efforts with the others. But certain people are still awakening in this group, so it's like you're kind of being called . . . I guess to bring them all together . . . kind of like the spokesperson for the group. I wouldn't say there's any leader, but you're kind of like the coordinator, I guess you might say. More accurately, the person that's . . . making the connections . . .

When transcribing this, I discovered that the tape had been dubbed over by accident, so about ten minutes of dialogue was lost.

[Two loud military jets come toward us. The first one flies by.]
Sharon: (laughing) Is that the sign you were looking for?

John: That reminds me of . . . [he is interrupted by the second jet flying very loudly overhead] That's it. Remember Jesus Christ Superstar?

Sharon: No. No.

John: Judas on the hill in front of the big jet?

Sharon: (laughing loudly) Noooo! I've never seen the play.

John: The movie.

Sharon: The movie, yeah. (laughing disbelievingly) A big jet . . . ?!

John: So the energy was brought into me. How do I awaken to that energy?

Sharon: You're doing that right now.

John: By doing what?

Jesus: By asking for it. By standing still long enough to receive it. By feeling at peace with it and not hurried, harried, or worried. It's not something you have to do alone.

John: So who will be with me?

Sharon: Jesus. He'll be with you . . . it's like He's saying, **"Peace, be still."**

John: Peace?

Sharon: "Peace, be still." He's telling you . . .

Jesus: Be at peace. Be still inside of yourself. Don't work at it. Don't push for it. Open yourself up and allow yourself to receive it. Do not feel overwhelmed by this storehouse of knowledge. I will sustain you in the times that you will fear and doubt it the most. I will not desert you. Like an ebb and a flow . . .

Sharon: I'm being given a visualization of the waves coming in and going out. It comes in with this great energy and then it pulls away. And people's lives are an ebb and a flow. Let the wave come in. Be the shore that accepts the wave and the energy that comes in. The shore does not move toward the wave. The wave moves toward the shore. It's like a cycle of energy. It's like a spiral that reaches up into heaven. It goes up and comes down. It goes back up and then it comes down. There are cycles. You must receive before you can give.

Jesus: You must be washed clean before you can go forth. The purer the light within, the purer the light that will be projected outward. Do not be troubled, for the weight of the world is not on your shoulders. You will be my mouthpiece. You will speak. I will speak to you, and you will speak to others. You will receive this information and this love. You are the channel and the mouthpiece for this. I carry the world in the palm of my hand. I carry the world. (Sharon: [amused] He's holding this big globe!) Just as I reach down and touch your heart, so will you reach out and touch others. As I taught you to heal, you will heal others.

Sharon: I guess He just wants you to know that you don't have to worry about feeling pressured to get it right or to do anything. You just need to open yourself up to receive it. That's all you have to do…you just need to be the channel that brings it forth.

Jesus: Others will be looking to you for leadership. But this is a natural thing, for they have looked to you before. As I have trusted in you, so will they. It's not so much a matter of learning. It's a matter of remembering.

John: What's the best way to remember? How do you remember?

Sharon: It's like I see Him touching your heart. Just by allowing His energy and love to come in. Just sitting still, like in meditation. It's like I see you in meditation. You're sending up this prayer. You're asking God to be with you, asking Jesus to be within. Just by being in your presence, people are healed. It's not something you have to struggle for. It just happens.

Jesus: And you know it's true. Just as that is effortless for you to impart love and understanding to others in your daily life now, so will the next step in your awareness, and in your work, be just as easy, just as effortless. Trust what's coming to you. Many times you've asked, and many times you've been told that the pathway to God is through your own door. Your own door. These channels of light that are imparting wisdom are limited in their ability to impart to you the true power and knowledge that are yours. They are reflecting small beams of light back to you. Collectively this makes light, but it is nothing compared to the internal light that you are connected to. Don't go outward for this, but go within.

Sharon: I'm just having to ask this question, so don't get mad at me. What are you waiting for?

John: I don't understand the question.

Sharon: What are you waiting for? What…like internally. What are you waiting for to give you information or permission to receive the information?

John: I have no idea. The knowledge of it?

Sharon: What are your fears or concerns about playing this role, of activating this energy, this knowledge?

John: I, uh…I don't have any fears or concerns about activating this knowledge or energy. My concern is that it's not going to be coming soon enough.

Sharon: What do you mean by that? Are you talking about in terms of things that transfer into a monetary…?

John: I'm just talking about physical subsistence . . . existence. I feel that . . . I'm done with the things that I am doing, a hundred percent. I don't feel at all inspired to [do] . . . what I am doing now. And I don't see the need nor the . . . uhmm . . . I don't see why I should . . . I feel that I'm going to be struggling through more of that to get to where this is. And I just don't understand why I need to struggle.

Sharon: It's like you've got those two things . . . together in one box. They don't have to necessarily be there. You can be channeling now. You know, the worries you have—[the] concerns for . . . physical [support] . . . should not be confused with the work you are doing now. That can come when you are ready for it. It's not . . .

John: What can come when I'm ready for it?

Sharon: When you're ready to channel…to channel the stuff that is coming to you. The focus should be on—taking care of yourself, of course. But, also, it's like that overlapping that they were talking about in the beginning. It's starting to happen now. Now's the time to start recording the information that will be coming to you—that will be channeled to you. Whether or not you're working at the Renaissance faire . . . [or] whatever you're doing . . . . Just like I'm writing the book [now], but I'm still doing sales [for my husband's band] on the weekends. I'm working during the week on the book. You'll be doing the same thing. You'll be doing what you do for your physical existence, but in your spare time . . . that time should be devoted to receiving and doing the writing. When you wrote e-mails to me during the spring, were you struggling to write that information down?

John: Uh uh.

Sharon: Were you concerned about your physical support?

John: No.

Sharon: Uh uh. That was a separate issue. So that's what they're trying to say: is that you don't have to . . . lump those [into the same box]. In your mind, it's like, "I'm going to be channeling and writing books, so therefore I'm supporting myself with this." The information is independent of anything else. Don't wait. Let that start pouring forth now and start recording that stuff now. Because what you're building now will be the future. By the time you get there, you will have all this stuff—this information. You see what I'm saying?

John: Uh huh.

Sharon: You'll be building a crescendo. And then by springtime, that's when it's going to be breaking forth in a major way . . . like a huge [way]. You'll be a part of this energy that comes out and you'll be imparting this energy. You'll be like a conduit for it. But you'll also . . . you'll be receiving it and then letting it flow forth from you. So I think they're trying to say just think of what you did before. That's the way you will be doing it, but even more in the flow—more of it for a longer period of time for a more sustained period of time, instead of just bursts—[like] a paragraph here or a page there. It will be, "Oh my god, where did the time go? I've been sitting here for . . . two or three hours writing stuff."

John: So what you are saying is, don't worry about my existence.

Sharon: Uh huh. Do what you need to do for now. Go along as if this is what you're doing . . . . [As you] consider what you want to do with your life . . . go on with your life, supporting yourself. But at the same time [there] will be another line—a parallel line—going along above [what you are doing now]. That will be your spiritual work. It's like when someone starts a business, if they do it wisely, they don't pour all of their money into this business and wait to have people come to them. They start having people come to them and the business just grows by leaps and bounds. They are trying to keep up with the business, not the business trying to keep up with them. They finally move out of the garage or the home or whatever. They can afford the office [now]. You see?

John: Uh huh.

Sharon: So that's sort of like that transition. You're in that transition stage. But it doesn't mean you can't enjoy what little . . . what your experiences are now. It doesn't mean that you can't say, "Oh, I'll enjoy this now because I know my life will change later. The things that I do love about this work I know are coming to an end, but let me linger here and enjoy what it is that I do best—what I've done best." Enjoy all of those things. And I'm thinking like . . . your stage combat . . . . your choreography, you know, the costumes, the script writing—all those things that you are so good at. It's like . . . a swan song . . . you know? Not really, but you know what I'm saying. It's like: "This is it. I've achieved this. Okay, this is what I've achieved and this is what I have mastered in this stage of my life. Let me enjoy these last fleeting moments like a sunset going down. Let me enjoy the last rays of light. Because tomorrow will be a new day, and the sun will rise and it will be a different horizon. It won't be the same scenery as it was before." But this is a . . . transition. You're in transition. That is an uncomfortable place for many people to be. Especially if you are very anxious for it to already be happening. But everything…the energy needs to build in that direction, first. The stage needs to be set.

John: So I need to be located somewhere, obviously in the April time frame.

Sharon: You need to be in a space within yourself that you can receive this information however that looks for you. If you can allow the time and space within your traveling trailer, where you go, to receive this information, then that will be . . . enough. But if for you to do the work, you need to be centrally located, then so be it. [So] . . . what they're . . . saying is to open up every morning to meditation . . . . Whenever you meditate, ask for the knowledge for that particular day. It's a trust process. "Okay, what's the next step? All right, I've done this, now what's the next step? Okay, what's the next step?" They're saying go within. Go within for these answers. Not out there, after this reader and that reader or whatever reader. It's a nice confirmation, but it needs to come [from] within first. It's like, don't put so much credence into what everyone is telling you and trying to come up with a consensus. Each person is lending their individual perspective. Take what you want from that, but also go within, so that you can feel within yourself what is true first.

On that note, our much anticipated reading ended. We left right away and headed back to Maryland. I leaned against the window and closed my eyes. I was disappointed that it had not been a straight channeling session from beginning to end as I had expected it to be. I did not feel that I had been any more connected to Jesus than when I had channeled Him before. However, John felt that the reading had gone phenomenally well, and he had not been disappointed at all.

When I later transcribed the tape we made of the reading, I was amazed at the amount of quoted words from Jesus that we were able to get down on paper. This was the first time we had ever tape-recorded His words and there was more on there than I had expected. In the weeks to come, I was astonished at how some of the strange information we received was confirmed or explained.

CHAPTER ELEVEN

John of Old

On Wednesday, September 15, 1999, Maryland was under a hurricane warning, so John rescheduled his regression appointment for the following Wednesday, September 22. Incidentally, that night would be John's last night in Maryland, as he and Spencer would be leaving for Georgia the next day.

A few days before his regression was to take place, John had some extraordinary experiences. Some significant things happened on Sunday, September 19, during a work day at faire. First, John ran into a fellow performer named Tasha. She remarked how much growth she had seen in John in the last few years. John had never shared any of his past-life discoveries with her before, but he decided to fill her in on what had been going on with him, spiritually, in those last few years. Just as he spoke the words, "I've remembered a past life," she blurted out, "John the Apostle" with no foreshadowing or forewarning whatsoever.

When John told me what she had said, I was truly astonished. Apparently she had an incredible gift that none of us knew about. In a strange way, her confirmation of John's past life as an apostle meant more to me than anyone else's because it had come so unexpectedly.

Later that day, a fellow performer named Tony told John that his back had gone out, and he was experiencing a great deal of pain. John placed his left hand on Tony's back and his right hand on Tony's shoulder. As he had done with Jennifer earlier that summer, he called on Jesus to help heal Tony. John felt this sudden rush of energy come through him and go into Tony's body. About a half-hour later, Tony came up to John and said, "I don't know what you did, but you did *something* because my back feels better."

I was sitting in John's trailer that evening, discussing all the great things that had happened to him that day, and we were about to add another extraordinary experience to the list.

John did some healing work on my hands, but after awhile, he told me the problem was not in my hands but in my head. So he worked on my head, and I could feel the warm energy surround my brain and infiltrate it. The energy felt so good that I didn't want him to stop. As soon as he did stop, I felt the energy that had been present leave immediately. However, I could feel a warm glow linger. It was very powerful.

During this whole episode, John was experiencing a transformation. He said afterward, "Jesus heals using a pure love energy and that was what I was channeling to you." I said, "Wow! I could feel it!" Then he received another message. As he was searching for the right word, I intuited that he would say the word "ascend," but instead he said, "This is how people…receive *enlightenment*." Then he added, "This is how people *ascend*." This confirmed what I had received. I could see a transformation in him that was quite remarkable. He was a different person. When I told him this, he said that for the first time he truly felt like an apostle that day.

I was so moved by the recent experiences and confirmations we received concerning John's mission, that I felt compelled to write this in my journal:

> I am just so overwhelmed by the influx of energy coming John's way. I feel humbled and deeply honored by my friendship with John and my continuing role in his awakening. I feel that John has reincarnated many times carrying [Christ's] energy. Maybe that is why John's energy only split three ways instead of millions of ways. It had to be carried intact because of its intensity.
>
> Now [I know] I must finish the manuscript. I just have to get it all down . . . . And the sooner I do, the sooner I will have accomplished what I have come here to do. I am resolved to continue telling this story, no matter what anyone thinks. I can't worry about anything else but doing what I am told I should do by my own divine guidance.

The day of John's regression finally arrived. This was something that we had discussed several times over the last two years and now the hour of truth was here. I really wanted to be there for John after this momentous occasion and knew that he would want to share with me what had happened. However, his regression, which was scheduled for the evening, was more than an hour's drive away. I knew that he would be getting back late that night, and I didn't know what state of mind he would be in afterward or if he would feel like talking about it.

Jennifer had come back to Maryland to be with John, and they drove to Carol Berman's house in Bethesda. Jennifer waited while John had his regression and drove him back to the campsite when it was over. He said

Sharon Prince

he felt too woozy to drive himself, and I knew just what he meant. They arrived late, but when John saw that I was still awake, he invited me over to listen to the tape Carol had made of the regression.

John put the tape into the player and stretched out on the floor, while Jennifer and I sat on the couch. As we listened to the tape, the intensity of the emotion in his voice was overwhelming. I should have been prepared for what I heard—having been through something similar myself—but when I heard John crying loudly on the tape, I felt great empathy for him. There were times when I just had to reach out and touch him on the shoulder.

After John had been hypnotized, using relaxation and visualization techniques, he regressed to his lifetime as John the Apostle.[32] The following is a transcript of his regression with Carol Berman, M.A., C.P.L.T. (Certified Past Life Therapist), in Bethesda, Maryland, on September 22, 1999:

Carol: Does it seem dark or light? When you know let me know by telling me.

John: It's light.

Carol: Okay, it's light. Does it feel like a small area or a large area?

John: It's a beach.

Carol: It's a beach. Why don't you start to describe it?

John: The water's flat and there's some mountains on the other side. Uhmm. There's boats with tall spires on the end of them. It's white sand.

Carol: Do you get a sense of where you are?

John: I'm standing on the beach. Uhmm. (sighs)

Carol: You're standing there. Get a sense of what you look like. Anything on your legs?

John: I have…I have sandals.

Carol: Uhm hmm. That's good. Start with your feet. And move up.

John: I have bare legs. I have a reddish, rusty colored tunic, I guess is the word. It goes to my mid-thigh. Uhmm. It has like short sleeves. My hair is sandy blonde—reddish and wild. I have a full beard. I have something tying it at the waist.

Carol: How big are you?

John: I don't have a sense of height. I'm very strong…very strong.

Carol: What are you doing there?

John: I have nets.

Carol: And are you holding the nets?

John: They're by my feet. I'm just kind of standing there.

Carol: Do you know what they're for?

John: They're fishing nets.

Carol: Are they yours?

John: Yeah. Yeah. They're heavy.

Carol: Is there anyone else there?

John: My father's . . . he's got a big white beard. He has some cloth on his head. He's got a gray, long . . . thing on. And he's leaning on a stick. He's very old. He's very old. Yeah. He can't do the work anymore . . . so I do it.

Carol: Uhm hmm. So he used to be a fisherman.

John: Uh huh.

Carol: And you've taken on the job.

John: Yeah. It's hard work. His back is hunched. His back is not good. He relies on the stick to hold him up.

Carol: What are ya'll doing? Just standing there?

John: He's . . . he's saying something.

Carol: Listen very carefully. What is he saying to you?

John: (laughs) Eh, I don't understand him.

Carol: Imagine you have a megaphone to your ear and see if you can hear it better.

John: He's talking about selling. And he keeps [saying] market. I keep hearing market. I guess he's talking about the fish.

Carol: You feel like there's anything else in this scene that seems important?

John: Uh-uh.

Sharon Prince

Carol: Okay. Well, I'm going to count from three to one and we're going to go to the next important scene. When I get to one, it will start to come into focus. Three, two, one. Slowly come into focus.

John: (groans slightly)

Carol: Are you inside or outside?

John: I'm still at the beach.

Carol: Okay.

John: There's like lots of boats on the shore and people walking in front of them.

Carol: When does it seem like?

John: Uhmm. I don't know. It's daytime. There's a small crowd by the boats, and I don't know what that is.

Carol: Do you want to go see what it is?

John: Uhhmm. All right.

Carol: Okay, walk on over and see what it is.

John: (groans twice, chuckles) [John is smiling and chuckles again. Through the eyes of John the Apostle, John saw himself walking over to the group of people. As John walked up, the crowd parted and he saw Jesus standing in the center of it. John's first thought was that Jesus was shorter than he had expected him to be. Jesus had dark brown hair with reddish highlights, due to sun exposure. His hair had slight curls in it and His eyes were blue. John knew who Jesus was immediately. He had felt His energy from several feet away.] Uhhh. It's Him! (sighs)

Carol: Say what you want to say. (John: Oh!) Tell us out loud what you want to know.

John: Uhhh! [John's voice is full of emotion.] Right now I can't ask anything! [John's breathing is heavy and he's very excited. At that moment Jesus has reached out with His right hand and touched John's left shoulder. John felt a wave of love energy overtake him, and in that instant he knew what it was to be Jesus and to feel what He was feeling.]

John: (swallows hard) Oh, I can feel him! (several gasps and breathes heavily)

Carol: Are you watching him or are you him? [At this point Carol is trying to confirm if John was looking at himself from the outside as John the Apostle, or if he was inside John the Apostle's body, experiencing his life firsthand. John was definitely observing his past life through his own body as John the Apostle.]

John: I'm with Him. We've been hit and miss. Oh…it's…uh…it's love. All of it? It's all…everything. It's…oh! Oh! (breathing in gasps) I am…uh…[John is experiencing what it is to be pure love. He is in a state of ecstasy.]

Carol: Be with it as long as you need.

John: (long pause; sighs) Ahh. Okay. Uh. [John is experiencing something incredible, but he is not sharing what he is experiencing. All that can be heard is the great emotion of awe in his sighs and groans. As he told me later, "I found myself not needing to see or hear but to just be. It was as if I was overflowing with love: a state of bliss."]

Carol: What is that message to get out to the world?

John: Everything is love. There is nothing else. All else is illusion. Everything is love.

Carol: And what are those steps to teach that?

John: It's simple. Just feel the love within. Now align yourself to that energy. Feel it. Be it. Release fear. Fear [is] not a reality. (inaudible) The world of man creates illusions. God is love. Don't fear God. He's nothing but love. (sniffles) You must not only feel it but emit it. Align yourself with the grace of the love, and that is what is healing. That grace of love moves the fear. The fear of the free will is what holds onto the illusions. That's how you teach love. Hmmm. It's simple.

Carol: What about the free will?

John: I don't understand. What do you mean?

Carol: Free will in man.

John: Free will…is a gift, that you may experience the lack of love. And in experiencing the lack of love, we come to know God. You have to have contrasts to understand. The problem is that we have become mired in the fear, and we feel separate and alone—far away from the love, far away from God. He's…He's the example. He's done it. He has no fear. He is only love.

Carol: What about justice?

John: There's only two things. There is only love and fear. Justice is a product of fear.

Carol: Uhmm hmmm.

John: That's it. It's fear. It's knowledge (inaudible). There's only love. There's only perfection. (laughs) All fear stems from the fear of not having love, not knowing love, not being love. (inaudible)

Sharon Prince

Carol: Where are you now?

John: I'm at . . . I'm at the beach still. And He's walking away.

Carol: Is there more you want to ask?

John: (laughs) I want to call Him Rabbi! [At this moment, Jesus is walking away and John feels a sudden emptiness. He had felt Jesus' love energy before and now He was taking that love energy away with Him. John felt that this was Jesus' way of getting him to follow Him.]

Carol: Ahhh!

John: (chuckles, sighs) Uhmm, I have to go with Him.

Carol: You have to...?

John: I have to be with Him. I have to be near Him. He . . . He gave me a glimpse of everything and (chuckles) I understand what He means about the contrast now. So now I need to be around Him. I need to be with Him. (breathes deeply and gasps)

Carol: You've separated from His body, now. Right?

John: Uh huh.

Carol: You're watching Him still?

John: Uh huh. (sighs heavily)

Carol: What would you feel about . . . how would you feel about seeing his death? [Carol is suggesting that John might want to observe his own death; however, John goes to Christ's death instead. Her comment later was "People go where they need to go."]

John: (gasps) Oh,...uhmm. I couldn't imagine that.

Carol: Would you like to try?

John: (apprehensively) Sure.

Carol: All right. You're really John. You are within him. You channeled with him. You connected with him. You're still John now, but in this past life with John the Apostle, he lived and he died. I'm going to count from three to one, and when I get to one, you'll be able to view his death. Three, two, one. Becoming aware.

John: (gasps sharply, sobs and gulps) [John is emotionally distressed. It becomes quickly apparent that instead of regressing to his own death, He is witnessing Christ's beating before the crucifixion. It was devastating for John to watch the person he loved more than anyone being tortured. He noted that the Roman whips were short and had several tails attached to a long handle. Attached to the end of each tail were beads of some sort. He was witnessing Jesus on His hands and knees on the ground as a crowd of people closely surrounded Him to witness His being whipped. John noted that His clothes had been ripped apart, and His back was all bloody.]

When the tears welled up in John's eyes as he relived the moments of Jesus' beating, it was gut wrenching to listen to. I had never heard him cry like that before, and it moved me to tears myself. I could only imagine the horror of seeing his best friend being beaten, tortured, and there was nothing he could do about it.

Carol: You know what you need to feel.

John: (cries loudly, deeply, soulfully)

Carol: [talking above his crying.] If you want to come above it, you can rise above it and not feel all the feelings. You can rise above and watch. [John's crying subsides to gasping and very labored breathing.] You can know, and you can watch.

John: (gasps. Sighs emotionally) Ugh. Oh.

Carol: You can also go to the other side. And allow him to look down on that life and see what he sees from the spirit realm. [John gasps.] Allow yourself, when I count to three, to go to the other side and experience his experience in the spirit realm after his death, so he is able to assess the meaning of that life. Three, two, one. Becoming aware. What do you see? [John noted that he saw the afterlife as the colors blue and silver. Later he learned that blue is the color of the afterlife in the Jewish religion and that silver is the color of the Christ energy.]

John: (deep breaths) (sniffs) It's over.

Carol: What was the meaning of that life?

John: To give an ideal—an example to follow. To understand that we can be love.

Carol: What is your mission? In an all-knowing spirit realm, ask your mission . . . to God.

John: (chuckles in disbelief) To carry His essence. To be grounding points to return to—a beacon. Since everything is love, you can be the reference point within itself to bring the essence to that point. (chuckles) I carry his signature. He needs me to return to this plane of existence . . . plane/existence. [Carol asks John what he thinks is the purpose of His mission.]

John: Uhmm.

Carol: Ask.

John: [Long pause, followed by a quick burst of words. John's voice changes, as if he is now channeling the information.] [This] knowledge is a gift to the world. Consciousness is raising to a point that it needs to have an awakening in the mass, in the whole. And there [are] connections [here] to other dimensions . . . and it will bring an infusion of the love energy into the consciousness of all. It's a direct connection to a higher plane—a higher understanding of love. And I have to be [here] 'cause I'm the only interdimensional doorway [in this plane]...if that makes any sense at all. [Carol: Uhmm hmm.] I'm the only one who can take Him in and not cease to exist in this plane. I'm the only one who can carry it in this plane. [Tape is flipped to other side, some dialogue is lost.] . . . to keep the love in this plane that I carry from Him. He is within everyone, but there is something in me that is needed for His manifestation of the physical. It's that beacon thing, that point.

Carol: Is there anything else you want to know?

John: (laughing) I asked Him when, and He said, "Sooner than you know." [both laugh]

Carol: And when you say "him," who do you think that is? Who are you referring to?

John: I asked Jeshua.

When I heard John say Jesus' real name, I knew he had really connected to Him because, up until this moment, John had flatly refused to call Jesus "Jeshua." I nudged John on the shoulder and laughed. "Jeshua?!" I ribbed him. He gave me a sheepish grin. He knew exactly what I was getting at. "It's true!" I said to myself. I could feel the tears well up in my eyes. They were tears of joy this time.

John: (laughing) Sooner than you think....He's got a great sense of humor!

Carol: I know. It's interesting, isn't it? (laughs)

John: Yeah, uh . . . (sighs) Oh, my. (sighs) I think I'll ask Him. [He addresses a question to Jesus.] He said something about Peter . . . Peter is [bringing in the energy that represents] the masculine and I am [bringing in the energy that represents] the feminine and it has to come together. (long pause) I don't know what that means.

Carol: Do you want to say it, and then you will have it to study? [Carol is asking John if he would like to ask the Master about what his bringing in the feminine energy means so he can have the answer to study later.]

John: When they come together...the word unification...is like global unification or universal unification. It's like the masculine has been, uh…the masculine has been, but it's time for the feminine, if that makes sense.

Carol: Okay.

John: (laughs in disbelief) I have no idea what any of that means.

Carol: Is this masculine—this Peter…ask about who you think this is.

John: Ask who is Peter? Sah-oo-ell. Sah-oo-ell. That's all I get.

Carol: Ah-oo-el?

John: Sah-oo-ell. I have no idea.

Carol: Okay, well. It's good to know.

John: Uhmm.

Carol: From what country?

John: I'm not even sure it's from this time.

Carol: Uh huh.

John: Uhmm. (laughs in disbelief) It's got…Sahooell is a name he had in another time.

Carol: Uh huh.

John: Uhmm. It's really Sa-oo-ell [the "a" is pronounced like the "a" in "sad"] is what I have, by the way. I keep getting this picture of a relay race—handing it on.

Carol: Ask what that means.
John: Uhmm. When the teachings were…distributed is the word I get…there was a split. Uhmm. And…the masculine…this is weird…the masculine went public, and the feminine went underground. And all teachings, all…it's been a one-sided view since…(inaudible)…it's been a very heavy-handed, one-sided view, and it's ending. It's…the knowing is coming. Everyone's going to know, and (laughs in disbelief) religions are falling by the wayside…for a…just a know-ing—an understanding.

Carol: An all-knowing kind of…

John: Yeah. Yeah. An all-knowing.

Carol: Rather than needing different religions. (John: Yeah. Yeah.) It would be more of a universal religion.

John: It's a total understanding. [John's voice changes and he is speaking more quickly, as if he is channeling from Spirit again.] And with a total understanding, everything—wars, disease—everything created by fear ceases…and the true knowledge of the…how this understanding is from the feminine aspect of the teachings.

It occurred to me that Christ had brought the feminine aspect of the teachings to this world even though He came in a masculine body. Perhaps this was necessary to show us that the masculine and feminine could balance in one's self regardless of a person's gender.

Carol: Compassion?

John: (chuckles) It's love. (Carol: Uh huh.) They keep saying there's nothing else. There's only love. There is…I mean…it has many, many…there's many words. There's many meanings. There is only love, and a lot of people have forgotten that. (barely audible) It's the only mission.

Carol: Do you mind if you ask why you were supposed to find me?

John: I'll ask. (pause, sigh) I keep hearing the word understanding, meaning an understanding. (chuckle.) A religious understanding. I get that a lot.

Carol: Uhm hmm. Uhm hmm. That makes a lot of sense. (pauses) Is there more for you here? In this place? [Carol was well-versed in religious studies, especially Judiasm.]

John: You mean now?

Carol: Yeah. What you're asking and what you want to ask. Is there more that you want to do and ask and know?
John: (lets out a big sigh) Yeah. (chuckles) I asked about my seeing Mary.

Carol: Uhmm hmm.

John: And…(chuckles disbelievingly) It's interesting. It's like because I'm a beacon for the Son, I'm a beacon for the mother…if that makes any sense.

Carol: Uhm hmm. A light to the world.

John: She…(chuckles) . . . She's around me all the time. (chuckles again) In spiritual and physical. (laughing a lot) She's looking after me now, as I did after her. (both laugh) That's kind of funny!

Carol: Souls travel together.

John: Yeah. She's telling me she's proud . . . (sigh) whew! . . . wow. The . . . (chuckle) every . . . every religion has had Christ [by] a different name. Different name, same energy. We see . . . (John's voices changes to direct channeling again.) When divine revelation—inspiration—comes, it's through a filter. And we . . . we see what we expect to see. We see what we want to see. And we create our own illusion around the divine. The time is coming when the illusions will fall away; the creations will no longer be needed. And . . . and it's the all knowing thing. Yeah.

Carol: So it's your understanding that the energy is [the] energy of the essence of God? And different people are translating that into different ways? (John: Yeah.) Into different religions.

John: There's only love. There's only fear. And…there's only love, and we created fear. And love is God. (Carol: Okay.) And so all religions are based on God—on love. And the various symbols and symbolism of the…sects…

Carol: Uh huh. Uh huh. I call it different people's baggage…(John laughs)…of their religion.

John: That's go . . . it's going away. It's falling away. This awakening in Egypt is important. Uhmm. The understanding of that civilization was far more knowledgeable of that . . . there [were] only two religions and one of them was created in the earth plane as a . . . contrast, and one of them was of the other plane.

Carol: Uhm hmm. The spirit realm.

John: And so you have (sigh) the Law of One and Sons of the Belial. (He pronounces it "be-lie-al" then "be-lee-ul". He settles on "be-lie-ul" with a long i sound.)

Carol: Sons? S-o-n-s?

John: S-o-n-s. The law of one understands the love connection. There's only one thing. There's only love. There's only love. Everything is love.
Carol: Have you ever heard of the Sons of Belial before?

John: Nah.

Carol: Or the Law of One? Have you ever read or heard of that before tonight? (John shakes his head "no.") No?[33]

John: You've got me! (laughing)

Carol: It's just coming to you. (John: Yeah.) That's what I am checking.

Carol: No, that's…okay.

John: Yeah. I don't know. Uhmm! (laughs) But when I say there's only love; there's only fear, I mean that literally. Very literally. It's very simple. This is not . . . this flesh is not—it's an illusion. (Carol: Uh hmm. Uh hmm.) There is only love, and fear was created to experience the contrast. To experience love, you have to know the opposite. And what's happened is . . . when the lesson learned was originally started, we fell away. We've gotten too mired in the fear. Simplicity. (chuckling) I keep hearing simplicity. It's simple. Everything is simple. We've put too much thought on it. It's simple.

Carol: It takes a lot of effort to get people at the love level...

John: (chuckles) Yeah.

Carol: . . . and out of the physical.

John: Yes . . .

Carol: Are there any . . . ?

John: There's two paths to follow.

Carol: Okay.

John: It's the fact that...it's love and fear again. There's love and there's fear. It takes courage to walk out of the known...but once you've done it, you realize that you were walking the harder path before. You step into the...once you step into love, each—and when I say fragment of love energy—once you step into love, you accelerate very quickly in understanding, and we are fragments of love. Does that make sense? (Carol: Uhmm hmm.) And, we're supposed to awaken to that. We're supposed to understand that. Step out of fear. God provides everything 'cause He is love. Does that make sense?

Carol: Uh huh.
John: (sigh)

Carol: How do we calm the demons of criticism?

John: (chuckles)

Carol: 'Cause that's what helps you not get to this.

John: (voice changes) Create within yourself the remembrance of love. Feel that love energy, meditate upon it, and go into it.

Carol: Uh huh. Uh huh.

John: And once you've experienced it fully, the criticism is gone. It's destroyed. The criticisms are...interesting. (He chuckles) The criticism is the fear of the separation. And it's the fear manifesting. All fear . . . all forms of . . . all fear stems from the fear of being separate from God or love. And all fear . . . all violence . . . all those things come from fear. And the fear of being separate from what we are is what creates that criticism, that doubt, that harshness. When Jeshua did healing work, he was love. He is love. He is the embodiment of love. When you are around or in the presence of pure love, there can be no fear. And that is how he healed. By . . .

Carol: Unconditional love.

John: Unconditional love. And it's the vibration . . . (Carol: Uh huh. Uh huh.) . . . it's that . . . once you feel that vibration—that energy, and you become one with that energy—that vibration, the fear . . . there can be no fear, because it's [love is] everything. And by Him being a pure channel of that divine love energy, whenever He would come into the presence of someone who was willing to accept or to feel the love from Him—to accept it and become aware of it, then they would lose all fear and hence all sickness because sickness is the manifestation of fear in the physical. And so his healing was done by . . .

Carol: Removing the fear manifestation?

John: Removing the fear out of the vibration because that's all we are is love vibration or fear vibration or both. There is love in everyone. And there are those who have wallowed in the fear to the point of needing to separate from their existence. (a chuckle of disbelief) He's talking about drug users, drinkers. The fear has scared them to the point of . . .

Carol: . . . the pain . . .

John: . . . needing to separate from the fear.

Carol: Because the love was absent?

John: Because they couldn't feel it any more. Love is never absent.

Carol: From them?

John: From anyone.

Carol: I mean, they couldn't feel that. (John: Yeah.) They weren't . . . right.

John: It goes back to the fear of being separate. Yeah. It's simple. (laughing) It's really simple. You see, you sit there, it's . . . you say it's simple, I guess, but . . . (laughing) . . .

Carol: You heard it very eloquently.

John: They say it's simple, but I think the hardest part is releasing the known. Releasing what is familiar.

Carol: Uh hmm. And convincing the masses.

John: (big sigh) Whew! Big job.

John was suddenly aware, for the first time, what had taken place during his Fatima experience as a child.

John: I don't recall it, but I think I'm being told that I was told this when I was five—what I am to do. And I shunned this, actually.

Carol: To do?

John: (chuckles in disbelief) To be a forerunner.

Carol: Uh huh.

John was obviously referring to being the forerunner for Christ's Second Coming. I was simply overcome with emotion when transcribing this. The words that Jesus had spoken to me over a year and a half ago came back to mind:

> *If this had been presented to you as an enormously important task for which the world was waiting, it would have seemed too daunting.*

John: He's returned in the consciousness already. And He is returning in the physical to prove it. And that I'm the forerunner. I'm the beacon for His return.

Carol: He is?
John: Jeshua. He is…the physical manifestation of God.

Carol: (with reverence) Uh huh. We call Him the Messiah. Same thing.

John: Yeah.

Carol: Pretty awesome guy!

John: (loudly) Uh huh! Both. Hmmm.

Carol: I don't want to rush you, but I want to know if you want to try and go to when you were five, or do you want to let go of that?

John: I don't need to.

Carol: Okay. I felt that, but I wanted to give you the opportunity.

John: Yeah, I've seen it.

Carol: Okay.

John: (sighs resignedly) Well, I know why I am here. (sighs) That's pretty intense.

Carol: Are you ready to come back?

John: (softly) In a few minutes.

Carol noted in the conversation that followed the regression that at first John's face had the expression of pondering a question, followed by a peaceful look, and then a huge expression of joy. All these emotions bore witness to the incredible experience of visiting his lifetime as John the Apostle.

As John became aware of his environment again, he knew beyond a shadow of a doubt that that he had known Jesus as Jeshua. He had walked with Him, talked with Him, stood by Him, broke bread with Him, and ultimately witnessed His death and resurrection. John had had the great privilege and honor of knowing, and being friends with, the greatest Master who had ever lived on this earth.

The enormity of what John was here to do suddenly hit me harder than ever before. I felt so very humbled to be even a small part of assisting John in bringing this incredible gift of Christ's love and energy to the world.

CHAPTER TWELVE

Angels Speak

The morning after his regression, on September 23, 1999, John traveled to Georgia with Jennifer, where he and his comedy partner, Spencer, were going to perform at the Georgia Renaissance Festival. I would not see John again until February, but we would stay in close contact by e-mail and phone. I later asked John how his regression had affected him. He said that he felt a grief deeper than he had ever known in his life for the two or three days following. "I cried a lot," John admitted. Mostly he was grieving as the result of remembering Jeshua's beating and death, and yet part of the emotion was the result of the revelation, during the regression, that he was to be the forerunner for Christ.

Randy and I left Maryland in late October and headed back to Texas. The band was contracted for three weekends of performances at the Texas Renaissance Festival, near Houston. We had been in Texas for a week or so when I heard back from Nick Bunick. He had sent me a letter on The Great Tomorrow stationery in response to my Felix regression:

October 29, 1999

Dear Sharon,

    Thank you for sharing the transcription of your regression as Felix. I found it very interesting. It certainly rings with a great deal of credibility and validity.

    Sorry I haven't answered you earlier but I have been traveling all around the country doing speaking engagements as well as humanitarian projects. I am finally now able to stay put for awhile and hope to catch up with things. Please say hello to John for me, and God bless you as you continue to stand in His light.

Sincerely,

Nick Bunick

At some point, before I sent the transcript and tape to Nick, I felt that he had already received his own personal confirmation of our past lives together. It is hard to explain, but I felt a stronger heart connection to Nick *after* the regression. No longer did I see him only in his current life roles of spiritual leader, author, and successful businessman, but now I knew in my heart that he had also been my friend in that past life. I felt this knowingness in the deepest part of myself.

I responded to his acknowledgment with a follow up e-mail:

November 6, 1999

Dear Nick,

I received your letter earlier this week, and I am very grateful that you took the time to read the transcript of my Felix regression. [I hope] you were able to listen to the tape as well. Thank you for your willingness to believe it is true. The way this knowledge has been revealed to me leaves me no choice but to believe it. Until the angels sent to me—at my own request—the name Felix, I did not know he even existed. Now I am holding open a multidimensional bridge of light between my lifetime now and this lifetime of the past.

I realize now why I must write the book that I am currently writing. I am allowing Felix to balance his karma and to be the "apostle" that he regretted not being in that lifetime by giving him a voice through me. [Sara] said, via her reading for John Davis, that there were two things driving me karmically in this lifetime. I believe I know what those two things are. The first one was to face up to what happened between Felix and and Paul and to tell you how I truly felt about you as Paul and the impact you had on my life as Felix. The second is to finally have the courage to speak out the truth about Jeshua, through this book, in spite of the possible ridicule or censorship it might bring upon me. (At least in this lifetime I don't have to worry about being imprisoned or killed for speaking out.)

I honestly do not know the final result of the effort I am making. (My angels told me it would get published.) Nevertheless, I know one thing is true. I must write it. My angels will not let me ignore this. Every day I think about it, and I feel bad when life's mundane tasks get in the way. Jacquelyne Ellis was right when she said she saw me writing in a book and putting it away and picking it up again until I could no longer put it away. The book would keep magically appearing on the table, waiting for me to write in it. It feels much like completing course work in college. It is always hanging over my head, and I will not feel relief until it is completed.

The letter continued with my asking Nick's permission to use his real name and to quote him in the book. I offered to send him a manuscript first, so he would have the opportunity to read what was said about him before he decided. I even offered to give him a pseudonym if he felt uncomfortable with my using his name. I told him I would be "honored beyond words to get your feedback on this project."

I updated him on the fact that John had finally had a past-life regression and how he had finally referred to Jesus as Jeshua. I gave him my own impressions of hearing the regression tape and how it had moved me to tears. I told him that seven readers, including myself, had confirmed John's apostle lifetime (and soon there would be another), and that the regression had "sealed the deal," so to speak. I concluded by telling him that, "I now feel confident that we have enough credibility to share this story with others."

About six days later, I was walking my cat Rommy when my angels spoke to me again. I shared their message in an e-mail to John:

November 11, 1999

Dear John,

I touched base with my angels today as I was walking Rommy—the lightning rod for divine guidance—in the campground. When I asked them why it had been so long since they last spoke to me, I was told that there had been many distractions in my life. I asked them if this book would get published and they told me "soon enough." They told me that Nick would be "delighted" with the story. I asked how the book was coming and was told I was on the right path. They said that there would be a few more adjustments made to the current text. They could not yet determine if [Jason] would come around to help this book get published, but they said he would be helping you with your second book (whatever that means). They said I would be put in contact with people who could help me get it published. We'll see!

Thought you would want to know about this. How [are preparations for] FLARF [the Florida Renaissance Festival] going? Tell me you aren't as busy as you were last year or as stressed out. Having Jennifer there should be good for helping to balance things for you. I wish the two of you well.

Call me sometime, all right?

Love, *Sharon*

John replied later that evening:

Well, here I am in South Florida. I started work on Wednesday after several days of exhaustive travel. Things are going well for the show . . . . I'm glad the guides are still so favorable to the project. Sometime, if you could, I would like to ask the guides for some advice on what to do next. I think I am in a holding pattern right now and am curious if this is correct. I feel anxious in my stomach. That is how I feel when the holy [expletive] starts coming. Jennifer says to say hi! I am looking forward to your arrival in Florida. It will be good for us to be together again.

Then John suddenly started to channel a message from the Master as he had done in the past:

> Dear Sharon,
>
> At this time you are feeling unsure and unstable. This is all for the best. The fear you are experiencing is the effect of important work to be done. Worthiness is a struggle for you, and you are feeling a little shaky in this area. Your guides are guiding you correctly. Trust and continue. Our hands are on yours and will guide your pen in the messages to come forth.
>
> Love . . .
>
> Well, there you go. *John*
>
> P.S. Couldn't have said it better myself

Soon after this, I received word that my father was going to need quintuple bypass open heart surgery. I left Houston before the last weekend of faire to travel to my parents' home in Longview, Texas, so that I could spend some time with my dad before he went into surgery the next week. This was an intense time for everyone in my family, but many people sent him their prayers and good wishes, including Nick Bunick and his daughter, Kim. My dad felt it was those prayers that helped him get through the surgery and to recover so quickly.

My dad's surgery took place on November 17, 1999. With everything leading up to the surgery and afterwards, eleven days passed before I had the chance to e-mail John or Nick again. Then I shared with John how I had heard from Nick's office in response to an e-mail prayer request I'd sent out for my father, and how touched I was that both Kim and Nick had sent personal prayers.

November 22, 1999

> Dear John,
>
> I thought I would send you a copy of the e-mail Nick sent [me] and my response [to him]. I guess I was right. Nick does "remember" me. I could feel in my heart that we are connected and will remain so. His friendship is not something I feel I must seek out. In time, I believe we will become good friends, and it will evolve on its own. I believe this [connection] may be helpful to [both of] you in the future.
>
> John, it occurred to me last night that I have been put in touch with some of Jesus' dearest friends: you (John the Apostle), Nick (Paul the Apostle) and [others]. It's pretty astounding. I have to believe that there is a reason for this. I'm not completely sure why, but I am honored by it.
>
> Hope all's well. Love, *Sharon*

Letter from Nick's office earlier that day:

Your letter touched us deeply. Many of us here have been with family in similar situations. I personally remember the pain and exhaustion of it. But how it makes us grow, and [be] thankful and more connected with the divine spirit. This is the divine plan, and we are apart of it. Much love to you and your father and your entire family . . . a big hug to your father.

Nick Bunick and the entire staff of The Great Tomorrow

My response back to Nick:

November 22, 1999

Nick,

Thanks so much for your thoughts and prayers. For me, the hard part was not in believing that he would make it. I knew that he would because my angels told me so, and I trust them completely. The hard part was watching him suffer. I am very empathic, and I hate to see anything suffer, even a bug! You can imagine how frustrating and helpless it feels to watch someone you love lying in pain and feeling totally helpless and there is not a thing you can do for him other than hold his hand and tell him you love him. Some things, like going through surgery, must be done "alone" and no one but our angels can travel down that road with us—much like birth and death. In those moments it is our faith that we are truly not alone—that God is always with us—that sustains us.

Thanksgiving will have a whole new meaning for us this year. I wish blessings and happiness for you and your family this Thanksgiving. Tell Kim thank you for her love and friendship. It has meant a lot to me.

I would truly love to come up to Portland again. Your neck of the woods is so beautiful! I may have an excuse this spring because my friend Lauren is about to get engaged and will probably be getting married around June. It would be nice to come when all the roses, tulips and daffodils are blooming. When I came in early April for the [444] Easter Prayer, it was a little too early to see all that.

Take care. Thank you for sharing your love—all of you!— with my family and me.

Love, *Sharon*

Then I heard from Nick about a week later:

Please forgive me for not having the opportunity to write a lengthy letter. I did pray for your father's recovery during the surgery as well as his healing. As you are well aware, many times our health is separate from our spiritual being, and that when a person truly becomes seriously ill, death is the ultimate healing. We must always be willing to accept what is best for the individual. But I do hope your dad's physical body is on the way to recovery.

I would be glad to read your manuscript. Feel free to use my name as well as to quote me in your book. I am flattered that you want to do so, and I look forward to you sending me a draft of your manuscript when it is completed . . . .

My heart was overflowing from the love that Nick and his staff were sending to my dad and me. I felt that I needed to express this and to thank him for his kindness and his willingness to let me share my experiences with him in my book.

Dear Nick,

I am always delighted to hear from you. Ever since I had the Felix regression done, I've felt a deep heart connection to you. I can't explain it, but I know this connection is real. I feel it and know it in my heart.

Thank you for praying for my father. I know that it helped him a lot. The surgery went well with only one small complication of a partially collapsed lung. He came home five days later and had two very bad days of extreme nausea that was treated with a strong drug that knocked him out. He was looking very badly, so his doctor took him off the drug and put him on something else that has allowed him to recover his appetite and strength. Now he is getting up and down much more easily, and walking around and talking on the phone, etc.

The most important gift to him was that so many people whom he didn't even know were praying for him and sending him love and good thoughts. This has been a life's lesson for my dad, who, although he will give the shirt off his back for his own family, has never [felt comfortable helping] strangers. He was simply overwhelmed and moved beyond all expectations. He received so many e-mails and cards from my friends that I collected them for him in an album. He's had a bit of a conversion. Before the surgery, he scoffed at the thought of angels and felt uncomfortable when I spoke of them. Now he refers to how his angels have helped him get through this whole ordeal.

I greatly appreciate your interest in my book and giving me permission to mention you and quote you. I have nothing but love and respect for you, and I hope this will come through in the story. I also value your taking the time to lend me your insights on what I have sent you.

I will tell you that the book has practically written itself. I have felt, for the most part, "in the flow" as I have written John's and my story. It has been hard work—don't get me wrong. It requires very intense focus, and there is a constant fine-tuning process that is going on inside me, but I'm getting lots of help from the angels. This story is not about flowery language but about getting to the point, which is hard for me. I naturally want to give too much detail. I feel my angels have guided me to be succinct and focus on the important stuff. I've tried to be completely honest about my feelings in this whole process for I believe that this is necessary if the story is to touch people in a real way.

I am currently writing Chapter Six, which details the experiences of my trip to Portland this past spring. I'm hoping that I will be finished with the manuscript by the end of January. It would be an honor and privilege to hand it to you in person—if God wills that we should be in the same city at the same time! (Remember last year's schedules?) My angels told me that you are really going to like it—at least that's what they tell me. I, for one, don't dare make any assumptions. If I'm wrong about this, you can blame them!

I wish you and your family a joyful and safe Christmas. Thank you once again for sharing yourself in the way you do so well—by truly caring!

Love and blessings (and lots of them!), *Sharon*

I felt blessed to have made a real connection to Nick in this lifetime—my apprehension of his knowing who I had been from our past lives almost two thousand years ago was finally put to rest. I was also very grateful for the time he had taken out of his busy schedule to correspond with me in the past year. Little did I know that that connection to him and those who worked for him would grow stronger in the future.

Some strange and amazing experiences took place that winter while I stayed at my parents' house. John and I continued to maintain close contact. We shared our individual spiritual experiences. Although our experiences were separate, many of them seemed to parallel one another.

John again saw a vision of Mary in the clouds as he was heading to his parents' new house in Florida for Thanksgiving.

November 22, 1999

Had an interesting ride home. Saw Mary again . . . this time she was standing again in the clouds and far to her left was an angel. Both were facing to the center. Between them was a flat cloud that seemed to look like a stage. As I watched this "stage," it began to [rise] in the middle. It continued to [rise] up, and then out, forming the shape of a cross. A feeling of calm came over me, and I felt a tingling in the front portion of my skull behind the forehead. I am kind of lethargic now, but it feels good. Let me know what you think.

Dear John,

Wow! Mary in the clouds—again! This time she brought a friend with her and the essence of Jesus. The cross symbolizes what you got from that experience when Jesus looked you in the eyes and transferred all that information to you from the cross. Mary and your angels are going to help you awaken to that knowledge. In fact, you need to start a dialogue with her! She wants to communicate with you. You know you've [wanted] this for a long time. You have been yearning for it—to talk to her. Not that you've ever told me you wanted this. I'm just feeling it. You don't need to be "chasing" her in the clouds . . . She is with you all the time. Her cloud manifestations are to remind you she's there. Talk about some big spiritual guides, dude! This is what I got from this.

Love, *Felix the Cat*

We seemed to be getting confirmations from all sides "telling" us that we were on the right path. One in particular came from an unexpected source. A woman in her mid-forties, named Barbara, whom I met at Brenda's Messengers group in Houston, had remained in contact with me via e-mail. She shared with me an interesting story, which I passed along to John:

Here's an excerpt from Barbara's e-mail:

December 7, 1999

Dear Sharon,

You aren't going to believe this, but I just got back from Denver last Tuesday. I went to Barnes & Noble in Denver to pick up a copy of "The Epic of Gilgamesh" for Bill [her husband] to read when I found a book written by Jess Stearn called "Edgar Cayce on the Millennium." I finished it in one day, last Monday, while Bill was in meetings all day. I recall the part where he mentioned John returning and being called John once again. I will have to pull out the book and review that portion.

You are so fortunate to experience direct communication with Our Lord. I have only had one encounter in the dream state and two with Mary in dreams.

Where and how did you find John? Will we ever get to meet him? I look forward to hearing more.

Love, *Barbara*

Barbara would finally get to meet John the following spring.

John, Atira, Michael Baumann, and the author Jason were planning a trip to Egypt for the fall that involved doing some important spiritual work over there. During the next few months, there would be some exciting correspondence between them and intuitive Judy Goodman, of which I would unknowingly be a part. Egypt would be the first of three sacred journeys that John and Michael would make together in the coming years.

At this time, Randy and I were staying with my parents to help out around the house during Thanksgiving and Christmas. While I was there, I channeled what seemed to be a pretty "far out" message concerning John's trip to Egypt, which I nicknamed "Mumbo Jumbo."

December 16, 1999

Beloved John. Now has come the time for you to awaken. Your activation is almost complete. Once the portals of your mind are fully open, you will receive great storehouses of knowledge. This will be completed in five stages. Portal 1: The receiving of a letter will trigger a memory within you. Portal 2: The connection to Peter will bring a greater energy flow. Portal 3: The words of a famous reader will point you in the right direction regarding your role in Egypt. Portal 4: Information received by others will come together as a whole picture. It will fit together like puzzle pieces. Portal 5: A message from someone afar—someone with clear intentions—will be making the necessary connections for you.

You must go to this with inner knowledge that has not fully awakened. As you trust, things will be revealed at the precise moment that they need to be revealed. This will give you the information you need without allowing your mind to betray you. You must trust on this one, my son. You must walk in faith, knowing that we are leading the way. It will not be something for which you will have all the answers.

Shifting sands. A place in the desert where nobody goes . . . not hospitable, but not impossible. A flow—an organization of path/walkways. A maze-like structure that has many openings, some leading to false entrances and others leading to dead ends. Someone knows the way through this maze and will lead you to the sacred chamber. You will be guided intuitively. You must act on this impulse to be led. Retrieval of information will come in stages, each building upon the other.

The opening is the mouth of the lion. [I have the feeling that this is regarding the configuration of the maze, not necessarily a reference to the Sphinx.] Go in through the mouth into its belly. There you will find a safe chamber, untouched by time. There will be a golden arc, a vision of the future. When the time is right, this arc will be opened, to be shared with all. This is the opening of time itself. A portal of mind, body and spirit. An awakening for the world. In truth, it is the ending and the beginning—the alpha and the omega. Not to be feared, but to be cherished. Secrets [will be] unveiled and mysteries explained. Once this veil is opened, there is no turning back. It will be for all time. A testament of our people. A covenant from our people. A bridge through time and space. Be at peace with this though you may not understand all the variables and how they come together.

The empowerment process begins here. You will receive this awakening and knowledge that you have been prepared for. You will not be the same [coming out as you were going in]. You will have transformed yourself and will see interdimensionally. The keys of knowledge will have passed from my hands to yours. You must guard these keys as if with your life. You have been entrusted with this sacred knowledge for the pureness of your heart and the honest intent of your mind. Do not labor over this. It will be pointless. You must trust that all will be revealed when the time is right.

John sent my e-mail to Jason, who responded the next day. He said that he felt that it was "an excellent beginning" and wanted to know what the others in the group thought. He mentioned that he knew someone in Egypt who was acquainted with the tunnels under the Giza Plateau and would ask him if he knew anything about "the Mouth of the Lion" that I had channeled.

Again, I felt the way I had when John and I first discovered the confirmation of John's past life from the Edgar Cayce reading. I felt as if I were getting into something way over my head and felt compelled to ask John on what crazy ride he was taking me. He responded by saying that this was the ride I had been waiting for my whole life. He also channeled a message for me:

December 17, 1999

When things seem out of thy control, a thought should bend to thy spirit. Thy spirit is one with all and thus being, all is in control but unaware. All is on course and all will come to pass as is needed for the enlightenment of all.

My children, fear not, for the task is a sacred one that is to be for the wholeness of the one. The power of the united is to be purified in the act to come. My love is with you always and know that we are as the one. Sharon...the smile that comes to you is a reflection of pure love. Hold this feeling within, and soon thy purpose will be made clear. Be the love. Be the one. The one is love.

Shortly after my channeled reading for John, which he had shared with Jason, Michael Baumann, and some others, I received a call from Michael requesting a reading. I had never met Michael, but I knew who he was from John. I sensed that Michael might receive a message from the

Master, but I was concerned about being able to channel Him over the phone for someone I had never met. In the way that I do readings, it is absolutely necessary that I am able to connect with a person's energy. Could I connect to Michael's energy field having never met him before? I didn't know the answer to that, but I was about to find out. I was very concerned about getting it right. The last thing I wanted to do was disappoint Michael.

To prepare Michael for the reading, I sent him a preliminary e-mail asking for his help:

> Although I have given many readings in person, I have only given about two or three readings over the phone, and those were with people I either knew or had met in person, first. Your reading will be the first one I have given to a "stranger" although it is my feeling that we might have known one another before this lifetime.
>
> Therefore, in order to help me make a stronger connection to you, I would ask you to pray and meditate before the reading....You don't have to tell me anything in advance. Just allow your energy to be open to me....I don't know if you ever speak to Jeshua, but if you do, you might ask Him to be present during this reading and assisting us.

Michael was wonderful when he called me at my parents' house on December 22. He put no pressure on me at all. He told me to let whatever messages that needed to come through to come through and if nothing came through, we would just have a nice chat.

I said my usual invocation to start the reading. The energy I felt was the same as when I channeled the Master for John. I felt the Master's energy come down around my head and face. I closed my eyes and tuned into the words that I was receiving.

The Master wasted no time in speaking to Michael. In fact, the whole reading was this channeled message:

> **There is much information being received at this time. It is important to assess and evaluate information accurately. We are in oneness at this time, and you can feel my spirit with you. This longing in your heart, this feeling of oneness, you know it's there. I would ask that you bring this feeling closer to your heart, closer to your being, and be present with that. This one, the one I'm speaking through, is a little nervous.** [I paused to take a deep breath. My voice was quivering a bit. As if to reassure me, the Master interjected this one-line message for me, to which Michael responded by encouraging me to just speak whatever came through me.]

It's important that the information be received. It's important that the fulfillment of the oneness take place on all levels. In times past, this communion with me would fill your being. Let this fill you now, let this remembrance embrace you, and this sweet love touch your heart.

You are an accurate channel. You do receive the messages clearly. You must trust this guidance you are receiving at this time. This awakening that is taking place between you and the others has all unfolded, and is unfolding, right now at the right time. Let this feeling lift you up. Be joyful and rejoice with this knowledge.

Never doubt that we are one. You have come to a point in your life where you are ready to experience this, and to accept this, and to bring it into your being. This love energy, that pours forth out of your heart like the rays of the sun, this is a blessing, this is a gift that you give to others. Though quiet by nature, you must share this feeling of love with others, and these messages of truth and peace with others, as you receive them. This natural shyness has always been a part of your being. You must loosen its hold on the bounty of information coming forth at this time. You will be guided within to share this information, and you will feel within your heart that this is so—that this is the right thing to do.

Never has there been a time in history where this love energy has been so important. This is the saving grace of this universe. These beings of light that are coming into existence, and into your world, are connecting with all of you who are awakening, and together this magnificent and brilliant light that you are creating with one another is being sent out like a beacon into the universe. This beacon is being received and understood.

There are those that will be coming to visit you—the ancient ones. You are preparing the way for this to take place. This ancient knowledge is awakening in you and in all those that have been called forth for this mission, to serve this higher purpose.

Do not deny me. Do not deny what you are receiving. It's very important for you to be awake and to transform this energy, this knowledge, this awakening inside of you, for fulfillment of a greater purpose—this sharing of this knowledge, of this love, of this gift with others.

Be at peace with this and know that you are ready. Let this trouble your being no more, for it is time. The path is being laid, the way of seeing made clear, for this important work to go forth, and you will be joined by others with the same purpose. Fulfill and support one another on your journey. Each of you holds a key to this awakening, this unfolding of knowledge; each of you play an active and important role. It is necessary for all the keys to be fully activated, that all of you stand in oneness, one in purpose, one in mind, heart, [and] spirit.[34]

You must trust one another and know that you have come together at this agreed-upon time, for this sacred mission, your sacred journey. All will be revealed when the time is right and when all are present. Be at peace my son and go on your journey, with a fully awakened heart, mind, and spirit, and know that my love and my blessing go with you.

And that was it. The reading lasted only twenty-five minutes, but the message that had "needed" to come through had come through me in a very powerful way. I was accustomed to giving hour-long readings, but, since Michael had no questions, the reading ended much sooner than I had expected. "That was great," he said.

"Since you don't have any questions," I said, "I don't know what else to say. I think that was it."

"We can just talk awhile. Why don't we try to reach our friend, John?"

"Okay."

Michael tried to call John and connect him to our phone call but he didn't answer his phone. "I'll try again later," Michael said.

We spent some time talking and getting to know one another. Later, Michael was able to reach John, and we had a three-way conversation. I enjoyed listening and talking to both of them at the same time. I had fun teasing John by telling Michael some "John" stories.

Michael told us of his plans to bring his wife Cheryl to Florida where John was directing a faire. I was excited to hear this because Randy would be performing with his band at the same faire. I would finally get to meet Michael and Cheryl. In an e-mail I sent to him later, I offered to give him a reading while he was in Florida.

December 27, 1999

Dear Michael,

I received your very generous love offering and beautiful Egyptian card today. Thank you so much! Although I prepared carefully for the reading and I could sense its importance, I was disappointed that it was short, but who am I to judge? I guess the Master knew the points He wanted to make, and perhaps the first message was to be a simple one. I know for the six or seven times I have channeled Him for John—five of which have been in person, and two that have been long distance—I have learned something new about Him each time. Perhaps the distance had something to do with its simplicity. I believe the message would probably be stronger in person, which would be related to me making a stronger connection to your energy field.

I first learned the Master had a sense of humor during the third reading I did for John in Ohio in the summer of '98. I even channeled some simple poetry from Him during the fourth reading at Rehoboth Beach. It made me giggle at the time because I didn't realize I was reciting poetry until the words started to rhyme. If the message—which talked about when He and John would meet again in this life (in the body he possessed in Galilee)— hadn't been a serious one, I would have thought He was just being humorous. Perhaps He was delivering a serious message in a non-intimidating way. So like Him to put things in a way that gets us to let down our defenses, so we can hear the message and not be afraid of it.

Can't wait to meet you and Cheryl in person. I really like your calm, gentle, loving energy. You seem to be a reserved person, but open at the same time. I find that an interesting combination. I sense that you were much the same way in your past life with John. I think you made a nice balance for the "son of thunder." Speaking of which, get John to tell you about this guy who called him named Bud who has a singing monk group called "Sons of Thunder"—Jesus' nickname for James and John!

Say hello to Cheryl for me. I really enjoyed talking to her on the phone the other day. I think she and my husband, Randy, would have a lot in common being married to people who have so much spiritual "craziness" going on in their lives!

In love, Sharon

With my dad's surgery and the hustle and bustle of Christmas, another promised reading for John had been delayed. I finally found time to do the reading, but I wasn't sure how John would receive it. I reluctantly sent off the reading, which had been a channeled message, on January 8. I felt I needed to soften the blow, so I sent a forward to the channeled message:

> Please don't be mad at me. They did not give the specific information that you requested . . . . it looks like they're telling you that you need to channel your own information. Some of this is coming together right now. I guess everyone [including those reincarnated apostles who will be coming together again] needs to be a fireman, so to speak, and be ready for the call when it comes.
>
> Looks like [the person who was] Peter is still being prepared as you are and that a lot of things look like they depend on other things happening first. I guess everyone's free will enters into the bigger picture and that it will all come together when everyone is in place and ready to go. I guess everyone involved needs to listen to their own internal spiritual guidance.

The following are excerpts from the actual reading I did for John. He had asked about the sacred journey to Egypt he would be taking at the end of the year and about when he would be meeting the person who had been the Apostle Peter. This is a channeled message:

What one wants to know is often a reflection of one's own hidden fears. The fears that dwell within are those thoughts that have no meaning. It is up to each of us to come to terms with the knowingness and trust that dwells within. The knowingness will tell you when to go forward and when it is time to stand still. This is your time to stand still and be at peace. It is not necessary to push the envelope, so to speak.

Many factors must take place and many inroads must be made before there is a completion of energies that make the time right for such a journey. The journey begins within. You must clean your own space before you can serve the world. This space must be prepared and made sacred, for the time will come soon that you will need it.

No one can possibly know what lies ahead. We are orchestrating it as it proceeds. There is a blueprint for what is to take place and an awakening that must transpire before all the necessary elements come together. When the time is right, you will know it. You will have the urge and the call to go. Do not depend on others for this information. They may extrapolate as they wish, [but] when the time is right, all will know it and at the same time. The coming together will be beautifully orchestrated. There will be others joining you whom you have not met yet. Some dear old friends will pop in to herald your arrival....

You are ready to know who you truly are. You are ready to unlock the gifts that lie within. You must follow your guidance, my son. What does your heart tell you about the wonderful things that you have heard? What do *you* think the purpose of your mission really is? You know the answers to these questions already. Do not look without but within for these answers.

Your connections to Peter are being made as we speak. You must understand that he is fully awakening himself as well. It would not be right to hurry him anymore than it would be right to hurry you. Have you not felt hurried enough already? We do not want anyone to combust.

What we are telling you is that you must seek the answers from within. There is a danger of too much verification and not enough inner guidance leading the way. There will be those looking to you, very soon, for the very answers that you seek. You will be the wellhead for such information. You need only sit down and transcribe the answers for yourself. This is how you will receive your verification. Now do it.

John's reply to this was: "Kick in the butt received! I will never be mad at you for giving me such a reading! It obviously is what I needed to hear!"

The following month, in February, Randy and I traveled to Florida, where John was directing a Renaissance festival near Ft. Lauderdale, where Randy's band would also be performing. It was here that Randy and I would have the privilege of meeting Michael and his lovely wife, Cheryl. On February 4, we had dinner with them at John's favorite Italian restaurant in Ft. Lauderdale. Unfortunately, John was too busy getting ready for the first weekend of faire to join us.

After dinner Randy and I parted, and I went with Michael and Cheryl to their hotel room to give them both a reading. The first part of the reading was for Cheryl, which is not included here. The last part was for Michael. I felt the presence of the Master almost immediately. The following is the message that He gave to Michael. The energy was very strong. Just like when I channeled for John, I could feel the close connection that Jeshua had to Michael. The following is a transcript of the reading:

> Beloved one, ageless and timeless. What a great heart you have. What a wonderful presence you are to this Earth. You are tried and true. As I have called on you in the past, you have been there, as you are now. Always willing to follow, always willing to listen, and to learn. These are your greatest gifts.
>
> As you trusted me before, trust in me now. I am guiding your way at this time. The people that you're coming to know, these are trusted friends. You know in your heart which ones are true. You've always known by your heart the things that are true. You have heard my words spoken and knew that they were true. You know when words are spoken that are true.
>
> Trust in this great presence, this gift that you have. You have a profound connection [to] humanity. You've come here with a wonderful purpose, to serve humanity in the greatest way, by bringing more love and light and energy into this world.
>
> You are ready for this. You are ready for the love and the understanding and to teach this to others. This great healing Light, that you carry within your being, I could see this light many years ago, and it has grown, and glows even brighter today.
>
> You have come here at this important time in history, into this world, to bring greater presence. To bring my love and light into this world, to pave the way which others may follow. This path that you are going down, you are leading others. As you blaze a path before you, others will follow in your footsteps. These are my footsteps as well.
>
> All of you who have come to serve me at this time are being guided by my presence, and by the presence of your Angels. All of this has a very important purpose at this time. You must understand, [that] the trust that you have—this innate understanding—is a part of the gift that you have been given. It's not something that you have to struggle with, it's something that's a blessing to you. It is yours, free for the taking.
>
> This open communication is a gift that not everyone has. Not everyone can feel this connection to me. You do not need this person

to speak for me. You can speak to me yourself. You have been longing for this for the greatest amount of time, and it's now time for you to have this personal communion with me. You no longer have to go through others to hear my words, beloved, you hear them inside of your heart, and in your mind.

This great wisdom that you have, this has always been there. You are learning to share this wisdom with others, and learning to speak your truth. It is so important, you understand, that it is not for you to hold onto this, but for you to share with others. So, as this love and wisdom comes through you from me, you are being guided to share this. Do not hold onto this, this is a blessing for everyone. Please share what you know with other people, so that they may benefit—to learn and grow as well and to be blessed by your presence, and your healing energy, and love, that is connected to this greater heart.

Trust in this knowingness; trust in this love. This will guide you through all of your days, Michael. You are my trusted guardian, and I am well pleased. I am well pleased in you.

Wow, the energy in the room was phenomenal! I could feel it bouncing off the walls. I felt humbled and privileged to be able to deliver another message from the Master to Michael.

"I want you to take a look at something," Michael urged. While I was still under the "influence," Michael led me across the room to a map of the Giza Plateau he had spread out on the desk top. It had markings and graphics indicating where the pyramids and different buildings and structures were located. "See if you pick up on anything," Michael requested, cryptically. I got the distinct impression that he was wanting to locate something specifically related to their upcoming trip.

"What are you asking me to do, Michael?"

"We're looking for the entrance to the tunnels, and wanted to see if you knew where we should start," Michael said with more than a little anticipation.

I had never seen a map of the Giza Plateau before, and I had no idea where this opening might be located. Feeling a little under the gun by this sudden request, and still woozy from the powerful energy I had just channeled, I silently asked my guides for help. Looking down at the map, I moved my hand all around and just above the surface to see if I could sense a vibration of where this might be. Finally, my hand stopped over a certain spot, and my eyes rested on a small, inconspicuous rectangular structure that hardly seemed significant. Doubting that I was receiving correctly, I almost didn't want to say it aloud. Finally I said, "I'm getting a buzz here" as I pointed to the little building thingy.

"Precisely!" exclaimed Michael with glee on his face. "You nailed it on the head!" he affirmed. Nailed what, I wondered? I would come to learn that it was typical of Michael to ask a mysterious, vague question during a psychic reading, leaving the poor reader wondering what the purpose of the question was in the first place. I think it was his way of keeping things pure. The whole experience was incredible and well beyond a normal reading. Michael was the second apostle I had read for, and somehow, I had the feeling that he wouldn't be the last.

The next night, John and Jennifer were able to join the rest of us for dinner. Watching John and Michael interact was like watching two very old friends carry on about the good old days. Everyone had a great time. John and I discussed the upcoming book and the messages we had gotten in our readings. Michael shared some of his spiritual experiences of awakening. The next day, Michael and Cheryl departed and flew back to their home in Missouri.

During our time in Florida, my husband's band was also perform-ing in a Celtic variety show, called a ceilidh. We were heavily involved in the preparations for that, but I took a moment to follow up with the Baumanns the next week. At the same time, Michael had written his own follow up e-mail. Our e-mails "crossed" in cyberspace. I actually read his e-mail after I had sent him mine.

February 8, 2000

Dear Michael and Cheryl,

I wanted to wait and get you a lovely card to say "Thanks for a great time," but my schedule's gotten so busy with the ceilidh we are doing in Vero Beach that I am sending this e-mail instead. Otherwise, it would take at least a couple more weeks [to write you] since we have a cruise the week after [this]. I don't know when I will get to spend time with John!

It was a great honor to meet both of you. You are very special people. I could not believe the incredible spiritual energy the both of you carry!

Thank you, thank you, thank you for sharing your gifts with me!! It will be a night I will remember forever!

Also, it was a very humbling experience and a great honor to chan-nel Jeshua for you. As soon as I felt His "hands" on my hands sending me that intense love energy, I knew He was with us.

It is remarkable to me that I was able to channel Him for you in the same way that I do for John. I know that sounds strange, but since His energy is the same, it verifies for me that it is Him and that I am able to channel Him consistently for others. Being fair and consistent is very important to me. And of course, I benefit from that love energy by allowing it to flow through me! My goal is to be able to bring more of

His loving, healing energy inside so that I can impart it more strongly and clearly for others. I am not ready to "see" Him yet, but I hope I will feel worthy of such an encounter some day. Maybe Judy Goodman could help me with that . . . [I had not met the well-known intuitive, Judy Goodman, yet, but was hoping to meet her soon.]

I hope that our paths will cross again some day soon. I know Randy thoroughly enjoyed meeting you both and had a lot of fun the second evening when we all had dinner with John and Jennifer. It's so wonderful to be among "family" again! Take care and continue to walk in His light, as I know you will.

Much love to you both, Sharon

I shared my impressions of meeting Michael and Cheryl with John in an e-mail immediately after:

February 8, 2000

Dear John,

I miss you so much! [I wish we could] spend more time together! It was so good to receive your loving hugs! I really needed them! It was also good to spend some more time with Jennifer to get to know her better. I had no idea how much she and Randy have in common. Isn't that perfect that we would each have a spouse opposite of our temperaments to balance us! How wise Spirit is to give us this great gift. Otherwise, you and I would be floating off into the ethers!

I sent a thank-you e-mail to Michael and Cheryl. The experience of channeling Jeshua for Michael was pretty powerful. Michael is pretty powerful! I'm telling you, he is a BIG player in the cosmic scheme of things. I can tell by the energy he carries. Cheryl is phenomenal though I don't think she has fully realized her power yet. She will be doing some incredible things soon! I felt immediately comfortable with them, as if they have been old friends forever! John, the "family" is getting back together again!

It's gotten busy over here. I am answering the phone and the door for the ceilidh.. Gotta go . . . see you Friday afternoon.

Love you bunches, Sharon

Then I saw that Michael had sent me an e-mail. I opened it up. The e-mail focused on my impending book. He expressed concern for John and the effect that fame would have upon him:

February 7, 2000

Dear Sharon,

Thank you for the little get-together last weekend. It was a wonderful warming for the soul to meet and talk with you in person. Now, I can place a face with the voice and soul I already knew.

You needn't concern yourself with reading any of the letters or info I have sent John. I know one must protect certain things that may eventually end up in a book. I place my trust in you fully and bless your judgment on what to include on your own and what not to.

Now, on to the subject of your book:

Maybe it is not time for John to be pushed out to the front of the stage. I know that sounds pretty stupid for a guy who has been there for a dozen years or so now, but I don't know. We all know it hasn't been a bed of roses for Nick through this whole ordeal. Maybe you should present that question directly to your guides sometime (if you haven't already).

I would ask is this book the one for John Davis to step forward? Perhaps you will need to save this for the next one.

If it is not this one, we all still know who is responsible for reaching out to guide someone in the right direction, and no one can take that from you. It's tough being the unsung hero sometimes.

I keep getting the feeling that you have enough going on with your own self-discovery to present a book already. I also feel that maybe putting John [in] public may get in the way of his own work to do at this time. Like maybe it needs to wait for a few years.

I don't know if John has considered this either way . . .

Maybe they would be fine with a two or three chapter mention of your encounter with him, but not reveal his exact identity. I don't know Sharon. I'm just opening my heart up to you, in hopes that you will publish soon, and it will be successful in any case. You deserve it.

Just review each subject with the higher authorities, trust that only the truth will be written, and continue to give Light and Love to others as you did this weekend to Cheryl and myself. And thanks for pointing John in the right direction.

Bless [you], talk to you again soon, and write me about anything at any time.

Always in the Light, Michael

At first, I was very discouraged by Michael's letter. I had to think about my response to him. I had barely met him, and yet I *knew* him. I knew his heart. I knew he truly cared for John and me. I had to search my soul. Was this book too much about me, and my own personal journey? Had I given enough time to John? Was I really serving John's overall purpose or only serving mine? Was this project premature? Should I ditch the whole thing?

Sometimes our friends are there to reflect back to us our own hidden fears and concerns. Their probing questions help us to get clear about our motivations and intentions. Perhaps this was what Michael was doing. I searched my soul and knew, in the deepest part of it, that John and I were being guided through this whole process. No matter what, I knew that I had to write the book.

February 10, 2000

Dear Michael,

Your letter caught me a little off guard and has given me some things to think about. I appreciate your sharing your concerns with me about the book. I also appreciate your wanting to protect John. The thought of making him anonymous may be a good one. That way he would have the option of "coming out" whenever he wanted to. However, to completely scrap the project when I am so close to finishing it would be contrary to what I (and John) have been working toward for all these months and what Spirit has asked me to do.

It is impossible to eliminate my perspective from the story because I am the one telling it. John has asked me to tell the story because I was there and have intimate knowledge of what transpired. I am hoping, by including my own spiritual insights in this story, that the reader will be able to identify with the struggle each of us goes through when we are learning to trust our spiritual guidance. I feel that I must finish the project (as I have been guided to do) and let the powers that be decide if and when it should get published. I will review what I have written and ask Spirit if I should change anything as I have been trying to do all along.

Believe me when I say, I am struggling with the consequences to my own private life of bringing this story forward. I know in my heart that I have been chosen [through writing this book] to be the forerunner for John, who is to be the forerunner of Christ in this millennium. That is a daunting responsibility and one that still has me asking humbly, "Why me?" But I know that this is what I have come here to do. I am a part of this mission. I would never want to harm my beloved friend by forcing fame on him before he is ready for it. I believe, however, that Nick has prepared the way for John by coming forward first. And, I believe, in many ways, John will be more ready to handle this responsibility as a result of Nick's efforts; and I believe he will be effective in helping people reach Jeshua in a personal way, simply because he is a conscious channel for Christ, and he bears Christ's energy signature. In fact, John's goal and future plans are focused on bringing this book forward.

I would be very happy to send you (or any other interested parties) a copy of my manuscript when it is finished and has been edited. I feel protective of this project because it is my heart and soul going into this. However, I have let those people I know and trust, and whose opinion I value, read it and so far I have gotten overall positive feedback and have received constructive suggestions which I have taken.

Michael, I must follow my own guidance on this, no matter what any outside party may believe about it. This is my test of faith. (Incidentally, Sara, Jacquelyne Ellis, and another reader from Florida told [John that] the book would be published as well as my guides on three separate occasions.) However, if it is not meant to be, then it will not go forward. If it is meant to be, then it will. Either way, I am off the hook when I finish this project. I will have fulfilled my karmic debt by awakening John and sharing the story. Ultimately, Spirit will have the final say, no matter what any of us think about it. I trust that it will be as it should be.

I give my blessings to you both. If you don't mind, I want to send your concerns about the book to John to get his feedback on the subject as well.

In love, Sharon

When I spoke to John, he was very supportive. He had complete faith in my telling the story and that the work would go forth.

I would give one more phone reading to Michael and Cheryl in March. Afterward, I e-mailed Michael to ask his permission to use his real name in our story. I was a little hesitant, considering our previous discussion on this topic. Michael stunned me by saying yes with no strings attached. This was a big step for Michael who was extremely private and who had been reticent about sharing his past life with others. As he said in a follow-up e-mail, "Well, my dear, they're saying yes. The name is Michael Baumann, wife is Cheryl. Three boys are 12, 11, 8. Don't misspell the name, either, they say!!![35] I would be proud to be a footnote in your book, and they confirm that my real name should be used."

When I asked him if he would be okay with me sharing stories about him and John, he said, "Yes, I'm at your service. [The] only [past life information] I've heard for sure is that John and I have hooked up together during Renaissance times to do battle against the powerful church, and we were also together during the Crusades. (Never again for me.) They say we always manage to find each other for some just cause. The uneasiness of meeting took about two seconds, much like meeting up with you again in Florida. It was such a release to be able to see you guys again. It was like finding friends you thought were lost forever."

In April 2000, John drove to Georgia to visit intuitive Judy Goodman, to whom he had been introduced by a mutual friend. John spent a day and a half visiting with Judy, which he says was like a continuous reading. She would be the eighth psychic and the most famous to confirm John's apostle lifetime. At one point, they were visited by the Master. Judy, who is very spiritually gifted and is able to see the Master, told John that He was present. This was confirmed when the entire interior of the house suddenly became very bright, but not from any light source.

As John was led into meditation by Judy, Jesus came to him. From his higher self, John could see the Master—through his third eye—place

Sharon Prince

His palms on top of John's palms—as He had done with me in North Carolina—and send him energy this way, which John felt throughout his whole body. There was no denying it. Something profound had happened, and both John and Judy knew it.

Judy and John felt like old friends. She invited John to visit anytime. In fact, she told him that, in the future, he would need a place to get away from it all and that he was welcome to stay at her house even if she wasn't there.

Within a month, John would have his past life confirmed yet again, this time by a reader at the faire he was doing near Dallas, Texas. As he was walking away from his stage, a reader was compelled to pull him into her booth. She made a comment about how incredible his energy was. The reader, Rita, whom John had never met before, told John that he would be leaving the Renaissance circuit soon and would be selling a book and speaking to large groups of people. Without prompting, she told him that he had been "John" and that he had an important message to deliver to the world.

CHAPTER THIRTEEN

Windows of Time

The spring of 2000 found me planning a trip to Portland to be the matron of honor for my dear friend, Lauren. The timing seemed too perfect as I was nearly finished with the manuscript anyway, and this would be an opportunity for me to personally hand the manuscript to Nick. I felt very honored that he would want to read it as he gets many manuscripts and cannot possibly read them all.

After my friend's beautiful, Irish wedding, held at a quaint old church in Portland on May 1, I went to stay with my friend Peggy Keating, whom I had gotten to know on my trip to Portland for Nick's 444 Prayer Ceremony the previous year. Upon arriving at Peggy's house, I tried to call Nick's office with the number I had been given, but I only got an automated message stating that the number I was trying to reach was out of service.

"That can't be right," I told myself. I dialed the number again and got the same message. "This isn't good," I thought. I couldn't believe I had come so far to bring a copy of the manuscript to Nick only to reach a dead-end now. I decided not to panic. "If things are meant to work out, they will. I will trust the higher power that brought me to Portland in the first place," I told myself. I asked Peggy if I could borrow her e-mail account to send Nick a message through the The Great Tomorrow e-mail address, which I had remembered through prior correspondence. I included Peggy's home number in the message and asked someone to call me.

The next morning I waited a little bit for someone from Nick's office to call, but they didn't. I had only two more days in Portland, and my appointment with Nick was the next day. So, I had to make a choice: I could either sit around all day waiting for the phone to ring, or I could trust the powers that be to take care of things for me, and spend the rest of the day touring the Willamette Valley. I decided upon the latter. Peggy and I had a wonderful time visiting the orchards where she grew up and driving to Mount Hood, where we paid a visit to the famous Timberline Lodge. I tried not to think about whether The Great Tomorrow would call, but it was in the back of my mind the whole day. As it turned out, I needn't have been concerned because when we got back to Peggy's house, there was both a phone message and an e-mail waiting for me. "Sharon, this is Heather from Nick's office. I am sorry you've had so much trouble reaching us. The number we gave you was off by one digit." She gave me the correct office number and detailed directions on how to get there. "Yes, we are expecting you and look forward to meeting you tomorrow."

The next morning I got up and put on a tartan dress with a velvet collar. I wanted to look nice, but not too business-like. Peggy drove me to Nick's office and I invited her to come in with me. Nick's office was in a very plush building, with big glass windows looking out on a stand of willowy trees, wood paneling along the hallways, and beautiful artwork all around. As I ascended the sweeping staircase to the second floor, I took a deep breath and tried to swallow the little lump in my throat.

I found his office door and knocked lightly before entering. There waiting to greet me at the front desk was a classy, blonde-haired woman who had the manner of a gracious host. "Hi," I said. "I'm Sharon Prince Wothke and this is my friend, Peggy Keating. We're here to see Nick?" She stood up to greet me. "Hi, I'm Heather. I'm Nick's assistant. It's nice to finally meet you! Nick has asked if you could wait a little while. He is on a long distance call right now. It shouldn't take too long. Can I offer you something to drink?"

Just as we were getting ready to take our seats, Beth Ayers, an attractive woman with short, brown hair appeared around the corner. "Sharon!" she said. Her voice exuded positive energy. "I'm Beth!" Beth was responsible for circulating The Messenger Newsletter that The Great Tomorrow put out every month. She gave me a big hug as if she already knew me. There was genuine warmth coming from her eyes, and I felt instantly comfortable with her.

"This is where it all happens," she said, showing us an office area which she shared with Melissa, the editor, and Kim, Nick's daughter. "Melissa's had to take her son to the doctor, and Kim is on vacation. They're going to be disappointed they missed you!"

We continued to visit until Nick came out of his office. He was clearly very busy handling a sensitive situation for one of his charitable organizations. (Nick was the director for several foundations and worked tirelessly on their behalf.) He apologized for keeping me waiting. We all chatted for a few minutes. He asked me how John and I had been doing and explained how busy he had been recently, but, he said, he was on the verge of making some real progress with one of his charitable efforts in another country.

This is as good a time as any, I thought. "Here is my manuscript. It's only a first draft, but you can get an idea. . . I have marked the pages that mention you," I told Nick as I handed him a blue binder. He very graciously accepted it. "Thank you, Sharon," he said, holding it respectfully and looking at it as if I had given him a very valuable gift. He promised to finish reading it within the next three weeks.

Peggy volunteered to take a picture of all of us standing in front of the open, glass wall of Nick's office. As we tied things up, he explained that normally he would invite me to have lunch with him, but that he was in the middle of something important and couldn't break away. I assured him that I completely understood and that no apology was necessary. He gave me a hug and the now familiar kiss on the cheek and thanked me for coming. Then he disappeared behind his office door.

It had been brief, but mission accomplished! Now it was just a matter of waiting to hear back from Nick as to whether or not he would allow me to use his name. On the way out, I left an extra copy of the manuscript for Kim at Heather's desk.

The next night was Peggy's Messengers Group meeting. She had invited me to speak about my "book" to the group. There was a lot of interest in the subject of another person who had discovered his past life as an apostle. I read some excerpts and answered their questions about John. The group seemed very excited about the book and wanted to know if John might be able to come there to speak in the future.

———•••———

That evening, Randy called, concerned about his eye. He told me that while driving that day he'd realized that he had a huge blind spot in the center of his right eye when he suddenly lost vision in that eye and had to pull his car over. It scared him enough to see a specialist in opthalmology. The doctor examined Randy and discovered that he had a serious condition in his right eye that was threatening his eyesight. His retina had a lesion that was allowing fluid to seep out of the eye thus obscuring his vision. The specialist didn't know what to do. He said laser surgery does not always help and often worsens this type of condition. The doctor said he wanted to wait a month before he did a radiation treatment on the eye. I was very concerned for Randy and dreaded the thought of him having to undergo surgery, especially since there were no guarantees. I suggested that John might be able to heal him and wondered if he would be open to this. After all, what did he have to lose? Randy agreed it couldn't hurt, but he wondered how John could possibly heal something that serious.

When I got back to Texas, Randy and I traveled toward Dallas, where his band was performing at the Renaissance festival. John had just finished directing a faire in Tennessee and had flown to Dallas to join Jennifer, who was selling beads at a shop she was renting at that festival. We were staying at the same campground, a couple of rows away from John's fifth-wheel trailer. When we arrived at the campground, Randy announced that he wanted John to do some healing work on his eye. This was a big step for my skeptical husband.

When John came over that evening, he told Randy to focus on the feeling of love. "Try to remember how you felt when you first fell in love with Sharon and re-create that feeling inside yourself. Being in a state of love will allow the energy I'm sending you to heal you," John said. He had me put my left hand on Randy's forehead and my right hand at the base of his neck to send him energy. I tried to focus on the feeling of love, too. John then held both of Randy's hands and sent a powerful energy through him that I could feel as well.

As Randy closed his eyes, he remembered the shape of the shadow that had appeared in his field of vision. Suddenly he saw a flickering light, like a flame dancing around, that went all along the outline of this blind spot. Afterward, he said he felt the energy travel from John's hands and go into his eye. He believed that something significant had happened.

After the healing session, John and I stayed up. We both felt the presence of the Master with us, and we both channeled a message from Him to each other. Tears welled up in John's eyes as he felt the Master touching the left side of his body as he "stood" next to him. I tried to see Him, but I wasn't fully ready yet. I could see energy and the very basic outline of a face, but not clearly.

The next day Randy's eyesight, which had been steadily getting worse over the last week, greatly improved to the point that the condition was nearly gone. Nothing short of miraculous in my mind. This was just the beginning of the manifestation of incredible healing energy that John carries. He would be healing many others in the future by bringing in the powerful Christ energy.

———•◦•———

Knowing that John would be in Texas, Brenda took the opportunity to invite him to speak to her Messengers group in Houston. She sent out this message to the group:

May 10, 2000

As I mentioned at our last meeting, John Davis, "John the Beloved," is in Texas for the month of May. I talked with him and he
would love to come and meet our group and share some of his experiences with us. We will have a special meeting this month. He will be
here on Wednesday, May 17 at 7:00 p.m. We will be meeting at my
house as usual. I hope to see all of you there and feel free to bring any of
your friends; we would love to give John a very warm welcome to Texas!!

Since we have been brought together through *The Messengers* I feel
that all of us have a connection to the time of Jeshua. Last time, Sharon
Wothke spoke to us about John the Beloved, [and] we shared in a meditation in which Jeshua came through...it was a very loving experience
for all. I know this will be a very special evening for all as we are united
once again with a friend from that time so long ago...

Here was another Messengers group that wanted John to speak to
them. There was definitely an interest out there. John began to feel the true
purpose of his mission and was looking forward to it.

May 15, 2000

Dear Sharon,

I felt compelled to sit and write to you. I find myself amazed at the
interest of these Messenger groups in our stories. It is quite daunting to
think of what to say and how to do it. I know that I will go there prepared with the stories I already have. The rest I will leave to the higher
realms. If it is needed, I am sure that I will find the "inspiration" to
speak the words I hear in my head.

My Dear, the thoughts [that] you hear are from Higher Sources,
and it seems that the trust I had been needing to accept the thoughts [I
am receiving] is coming to me rather rapidly. My faith has been tested
and my faith is coming through with flying colors. Jesus works with me
in an intimate way. I am becoming very aware of this connection. I once
heard Jacquelyn say, in her reading for you, that I have been, "anointed
and sent into service." Judy [Goodman] anointed me with oils at Jesus'
request. There is no looking back at this point.

It's funny [that] this past weekend someone came to me about a
project. The project was a large stage combat show that would tour
theaters. This type of project at one time in my life would have been a
dream-come-true. It held no interest for me. I think that I have risen to
the top of that field; I have the respect of many and I could at this time,
more than any other time, turn that into a lucrative career, and yet my
path lies elsewhere.

Many times, I have been told the pathway is through my own door,
and this time I am listening. I am putting one foot in front of the other,
and now I am walking through the door. My path is that of God. I am

experiencing God within me. I am God. As are you, and as is all [that] I survey. It is One. There are things called the laws of physics. In faith, there is only one Law: The Law of One. All is one and, with that understanding, anything can be affected by thought. It is more than thought though. It is knowing, and having, complete faith that it is so.

Thus Manifestation can be instant. Healing is Manifestation. Had Randy full faith in the healing it would have taken nothing but himself to heal his eye. My touch was just a gesture that he could put faith in as it was outside of himself. Love and its vibration are the keys to realigning perfection. The fear dissipates and the perfection is realized. We are perfect, as God is perfect. Blessings to our journey as it is also perfect. It comes forward out of love. It is a universal truth that all will hear.

Love. JOHN

John came to Houston to speak to Brenda's group on May 17. Over twenty showed up to hear John speak. Brenda introduced both of us and informed the group that I had written the manuscript for a book about John. I gave a little background and told the story of the reading I gave for John that indicated his connection to Jesus two thousand years ago. Then John began to speak and recount his experiences.

In the middle of his talk, an attractive, petite, blonde-haired woman in her thirties let herself in, quietly, through the front door and sat at the back of the room. She looked a little uncomfortable. Perhaps she was embarrassed for arriving late. It was my impression that she just wanted to blend into the background and not attract any more attention to herself. John immediately noticed an angel standing behind her. It was only the second time he had ever seen an angel—the first time being when he had met Nick Bunick at the symposium in Florida.

John and I were sitting next to one another, at the front of the room, about four feet apart. Even before he began speaking, I could distinctly feel the presence of the Master with us. John said later that he could also feel the Master, who was standing behind him the whole time. As John came to the end of his talk, I could tell he had everyone's rapt attention.

At the conclusion, Brenda stood up. "John, there is someone here tonight who would like a healing. Are you willing?" she asked.

John was caught off guard because it hadn't occurred to him that anyone would be asking him for a healing that night. "Uh, uh . . . I'll try," he stammered.

"Leslie," Brenda called. "Come sit here." She indicated a chair in the center of the room. "Why don't we all send her light?" Brenda suggested to the group.

John watched as the beautiful woman, with the angel behind her, stood up. Leslie nervously walked over to the chair provided for her and sat down, her face slightly flushed. She was sitting about ten feet away from John.

Unknown to us at the time, Leslie had been through an ordeal with some serious health problems. She had been feeling extremely tired all the time and did not have the energy to engage in normal activities. Often she would sleep twelve hours a day, sometimes more, just to muster enough energy to take her kids to school or to run a simple errand. Her doctor had run various diagnostic tests but couldn't determine what was wrong with her. Her symptoms were lupus-like; however, the tests they ran for that particular disease came back negative. She was asked to return for further testing. Frustrated and depressed, it took all of her strength just to drag herself to the meeting. But her good friend, Brenda, who had insisted that she come, told her that John might be able to help her.

Everyone sat up straight and closed their eyes as John led all of us in a relaxing, healing meditation. He asked everyone to focus on love and to send love and light to Leslie, who was sitting in the center of the room. Breathing deeply and sending Leslie all the love and light I could, I suddenly felt the Master, who had been standing near John and me, pass between us and walk over to Leslie. I didn't say anything to anyone at the time because we were in the middle of a sacred moment.

The energy in the room increased greatly, and everyone could feel this huge buzz. We all basked in this magnificent light energy for several minutes. Then John brought everyone back slowly. When everyone's consciousness had "come back into the room," he asked Leslie what she had felt.

"I felt this energy, and I felt someone holding my hands," she confirmed.

"You know He was here and He healed you, don't you?" John said, referring to Jesus.

Both Leslie and Brenda looked at one another, completely overjoyed.

"All you have to do now is accept the healing. Do you accept?" John asked.

"Yes," she responded with tears in her eyes.

"Do you want to know what I saw?" asked John. Leslie shook her head "Yes."

"Through my third eye I saw Jesus, who was standing behind me, walk over to you and touch your hands," John offered.

"Wow, I sensed that, too!" I exclaimed. Two other people in the group, who had sensed the same thing, concurred.

"It's wonderful, isn't it?" John asked.

"Yes," Leslie said.

Brenda gave Leslie a big hug. I could see complete bliss on Leslie's face, and I knew that she had experienced something very special. Leslie shared the details of what she had been through with John. Other people also came up and wanted to hug John and share their stories, too.

After everyone left, John and Leslie and Brenda and I all stayed up talking. Normally, Leslie would have been too exhausted at ten o'clock in the evening and would have had to go to bed, but tonight she felt light and energetic. She laughed and talked with us until two o'clock in the morning. The fatigue that had plagued her for so long was completely gone! She had energy to enjoy her life again. Leslie, whose spiritual background was not particularly metaphysical in nature, became a believer in the power of the divine to heal us all.

———•◦•———

Unknown to me, while John and I were at Brenda's house, I had received an e-mail from Michael Baumann. Earlier that month, I had sent him a copy of the manuscript, so he could correct any mistakes and also give his approval on how I quoted him. His positive response overwhelmed me in its support:

May 17, 2000

Dear Sharon,

I got your book the other day and finished reading it quickly the other night. Now I know the time frame of all the stories I have heard from you and John and can put most of them in some kind of order. I also learned quite a bit that I had not heard before.

You have done an excellent job of putting all your thoughts and events down on all these happenings. I also believe that it should be edited with the most reserving of pen, as this is how things were encountered and perceived by you and John, and that's that.

Somewhere toward the back, you mention that [Jason] introduced me to Sara. Actually, Atira connected me up a month later to [Jason] after she and I met in Seattle at Nick's seminar. I met Nick only as an audience member earlier that same day that I met Atira.

[Remember when] I mentioned that [my Guides] said to get my last name spelled right? Well, at the beginning of the book [on the Acknowledgments Page], my last name is spelled Bauman, instead of Baumann. Elsewhere it is correct. Quite a coincidence, wouldn't you say? I think you should leave it though!

Thank you for the privilege of reading the work in advance. I will be sending Love and energy to assist in getting it out there to be heard. There is an energy behind this that has been dormant for a long time, and when it hits it will be something to behold.

Let me know if I can be of help, and blessings on your mission.

Always in the Light, Michael

When I got back to my computer after the trip to Houston, I was eager to share with Michael our experience at Brenda's house:

May 19, 2000

Dear Michael,

Thank you so much for your support of the book! I can't tell you how honored I am to have this!

John and I went to Houston so that John could speak to Brenda's Messengers group meeting and John was a hit! He shared his story with her group (with me riding sidecar,) and it was very well received. At the end, the twenty-two people present at this special meeting (called just so people could meet John) sent light to a lady who has a life-threatening illness. We put her in the center of the circle and John sent her energy. I felt Jeshua standing behind John and me, and then I (along with two other women and John) sensed Him going to the lady in the center of the circle and putting his hands on top of her hands and sending her healing energy. Later, the lady, whose name is [Leslie], said she felt some warm hands holding hers!

I am very excited for John. He seems to be coming into his healing abilities. Can't wait to see what happens next! John has been invited to speak at another Messengers group in Austin next week.

Thank you for your feedback on the book. I will make the necessary corrections as soon as possible. That is why I must send this manuscript to those who are featured in the book: to correct any misperceptions or inaccuracies. It is important to me for this book to reflect as much accuracy as it possibly can. Thanks again. Your support is the biggest help you can give us!

Love, Sharon

A week later, John and I traveled to Austin to talk to Julia Hanson's Messengers group on May 24. That same day, Brenda sent an e-mail to her group announcing John's trip and the miraculous results of Leslie's medical tests:

John would love to hear from you. He is speaking tonight at the Messengers meeting in Austin. I so enjoyed meeting with him and sharing his experiences. It was really quite a night. [Leslie] went to the doctor the next morning and received a clean bill of health. She truly believes that she received a healing that night. She felt a presence as she was sitting in the circle and felt someone touch her hands. What a blessing. I truly believed that Jeshua was with us. That morning she woke up at 4:44—her first 444-experience. What a wonderful confirmation. What a special evening . . . wish John could come back!!!! He will be leaving Texas soon. This is his last week here. He will be heading for Egypt in [October] with [Jason, an author], and Atira to participate in a very special spiritual event.

When we arrived at Julia's house, a bubbly, petite, athletic woman with strawberry-blonde hair, and a large, friendly dog met us at the door. "Jewls," as her friends called her, greeted us with the enthusiasm of a long-lost friend.

"John!" she cried, as she opened her arms wide to give him a hug. "I am so glad to finally meet you!"

"Likewise," chuckled John.

"And you must be Sharon," she exclaimed as she also gave me a hug. Julia is the kind of person who never meets a stranger. Her heart is as wide as the state of Texas, and so is her smile.

"Well, ya'll come in. Have a seat. So how was your trip? How do you like Texas so far, John?" Julia was a kinetic ball of enthusiastic energy. She sat cross-legged in a big, overstuffed chair with her bare feet curled under her legs, eyes sparkling with excitement. Baxter, her large brown therapy dog, curled up in a ball and lay on the floor beside her.

We talked for the next few hours as if we had known one another forever. She spoke of her healing work and some of the messages that she had been receiving from her guides. We shared our adventures and, all in all, it was a very pleasant afternoon.

Julia's house was beautiful and well appointed, but not stuffy or pretentious. It was the kind of environment in which one feels instantly comfortable, like the feeling one gets when taking in a deep breath and letting out a big sigh.

That night about fifteen people gathered for the meeting. Julia introduced us. John shared our stories and his early spiritual experiences. The group was fascinated, but there was one woman in particular who kept interrupting John and challenging him on almost every point he made. Her energy wasn't particularly pleasant to be around, but the encounter helped John solidify his beliefs, and later he said he was very grateful for this exchange.

John's back had gone out on him due to a condition he has had since birth, so Julia and her good friend, Cindy Shelton, both of whom are healers, had John lie down on the floor to do some energy work on him.

Julia was at his head, and Cindy was at his feet. They were amazed at the size and strength of his aura. At one point, they asked everyone in the room to connect with John and send him energy. He seemed so open and vulnerable, lying on the floor with his eyes closed. I felt very protective of him because of the woman who was being so negative.

Finally, Cindy, who is very tuned into the energy around her, stopped and looked over at me. "I can feel your energy standing guard over John. I sense that you are protecting him." She was absolutely right, and it was interesting to me that someone else in the room could sense energy from other people the way I do. "You're right," I said. "I was."

Then I received the confirmation I needed to let go when I heard John say, "I'm fine." I released my protective energy and allowed the group to work with him. Several people sat around John in a circle, holding their hands out in front of them and sending him light.[36]

Afterward, everyone shared what he or she had experienced, and each seemed to have enjoyed the interplay and exchange of energies. I took John aside and told him why I had been protecting him, that I had been worried about the disruptive woman sending him her negative energy. He assured me that he hadn't been worried in the least, that he felt he had tremendous protection around him. Then I remembered how Sara, the reader, had described it: "The ground you walk on is holy. The angels want to be where you are. Wherever you are, you are definitely protected." I learned some important lessons that night, one being that I didn't need to protect John. He came with his own special protection!

Julia wanted to put John in contact with her friend, author and spiritual leader James Twyman,[37] who had written a book called "The Secret of the Beloved Disciple." She said that John and "Jimmy" carried the same type of energy and knew that they would "hit it off" as soon as they met one another. She e-mailed James a couple of days later to see what he had to say and sent us a copy of the letter.

May 26, 2000

Hi you guys. This is the letter I sent to Jimmy. I talked to him last night during [our phone] class, and he said to email him with the info. I hope I have presented it in a manner that you would agree with. If there is anything incorrect in this letter, I apologize. I love you two, and can't wait to see you again!!!! Please don't forget to drop by, when you get a chance. I love you both!!!!

In Love and Light. Jewls/Julia

Julia's e-mail to James Twyman:

Dear Jimmy!

Thanks for the wonderful session last night... wow.... am still float-ing on the ceiling!

But as to why I am writing . . . I have had [Jason, the author], and Nick Bunick say that you need to meet this wonderful soul I have just had the pleasure of meeting in my home. His name is John Davis. He has the energy of John the Beloved Disciple.

He has had nine incredibly talented psychics (including Atira H., [and Sara] . . .) tell him that he has this wonderful energy. And he also has many of the memories of that time.

They both say that you two probably should meet. I agree and told him I would contact you and give you the information to contact him.

As I met him, I was reminded of the wonderful energy we had in Colorado. He is truly a beautiful soul (and a dead ringer for you—just bigger). I was a bit taken aback when he first came here. I truly thought it was you for a second, except I wondered how you had put on quite so many pounds!!! But he does have that beautiful energy shining thru his eyes.

He is going to Egypt in [October] with [Jason], Atira, and a man named Michael . . . My guides say that he needs to speak with you before this trip. As he was here I had a vision of him being the key that unlocked the energy in Egypt, for the benefit of the entire world. (Actually I had this flood of info from the guides and as I told him what I saw, he simply showed me the passages in [Sharon's] manuscript that I was describing). Nope I haven't read any of his experiences either. Sooooo. I truly believe you two need to meet.

Anyway, if you would like any more info on what my guides said about this, I will send it to you . . . Thanks Jimmy. I truly feel that this meeting should take place. I FELT his energy and it was our (the Beloved's) energy. And as he spoke, the feelings of peace and joy at his words spoke to me in a way that few have. Thank you bud, can't wait to walk on the ceiling again next week!!!!

In Love and Light Jewls/Julia Hanson

John wrote Julia a nice note in return, thanking her for doing such a good job of hosting his talk and how impressed he was with her spiritual connectedness. Julia responded to him with this [the emphases are mine]:

May 30, 2000

Thanks for the wonderful words of encouragement!!! As I am kinda new at this "spiritual coming out of the closet" stuff, that was very kind of you. Oh and sorry about the mix-up on Nick, but as I have met him and talked to Kim myself, I feel they are family as well. And I DO believe that you should meet Jimmy asap!!!!! It just takes forever to get his emails to him.... he bounces all over the durn burn country!!!!

But as to the readings, the only one I am consistently getting is that you are a key to a "Gateway" and some word like Sharinah or Shekinah[38] . . . or something like that . . . . and singing. But YOU are the key that will make this all happen in Egypt. You have the correct DNA structure for the work ahead. I believe that all three of you must have this same DNA structure (of divine origin); however each of you has a different encoding (or gene that is turned on) to do your individual work there. This is so hard to explain. I can see it clearly in my head . . . just hard to write.

Once this gateway is open, it will facilitate the coming onto Earth of the fifth dimension or a planetary raise in vibration and consciousness. This I do see quite clearly. I am still seeing you like (I wanna say turning) turning a huge pillar until it makes a loud clicking noise but kinda cavernous sounding . . . and that turning will then open a "hallway." I am gonna have to think about that one for a bit as it seemed metaphorish for something bigger than that.

Well that is it for now . . . hope this helps. I keep feeling like I am forgetting something . . . but will email you back with it as it comes . . . so this may be a two-parter. LOL

Hope all is well with you and Sharon. I love you both!!!

In Love and Light Jewls/Julia

The next day, Julia got an e-mail from Jimmy saying that he felt he should contact John and had been hearing about him for some time. He promised to call John soon.

———•‑•———

Meanwhile, the buzz about the trip to Egypt continued between those going over and those of us who were supporting them. Julia and Cindy[39] had a powerful channeling session on May 31 with a huge entity who brought a message for John. I can only assume this message was either from the Master Himself or someone acting on His behalf. The following is an excerpt of that session:

Your DNA structure is such that when you enter the hallways of Egypt, your body will automatically vibrate in resonance to a particular tune . . . Your body will be creating a song . . . that will open the door. You are the key. Without you the door will not open. You carry the resonant harmony in your DNA structure. [This song was implanted] within your genetic structure two thousand years ago. More than this you do not need to know at this time.

The song is named Sekinar (or something sounding like that). A rocking trip to Egypt! For some reason [He] wanted me to include that last line to you. Said you would know why!!!

Well hope this helps you . . . I am of course still confused. But the energy that came in last night was truly unbelievable. Cindy's face was flushed red as a beet as she was writing as fast as I was talking. Was probably pretty funny to watch!!!!! For some reason he/she/it wanted me to include that last line to you. Said you would know why!!! So there it is dear ones. If I get any other neato stuff, I will keep in touch with you. (Or even if I don't get any good stuff, I will still keep in touch) Good luck with Jimmy.

In Love and Light. Jewls/Julia

John and I would part ways after our visit to Austin and would not meet up again until July, at the faire in Ohio. Meanwhile, Randy and I traveled around the country with the band and had a mini-vacation driving up to Montana, then over to Pennsylvania, and finally to Ohio. I stayed in touch with my friends via e-mail whenever we got to a campground that had online access, a true luxury when traveling as we did.

Kim Bunick wrote and asked me how things were going. She had returned from her vacation to Hawaii where her fiancé Todd had proposed to her again (officially). I wrote her back to catch up on things.

June 21, 2000

Hi Kim,

I am doing well. Randy and I are about to go on the road again. We finished up at a highland games in Montana this weekend and will be leaving for Ohio tomorrow.

How was the trip to Hawaii? So did you say yes [to the proposal]? (Of course you did!) And when is the big day? Have you picked out a dress? The church? Are you registered? I do love weddings! My friend Lauren's wedding was so beautiful and special. It was it rich in Spirit! I was very honored to be there for her on her special day.

I hope your dad is doing well. I sent him an e-mail not too long ago. I haven't heard back, but I know how busy he is. As you know, I am not one to impose, so I will not bother him about it. I am concerned about his health. He looked so tired and worn out when I saw him. We were not able to do lunch because he was in the process of doing some important work. I just hope he slows down a little, so he can stick around longer. Tell him I said hello and send my love to him. Even though he does not know me well in this life, I consider him a friend, and I care what happens to him.

Send my love to the girls in the office. I hope you all got the picture I sent to you of my visit there. There were two faces missing from that picture—yours and Melissa's! Maybe next time . . .whenever that is. Who knows when Spirit will send me back up to Portland again. Spirit doesn't have to try very hard on that matter. I will willingly return to the Willamette Valley and Mount Hood any day!)

Thanks for staying in touch. I know you are very busy!!

Love, Sharon

Kim responded back that very day:

June 21, 2000

Sharon,

Everything is going well here. My dad has slowed down a bit, and he is looking a little less peaked than he had been. He really drives himself hard, and it has definitely taken its toll.

Hawaii was fantastic! Yes, I agreed to marry him! I am so excited and the wedding is going to be outside in September up at the Columbia River Gorge, which is absolutely beautiful if you have never been there.

I have not seen the copy of the manuscript, but I will ask the girls about it.

I really appreciate all your e-mails and our correspondence. I hope you have a fantastic summer. Todd (my fiancé) and I are going up to the mountains to go camping this weekend. I LOVE SUMMER!!!

Take care, Kim

When Randy and I arrived in Ohio several days later, I replied to Kim's letter:

June 26, 2000 [Excerpt]

Hi Kim,

Randy and I have been on vacation traveling the great west. We are now in a campground in Jefferson, Ohio, which is about an hour's drive east of Cleveland. We will be here all through the end of July and possibly the first week of August. Randy's band and my friend John Davis and his partner will be performing at the same faire . . .

I'm so very happy for you! Congratulations! I asked about your guy to see if he was a "good guy" and both Heather and Beth vouched for him! :) I finally did get to see the Columbia Gorge when I came to Portland this May. Peggy Keating took me on a daylong tour of the gorge and up the mountain. It is spectacular! What a backdrop for a wedding! Your pictures are going to turn out fantastically! My friend Lauren had some outdoor pictures done of her wedding party and, boy, did they turn out great with all the colorful flowers in the background. Just pray for a sunny day, girl, so you can see all those beautiful mountains and the river!

I wish you all the happiness in the world with Todd. I pray that you will have a long and happy life together. I hope your wedding is all that you've ever dreamed it would be! Take care and stay in touch.

Love, Sharon

In early July, I contacted well-known intuitive Judy Goodman to ask her permission to use her name in my book. I told her that I understood that she had an excellent professional and spiritual reputation and that I would be honored to meet her some day. A few days later she wrote back:

July 6, 2000

Sharon:

How nice to hear from you; thank you for taking the time to write. It would be a privilege and honor to meet you one day soon. Where do you live?

Your work would be of interest to me, particularly if you wish to mention me by name in your material. I am accustomed to working with 'drafts' and would appreciate receiving a copy of your work. You are most thoughtful in affording me an opportunity to review the work prior to the release of the materials. If this is about my good friend John Davis then it will be of interest to me.

You may forward a copy to me at this address . . . Here is my phone number in case we need to chat at some point . . .

My schedule is very hectic; do not give up on me if you send emails or leave a phone message. I have been geographically near home this month even though the time has been consumed with many people coming into Georgia to see me. July will find me being away a great deal attending to a very busy schedule. I look forward to hearing from you again, soon.

In light and love, Judy

I was so happy to make the connection with her—someone who was very loved and respected by people whom *I* loved and respected. She was so gracious. I just knew that I would love meeting her some day. I told her a little about myself and that my home base was in Houston, Texas. When she responded with the following e-mail, I knew that my chances of meeting her soon were very good:

July 10, 2000

Sharon:

Thanks for your sweet note. I have always gone into Houston a good bit in my work. I have some real good and treasured friends that live there. Hopefully, we will meet soon, [and] am sure we would have lots to talk about.[40] Give my love and greetings to my good friend John when you see him.

Will look forward to receiving your work and having an opportunity to read over it.

Judy

For the next four weeks, Randy and I would be staying at the campground in Ohio in order to work at the medieval faire. I was able to spend a little time with John during the weekends. We would hang out behind his stage in between our shows and talk about our future work together, his

Sharon Prince

mission and what we needed to do to get the book published. We also did some readings and healings for friends on the cozy deck he had built behind the stage—outfitted with some soft camp chairs and strewn with swords, and various props, and costume pieces.

During this time, and right after the faire in Ohio closed, I was in the process of making final changes to the manuscript. Since I hadn't heard back from Nick to know if he would allow me to mention him by name, I called his office and left a message. The next morning I had an e-mail waiting for me from The Great Tomorrow. I was very interested in knowing what he had thought of the book. I anxiously opened it:

August 11, 2000

Dear Sharon,

We received your call this morning. You certainly get around gal!!! Hope you're having a fun time there . . . .

It is good news to hear you are in your final edit phase of your manuscript. I think it is such a fun, and curious piece of work, so many people are going to just eat it up. It is a really good read. Nick is more than okay with how and what you wrote about him in connection to everything; rather, he is honored that you shared so much and it meant that much. He would be more than willing to write an endorsement for your book if you would like. Just let us know.

Sharon, thanks so much for being such a good messenger and for joining hands with us. It truly does touch us. It is the energy and passion of people like you that help us continue on our mission.

God bless and always keep in touch. Heather

PS: Kim, I know, says hello as do all of the girls. Kim is busy, busy getting ready for her wedding the first of September. That will be fun for all of us.

An endorsement? Had I read that right? In disbelief, my eyes scanned over that word again. I hadn't even asked him for an endorsement and here he was offering me one! I was honored beyond words. I couldn't wait to tell John. "That's really cool!" exclaimed John when I told him.

———•◦•———

The weeks in Ohio had passed quickly, and we were back in Maryland again for the faire, which started in late August. Both of these faires were our favorites, and it was good to be able to see my friend again, though he was busy with wedding plans. He had asked Spencer to be his best man and Michael and another friend, Brian, to stand up for him.

It was probably the most unusual wedding I had ever attended. John got married outdoors, at a state park in Pennsylvania, in an Eastern Orthodox ceremony on Saturday, August 26, 2000. It was the religion of Jennifer's father's family, who had emigrated from Syria. I had driven across Pennsylvania with a friend of Jennifer's, whom she had met during her days in the Peace Corps. The drive through the mountainous terrain was beautiful.

When we arrived, there were chairs set up next to a large tree. Jimmy, John's younger brother was playing on his guitar, which set a nice ambience. I sat next to Michael's wife, Cheryl, who was busy taking pictures before the ceremony started.

The bride and her bridesmaids, who wore pale green gowns, walked down the grass "aisle" in their bare feet. John was standing at the altar in a handsome, black suit. The priest chanted (or sang) almost the entire ceremony in a language I didn't understand, and blessed the ceremony with liberal doses of wonderful-smelling frankincense incense pouring from a silver container, which he swung back and forth. The bride and groom walked around the altar three times. Then the priest, who had a great sense of humor, put a ceremonial crown on John's head and chuckled, "You look like a czar!"

After the wedding, they had a nice reception at the local country club. I sat at a table with Cheryl and Gracie (John's friend who had prophetic dreams; she had flown in from Canada) and the lady who had traveled with me to the wedding. John and Jennifer looked happy together and were occupied most of the night receiving people's congratulations. I could barely get in a hug before the next person came along with ready felicitations.

The time arrived for the wedding toast. Spencer, the best man, had decided to play a joke on John and Jennifer with the help of some accomplices. After he made the official toast to the bride and groom, he followed up with this announcement: "Now that John is a married man, it is only proper and fitting that anyone who still has a key to John's place, return it to him out of respect for his new bride, Jennifer." He held up a glass bowl and set it down at the head table, between the Davis's. "Don't be shy. If you have a key, please turn it in now."

Unknown to them, Spencer had passed out a bunch of keys to several ladies in advance. One by one, each woman got up and walked over to the bowl, pretending to return his key. Then suddenly, one man popped up to return "his" key and the whole room erupted with laughter.

There was dancing and a general feeling of levity. The party went well into the night, but John and Jennifer didn't leave early, as most couples do to start their honeymoon. They actually stayed at the same hotel as most of their wedding guests. Their honeymoon would come later when they would go to Egypt with Michael and the others.

———•◦•———

The next day I returned to Maryland to work for the band. It was the first weekend of the festival. The band only performed four weekends there that year, and then two more weekends at two other faires, before returning to Texas for seven full weekends at the faire near Houston.

———•◦•———

In mid-October, barely two weeks after we had settled back down in Texas, Michael flew into Houston for yet another reading. He wanted to know if there were any last-minute messages that he needed to hear before embarking on this much-anticipated trip to Egypt in late October with Jason, Atira, John, and Jennifer. Michael seemed to be the one making most of the arrangements and coordinating all the details of what would take place once they got there. Like any good tour guide, he was just checking in with the "home office" for guidance before their departure. He didn't have to wait long for the big guy to come through though. As Michael would later recount: "This time Jeshua's presence was instantly there. There was no need to prepare or still the mind, His Oneness was instantly there, waiting to burst forward."

This is the message that I channeled from Jeshua to Michael on October 13, 2000:

Jeshua: Dear gentle true spirit, beloved one, whose heart is wrapped inside my own.
The path lies before you beloved, just walk down it.
Each step you take, in faith, is a testimony between you and I and that greater presence. Many times you have called out, and many times I have answered you. Trust this knowingness inside of you, and know that you have all of the answers.
One day will be soon, and we will stand face to face, and you will speak to me as you are speaking to this person, and all those memories will come back, the oneness, the presence, the love. All of those are still locked inside. Only you have the key to unlock this. Only you have the Oneness inside of you; and you know how to bring this forward, in faith.
This greater heart connection that you seek, Michael, is already there. I am NEVER away from you. You are NEVER not in my presence. We are always walking hand in hand.

The time has come for you to bring forth the work and the knowledge you have inside of you. It is time for you to come forth with what you know to be true. Do not fear, for I am always with you. Trust in yourself, Michael. You know all the answers for the questions that you seek. It is not necessary for you to speak to me through someone else. I am always in your heart, and you are always in mine. We are never separated.

What you have come here to do is a very courageous deed, and you will know the right things to say, and the right things to do, because you will be coming from the heart. The heart never lies. It will always guide you truly.

You have come here to share my heart with the world. It is a very sacred duty, and one I have entrusted you with because I know you are true. You cannot fail me, Michael. It is impossible. In the very fibers of your being is this love energy that knows no wrong and that knows no harm. It is complete and whole within itself.

Your sacred duty is to love and to be loved. You can do no harm, you can do no wrong, as long as you are in that love, as long as you are in that presence.

You are taking a special part of me with you to Egypt, to be completed upon your arrival. On some level, you will feel this union, in the deepest part of yourself. You have come here to awaken a part of this world, and the knowledge and the power.

Things need to be set right; plans set into motion long ago will come to fruition, and all this knowledge will come forth into the world, that all may see, that no one can deny. It will be a bridge of light from the present into the future, but it spans much further beyond that.

Michael: (Question re: Egypt energy work)

Jeshua: The most important part of this journey is connecting the energy of the three. You will be given instructions when you get there. You will be meeting those people at the right times and places that will bring you to the points where you need to be.

You must have faith that everything will turn out as it should be.

The work that you do now will be laying the groundwork for future journeys to Egypt, but yes, something very significant will happen there, and everybody will know it. A powerful synergy, a connection with the Oneness, this will be for all to know and to experience at the same time. You will have no doubts after this journey as to why you've come here. There will be no more hesitations, no more fears, no more doubts. You will know beyond a shadow of a doubt, that you are loved, and that you are in oneness with your Creator.

It is not necessary to have all the pieces of the puzzle set before you at this time. Part of this will be a matter of trust. Too much information may distract others in your journey and your purpose. Know that everything will be set in place, and those things that need to be set in place on this particular trip will be set. This will not be the last time that you go to the Giza Plateau. There is much work to be done there. This is an opening, the very beginning of the opening of the room. There will be other journeys that will seek other passages to other places that you know not of at this time. Other records.

And so it will be. Worry not, for all things are coming along as they should, and I am very proud of the work that you have done, very proud indeed—of the spiritual being that you are and the man that you have become.

Michael. (Question about a very elderly lady friend of Michael's, incarnated from 2k ago.)

Jeshua: As I said beloved, your heart never lies. There is a connection. There is an understanding of what is to take place. Worry not, for nothing is lost. You and this being are fully connected, and you will continue to be connected. Do you understand?

Michael: Yes.

Jeshua: It is a heartfelt thing, and it is all right to grieve. This is part of your human understanding, and all is well.

Michael: Thank you, and I ask for blessing on all of us on our mission to Egypt.

Jeshua: It is so.

Within the next two weeks, Michael would be boarding a plane for Egypt, joining up with Jason, Atira, and John and his new wife, Jennifer, in Cairo. The many months of preparation would culminate with an experience over there that still haunts them today. For Michael, Jason and Atira, this would be the second sacred journey to the land of the pharaohs. For John, it would be his first sacred journey to a land of ancient mysteries and the beginning of a spiritual odyssey—a trip that neither he, nor the others, would ever forget.

CHAPTER FOURTEEN

Sacred Journey

When Michael first received the "call" from his guides that it was time to make another trip to Egypt, Jason, who was knowledgeable in ancient Sacred Geometry, [41] decided to join him. Both Jason and Michael believed that John would be an essential part of this second sacred journey, which Michael now refers to as "Phase II." They invited John to join them as well as Atira, who was a natural escort for the group, being psychic and having done business in Egypt for many years.

Scholars in the study of Sacred Geometry say that there is an invisible energy grid around the earth. Imagine, if you will, a spherical cage with crisscrossing lines, that encases the earth like a shell or a second skin. Within this grid, there are certain spiritual energy spots that are more powerful than others. Sacred Geometry is based, in part, on the location of these power spots and energy lines. Thousands of years ago, the builders of ancient Egypt somehow perceived a sacred energy coming off the Giza Plateau and used this to determine the placement of certain pyramids, buildings and other structures, which would be in harmonious alignment with, and even take best advantage of, one of the most powerful energy areas in the world.

Apparently, when the pyramids were built, these ancient energy "ley lines" were still in harmonious synch with the Egyptian structures there, but in the past few thousand years, there has been a shift, and the energy patterns which made up the original grid of the Plateau were now out of alignment with the present structures, creating an energetic disharmony, to put it in very basic terms. To re-create balance and spiritual harmony, the energy needed to be brought back into its original position.

The objective of the first trip to Egypt by Michael, Atira, and Jason, for which Michael coined the term "Phase I," had been more to determine just where the energy had drifted to—based on the alignment of the original grid pattern—in order for the group to know where to bring the energy back. On the first trip, the three of them had formed an energy triangle, with each person being at one of the three end points, and then they carried the energy to the center by walking toward it simultaneously.

On this second trip—Phase II—the objective was to form an energy triangle in the *reverse* direction of the first. This new triangle would be the same size and shape, only inverted and superimposed on top of the previous one. In other words, if you could see the placement of the second triangle on top of the first, the two of them would appear to form a Star of David.[42] However, there would be one major difference: this time there would be someone standing in the center as the other three, who were stationed at the three outer points, walked, simultaneously, toward him.

The role of the central person would be to act as a grounding point for all the converging energy. The group decided, unanimously, that the only person who would be able to hold all this energy was John.

Simply put, the group's intention was to realign the ley lines for the purpose of activating the higher spiritual energy associated with this powerful place and its connection to other dimensions of reality. In other words, when these grid lines, that run the length and breadth of the Plateau, began going out of alignment, they affected the energy grid of the entire earth. The Giza Plateau needed to be realigned in order to start creating a place of spiritual balance from which the world would greatly benefit.

For some in the group, this work was being done in preparation for the eventual discovery of a secret room, known as "The Hall of Records,"[43] which houses the sacred knowledge of the ancient world. For John, it was a journey of faith that, once over there, he would discover his purpose for going. He had no expectations or agenda other than to do what he was guided to do—in the moment—and to assist, energetically, in whatever way he could.

Edgar Cayce, many years ago, had predicted that the reincarnation of John the Beloved would be the person who would open up the ancient Hall of Records, supposedly located in the area of the Giza Plateau; hence, the interest within the group in finding a secret room in the maze of tunnels located under the Plateau. Another modern prophet named Paul Solomon also predicted that the reincarnated John the Apostle, who would also be referred to as "John of Peniel,"[44] would discover—or in some way unlock— the secrets of The Hall of Records. This room, or chamber, allegedly contains a time capsule from the ancient time of Atlantis[45] and other enlightening knowledge, which, upon being discovered and "opened," would awaken the spiritual consciousness of mankind and have a dramatic effect upon our perception of the world as we know it.

The day before the big event, the group made a pre-visit to the

Plateau to scout out the energy spots to determine where they needed to stand to initiate the realignment process. The group visited each of the four places they would be standing—the three outer points, and the center point—and confirmed with one another that they had each found their correct place to stand.

Atira would stand at the point of the triangle where the feminine energy was the strongest—northwest of the two larger pyramids, Khufu—the Great Pyramid—and Khafre. She would have to take the most circuitous route to the center, zigzagging around several buildings along the way.

Michael would stand at the northeastern point, in an area known as the Mastaba, where the burial grounds are located. The only evidence of life in this deserted place were the local horsemen that traveled down a coarse road back to the tourist area.

Jason would stand at the southern point of the triangle. He would have the quickest, most unobstructed route to the center, where John would be standing. John's spot was east of the second largest pyramid, Khafre, and south of the Great Pyramid, where the southern edge of Khafre and the eastern edge of Khufu make a right angle. He would stand facing the central area between the two pyramids, which was west of and behind the Sphinx.[46] (Jennifer planned to spend the day on her own, touring the sites, as the others did their spiritual work.)

The next morning they all shared a taxi to the Giza Plateau, but each had a different attitude on the way there. Jason was as solemn as a soldier going to war. He had no time for frivolity. John, on the other hand, was completely the opposite, cracking jokes the whole way. Atira, the seasoned pro, was nonchalant, having made the journey numerous times over the years. Michael, the detail organizer, was giving the rundown of how the scenario would go, and making sure that everyone knew exactly where he or she was supposed to stand and what they were to do once they got there. To make sure that this event took place exactly as planned, he had procured four special watches that were exactly synchronized with one another, down to the millisecond. He didn't want to leave anything to chance. Just as the cab pulled up to the visitor's entrance near the Sphinx, Michael handed everyone a watch.

In spite of John's joking around, he knew he had come there for an important purpose, but he wasn't worried in the least. He trusted that things would happen exactly as they were supposed to. "You need to stay on this planet, John. Don't check out," warned Michael. "We will be there to try to hold you here in this dimension."

"Oh, I don't plan to check out," reassured John, who after all, had just gotten married and had every reason to stick around.

Everyone climbed out of the cab and stood for a moment surveying the vast desert around them, the Great Pyramid looming in the horizon. This was it. The time had come. After a brief pep talk from Michael, and a reminder for John to visualize a column of light coming straight up out of the ground from where he would be standing, they all began to walk to their predetermined spots. Their various treks would take up to half an hour, except for John's, whose spot was the closest to the entrance. As Michael described it, "We were walking up and down in all these rolling little hills in the Plateau. It's not flat like one would think." As John walked to his place behind the Sphinx, he watched as Atira disappeared out of sight. He would be facing in her direction and concentrating on her the whole time.

Jason reached his place rather quickly and had the longest time to wait before they began their walk to the center. Michael took his walk at a brisk pace and entered an area that was not usually frequented by tourists—a ditch near the horse trail. He hoped to be somewhat inconspicuous as he meditated there for the few minutes before walking. Atira had to weave her way around the second largest pyramid and in between many building ruins to reach her spot.

John stood at his place and began meditating several minutes before the start time. He would be the lightning rod that would sustain and hold the energies coming from the other three as they brought those energies to the center. He wanted to be all set before the others began.

The anticipation was building as the start time neared. Everyone kept checking their watches. They couldn't afford to let their attention stray even for a minute. It was important for all of them to start at once, so the energies could converge equally.

About five minutes beforehand, a local spotted Michael standing in this ditch and began to question why he was there. Michael couldn't allow his attention to wander, and so tried to ignore this person for as long as he could while he prepared. It didn't work. The man came closer, so Michael gestured with his hands in front of him, palms facing outward as if to say "Leave me alone." When that didn't work, Michael made a gesture with his hands which indicated prayer. Finally, the man backed off. With his eyes barely open, Michael looked at his watch. One minute left. It was about to begin. He took a deep breath. He was feeling a little anxious about timing his arrival to coincide with the others and would be impeded only by the up and down of the hills he knew he had to face. The terrain would be challenging, and he knew he had to walk fast.

Atira was hot and tired. It had been a hard trek for her. She wondered how she was going to make it to the center on time in light of the fact that she had the most convoluted route.

Jason was getting nervous as the hour approached. For him, it seemed as if time were moving in slow motion. Everything they had planned for and had worked toward these many months was about to culminate in just one minute.

Meanwhile, John had begun to meditate in order to center his energy before the others began their walks. About fifty feet away from where he stood was a little building where several local men were congregated. One of these was a tourist policeman. As John closed his eyes to meditate, he could feel the policeman walk up to him and stand fewer than two feet away. He could feel the man eyeing him closely.

John had been warned that this might happen. Jason had suggested to the group that if any of the tourist police tried to bother any of them while they were standing and waiting, they should say that they were meditating. For some reason, that term wasn't working for John, so when the policeman asked him what he was doing, he said, "I'm praying."

"How long?" inquired the policeman.

"Soon," John replied.

"Soon?" the policeman asked.

"Soon," John responded.

The whole time that John stood waiting for the others, this policeman was standing right by him.[47]

Finally, the appointed starting time arrived. Michael, Atira, and Jason, from their various spots, began walking toward John at the same time. Atira began her long walk, as she headed straight toward the pyramid that stood between her and John. She struggled with maintaining a good pace as she wasn't feeling well. Jason had a straight shot to John. He had to walk very slowly, so as not to get ahead of the others. Michael had to walk really fast across the Plateau, up and down over the many rolling hills, which, of course, added distance to his walk.

As each began their individual treks, they each could feel this powerful energy that they were carrying with them. Michael describes it like this: "It was like I was carrying this energy column with me the whole way. It was about six feet in diameter and twenty or thirty feet high." The others described feeling wave upon wave of energy as they walked.

Meanwhile, John had been meditating the whole time. He described to me what it felt like before everyone started walking toward him:

John: The way I described it is kind of funny. Imagine if you were in a gigantic bag of
popcorn and everybody—like twenty, thirty people—was standing around
outside this gigantic bag of popcorn and all of them pushed at once from every
side. It was like a big push of popcorn. So I feel this giant push and I looked at
my watch and it was exactly nine o'clock, the moment when they started
walking. I felt it pulse. As they kept coming, I kept focusing on Atira. I kept
thinking of Atira . . . focusing on Atira . . . thinking of Atira. Meanwhile, the
pressure is building and getting bigger and bigger, and I'm starting to get really
woozy, really out of it.

John had been standing in his spot for almost an hour when the
others started to appear. By the time Michael reached the center, he could
see Jason taking baby steps, as he tried to balance the distance between
himself and the others. Atira had not yet arrived, so Jason backed off a little
and waited. A few minutes later, Atira appeared over the horizon and, with
all the energy she could muster, pushed herself on toward the center. All
three of them started to converge upon John from a near distance. John was
standing there, eyes closed, doing his meditation.

As the other three approached him, John was struggling to remain
conscious. He had no idea that he was causing a crowd to gather around him.
All he was aware of, at the time, was the policeman standing next to him:

John: And so [the policeman] stood there right beside me and then [Jason] and Michael
come up behind me. So, I'm behind the Sphinx facing the second pyramid.
[Jason] comes up to my back left [at a] forty-five [degree angle], and Michael
comes up to the back forty-five on my right. And of course, I am facing where
Atira is. They come up behind me. Meanwhile, at this point, I am half way out
of my body. I'm not really fully coherent.

As Michael approached he became very concerned when he saw John:

Michael: As I came over the hill, I see John. And there's a crowd around him already. He was
out of it. He's just beet red and sweating profusely. He was rocking in a circular
movement, in all directions. You would think he was the Leaning Tower of Pisa in
high winds, and you could just see that the energy was just pouring through him.
[Jason] was standing back about twenty feet [as I approached]. I could see Atira
maybe about a hundred yards away. [Jason walked up another fifteen feet and]
remained five feet away, waiting for the other two of us to show up.

Although he was moving all over the place, John couldn't feel his
body or what it was doing. He was rocking back and forth, going back on
his heels and then up on his toes, back on his heels and back up on his toes.
He seemed to defy gravity.

As Michael, Jason, and Atira approached John, they tried to keep people away from him, but one person who wasn't budging was the policeman. John was almost out of his body when he heard Jason say, "Can you leave us?"

Just before John lost consciousness, he recollects the following:

John: I'm almost out of my body, but I'm still there. [Jason's] talking to the cop [and he says] "Michael, are you flush?" So then I hear money come out of Michael's wallet. I'm [standing] there and trying to open my eyes to see if Atira's around and [I'm having trouble opening] my eyes 'cause I'm not really connected to my body. [For a moment, I was able to] see her start walking around the corner and start walking towards me. And they walk right up to me and I was [standing] there and I'm crying. Literally, just tears running down my face, having a really hard time with the whole thing, 'cause really, I'm out-of-body, yet I'm in-body.

When enough people had backed off, Jason, Atira and Michael came up to John and all touched him simultaneously, which brought the energy to one common point. As Michael describes it: "If I could have seen it, it [would have looked like] a lightning bolt, coming out of the earth, shooting right through John, up to the stars." For John, it was a climactic moment:

John: The three of them look at each other, they walk in and they all touch me at once. They touch me at once and I fly right out of the top of my head. Poof! Straight up. Suddenly I'm standing face to face with Jesus and just having this divine experience of me and my higher self and Jesus and His higher self. Then I start seeing the shaft of light come out . . .

As John's consciousness shot up out of his body, he lost control of it. From an outsider's point of view, it appeared that he was very sick. The locals wanted to call the hospital because they thought John might be having a heart attack or a stroke. As Michael recounts: "At that point, he went into—for lack of better words—convulsions, still standing up, and just heaving and sighing for three to five minutes."

In spite of all the movement and convulsing, John was still standing because he was being held up by the others. Finally Jason said, "That's enough," referring to the need to get John out of the center, where a considerable amount of energy was still flowing through his body. "We need to break *now*. We've done our joining of the energies. It's aligned properly."

In order to release John from the energy that still held him, they all pushed him backwards, out of the shaft of light—invisible to the naked eye, but felt by those present. John fell to his knees and was immediately surrounded by thirty to forty policemen. As John puts it: "They were all around us and they were freaking out. So here I am having this issue and they're, like, trying to make sure I'm okay."[48]

Michael describes John's recovery process:

When we finally finished, as soon as we broke, John dropped to his knees. It probably took fifteen to twenty minutes [for him] to recover anything at all, where he could [even] start speaking. At that point, he did a small bit of channeling. He said he was set up to be a beacon for [this] time frame, so the time frame would have an alignment to know where to come back [to], when we did this type of thing—when he showed up here in this life time. It was a beacon, a time frame, an alignment point on the energy grids. So it would know where to find him and where to pick up. He did say that something was activated and that the Prince of Peace built the grid. There were a lot of very long pauses between each word. I believe he was too out of it to be an effective channel at the time. It was probably more than he should have handled, but he did make it through it.

Finally, Jason said to the others, "We need to get him out of here. We're making too big of a scene." As the four of them started walking up this hill to leave, they encountered a little Muslim man who had witnessed the whole thing. He came up to John with a huge smile on his face. He touched his heart and pointed to the sky. "Allah!" [God!] he said. He pointed to John and touched his heart again. "Allah! Allah!" This was a huge confirmation for John. It was like this man knew John had just touched God.

As they were ascending the hill, Atira was having a hard time walking. John's instinct was to reach out and assist her. "Here, I'll help you," John offered. "Oh no! Don't touch her, John," warned Jason. "You're just buzzing with energy right now."

Within a half-hour, they were leaving the Giza Plateau, taking the twenty-minute cab ride back to their hotel, located right on the Nile River. John could not really enjoy the beauty that surrounded them. He was completely wiped out. He looked like he had just done hard labor. When he got to his hotel room, he collapsed on the bed from total exhaustion and slept soundly for sixteen hours.[49] He didn't show himself again until the next morning.

The next day, everyone got together to recap and process the events of the previous day. John's wife, Jennifer, who had not participated, was filled in on the details of their experience over breakfast.

What really happened there? It is Michael's belief that they opened The Hall of Records energetically, which may preclude the actual need to physically open The Hall of Records later. John agrees with this. Michael later shared his thoughts with me on this subject in an interview I did with him. The following is an excerpt:

Michael: After [our energy work on the Plateau], the feeling was that Egypt was done for now, that the energy was aligned. People say The Hall of Records was a physical opening. I believe The Hall of Records was a dimensional opening and a realignment of the energies. From my perspective, I believe it was completed, and for now, Egypt is as it needs to be: as much as [the energy grid] can stand, as much energy that can be sustained at this point.

Sharon: So does this mean a dimensional opening, which will happen later in the physical?

Michael: Yes, possibly. But I believe it was something that was planned long ago. Something we certainly agreed to when we came here. And it was a quest that I had to do, probably since '92 or '93. At this point, it felt like this is the accomplishment [of that goal]. It was a little bit difficult to accept that all that needed to be was an energy opening. But that [recognition and acceptance] came in time and definitely resonated [with me], that it was an energy opening, not so much a physical opening.

Cayce said that John's biggest work would be opening The Hall of Records. John agrees with Michael that it happened on an energetic level and it may or may not happen on a physical level, but it has already been opened. I personally believe that the energy work done there has set into motion events that may culminate in an actual finding of the physical place sometime in the future.

Whatever the case, something profound did happen over there, and everyone has been changed by this experience, each in his own way. Atira, who has been in close communication with her guide ever since she was a small child, lost contact with him for two and a half to three days after the event on the Plateau. When her guide finally came around, he explained that her vibration level had increased so significantly that it was necessary for him to make energy adjustments to himself, so that he could continue to speak to her.

John's healing abilities have increased ten-fold since his experience in Egypt and his connection to the Master is stronger than ever, but he has not spoken much of the things he experienced when he saw Jesus, even to me. To this day, I feel that the communion with Jesus was so intimate, so personal, and so extraordinary that his conscious mind is not yet fully aware of everything that took place during this exchange. It is my personal belief that the details of Christ's Second Coming were revealed to him and instructions and guidance for John's personal mission were also given.

Back home, some of us could intuitively feel that something significant had taken place. I could sense when the work had been completed on the Plateau the day it happened. I was going about my business when suddenly I looked up and said to myself, "Wow, something major just happened over there." I later confirmed with John that it was the same day that they did the energy work.

Meanwhile, a good friend of John's had a profound dream during the time of the energy convergence. In her dream, she was walking along on what seemed like a bridge in some giant, black expanse. All of a sudden this huge surge of white light came rushing forth, like a wave, from one side of this expanse across to the other. She felt this energy flow around her and heard a voice say, "I'm with you now."

Some friends of Atira also experienced "something" during the time that John and the others were doing the work over in Egypt. One of her friends called her and asked, "What did you do over there? We all felt a huge shift!"

The group stayed on a few more days, visiting the King's Chamber in the Great Pyramid, the Temple of Saqqara, and other sites. On the eleventh day, Jason, Michael and Atira were on a plane heading back home, but John and Jennifer stayed on for another ten days. At last they were alone, and, for the first time during the trip, it felt like a honeymoon. They went south to visit the mysterious and exotic places of Karnak and Luxor. Their trip culminated with a climb up Mt. Sinai.

While John was lingering in this idyllic setting, those of us back home anxiously awaited his return, eager to know everything that had happened. We just had to be patient, but three weeks seemed like a very long time!

Michael called me when he got back to give me a brief overview of the trip. No, they did not discover a secret room in the tunnels, he confirmed. My first thought was, "Then what was that 'mumbo jumbo' reading I gave John about?" The only answer that I could think of was that it might refer to some future trip to Egypt that John would make. Michael described John's rocking back and forth and how they had brought him back to the hotel afterwards to recover. It might even have been a disappointment for some that they didn't discover The Hall of Records, but I knew that something very significant had happened over there because I could feel it.

Another cue was the fact that John couldn't remember a lot of it nor was he especially inclined to want to explore it at first. Although he did his best to convey the details of what he had experienced that day on the Plateau, more of it would be revealed to him in bits and pieces over the next several months. He did ask me for a reading, though, to help him put into perspective what his purpose for going to Egypt had been. He wasn't knowledgeable of, or even invested in, any of the Sacred Geometry the group had used to locate the energy on the Giza Plateau. He wanted to know what he had really accomplished over there. Curious to know myself, I was only too happy to receive a channeled message from the Master regarding this subject. The following is a reading I did for John on December 5, 2000:

> Beloved one. You have stepped forward to the plate. You have called on my name and in faith you have been guided. You have appropriately withheld information until the time is right to share it with others. Some of the things, which have been revealed to you, are in strictest confidence. You will know when the time is right to share these precious and sacred things. Your memory is whole, but a part of you is healing with this sacred knowledge.
>
> You know in your heart that the things you have heard are true. It is your duty to hold sacred any and all information that is revealed to you concerning our union. Things will be revealed to your conscious mind when the time is right and not before. There are many clamoring for details. These details are not theirs to know. Although it would satisfy their curiosity, the divulgence of such things would not fulfill the wholeness of the plan and would not be wise.
>
> The need to hold these sacred principals and truth in a place of confidence supersedes any need to rush forward with information that has not had time to mature. You must seek those principals and truths that would support the experiences that you have had. [This is how] you will find the peace you seek.
>
> There is someone who will be assisting you in awakening these memories and experiences that have been recorded in your soul. You must find this person and seek her out. She will be of utmost benefit in helping you piece together the pieces of the puzzle. You already know her and trust her. Seek her counsel.
>
> We must wait until you have uncovered those memories and experiences before we can proceed any further. They [the memories] hold the key to the next step. You were given solid instructions as to how, why and when you will open the sacred door. You will bring others with you—those who have been chosen, hand-picked for this assignment. It is your honor and duty to lead these precious souls to assist in the awakening of the soul of mankind. When you have fulfilled this sacred duty, then my return will be heralded.
>
> Do not stray from the path, but be steady in your countenance and bearing. Know that all things come to pass in their own time. It is time to focus on those things [that] require your attention. Take time to listen to your inner guidance and to take instruction. Do this, and we will not fail you. You will be protected and assisted throughout this journey. It is so.
>
> Amen.

I still wasn't completely clear as to what had actually taken place over there, but I found a reading that someone had done for Michael about a year before the group went to Egypt. It was hiding in one of my e-mail folders. I don't remember ever reading it before now, to be honest. The following is a transcript of a conversation between a reader named Joyce and Michael, which took place about a month before my "mumbo jumbo" reading for John. I found this after the fact, and I think this may shed some light on what the significance of the work in Egypt was. Michael describes Joyce as being "highly accurate."

November 11, 1999

Joyce: A few weeks ago I got woke up about [half past two o'clock] in the morning. What I saw was the pyramids. And I [saw] the ley lines, if you will, and the triangle that you all created, then something else popped into view. You guys will have to figure it out mathematically. You'll do this again, and it has to be after the beginning of the New Year. It has something to do with the millennium and da de da. I saw a white line, which was your triangle point that you did, and you've got to do another triangle, and what you've got to create is a six-pointed star. You've got to do the same thing, only angle it differently so it's creating a six-pointed star. Now, why, I have no idea, but you've got to create a star with this, even if the pyramids would happen to be in the way. It may be shorter. The six-pointed star has always been a very powerful symbol. I saw these lines in white light, and then instantly it was drawn into it. It kind of shifted and those lines became brighter and created a star. So, that is something that's going to be an extreme energy point, and I think it has something to do with preserving the earth. Okay, something, somehow, that's going to have a counterbalance to the ring of fire. This star has to be done.

Michael: And you say after the first of the year?

Joyce: After the first of the year. You've got as far out time wise as . . . I think just as long as it is in the next year. When did you go this last time?

Michael: April 13.

Joyce: Okay, you've got the same amount of time from January first, so about eight months. It's something that's important. Again, I couldn't even go back to sleep. It woke me up, I'm clearly seeing this, and, the weight, the...the magnitude I felt was phenomenal. The only thing that I can figure is that this has something to do with preserving the earth. I don't know if this is going to bring in a totally different energy field around the earth, but if it isn't done we're looking at bad things, and remember all the bad predictions....

212   Sharon Prince

Michael: An alternative reality. You've mentioned us finding a tunnel before; anything on that now[?]

Joyce: Now the tunnel is important, but before you even search for the tunnel, do the lines.

Michael: Can we accomplish this in the same trip?

Joyce: Quite probably. Not in forty-eight hours, but if you're going over there for more...

Michael: Ten days.

Joyce: Yeah, ten days, you can accomplish that. But, like I said, that has to be done first. You're not gonna find that doorway until after that is done. That's of major importance. You've got to do it the same way, and you've gotta figure out your points. And it's got to create the Star of David. The six energy points will balance.

(They look at a Giza Plateau map for a minute.)

Joyce: Even if you have to walk around something, get your points so it's creating a star. Like I said, the magnitude of that—I haven't had anything that over-whelming in ages.

Michael: And who brought that to you?

Joyce: Beats the heck outta me. I just said, okay, got it, got it.

Michael: Any idea on our tunnel opening?

Joyce: Again, look very close to one of your points, and very close to one of your lines. [Pointing down to an area south of the center spot.] You may be looking down in here. I still feel it's out in here somewhere.

Michael: [Pointing to the mini structure just south of the second pyramid.] What's the significance of this building here? A couple people have got some hits on that.[50]

Joyce: You could end up with tunnels connecting at that point. Is that a building you can go into?

Michael: No. It's a very small ruin.

Joyce: That very well may be over the connection and series of tunnels you're looking for . . .[51]

As an exciting year full of changes for John came to an end, it was just the beginning of many more changes to come. The next year was a pivotal year for him as it was for myself and many others.

CHAPTER FIFTEEN

The Interim Years

John's marriage in the fall of 2000 brought a new focus into his life, which coincided with an abatement of our spiritual work together. We continued to stay in touch, but the days of our going to Rehoboth Beach for readings were over for the time, and when I did give John readings, they were mostly by phone or e-mail. He continued to heal people when the occasion would present itself, but the vision we had once had of his spiritual work seemed to get pushed aside by other things. We still spoke of our work together, but this was to be a time of transition for both of us.

Another significant event that happened that fall was that John finally got to meet James Twyman, the Peace Troubadour, who travels around the world giving Peace Concerts, especially in war-torn countries. Julia Hanson, who had contacted James earlier that year about John, had opened the door for the two men to meet. As it so happened, James was scheduled to give a Peace Concert on the steps of the Capitol Building in September 2000, during the time that John was performing in Maryland. John was given James's number and called him to arrange a meeting after the concert.

The centerpiece of the concert was a Peace Quilt. People around the world had contributed different sections of the quilt, which were sewn together to make one huge quilt, hundreds of yards long. That day the quilt was laid out around the base of the Capitol while thousands of people from around the world prayed for peace. James gave a concert on the steps of the Capitol Building to those people who were gathered, including John. John said that he felt a huge energy come in while James was singing. After the concert, James spoke to the crowd about bringing peace to the world.

After the concert, John went up to James and introduced himself. "He was wonderful to talk to," John remembers. "I was impressed by the work he was doing, and he was humble in talking to me." John shared his story of John the Beloved with James and told him about the enormous energy he had felt when James had been singing, about which James joked, "No wonder I felt like I wanted to preach!"

After a few precious minutes of talking with James Twyman, the two men said their good-byes. John went away feeling honored to have met someone who was so clearly on his spiritual path and making a positive difference in this world.

In the next five to six years, John and I would basically follow two separate paths, both spiritually and personally. I will touch on the highlights of the interim years in this chapter, beginning in 2001 and going through to late 2006 when John's and my spiritual paths finally started to come back together. Though the delay was frustrating for both of us, we believe that everything happens for a reason even if we cannot see the purpose of it at the time. Looking back, we both now believe the sabbatical from our spiritual work together enabled us to grow as individuals and to mature as spiritual beings.

2001

In January 2001, I finally got to meet Judy Goodman,[52] the most famous spiritually-gifted person to have confirmed John's past life as John the Beloved, when she came to Houston to give a weekend workshop. She happened to know a gentleman, "Bill," whom I had met and read for the previous spring. (Bill has memories of "walking with Jesus" and heard John speak at Brenda's Messengers Group meeting in the spring of 2000. He had come in quietly and then left early, so John didn't get to actually meet him until the following year.) Bill is a reserved lawyer, in his fifties, from a small town in Texas, who quietly does healing work on the side. When Judy found out I lived in Houston and that her friend Bill was coming to see her that weekend, she invited Randy and me to join them both for lunch.

Judy is a redheaded bombshell from Georgia with an endearing southern drawl. She is a completely charming and engaging woman who takes no prisoners with her wit. She is also a deeply aware person with extraordinary spiritual gifts. Sitting across from her was like having some-one gaze into my soul. She playfully gave Bill a hard time because of his serious nature, all the while winking in my direction.

I had never met someone whom I felt could completely penetrate my aura and read me the way I read others until I met Judy. In fact, there was quite a bit of telepathy going on between us at the table. I felt she could read my thoughts as I looked into her bright blue eyes. At one point, we even broke out laughing, for no apparent reason, as if sharing a private joke. I felt that Judy was a dear friend from long ago—like I had known her all my life. (Later, I would ascertain through Spirit that she had been one of my teachers and spiritual mentors from a past life.)

The feeling of knowingness I felt with Judy was mutual. She looked deep into my eyes and told me that she could see the important spiritual work that lay ahead of me. Her words gave me a chill that went right to the core of my soul. I felt humbled by this as it was coming from a great spiri-tual being for whom I had the utmost respect—a master teacher. Before we parted company, she gave me a series of her spiritual tapes and a book some-one had written about her spiritual work with a small child who was exor-cised, called *Enlightened through Darkness*, by Kelly Hartmann. In humble exchange, I gave her a CD of my husband's band's music. I felt privileged to meet someone who can actually see and speak to the Master on a regular basis, and who had, at the Master's request, anointed John into His service.

———•◦•———

During January, John was hired to direct his first Renaissance festival in southern Florida. He had been promoted from the previous year when he had worked as the fight choreographer. John was really in his creative ele-ment, writing some great scenarios and comedic dialogue for the shows, choreographing some fantastic fight stunts, and training a company of young, budding actors who really looked up to him. He definitely has a gift for taking raw acting talent and developing it, which he certainly did that year.

Randy's band was contracted to perform the last two weekends of John's faire. After finishing a show in Vero Beach, we drove down to where the faire was located in Deerfield Beach. I was proud of John's promotion and looking forward to seeing his directorial debut.

Another person who wanted to see John as much as I did was Michael Baumann. He knew that Randy and I would be in Deerfield Beach during those last two weeks, so he scheduled a trip to Florida to coincide with our first weekend there. That way he could visit John, get a reading from me, and enjoy the band's music all on the same weekend.

Michael scheduled a joint reading for himself and John to take place on the evening he arrived. I had never thought about doing a reading for both of them at the same time, but I liked the idea.

Michael flew into town on Friday. John, Michael, Randy and I all met for dinner. Afterward, John and I met Michael in his hotel suite for the reading. The energy created in that room was phenomenal! Perhaps the reason we had a very powerful session that evening was because of the increase in frequency of both John's and Michael's energies after the work they did in Egypt. Since that time, I always look forward to being with the two of them because the spiritual energy is just so incredible whenever they are together! I feel that I am being lifted up, and I always seem to learn something new each time I read for them, like I am getting another piece to the spiritual puzzle. Invariably, the Master will come in to say a few words.

The following excerpt is a channeled message from the Master for John and Michael:

Feb. 21, 2001

Lead these troubled souls out of the wilderness and the darkness. Lead them into the Promised Land—the promise that was made long ago by our Father, [that] the day of awakening would come. That all those blessed souls would return at this time, would be activated, and would remember who they were, who they are, and what they have come here to do. Now is the time to prepare yourselves with the one purpose in mind. Gone are the days when you had the luxury of time; the time is now. Arise to the occasion. Trust and follow in me. The plan is laid forth, now it must be implemented, each person playing his part, her part—their roles. You will get your assignments from me. Each person will be given a specific set of instructions to follow. Listen, and report in daily. You will have a message waiting for you. Listen and follow. Trust in the oneness. Trust that we are all connected. The day has arrived; the plan must go forth. What is at stake is the world—very high stakes, but a very large prize. You are my trusted few—the elite of the elite. And [my] trust has been well founded. You will carry out this plan, my plan. And you will touch all in my wake. The time is now; the moment has arrived. Go forth with this oneness, a purpose, my spirit and heart. Receive your assignments and do them well as I know you will. The connection cannot be broken. I will always be here for you. You will hear my voice whispered soft in your ear. You will feel my gentle touch in your heart. You will feel the oneness in your spirit. The communion is complete. It is there that you will meet me. You will know. You will know me.

The next day Michael came to the faire to hang out with all of us as he has done on many occasions since then. Getting to see John and my husband's band perform at the faire on Saturdays is always a bonus for him as he is quite the musician himself and loves the bagpipes. On Sunday, he flew back to St. Louis.

I got to observe John's directing skills for the first time that Saturday. I was impressed with the way the actors really looked up to him. John is a quiet, confident leader, a very good listener, and he makes good judgment calls.

Just how much the actors admired him was made clear on the last day of faire at the pub sing. The performance company surprised him with the ultimate compliment: they paid to have him "roasted" for a half-hour by an actor who brilliantly uses an outrageous mixture of eloquent Shakespearean prose and graphic bawdiness. The word got out, and a large crowd gathered to watch. The whole scenario amused John, and he chuckled the whole time. It was obvious that the entire cast adored him, and I was happy for his success.

When the faire ended that weekend, Randy and I headed back to Texas and John went on to direct the Renaissance festival in northern Florida in March. Upon completing this second Florida faire, John then went on to Tennessee to direct the festival there, in late spring. We would not meet up again until June.

In the meantime, I worked on a book proposal to send out to publishing houses and contacted Julia Ingram[53], a well-known therapist and the co-author of *The Messenger,* offering to send her a copy of the manuscript, which she accepted and promised to read when she received it.

In March, I flew to Portland, Oregon to speak to Peggy Keating's Messenger's group. It was another opportunity to share the story of John, do some readings there, and to spend time with my friends. I met some wonderful new people in Peggy's group who seemed to really be interested in John's story and who were looking forward to the book coming out soon. Little did I imagine that it would be more than seven years before that would happen!

While I was there, I contacted Nick's office. His schedule was so busy that he was not able to join me for lunch, but his daughter Kim came, along with Melissa, the editor of The Great Tomorrow newsletter. We had missed seeing each other during my last visit, so it was great to finally spend some quality time with these lovely ladies. We talked about many things.

They asked me about the book. They shared with me that they were nearly finished editing Nick's new book, *Transitions of the Soul*. I felt we made a real connection that day.

After my trip to Portland, I felt Spirit nudging me to give Nick a reading from Jeshua. I wasn't sure how to approach him about this, and, to be honest, I was a little intimidated by the prospect of reading for him for the first time. I had heard the stories from Nick's staff about how well-meaning people would call, write, or e-mail Nick offering him unsolicited readings or advice on spiritual matters. I certainly did not want to be perceived as a hanger-on, but the promptings from the Master would not go away. I wrestled back and forth in my mind about it. Finally, I determined that I was going to make him the offer and let him decide if he wanted to take me up on it. I plucked up the courage to e-mail him, first thanking him for his offer to write an endorsement and then offering him a complimentary reading.

He responded to my e-mail in late April, telling me that he would be "more than pleased to write an endorsement" and said that he was "very grateful" that I was willing to provide him a reading from Jeshua. He wanted to know what method I would employ, whether I would write down what was said to me and send it to him or give him a phone reading where I would be "basically channeling Jeshua."

It might not have been necessary, but I felt I should offer him references since he had never gotten a reading from me before. I asked Michael and John to give him their impressions of what it was like to have a reading with me and to have Jeshua "speak" to them through me. Michael was the first to send his letter to Nick, followed soon after by John. Each person's words really opened my eyes to the work we were doing together and put things into perspective for me.

[Abridged]

April 29, 2001

Dear Nick,

Sharon has asked me to describe her readings that she has done for me.

I don't know if you recall me, but I am the person who "came all the way from St. Louis" [to] your Messengers conference in Seattle of 1998. I originally had plans to go to the one earlier that year on the east coast, but Spirit had other plans.

During a break at the Seattle conference, Atira caught sight of me, a complete stranger, and would not let me go. She said that the entire hall [had] disappeared except [for] two fifty-foot angels, and a unique light that was surrounding me.[54] Atira sat next to me during the afternoon and within an hour remembered my identity from [two thousand] years ago.

That evening I went out to dinner with her and Mary Ellen, [an author of miracle books], and have been re-connected ever since.

Atira, [Jason] and [I] have traveled to Egypt twice for energy work on the Giza Plateau, taking John Davis with us on our last trip.

My wife and I have also briefly crossed paths with you at two Whole Life [Expos] in Chicago. You certainly are a busy person whenever you appear in public.

The first time I spoke with Sharon was in December of 1999. I had come to know her through our mutual friend John Davis.

Sharon and I talked on the phone for my first reading. For fifteen to twenty minutes she discussed many things that she felt were happening around me. During this initial period, it gave us time for our energies to attune to each other.

Then she began to channel the Master for me.[55] I have had countless readings in the past, and always felt more like an observer than a participant, but this time it was different, dramatically different. I could feel this energy. Not just coming from Sharon, but rather emerging from my own heart; an uncontrollable Love energy and Oneness that was not just my own, but that of all Creation.

A few months later, I met Sharon in Florida, and she gave me another reading in person. Immediately we could feel His presence in the room. Again, it was not simply Sharon bringing forth this presence, but something in our connection that allowed this Oneness to come from within my own self. As if something that has been lying dormant for many years had instantly returned as if it were just yesterday.

By the end of our reading, the energy flowing forth from our hearts was so strong that Sharon's hands were on fire from the exchange taking place.

Last October I met up with Sharon again in Houston for a second reading in person. This time Jeshua's presence was instantly there. There was no need to prepare or still the mind. His Oneness was instantly there, waiting to burst forward.

There is most certainly something unique when my energy comes together with Sharon's. Many other readers have channeled for me, but none as Sharon does. My connection to her brings out that direct channel to the Master. It brings out my own connection that already exists, with Sharon being the conduit for this Oneness to take place.

His words through Sharon are always kind and gentle, with only the slightest nudging from time to time. Each time he has stressed that I do not need Sharon to hear His words, as our heart connection is still intact from long ago.

The Master has spoken of many missions that he is directing me on in this life, but none as important as sharing His heart.

Again, there is still some incredible completeness that takes place each time I meet up with my dear friend Sharon, a true friend throughout many, many sojourns. I encourage you to search your heart, and consider if having a reading with Sharon is right for you at this time.

Many times I have asked the Master questions, questions I feel that

I already know the answer, and each time His response is the same:

"As I said beloved, your heart never lies."

Blessings to you, and thank you for the many, many seeds of Light you have planted upon this world once again.

Always in the Light, Michael Baumann

I was blown away by Michael's letter! Had our readings really meant that much to him? He was always so quiet. I had expected a paragraph, maybe two, but Michael had poured out his heart and even shared Jeshua's words.[56]

Upon reading Michael's letter, I realized that something very real was taking place whenever I channeled Jeshua, and that he and John could really feel that. In other words, it wasn't just my imagination. Jeshua's words and energy had real and deep meaning for them—a connection to both heart and soul. And this was true for whomever He spoke to. I couldn't imagine then—and I still can't—why the Master has chosen me to be one of His messengers.

Michael's acknowledgment of Nick's courage in sharing his past life and present mission with the world echoed John's earlier letter to him. John, Michael and I are all grateful to him, for he has laid the groundwork for the other reincarnated apostles to share their works and missions as well.

A few days later John sent his letter to Nick:

May 3, 2001

Dear Nick,

I am writing this on behalf of my dear friend and advisor Sharon. Over these past few years I have been going through quite a lot with the news of who I was and with the making of who I am now. It was Sharon's guidance and gifts that helped me through the beginning of this journey.

The first time I experienced the incredible energy of Jeshua's love was through Sharon on a beach in Delaware. The wind was blowing wildly and we were being pelted by sand. Suddenly a calm surrounded us that protected us from their torment. I was surrounded—for lack of a better word—by a vibration that embraced me and comforted me. Sharon then started speaking things that I had never heard before, beginning with "John of Old, John of New." The love of Jeshua was laid before me, with an eloquence and warmth that I had never felt in my life until then.

Over these years Sharon has read for me many times, some straight readings and some a direct channel of Jeshua's energy. Since then I have had a regression [to] that past life as John the Apostle and remembered a lot of that life. The first was the meeting of John and Jeshua. Jeshua walked to John and placed his hand upon his shoulder. John then experienced a glimpse of it all. That it is all love and that was it. Then Jeshua took it away and this is what made John follow [Him]. After the regression I still have a distinct remembrance of that feeling and the energy that comes through Sharon is definitely that.

Sharon has meant so much to me in my life that I cannot express in words. She is truly a person that is here to guide. I would strongly suggest (and have done so to hundreds of people) that you have a reading with her. It is an honor to call myself a friend of so humble a servant of the work.

John Davis

When I finished reading John's letter, I simply cried. As well as I know and love John as my friend, it is still an overwhelming privilege to be working with him for the Master. Our friendship is so natural and easy that I sometimes lose sight of how important a work he has come here to do.

I was grateful to John and Michael for their thoughtful and encouraging endorsements, and I was sure that their kind words helped to assure Nick that he could trust me to do a good job for him. He responded shortly afterward and thanked me for the references. He said he was looking forward to writing the endorsement, and we agreed upon a day and time to do the reading by phone.

The day of the reading arrived, and I was nervous. This was my first reading for Nick, and I wanted it to go well. If I wasn't able to connect to the Master and deliver the intended message, I was going to look really foolish, I told myself. What if something went wrong at the last minute? I squirmed a little in my chair as I watched the clock tick down to the starting time. I prayed one last time, and I felt the Master's energy come through. Intuitively, I felt Him assuring me that He was there and that He would not let me down.

At the agreed upon time, Nick called me for his reading. The Master came in as promised, His energy close to the left side of my face. His words echoed what He had said to Michael and John in previous readings. Here is the transcription[57] of the reading I did for him:

May 3, 2001

Dear Beloved heart, you have been working so hard to affect a change in this world. We do appreciate everything that you have accomplished so far. We are concerned at this time that your energy has been drained. We ask at this time if you feel our presence. Remember the love and the light that we once shared; recall that memory forth at this time. Bring this feeling into your being, let it embrace you and fill you up inside.

This longing in your heart has not gone unheard. But I am

always with you. I watch over you daily, I assist you when I can, when you are able to let me. You do not have to do this alone, for I am ever present, always here willing to assist you. Let your heart not be troubled at this time, but there is a burden on your heart; let it lift.

This is not your concern, Beloved. I will support you in this troubled time. All the worries, cares and concerns are not important. What is important is the oneness that we share. What is important is to take the time each day to commune with me until this Love and this Light fills your being. This is what will sustain you in the months to come. The burden is so much easier when you share it with me.

Remember I have called you forth to this mission and I will not desert you. Those things that require your utmost concern and care will be brought forth and made manifest to you. Those things that are a waste of time or a drain of your energy will become apparent. Delegate those things or let them go. Keep intact the Sacred Heart Energy that you carry within you. Do not let it be scattered and diffused by the many channels of energy and the many directions that your consciousness is going toward at this time. Unify that energy. I will help focus your attention on those things that require your energy, your time and your devotion.

You cannot accomplish everything in a day, and as they say Rome was not conquered in a day or within a year. There are many things to do and many things that may be accomplished at this time. Hold fast and steady to the course that you were meant to walk on. Take the bridge—the time and space. Walk across this bridge while I am waiting on the other side to embrace you. Open your heart. Leave your fears, worries and anxieties that do not serve your higher purpose. Hold fast to the purpose that you are here for. You will be guided in the coming weeks and months to projects that fulfill this purpose.

Listen and be still. Quiet your mind. For this is where you will receive all of your answers. Not after this psychic or that advisor, but from within. The answers dwell within your own heart. I am ever present. You may open dialogue with me at any time. Ask and you shall receive.

This longing in your heart from long ago . . . remember what this felt like. Remember what it was to serve me. You have not forgotten; you have carried this flame forward with great courage and great love. Do not let this flame die out. You must sustain this flame in this existence, in this plane, and in this dimension. That is where your focus needs to be at this time—to be present with that. Bring this love into your heart even greater than before. Let it magnify, reach out to those many who wish to touch this energy, that know what this love is.

You have been cloistered and protected for you needed to revitalize. It is time to go out now and to share this energy. Remember to feel love before you do and to keep replenishing, for this source is constant. It is never ending. You can draw from this well as many times as you wish. Do not be afraid of this; you do have the energy and you do have the purpose. In your heart you know these things are true, and you know that I will not fail you.

Speak words that you hear in your heart and share these with others. You know that these are my words. Yes, you ARE a pure channel of this Love and this Light. You are my messenger; you hear me clearly. Now speak clearly so that others may hear me. Yes, you will channel this Divine Love and energy and send it out to others in a way you have not done before, to a greater extent. This magnificent light will burst forth and reach everyone within your physical presence. This Love and Light will also protect you. It will renew your spirit; it will keep your energy strong.

Remember to go to the well and fill your own cup up first, before you share it with others. You have been forgetting to do this. Sometimes you forget to do this, but you will remember this and you will take this with you. Be the Love and be the Light and know that we are always one.

You will see me again as you did before—very clearly—when you are ready for this. It will be our great reunion and it will take place sooner than you think. Trust [and] know that all will be made known in its right time and in its right place. Go in peace and know that these things are true.

Feel the fire burning within your heart, and let it expand, my beloved one. Trust this feeling, my brother, my soul mate.

Nick's daughter, Kim, followed up with an e-mail saying: "I just read your reading from Jesus to my dad, and it was very beautiful. The Master speaks with such love and it totally comes through! My dad was very grateful for the information . . . [He] already intellectually knows what you said in the reading [is true] but his heart needs to hear it to keep him emotionally up to the task!!!" I was gratified to know that I had been able to deliver the message and that it had been appreciated.

A couple of days after the reading for Nick, I heard from Judy Goodman, who was doing spiritual work in Peru and was soon to return to the States. She e-mailed me some words of encouragement: "Glad Nick got the confidence to work with you. I hope you blew him away, as I am sure you did. Of course, when it is J.C., you don't have to worry about it at all. But I know this was difficult for you and I am so proud of you."

She was absolutely right on both counts. It did take a lot of courage to go through with it, *and* I should have remembered that when I channel the Master, I don't have to work hard at all. All I have to do is allow His energy and words to flow through me. It is always an intensely loving, calm, yet strong energy that envelops me when I communicate for Him. I truly believe that anyone can connect to Him if they are truly open to this. All they have to do is ask for His presence.

———— •◦• ————

John finished up directing the faire in Tennessee at the end of May and drove his truck to the campground in the Dallas area, where Randy and I, and John's wife, Jennifer, were staying during the run of the faire in Waxahachie. Jennifer had been staying in their fifth wheel trailer while she was selling her beaded jewelry at the faire. Now she needed John to bring the truck so they could tow their rig back to Ohio.

John's coming back to Texas was the perfect opportunity to make another speaking appearance at Brenda's in Houston. Several people in her Messengers group had been waiting for over a year for him to return. Since he was only a four-hour drive away, Brenda invited him to speak again at her house on a Saturday. John accepted, and in turn, invited Michael Baumann to join him.

John and I drove from the Dallas area down to Houston that Friday, and Michael flew in from St. Louis to meet us there. Brenda graciously offered to put us all up in her home, which was very convenient for the work John and Michael would be doing that weekend.

John, Michael, and I were all quite surprised by the turnout for the Saturday meeting. Apparently word had gotten out about how great John's last visit had been because over fifty people showed this time, more than twice as many as the time before. Had this been John's first time to speak, that might have been a little intimidating, but this time around, he was more prepared to handle that size of group.

When John had first spoken to Brenda's group, he had been a little nervous. It was the first time he had shared his story with a group, and he was only just beginning to make the transition from comedy fighter to spiritual speaker. It was all new to him. Plus, he had been put on the spot to heal someone of a potentially life-threatening illness in front of a fairly large group of people, which he had never done before. But John felt a lot more comfortable about speaking and healing now, and he would be sharing the stage with Michael. Now it was Michael's turn to debut his story.

"I was no longer the new guy in the room," John recalls. "I was now introducing someone else. I was the guy who had already been there."

Michael spoke first. He briefly shared his story of his spiritual awakening. It was the first time I had really heard it, and it was similar to John's in many ways. Like John, he had been grabbed and pulled aside by more than one psychic reader and told that he had been the Apostle Philip. After these unsolicited readings, and being told he had been one of Jesus' apostles, and various other confirmations, he did his own exploration of this and finally accepted it. And like John, he had to go through a gut-wrenching process to get there. In both their cases, neither of them had asked for it nor expected anything like this.

Then Michael began talking about their recent trip to Egypt. At one point in the story, Michael teased John about "crying like a baby" on the Giza Plateau to which John retorted in kind. They only spent a little time on their past lives because a lot of the people there had already heard John's story. They rest of the time, they focused on how each person could awaken to their spiritual gifts and purpose and how each could connect with God.

The rapport and camaraderie between John and Michael was great to see. They looked like a couple of old pros, so I was surprised to learn later that they had not planned what they were going to say in advance. Instead, they had agreed that they were just going to let Spirit guide them; and it worked like a charm.

In fact, John was amazed at how well things worked out. "As my thought was coming down, it would feather [Michael] into the next thought, which would bring him up. He would say something, which would feather me into the next thought. The speaking part of the evening just flowed." In fact, it flowed so well, that someone later made a comment that it seemed a bit too rehearsed, which really amused John and Michael as they had never even discussed what points they wanted to cover.

At the end of their talk, it was Michael who stood up and offered healings to all who wanted them. This really surprised me as I didn't expect this from the quiet and unassuming Michael. To be honest, I don't even think John was expecting him to do this. And, although I had never witnessed Michael healing anyone before, I knew he was capable of it. I knew he was a healer the first time I held his hands during our second reading together. In fact, I believe all the apostles received healing training from Jesus, the same way that John received it in that lifetime and that each reincarnated apostle carries that energy forward and is now capable of healing others.

Immediately following Michael's offer, people started to line up. Thirty people stayed after the meeting to receive healings. What was interesting was the way that John and Michael worked together. Michael would stand behind each person, anchoring and balancing their energy, while John would stand in front of them, holding their hands and sending them energy. Every person who touched John's hands received a personal message from him as to what was causing their illness or discomfort; and it was different for each person.

John was not only healing people but doing readings for them at the same time. As he would receive information for each person, he would share it so that each individual would not only understand what was causing their disease but how to change their thinking to support the healing. Coming from a psychology background, it made perfect sense to me, because the mind and body are closely connected. Our thoughts and feelings do influence our health more than we realize. I had to wonder if that was how Jesus had done healings so long ago, by talking to each person before he healed them, giving them the chance to let go of whatever they were holding onto that was not healthy.

Doing healing work with a group this large was a whole new experience for John. Each time he would begin to heal someone, he would ask, "Are you ready?" When the person indicated that he or she was, John would say, "Here it comes," and a great rush of energy would come through his body and go into theirs. "It was just like bing, bing, bing, bing," John explains.

One lady who came up to be healed had watched twenty other people receive healings before her. She had witnessed John receiving personal information for each person that he healed, things he would have had no way of knowing on his own. She had seen the tears flow when people sensed that they had been healed. As John took her hands, she looked up into his eyes with an expression of complete awe.

"Can you hear Jesus?" she asked. In her mind, John was listening to Jesus talk when he spoke to others.

The woman's question surprised and even amused John. He said, spontaneously, "Sometimes he lets me hear his thoughts." This is an interesting concept, when one thinks about it. When John spoke the words he was receiving during the healings, it was like channeling. Later, he would say, "It's like hearing someone else's thoughts and I'm just repeating those thoughts."

One of the women that John healed was a lady who was slowly losing all of her senses. She was losing her sight, hearing, and her sense of taste. John told her that this was happening because her family was limiting her. She was surprised to hear him say this, but heartily agreed. As she described the many restrictions her family placed on her behavior and how she was afraid of displeasing them, John exclaimed in a jovial voice, "To heck with them!" The woman sitting right next to them started to laugh.

She thought it was funny to hear these kind of words coming from the "spiritual" guy. But the message got through. John's "patient" needed to stand up for herself and start living the life she was meant to live.

Another lady who came up to John had a hang-up about money, which was affecting her health and life. She had plenty of money but felt badly about spending it. John was guided to tell her a joke about a spend-thrift couple. When he finished, the woman laughed with tears of recognition and acceptance. All her life, she had heard that it was "easier for a camel to go through the eye of a needle, than it is for a rich man to go to Heaven." John assured her that this scripture[58] didn't mean that money in and of itself was evil, but that it was telling us that what is important is *how* we live our lives, and what we put our value in. "If you are so wrapped up in your money that all you can think about is your money, then yeah, money is your god," he told her. "It's okay to have money, but it can't be your god. If you have money, enjoy it."

One woman got up and walked into the kitchen when the healings began. As she left, John turned to Brenda and said, "I need to work on her." Brenda went into the other room and casually said to this woman, "Come on back in with us," and led her to the living room where John was. John walked over to her, and he and Michael ended up doing all kinds of healing work on her. She had so many issues that she came back the next day for further healing.

One elderly lady, who was sitting on the couch, wanted a healing from John but couldn't walk over to him. When John heard she wanted a healing, he said, "You stay there. I'm coming to you." He and Michael walked over to where she was sitting and ended up having a powerful but fun healing experience with her.

The healings lasted all night long and the energy in Brenda's house was just buzzing. John and Michael worked on every single person who stayed for a healing. Some people had to leave before they got a healing because it was getting so late. It was well past midnight by the time everyone had left Brenda's house. It was then that John took the opportunity to get some feedback from Michael, who had been tight-lipped during the whole process.

"So what do you think, Michael?" John asked him. "How do *you* think it went?"

Michael got very quiet as he does during profound moments such as these. He shook his head slowly from side to side, as if in disbelief. He paused for a moment and then said, in his understated way, "Awesome." He was dumbfounded by what had taken place. The evening had surpassed both of their expectations.

The next morning, while still at Brenda's house, John and Michael took appointments from those who had not had a chance to be healed the night before or who just wanted to have a private session with them. The sessions were again offered freely, but people gave money love offerings, anyway.

The healings on Sunday were a mix of mental, emotional, and physical healings. One young lady was suicidal, and Michael and John talked her back from that. Another lady's husband was abusing her, and she found the courage to walk away from that situation. "Bill," who has memories of walking with Jesus, had come to the meeting the night before, but had had to leave early. He returned on Sunday because he wanted to meet John and Michael privately and feel the connection with them. He was overwhelmed by the energy coming through John. "Oh my God! You are so powerful! *So* powerful!" he exclaimed.

When John and Michael had finished their healing sessions, all of us—John, Michael, Brenda, her friend Leslie—who had been healed the year before—and I went to lunch to recap the weekend, which had been amazing. Afterwards, we all parted ways. Michael left for the airport, and John and I headed back to the campground in Dallas. John hitched up his trailer and left for Ohio the next day with Jennifer. Randy and I headed out in our motorhome for our annual vacation to the West before starting the band's summer tour.

A few days after the meeting at Brenda's house, I heard from Michael. Apparently, he had had no idea that he would play such a big role when he agreed to come to Texas. He believed he was only there to support John's work, but he ended up actually making his speaking and healing debut.

June 5, 2001

Sharon,

I had a great time this last weekend. Thank you for bringing both [John's and my] confidence levels up over these past few years, allowing us to stand there and speak our Truth. You had a very large part indeed! I hope your students made you proud.

I tried to acknowledge your special talents in channeling, without sounding too much like a paid advertisement. Hope that was enough to get a few more people interested in contacting you for a reading. However, as you know, many may feel intimidated or unworthy of speaking with the Master.

Thank you again for being there, and supporting us in many, many ways.
Blessing from my heart to yours, Michael

I thought it was ironic that he referred to himself and John as my "pupils." Nothing could be farther from the truth, in my mind, but it was Michael's way to humbly give credit to others.

Randy and I did quite a bit of traveling with the band from June to August, but I managed to keep up e-mail correspondences with Nick's staff and with John and Michael over the summer. About a month and half after we left Texas, I heard back from Julia Ingram, to whom I had sent a copy of my manuscript earlier that spring. In spite of her busy schedule and working on a new book herself, she took the time to read the original draft of *John of Old, John of New*, and to comment on it.

July 13, 2001

Dear Sharon,

I finished John of Old, John of New last night. I really enjoyed reading it ... it felt like a family reunion to me with all of your communication with Nick (can't mistake his writing style) and sweet Kim, Atira and Jaquie Ellis and others. It took me back to those heady years in Portland when all of our synchronistic events occurred.

I'm naturally curious how John and you are doing these days and whether you feel as strongly that all the Apostles are still going to gather?

Do you have a publisher or are you self-publishing as we did with *The Messengers*?

Thank you very much for sharing your interesting story with me. Blessings to you on your continued journey and for your sweet spirit of service.

Love, Julia Ingram

P.S. I forgot to comment on a portion of your book that really hit me. [In Chapter 11] you wrote about the split of men and women during Jeshua's time. It was a profound event and one that heralded the abuse of power of the Christian religions in my opinion. In my book, *The Lost Sisterhood* (which has not been published [yet]), I spend a lot of time examining that split, which you described very well. Thanks for that, and for understanding that balance must be restored. Jeshua was in balance and [He] taught that to come to the Kingdom (oneself) the male and female must be one.

I also enjoyed reading about your regression with Dr. Borg.

Best, Julia

By the time I met up with John again at the Maryland Renaissance Festival, I had submitted book proposals to five different publishers, and of those five, only one took the time to respond to me. I knew that before I would feel good about pitching the book again, I would need to have John read through the manuscript one more time to edit it and to add more of his personal comments and quotes. But tying him down long enough to get that done was another matter. He had a lot going on.

On Tuesday, September 11, I was sitting in a dentist's office in Annapolis, Maryland, having my tooth worked on, when the news broke about the terrorists' attack on the World Trade Center. The nurse rolled in a television, and I watched in horror and disbelief as the Twin Towers fell before my eyes. It was an event that would forever change history and send shock waves around the world. Ironically enough, three days before 9-11, John and Spencer had been invited by the Armed Forces Entertainment (which contracts for the USO), to bring the Hack and Slash Comedy Show on tour with the USO that winter. The timing of this seemed divinely planned. Now, more than ever, the world needed John's message of love and also his healing presence.

When the Maryland faire ended in late October, Randy and I headed back to finish out the season in Texas, and to get ready for a big trip the band was taking—with some of their fans—over to Scotland in late December.

———————————

At the end of November, John and Spencer began a thirty-four-day Christmas tour of Europe with the USO that would take them to military bases in England, Germany, Belgium, Norway, and The Netherlands. John would miss spending Christmas with Jennifer that year; instead, he would be spending it with Spencer in Amsterdam. On New Year's Eve, they found themselves celebrating with a group of fun-loving Bavarians on a secret military listening post in Germany. After an exhausting five weeks of shows, they returned home on January 4.

While John was still in Europe, Randy and I left with the band and a group of fans for Scotland the day after Christmas. We were over there for a total of ten days, visiting castles, monuments, seeing the countryside and performing for the locals at a traditional Hogmanay Celebration on New Year's Eve in Glasgow. Scotland is beautiful even during wintertime, and we enjoyed the sights and the company of some great people there. Ironically, John and Spencer returned to the States the same day we did.

2002

The year 2002 ushered in a new era. There were changes in Randy's band. One member left and a new one came on board, which changed the stage presence of the band quite a lot, but in a good way. I took a much-needed sabbatical from my involvement with helping to run the day-to-day business for the band. John turned his attention to trying to start a new entertainment business specializing in stage combat. The new year would not bring much progress on the book. Any attempts to finalize the re-editing of the manuscript with John fell short of the goal that year.

At the beginning of 2002, I was having some health concerns. The doctor told me I had a tumor, but I did not want to have the major surgery that the doctor recommended, so I reached out to John for guidance, reassurance, and healing. He sent me an e-mail with a surprise message from the Master:

> January 18, 2002
>
> Hey Sis,
>
> In the words of a good friend of ours, "This illness comes not for you, but for the glory of God":
>
> My dear child, know that nothing comes without reason and sometimes it comes for the most significant [of] reasons. The reason for this at this time is to show the true nature of healing and how fitting that it should come to one who will then put it into words. Do as thou art instructed, by those of science, but know that even in the asking art thou healed. When the time comes for secondary tests they will find there is no need for more; for that which is will not be. Even as my beloved friend writes these lines, art thou healed. Bless you for the work you do and for this demonstration of God's love. You have far more to do before your reunion. Blessings of Love surround you. Be at peace all is well. I love you.
>
> Well what else can I add, but I love you too. I am always amazed when this stuff happens. I can only say that what a selfless deed you have agreed to do. I commend you. Talk to you soon.
>
> LOVE JOHN

As soon as I read those words, I knew everything was going to be okay. If the Master said I was healed, then I was healed. I think this was John's first-ever e-mail healing. As of this writing, I have not needed the recommended surgery and that was six years ago!

In February, Randy and I were off to Florida for a big celtic show that I helped manage, but it took its toll on me. When I returned to Texas later that month, I felt emotionally and spiritually drained. I called up Julia Hanson in Austin and asked for an energy healing session. She said that she would be glad to give me one and that Julia Ingram would also be at her house during this time, if I wanted to get a past-life regression with her as well. How could I pass up the chance to have a regression with the therapist who had regressed Nick Bunick and given an account of it in *The Messengers*? So I scheduled a regression with Julia Ingram and a healing session with Julia Hanson.

When I arrived at Julia Hanson's house in Austin, I had a past-life regression with Julia Ingram first. It was very nice to finally meet Julia in person and to see how she worked. She has inspired me to get certified in past-life regression, and her support of my work with John was validating.

The past life regression I received from her shed some light on a relationship I had with someone at the time and gave me insights into my current situation. It was fascinating to actually be able to revisit two lifetimes during my one-hour session with her. One was a young teenage shepherd in ancient Greece, who was murdered because his father had angered a powerful landlord; and the other was a young Native American teenager who was gored to death while buffalo hunting in an impetuous attempt to prove his manhood.

It's always interesting for me to see how our present-life issues can have roots in our past lives. Any time we take a look at an ongoing issue, learn from it and release it, it only helps further us along our spiritual path.

After the regression, I had my spiritual healing session with Julia Hanson. It's always a joy to work with "Jewls." Her talents are quite amazing. While I was on her table, I felt all kinds of high-level energy moving around me and through me. My arms and hands jerked and twitched as she worked on me. I felt the presence of more than one spiritual being in the room. Toward the end of the healing session, I felt "someone" take my hand, and communicate that I had been initiated into a higher level of spiritual service, which could only help me to read better for John and the others whose missions I am serving.

I definitely felt that an energetic connection had been made inside of me and felt woozy and out of sorts afterwards. Julia had warned me that it would take a little time to adjust to the realignment. And she was right. I was barely able to drive back to Houston, and, once I got there, I slept all night and most of the next day!

In April and May of 2002, Randy and I did our normal spring gigs, while John was performing in Georgia and directing the Tennessee faire again. Just as we were heading out for our summer tour in June, John,

Jennifer, Michael, and Cheryl took a trip to Peru to visit Machu Picchu at Michael's behest. Michael had received guidance earlier that year that he needed to do an energy alignment there, and so he invited John and the others to join him. Now it was John's turn to support Michael, and hold the energy for him the way Michael had held the energy for John in Egypt. There are those that believe that the pyramids of Egypt and those in Peru are energetically connected, which would make sense of why John and Michael should do energy work in both places.

That summer, Randy and I traveled to many places. We went as far west as Montana and as far east as North Carolina for various gigs with the band. We finished out our summer tour in August with our return to Maryland by the end of that month. As usual, Michael flew in for his annual visit to the faire that September and to get a reading from me. He would later comment that these yearly readings had encouraged both him and John and pointed them in the right direction for their future work.

"Don't discount the significance of the three of us getting together every year at the Annapolis faire, because . . . from my perspective, it was realigning us on this track. Sharon, you were the center point that brought us back, that got us the connection and almost reaffirmed our connection to Jeshua each time."

"Really?" I had responded, quite amazed to hear him say this.

"Because of the ease with which you could connect to give us direct channeling," he continued. "To me, that aligned me every time. It brought me back and gave me the little boost—that inoculation that I needed periodically. I think we went four or five years in a row, getting together at the Maryland Faire, so that's significant for me, and also, I think, for John, because it was always the three of us getting together. You know what they say; 'When more than two are gathered in my name . . .' It was very important."

John and I didn't really didn't get to see much of each other that season. As soon as he and Jennifer finished working the weekend, they would drive back home to Pennsylvania, where they were lived. John was rehabbing[59] houses in Pittsburgh, which kept him busy during the week. I really missed hanging out with him like we had done in past years. I felt sad whenever he would leave on Monday mornings, knowing that our time together was so brief and that Maryland would soon be over before we knew it, and it was.

Toward the end of the year I had almost completely let go of the expectation of getting any further with the book and turned my focus, instead, on developing new promotional products for the band. Michael would send e-mails, on occasion, asking me how the book was coming along. Once in a while he would send me author's tips and print-on-demand publishing information, but as far as I was concerned, the project was shelved.

2003

The next year, 2003, would prove to be an interesting one. As Randy's band was just starting its usual spring gigs, John and Spencer were back in Europe doing their second USO tour. This time they were gone for forty-two days in February, March, and April. Their tour began in Iceland and took them to England, Norway, Germany, Belgium, and The Netherlands. It was while they were in Norway that something profound happened. It proved to be one of the most extraordinary spiritual manifestations John had ever witnessed.

As soon as they arrived in Norway, a bus picked them up and drove them to the military base near Stavanger. They had to perform their entire show without weapons, when it was discovered that their swords had been lost with their luggage. Instead, they improvised the fight sequences with fist fighting, which actually turned out to be quite funny.

Because there wasn't really a place for them to stay on the base, they had to get a hotel room downtown. This was a nice break from the grind and they had the opportunity to explore the area and do some sightseeing in between their shows.

Right across the street from the hotel was a town square with some shops and an old stone church. The streetlights around the square emitted a strange amber light. Under this eerie glow, the church looked mystical and beautiful. John and Spencer were drawn to it like magnets.

John had brought a small digital camera and began taking pictures of this old church. As he walked around to the side, he saw an old wooden door with iron braces and a Gothic arch above it. Intrigued, he snapped a picture. He continued taking pictures without reviewing them right away. He figured he could always delete any pictures he didn't want later.

Back at the hotel, John promptly uploaded all the pictures he had taken into his laptop computer. He was flipping through them when, suddenly, one image jumped out.

"What the…? What is that!" he shouted out in amazement. An

image of white, swirling mist was superimposed over the picture he had taken of the old wooden door.

"Oh, my God!" Spencer blurted out. "Look at that!"

"That looks like a face," John stated.

"Yeah, not only that, but look at this," Spencer said, excitedly, pointing to what looked like a moustache and beard.

"Oh my God!" the two of them exclaimed at once. Immediately, they grabbed their coats and John's camera and headed out of the hotel, running all the way back to the old stone church.

John describes what happened next. "We started trying to recreate this picture [of the face in front of the door]. So we're taking picture after picture after picture [but the image did not reappear]. We said, 'Okay, how are we going to get mist into this picture?' So we're starting to do things like, I would exhale like [this]. . . [John demonstrated the noise by making a long, deep exhaling sound.] We had Spencer hunched down below the camera, breathing heavily."

Exhaling from all different angles near the camera, they tried to recreate the same misty effect, but couldn't. They snapped frame after frame. One hundred pictures later, they were still not able to duplicate the original snapshot. They did manage, however, to get one picture with a very small amount of breath vapor in front of the church, but nothing even close to the massive amount of white mist that had appeared in the previous photo. "I was hoping something would show up again, but nothing ever did," John explained.

The next day, after their performance in Norway, the two of them went on to their next scheduled show, in Germany. While traveling on the bus, John pulled out the photo he had taken the night before and showed it to Mike, their bus driver, with whom they had become friends on their first tour to Europe.

"What do you think of this?" John asked him.

"I think you got a picture of one," Mike replied.

"One what?" John quizzed.

"A ghost," Mike offered because he had been able to see the "face" immediately.

(John thought he knew whose face was in the mist, but he had trouble believing it, so he was asking others, like Mike, for their opinion. Spencer, from the first moment he saw it, could see that the face that appeared in the misty photo of the church door was Jesus' face. Deep down, John knew that the photo was an image of Jesus' face, but not until he superimposed half of a photo of the Shroud of Turin[60] over the misty image a few years later, did he see the astonishing resemblance!)

When they arrived in Wertheim, Germany, John, Spencer and Mike decided to explore an old castle's ruins nearby. As they were walking around, they came across a part of the castle that looked like a cave. They walked inside this dug-out area; it was pitch black. They couldn't see anything until John used the flash on his camera to take a picture of Mike.

"What's cool in that picture is that I can see two very distinct angels working on him. I can see the one behind him, with wings up, and one standing beside him, touching his heart. The one touching his heart is the most important thing for me," John said, "because that's what Jesus did to me in the regression. He walked over and touched my heart.

"I have seen angels in energy form, like that, but what I find fascinating about [it] is that if you look at that picture of Mike, you will see, right at the neckline, where a white robe stops and where a flesh color starts. You can [also] see blonde hair. It's very faint, but it's there.[61]

"Then I snapped another picture of Mike and what I got [this time] was a shot . . . which I looked at and said, 'Oh, I know exactly what it is, it looks like a misty face, like an angel is now working on me. [The angel appears on the edge of the photo, in the space between where Mike and John are standing.] I have never had [that]. I have had orbs show up in pictures [of me] but I had never had that kind of stuff show up [before].

"For me, I was in a weird sort of place in where I was in my spiritual work. [When the picture with Jesus' face showed up], I said, 'Yeah, yeah, yeah. . . .' I was not doing anything about [my spiritual work] at that point. Spencer said, 'Yeah, but it's *Jesus*.' I was like, 'Yeah, okay.' I thought it might be, but I was in denial about it."

I asked John, after several years, "Do you still think that the image that showed up was of Jesus? "I absolutely believe it," he says.

While John was performing in Germany, he encountered a heavy-set man with a full beard who seemed very familiar to him. One reason he stood out is because one doesn't usually see a full beard on a military base. John kept looking at him, thinking he had met him somewhere before. From across the room, the man was also eyeing John. Finally, the two of them got together and introduced themselves. "I think I know you," John said. "But I don't know where I have met you." "I know you, too," the man responded, "but I don't know where from, either." Both of them were sure they knew one another, but neither of them could figure it out. They finally gave up trying and just laughed about it, but the strong sense of having run into an old friend lingered with John long after the tour.

When he got back home to the States, John sent out an e-mail letter to all his friends and family with an attachment of the picture he had taken that night at the church in Norway. He wanted to get other peoples' impressions of what they saw in the photo.

April 9, 2003

Hey Guys,

I just got back from the USO/ Armed forces Entertainment tour of Europe. It was quite an experience! I got to perform for the wounded soldiers from the war at Landstuhl Hospital. I was at Manheim when the soldier who threw the grenade into his commander's tent was brought in under arrest. I missed Colin Powell at the Supreme Headquarters for Allied Powers Europe (SHAPE) by one day.

While I was in Norway, I was taking some pictures of an old church and an image showed up in one of the pictures. What I find interesting is this was [taken] on a digital camera, so it can't be a film issue. Look at it and tell me what you see.

JOHN

When I opened the photo attachment, I saw the misty apparition superimposed over what appeared to be a building of some kind. Then I saw what looked like the image of a face. That's when it dawned on me whose face it was—Jesus' face!

About a week later, I would do a reading for John about the meaning of what had happened in Norway and Germany. John sent me some questions, and I channeled the answers and recorded the session on tape, which is transcribed below.

John's Reading April 16, 2003:

John, this is a reading for you that you requested back in March . . . in regard to the questions you had about the events that happened to you in Europe. I've asked the Master to be with me now, to be with us. Someone is holding my left hand. I believe it is the Master. He took my hand, which was up against my face, and brought it down. He says, "**Speak the words that I am speaking to you.**" This is what He is telling me.

Dear John. Dear special, Beloved John. We are quite impressed with your progress. You're learning to take our leads in finding paths where you must walk to discover the things you need to know, to receive the confirmations that you need to receive [and to] vocalize

the experiences that you are experiencing. Your participation in this great experiment is appreciated and honored. [This] communication with you is succeeding. You are listening to our instructions. The people you have come into contact with are special Messengers of Light—beings of profound awakening—of the places that you go to. You are being guided to go there, to these places.

There's a special, sacred site in Norway. A church. A church that was built on a sacred spot. This ancient church houses the energy of a very special soul, who has a very special wisdom. The priests of the early monastery understood that it needed to be protected. This area is a key archeological site, but it is much more than this. It is a sacred site. Both the experiences you had there . . .the light which you saw [and] the being which you saw was me. For I am the keeper of this place. There are others who work with me, who stand watch over this sacred spot. This portal is an entry point into the earth, which also connects to the heavens above. This is the place where I will come, where you will receive me—[and] the others as well. This will be the first of many places. For I shall appear to those who have been called to gather there. If you listen, you shall hear their voices, telling you the time and the place of gathering. There will be many places that will need my energy for the fulfillment of the one purpose: to bring peace and light back to the earth.

You must trust what you are getting. You must trust and you must know that we are with you always. Be at peace, my son. The time is at hand. Enjoy your "vacation," for soon you will be very busy with my work. Enjoy these last few months of freedom. For you and I are one purpose, one mind, one heart, and one soul.[62] Others will be coming to assist you in your mission. This man whom you met . . . a very old soul. A very dear friend of mine. He and I go back a long time as do you [and I]. For we were three, a trinity. It was necessary for you to meet this person to complete that energy, especially since you connected with me and that church.

The dove of peace. That has always been your symbol, beloved. The dove, and the lamb, and the rod. Those are all sacred symbols of peace in my kingdom.

Judge not a man by what he does, but by who he becomes on his path to oneness. There are many roads you will follow. All paths lead back to me. Cherish those moments when you and I are alone, and I speak to your heart. Remember these things and record them. For they will be necessary in your work, for you will refer back to them in future times."

Sharon: Okay, John, I'm going to read the questions now. That [channeled message] just came out, so I'm not sure if I actually answered them or not. Your questions were . . .

John: While in Norway I received a huge kick in the spiritual pants! And I have evidence of it!! Will you go in and ask a couple of questions for me?

1) What is the meaning?
2) What's next?
3) That was you right?

Sharon: And the fourth one, I think you wanted me to ask: who that person that you met was, whom you felt you had known before, and why did you meet him. I'm not sure if I answered those questions.

Sharon: [Question one.] What is the meaning? He says that: **you already know the meaning. As a clarification and a confirmation. A work together in the future.**

Sharon: He just wants to make sure that you can see him clearly; that you can feel his touch. We're getting closer and closer to the time where you two will meet face to face, and carry on a conversation as you would your best friend.

Sharon: [Question 2] What's next?
Enlightenment of the world through a series of manifestations, transformations, and awakenings of which you will facilitate by going to many different sacred sites and bringing people with you.

Sharon: The journeying is part of your mission—awakening those people who are working on a high level of spiritual awareness. These will be like leaders. You are like a leader for the leaders.

Sharon: Okay, the [third] question is: That was you, right? I think we pretty much covered that one.

Sharon: The person you met. . . I think he touched on that. I'm hearing the name Mark.

Sharon: Why did you meet him? A remembrance. As if to say "Aha, I know you. I'm awake, too, and you're there." So, you've met another one, so to speak—a person to that effect.

Sharon: The next step? The bringing together of the Ones who knew the Master. Time to start calling those persons in . . .
A conference or a meeting, perhaps, in a central location. A special conference of the Sacred Ones. An incredible reunion.

Sharon: And it doesn't necessarily have to be just apostles or disciples. It could be anybody associated with Jesus during that time, who remembers his energy. It would be like a private, not-for-profit conference, basically. This is not like a spiritual seminar, in the sense that you would sell to the public and have people sign up. This is just for you guys and gals. So, it's time to start planning that. And Michael would be just the person to lay the groundwork for that meeting.

John of Old, John of New   241

Sharon: And yes, at some point in time you must bring [name deleted][63] into the mix.

>It's time for him to fully awaken. Perhaps by being with the others, he will be put into a position of having to come to terms with his personal demons, and in the Light of the Love, understand that all is perfect, and as it should be. Perhaps he can uncover some of those memories that are locked within him, that he is afraid to let out. For you, all of you, are in this together. Everyone served a purpose. Everyone's mission was important [so] that all [the] pieces come together to complete the whole. For without one piece, there is not a whole. Every piece must be in place for there to be a whole. And if there is not a whole, ["w-h-o-l-e"] then there is a hole, ["h-o-l-e"].

(And I know this is the Master and his sense of humor.)

I hoped this helped you John. *I love you. Sharon*

I had no memory of giving John this reading until I found it hiding, almost five years later, in one of my e-mail files. As I was reading over it, I found it interesting that the Master had indicated that the "rod" had been one of his symbols. I had to do research to confirm whether this was true and was very surprised to learn that it was![64]

Shortly after John got back from the USO tour he called to inform me that Jennifer was pregnant. She was due in October, close to the time of my birthday. I teased John about the possibility that the baby might be born on my birthday, and if so, I would get to choose the name of the baby.

That summer John would direct the Tennessee faire again, while performing at the Georgia festival at the same time. This necessitated his flying back and forth every week. It took a couple of months to set up the faire—making out stage schedules, training the cast and setting up promotional appearances, setting up the faire site, and interfacing with vendors. Once the faire was up and running, he would leave it the hands of his Assistant Director, who took over for him on the weekends, while John performed at the Georgia faire with Hack and Slash. It was a very busy time, but he had fun doing it. Of course, he did a fabulous job, and all the actors loved him, just as the ones in Florida did.

After both faires closed, John spent the rest of the summer "rehabbing" houses. He and Jennifer fell in love with one of those old homes, and so John began fixing up the house for them to move into; they hoped to move before the baby was born. During this time, Randy and I were traveling for our summer gigs. We met up with John again in Maryland.

The fall was a busy time for everyone. By the time I saw John in late August, Jennifer was very pregnant. Even though she tried to work at a booth at the faire on weekends, it was just too much for her, so she had to "sit it out." I was busy getting ready to debut a new Celtic show that I was producing and co-directing in late September for my husband's band. John was running back and forth from Pennsylvania to Maryland, rehabbing houses during the week and performing on the weekends. Every weekend, for the first five weekends of faire, John was on "baby call," ready to leave at a moment's notice if and when Jennifer called to say she had gone into labor. (His nephew Eric, who knew all John's lines and had filled in for him as "Hack" before, was ready to step in for him if needed.)

So, every weekend I would ask John how Jennifer was doing and how he was holding up. He looked tired. I could see it in his eyes, but he was also extremely excited about their impending arrival. Finally, on October 10, Jennifer delivered a healthy little boy whom they named Kynan, which means "chief" in Welsh. (And no, I didn't pick out the name!) John couldn't have been happier. The next weekend he proudly showed pictures of his son to all his friends. Kynan is a handsome little boy; there's no doubt. And he looks just like John! I nicknamed him "John's Mini Me."

As usual, the faire in Maryland closed in late October, and Randy and I headed back home for gigs in Texas and Louisiana. John began to settle into his duties as a new father and loved every single minute of it. But before he could get too settled, he would be leaving for another USO tour in mid-November. This tour, thankfully, was short—only fourteen days—but intense. They would be touring the Middle East for the first time, stopping at bases in the United Arab Emirates, Qatar, and Djibouti. The USO/AFE wanted to field-test the Hack and Slash show in a new location to see how it played for the troops. As it turned out, John and Spencer were a hit! Plans were made soon after to bring them back to that area the following year.

2004

In spring of 2004, Randy and I made the regular touring rounds to Oklahoma and Texas. In April, I would return to Portland again to see our friends Jim and Lauren, but this time I brought Randy with me. Our friends had just had their first baby and asked us to be her godparents. We had a nice little godparent ceremony with our friends in the Rose Garden, on a hill overlooking Portland. Randy got hooked on the natural beauty of Oregon as I knew he would. We enjoyed exploring the beautiful Pacific coastline for the few days Randy was able to visit between his weekend gigs back in Texas.

While we were there, we had lunch with Nick Bunick. It was great to get a chance to finally socialize with him privately. During our conversation, Nick asked me if I had time to give him a reading back at his office. "Of course," I said. He asked me to ride over with him so we could talk, and Randy followed us over there.

His office was much like I remembered it, but all his staff, with the exception of his personal assistant, Heather, were gone. He was about to close down the offices of the Great Tomorrow, his non-profit organization for ten years, formed after *The Messengers* came out. His ministry—of giving symposiums, guiding the many Messengers group meetings around the country and abroad, and sending out The Great Tomorrow Newsletter—had touched many people's lives. I felt sad, but at the same time, I also knew that all things happen for a reason. Nick would still be working with charitable organizations, so his humanitarian work would still continue, but not so much in the public eye as before.

As I sat with him at his desk, I closed my eyes and began the reading. It was a normal reading in every way. He asked me some questions about his personal life, which I answered. At the end, Jeshua came through to deliver a message for him. I held Nick's hands so that I could convey to him the strong love energy that I was receiving from the Master, which poured through me to Nick. I was hoping that he could feel it, too. The intensity of the feeling made me cry. When I opened my eyes again, I saw tears in Nick's eyes, too.

He thanked me and offered to pay for the reading, which I declined. "Don't worry about it," I told him. "The Universe will pick up the tab." It had been a great privilege to read for Nick, and an even greater privilege to deliver a special message to him from Jesus. We gave each other a big hug and said good-bye. Before I left, Heather made sure to personally thank me for doing this for Nick. Getting her blessing meant a lot because she had been Nick's personal assistant and gatekeeper for so many years.

———•••———

During this time, John was performing at the Georgia faire, as usual, but that year his touring schedule was much lighter. He did not return to direct the Tennessee faire, but stayed closer to home. This allowed him to spend precious time with his newborn son and to do things he hadn't done in years—like paint. He painted several wonderful acrylics of landscapes and portraits that spring,[65] and continued to rehab houses.

In July, John and Spencer began their fourth USO Tour, which lasted twenty-four days. This time their trip would take them to such exotic places as Kyrgyzstan, Uzbekistan, Pakistan, and Qatar, and into Afghanistan for the first time. They had stepped into the big time, flying over and into war zones, and wearing full metal jackets on a C130 military transport plane. They performed at a very dangerous front line base known as an FOB (Forward Operating Base).

John and Spencer nicknamed this USO tour The "Stans" Tour, because the names of most of their destinations ended in "stan". They brought along their friend Todd, who is a comedian and juggler. He also filmed a documentary of their tour. When they returned to the States, they edited the video and put it on a DVD, which they named Operation Swashbuckle. It shows John, Spencer and Todd performing at the many bases in Europe and the Middle East and sharing some funny stories with their audiences. There is also a funny scene where they "steal" a Hum-V to take a joyride and then get "arrested" by the military police.

I saw John again in Maryland in September after the band's summer tour. We were both busy during the run of faire, producing and promoting shows. My husband's band and I put on the second Celtic Crossroads Show in late September (in which John made an hilarious guest appearance as a huge fairy in a pink tutu); and in mid-October, John and Spencer put on their first indoor theater version of the annual Hack and Slash Christmas Show—always a popular hit at faire. This type of venue allowed them to present a more professional-quality production, and to sell tickets, with the proceeds benefiting the Johns Hopkins Children's Center. The faire closed the next weekend, and Randy and I headed back home to finish out the year with gigs in Texas. The year ended on a very sad note for us. In early December, a very dear friend of ours lost his life while working security for another band. He took three bullets at point blank range in an attempt to stop a gunman, who ended up killing our friend and three others, including the lead guitarist. He sacrificed himself to save his friends. This singular, tragic event seemed to set the tone for the coming year, which would prove to be full of tumultuous change and personal hardship.

2005

Looking back, I can see there is no doubt that 2005 was a very difficult year for me, involving some major changes in my life. I decided to stop working for my husband's band. It was a hard choice, but I felt I needed to step away from the group and to pursue my own interests. I stayed behind that summer to work a full-time job in Houston. For the first time since 1997, I would not be working or traveling with my husband. This transition was hard for both of us. It was a year full of challenging experiences and some very hard lessons. I had to deal with an arbitrary, adversarial boss, and the impersonal, rigid mentality of the corporate world. But it was a year of a lot of personal growth.

In February, John asked me for a reading. He was restless and somewhat dissatisfied with the current direction of his life. He thought about his spiritual mission often, but did not know the path he should take to get there. He didn't feel he was getting support from home and needed some guidance and direction. The Master came through with a message for him.

February 22, 2005

Beloved One of Old,

Now has come the time for you to impart your wisdom to the world. You have been very careful not to abuse this privilege, and our faith in you is well founded. Please do not linger, for the time has come for you to fulfill your mission here on earth. There are those who are waiting for such knowledge to come forth—such beauty, such wisdom. The Truth is simple and yet unheard by those who will not listen. Give them a reason to listen, John. Give them hope of a better tomorrow. Bolster their fragile egos and wills to give them strength to hear your words, the words of the Ancient Wisdoms, so the truth can be heard from the mountaintops. The

Glorious Age has arrived when all men will know their Maker.

The Ancient Wisdom of the Ages is upon us. We can no longer turn away from it. It is time for it to come forth; for man to know who he is; to seek counsel in higher places; to connect to energy frequencies not of this world; to bring in a higher vibrational frequency [to the Earth]. You must trust this. To go forth in faith that all will be fulfilled is to seek the very purpose of your life. There are wondrous things that await you: wondrous deeds and works of miracles that await you.

For as you receive, so shall you give. As you give, so shall others receive. It is an interconnected cycle of awareness and energy exchange. Be true to your purpose. Be one with the Creator. Be one with Him who sent you here. Know that all will be well and your purpose will be fulfilled as was spoken of in ancient texts. For this is the way the world was meant to be to fulfill its purpose: a living library of hope and oneness with God. Intend not to harm those things that are sacred.

Believe in all things; know all things; be at one with all things, both in Heaven and on Earth. This is your purpose, John: to know all things whatsoever the Father would have you know. Believe in Him who created you. Seek the wonder and the miracles you are meant to bring forth. Have faith in all things that we give you, whose purpose serves Heaven and mankind here on earth.

Amen.

It would be a couple of more years before John's mission would start to really manifest, but his consciousness was beginning to move back in that direction now. He had the tools; he just needed to apply them.

In March and April, John and Spencer, along with other actors, did their fifth USO show—the third to the Middle East—that took them back to Kyrgyzstan, Uzbekistan, Afghanistan, and Qatar, but this time they would add Kuwait and Iraq to their itinerary. Again, they found themselves flying into war zones wearing full metal jackets in Black Hawk Helicopters in Iraq. This would end up being one of their most dangerous assignments.

But the dangers were offset by moments of profound healing. Todd, the juggler, had joined their tour again along with another performer named Dan. Their third stop was a base in Afghanistan. After their show, everyone went into the hospital tent to visit the wounded soldiers. There was a little girl there whom the soldiers had rescued and adopted. She had not spoken or smiled for several months since witnessing the brutal execution of her entire family. In a matter of minutes, Todd got this small child to smile, and even laugh, as he transferred a spinning ball from his fingertip to hers. It was moments like these that stood out for John and reaffirmed their purpose for going over there.

Later, when they were in Kuwait City, another healing opportunity presented itself. The previous year, John had told Dan about his "John of Old" story, so Dan knew that John could heal. As they were warming up for their show that day, Dan was having trouble with his side. Earlier in the tour, Dan had pulled his serratus anterior muscles while doing back flips during his warm-up for a show. It was a serious enough injury that it prevented him from doing any back flips in this show.

He decided to let John work on him, so he called him over. "Why not experience some of that healing energy that John is known for. What could it hurt?" he reasoned. John went over to Dan. He put his hands on Dan's side and started giving him some energy. Then he was guided to go to Dan's knee for some reason, so he sent healing energy there, too.

John didn't know it, but Dan had hurt his knee a long time ago. It was an old injury that he had just learned to live with, but he had never mentioned it before or complained about it. Without any prior knowledge or being asked to, John then moved his hands to Dan's knee, and sent healing energy to that area as well. It surprised Dan that John just "knew" to go there.

When John finished working on the knee, he went back to work on Dan's side again. When the healing session was complete, Dan asked, "Why did you touch my knee?"

John said, "I was told to heal your knee."

"But I never told you I had an injured knee," Dan replied.

"I was just told to go to your knee and work on it," John said casually.

Dan was amazed at John's healing touch. "Wow. I can't believe my knee doesn't hurt anymore," he said. "But the side will take longer to heal, I am sure. That's a more serious injury."

"Well, it will take as long as you believe it will take," John responded. And it did take a few more days for his side to heal because that's what Dan was expecting. However, the knee was healed instantly, probably because Dan wasn't expecting it at all and had no preconceived ideas about it.

They continued on their tour to Iraq, which proved to be rather exciting. While they were in Fallujah, waiting for a helicopter transport to whisk them away, they saw bombs blow up near them, and gunfire erupted close by them in Ramadi. But their closest call came at the base in Samarra. John and Spencer had just finished performing their show for the troops. They gobbled down a quick lunch while sitting on a Hum-V at the base in

Samarra—a place too dangerous to have even a mess hall, where soldiers would naturally congregate, making them easy targets. Shortly after packing up, they loaded their gear onto the Black Hawk helicopter that was waiting to take them to the next base.

Moments after lifting off, mortar shells exploded right where their helicopter had been. Immediately, the crew went into search mode, flying around, looking for the source of the bombs. The door gunners were poised, waiting for their opportunity to fire. John and Spencer were caught up in the middle. As John looked out of the chopper's window, he saw Iraqi villagers below running in terror, trying to find a place to hide.

During this trip, they would get the opportunity to visit some famous places associated with stories in the Bible, places like ancient Babylon and the Ziggurat at Ur—the birthplace of the Prophet Abraham. All in all, it was a fascinating journey.

When John got back home, he and Spencer performed their show at the faire in Georgia that April and May, and John spent the summer making swords for a vendor in Maryland. Our paths crossed only one weekend that year, when I flew to Maryland for my birthday in mid-October. I spent a few precious minutes with John in between his shows. Then, in December, Hack and Slash did their second Christmas show in a theater, this time benefiting the Make a Wish Foundation. They were able to raise thousands of dollars for that organization. Each year the show has grown more and more popular and has become somewhat of an institution in Baltimore.

It was during this time that Jennifer and John's relationship began to grow more distant. When the faire season was over, he decided it was time to refocus on his spiritual work. With the help of Spencer, who has a nice recording studio set up, they mastered and mixed a new recording of the cassette tape of John's past life regression. The original recording did not have good quality, but Spencer managed to mix out some of the static and bring more clarity to John's voice, which sometimes gets very soft. John added his comments and narrated what was going on during the regression.

He called me in November to ask my permission to use my name on the CD. I was in the middle of dealing with a crisis at work, and my mindset had completely changed from my spiritual work to one of survival in the corporate world. The first thought that came to my mind was, "Oh my God. What if they find out about this at work?" My hesitation was somewhat of a reality check for me. It made me stop and re-evaluate the path I was heading down. John assured me that he would not mention me if I had any reservations about it. What was I thinking? After all we had been through? "Of course you can use my name," I told him. "I just hope I am ready for all of this!" I laughed.

Two days before Christmas, John discovered something that would forever change his life. Jennifer wasn't happy and wanted to leave. He struggled to hold his marriage together in the aftermath of this heartbreaking news, and at the beginning of the New Year, they went to therapy to work on their relationship. But after only three sessions, the prognosis wasn't looking good.

2006

In January 2006, John sent me the produced CD of *John of Old, John of New—The Continued Path of an Apostle*. I was bowled over. It looked and sounded very professional, and he and Spencer had done an excellent job with it. He gives an introduction on it about how we met, our first readings together, and the influence our communications with the Master had had in his life.

"Well, I am for sure out of the spiritual closet now!" I laughed. If John had the courage to put his name out there and speak up for what he knew was true, then that meant only one thing for me to do. It was time to revisit getting our book out. "Wow, after so many years, this is really going to happen," I said.

During this whole time, John was also dealing with the ramifications of the breakup of his marriage. Jennifer moved out of the house towards the end of February, taking Kynan with her to Ohio, where her mother lives. It was a very difficult time for John. Only two weeks later, in early March 2006, he would leave with Spencer for yet another USO tour of the Middle East.

Their first show would be Kyrgyzstan, but to get there they had to fly through Moscow. Unfortunately, they did not have visas, and so they spent they eight long hours in the Moscow airport waiting for their flight to Kyrgyzstan. All the while, John was wishing he could get out and see Red Square. Finally, their flight took off. By the time they arrived at the base in Kyrgyzstan, they had only had four hours of sleep before performing their first show in a haze. It was grueling to say the least. "We were completely wiped out," John recalls.

The next day, as John and Spencer were preparing for their second show at the base, they discovered that one of the nails in their bed-of-nails prop had been damaged in transport. (One show they do has Spencer lying down on a bed of nails while John breaks a cinderblock over his chest with a sledgehammer.) John felt it was his duty to fix this prop, so that Spencer would be safe.

The performers were asked to go around and visit all the soldiers in the guard shacks who would have to miss the show that night. As Spencer and fellow performer, Dan, went out to fulfill this request, John went with a young corporal to the motor pool to find some tools to fix the bed of nails. During this time, John shared his story with the soldier.

After successfully completing the repairs, John went with his escort to the mess hall for dinner. Upon arriving, the corporal saw another soldier from his unit and began chatting with him. Just then, their sergeant walked into the mess hall. He was a big, strong, muscular man with a shaven head. Everything about him said, "I am not someone you want to mess with."

As the sergeant approached the table where John and his soldiers sat eating, he addressed John. "Hey, thanks for the show last night. It was great."

"Oh, yeah? Good. I'm glad you liked it," John smiled.

The sergeant got his food and sat down right next to John. Halfway through the meal, out of the blue, this big, tough sergeant broke down into tears, unburdening himself to John. He told him about the horrible relationship he had had with his abusive, alcoholic father. He didn't even know why he was compelled to share his story with a complete stranger; he just knew that he needed to. John listened intently and responded by reinforcing the positive choices the sergeant had made in his life. Afterward, the sergeant thanked John for listening and shook his hand.

"I have to get back to work," he said as he got up to leave.

What touched John almost as much as the emotional healing that had taken place was the reaction of the other two men who had listened to their commanding officer's story. "Oh, my God!" they gasped in disbelief. "I never knew that about him," the corporal remarked.

This tough sergeant had shown great courage in opening up emotionally and sharing his painful past. John carries such a love energy about him that a complete stranger opened up to him at great risk to his reputation and ended up gaining the respect of his men in the process. John was amazed by the whole thing.

He has touched many other soldiers, too. One soldier in Kuwait described John as "a larger than life individual . . . with many talents, and a heart larger than he." He added that John "always made sure that I kept a sense of humor, even when I was dead on my feet. Of course even when I told him I was good to go, he would just look at me and know I was running on empty."

By now, Hack and Slash were well-known in military circles, and the effect that they have had on the morale of the soldiers had been wonderful. One soldier summed it up like this:

> I'd like to say that between the other entertainers that I've escorted, [and] you guys, [you] were without a doubt the best so far, not only in entertainment value, but as people. All in all, this was one trip that will not be forgotten anytime soon; nor will the individuals that brought the laughter to Iraq.
>
> These are people that didn't have to travel to this godforsaken country, but did so, with great risk to themselves, so they could bring smiles, laughter, and a bit of home to all the soldiers here, and for that we are all grateful.

Another commented:

> Above all of that, you have shown that there are some people who support our troops even though they might not support the war.

It is true that John does not believe in war; however, he does support the men and women serving in the military. And I know that his presence in the war zones of Afghanistan and Iraq made a positive difference in the lives of both soldiers and civilians.

———•◦•———

Overall, John has participated in some pretty amazing healings, especially in the last three years. Some of those stories are found in the last chapter.

When John returned home from his tour, he came back to an empty house and no vehicle. [His truck had been sold while he was away].

I also was going through some personal changes at the same time, but fortunately they were good ones! In mid-March, I courageously quit the job I had been hanging onto, which wasn't right for me, and stepped out in complete faith that the Universe would support me. Within three days, I was working for a professional football team as a contract-hire. By the end of April I had been offered a full-time job, and I loved it. It was exactly where I needed to be at the time. I had a great boss who appreciated my talents and hard work. It was quite a contrast with my previous job.

Meanwhile, John had moved out of his house in Pennsylvania and into a cramped, temporary living space in Ohio so that he could be near his son. He put it out to the Universe that he now needed gainful employment and a house in Ohio in order to be near his son. Shortly after making this request, he was offered the job of directing a small medieval faire in Ohio, and the owner of the faire provided John a house to live in that was close to the site.

In April, his new website[66] went up, which offered his regression CD to the public for the first time. He was focused on his spiritual work again. I was excited for him, but I was in a completely different head space as I was still working in a corporate environment. However, in the back of my mind, I thought about getting the book published, but it was hard to find the time to work on it. John was starting up again, and now he had to pull me along!

That summer, he took over the directorship of the little faire outside of Cleveland with only a few weeks to prepare. He did a wonderful job with the time he had. Many thought the faire had declined in recent years and commented that John had brought the magic back.

I saw John only once that year, again during my birthday weekend, when I flew up to Maryland to visit the faire. It was difficult to be away from my husband for so many months at a time. I missed traveling and being with him. I also missed getting to spend time with John. Things sure had changed for me in two years, and they were about to change even more in the coming year not only for me, but for John as well.

In the fall, John and Jennifer were legally separated, and by year's end, she filed for divorce. Though John's life was changing so drastically, there was one bright spot in this very difficult year. Immediately following the faire, he would make the most significant spiritual journey of his life.

CHAPTER SIXTEEN

The Return

Michael decided that the time had come for him and John to finally visit some of the places which they had frequented in their past lives as apostles. He planned a whirlwind tour of Israel, Greece and Jordan for the fall of 2006 and invited John to join him. This was something that both of them had desired, and John was only too happy to make the journey to these ancient lands with his dear friend through many ages.

The incentive to explore Israel was apparent, but their intention of visiting Greece was less obvious. Ever since I told him about the cave at Patmos—where the Apostle John was said to have written the Book of Revelations—John had wanted to go there. This was the very cave that I had visited some thirteen years earlier, and The Master made a direct reference to it during our "conversation" in Maryland in '98: **"You were meant to do this work with John. Why do you think we sent you to Patmos?"** Here at last was John's chance to see it for himself.

Typical of Michael's propensity for research and meticulous preparation before taking a big trip, he sought the counsel of a psychic named Rena, who had worked for military intelligence for many years. Her ability to tune into past lives was uncanny, and he used her references to the places that he and John had been in their past lives to pick out locations to visit, especially in Greece.

In spite of all his careful research, the one thing Michael could not nail down before their departure was a confirmed ferry schedule to Patmos. Because their visit to Greece would coincide with the tourist off-season, the ferries would not be making their regular daily runs. Not knowing if they would actually be able to visit the island or not, they decided to include Greece in their travel plans, anyway. Michael would try to figure out the ferry schedule once they got there. Besides, Rena had told him that he and John had shared some other past-life adventures in Greece.

On October 26, 2006, they flew from New York City to Athens, arriving at sunrise. After landing, they immediately rented a small car and drove to the beautiful port town of Glyfada, just south of Athens. When they got to their hotel, they checked in their luggage with the hotel clerk, jumped back in the car, and then drove straight to the Acropolis for a quick visit to the Parthenon. Actually, their main objective was the Well of Klepsydra, which was located near the Acropolis, but since it was so close they figured, why not take in a little time sightseeing first? In ancient times, the Well of Klepsydra was known as the "wellspring of knowledge." Legend claimed that if one drank from the well, one would be enlightened with knowledge of the past. John the Beloved was said to have visited there once, so of course John wanted to go.

When they arrived at the Acropolis first, they discovered that a good portion of it had been closed off to the public for restoration. However, they were able to go right to the top of the hill, to the Parthenon, the most prominent building at the Acropolis, and look out at the ancient ruins. It was their first trip to Greece and this sight was impressive. After spending some time there, they decided to continue on to the Well of Klepsydra, which was just around the corner. Upon arriving, they saw a long iron gate at the entrance to the pathway that led to the well. It was wide enough for a car to drive through, but there was only one snag: the gate was closed. Unwilling to let this deter him, John decided to investigate the latch more closely.

"It doesn't look like it's locked," he declared.

Michael glanced around a bit nervously. "I'm not sure we should go in there, John."

But before Michael could say another word, John had opened the gate and let himself in. Michael hesitated for a moment as he watched John walk inside the fenced area. After all, they were in a foreign country, he reasoned.

"What if we get arrested for trespassing or something?" Michael proffered.

"They'll probably just tell us to get out, that's all," responded John, casually.

As he looked around the corner, John saw the Well of Klepsydra at the bottom of a small hill. He waved for Michael to join him. Michael scanned the area once more, then darted inside, and followed John around the corner.

When they reached the bottom of the hill, they looked down the well shaft and discovered, to their surprise, that it was completely dry. One thing was for sure: there would be no drinking from this well. But they did hear water running underground, so apparently the spring was still alive, if not accessible. They decided to meditate for a few minutes, and then left without incident.

They did a little more sightseeing, (this time, on the "proper" side of any latched gates) and then had something to eat before returning to their hotel in Glyfada that afternoon. They managed to snag a few hours of sleep before getting up very early to catch a two o'clock in the morning flight to Tel Aviv.

After their two-hour flight, they arrived in Israel around four o'clock in the morning. As they were going through airport security, three young ladies working for the Israeli military intelligence, probably no older than twenty, stopped them for questioning. Security was very tight because of recent bombings in Jerusalem. The army was trying to intercept any would-be terrorists through interrogation.

Michael gives his account: "They are questioning me and questioning John, trying to trip us up on our story of what we're doing in the country and where we're headed. They even asked, 'How are you going to get from here to [there] on this day? Who's your tour company?' So they were doing their best to find out if we belonged in the country and what our purpose was. After five minutes . . . we allayed their fears [and confirmed] that we were not terrorists."

They hailed a taxi at the airport. The half-hour trip to their hotel in Jerusalem proved to be an adventure.

"The cab ride was quite interesting," Michael recalls. "It was pitch dark. All we could see were sandy, rocky hills and fencing, and a cab driver that drove as fast as that little car could go. We had no problem with this because if we were going to be shot at, we wanted to make sure they missed us, knowing what the state of the country was. The driver was halfway falling asleep, so we tried to make as much noise as we could. He claimed he was rubbing his eyes . . . because he had dirt in them . . . [but] we know what a falling-asleep driver looks like."

When Michael and John arrived at the hotel, they found they didn't have a reservation. As tired as they were, they would not find respite until the next night.

———•◦•———

"We get to the hotel [at half past four] in the morning and felt we were going to check in, but I had forgotten . . . that the hotel was full," Michael recounts. "It was the King Solomon Hotel. I figured if we were going to stay somewhere, we're going to stay in the best . . . hotel. It was the most expensive, of course. So, I was wondering, why did they give our room away when it was guaranteed?"

"When we got there, we were both completely dead tired," John admits. "It was pitch black outside . . . We got there and there was no room. Michael was arguing with the guy . . . because he thought the day clerk gave the room to someone else. After about fifteen or twenty minutes, Michael realized it was his mistake. When he booked the room, he accidentally booked it for the next night. He figured we would be getting into town so early, that we wouldn't need a room."

It finally dawned on Michael what had happened: "It turns out we decided, and agreed, not to have a room that night because we'd get there late in the [night] and we knew the minute we hit Israel, that if we could, we were going to go to the old city and spend the day there, so why waste "x" number of dollars on a hotel? So, [the clerk] convinced us and showed us after twenty minutes that we were not, in fact, in there until the next day."

Without a comfortable bed in which to catch a couple hours of sleep before daylight, the pair had to make the best of the situation. Dragging their tired bodies and luggage through the enormous lobby of the King Solomon hotel, they searched for a place to rest. Finding some small couches in a far corner of the lobby, they arranged their bags and suitcases around them and began to settle in.

John tried to squeeze his large body onto one of the loveseats and barely had enough room to perch himself without falling over. Michael pushed two chairs together to form a type of bed. Both of them twisted and turned, trying to get comfortable. Michael chuckled to himself when he saw John's six-foot two-inch body squeezed onto the five-and-a-half foot long, by two-foot deep, couch. "He looked like he was sleeping in a crib," Michael laughs.

John soon drifted off into a light, fitful sleep. He would sleep a little, stir, then fall back to sleep again. Michael, on the other hand, was not so fortunate. As exhausted as he was, he could not sleep even a wink.

Finally, when John sat up and rubbed the sleep out of his eyes, Michael was relieved. "After an hour and a half of uncomfortably lying there, trying to fall asleep . . . with no buzz . . . it wasn't to be. So when John got up, I got up. We looked at each other and I said, 'Let's do it.'"

————•◦•————

It was six o'clock in the morning and daylight was starting to break over the city. Not wanting to waste another minute, they checked their luggage with the hotel clerk and then stepped out of the hotel. They had no idea what to expect, having never been there before.

In the days preceding the trip, there had been news reports about bombings and gunfire in different parts of the city. Michael had read all the U.S. State Department briefs that warned travelers not to go to Israel unless absolutely necessary; and, if one did travel there, what areas to avoid at all costs, and what roads to strictly adhere to. The briefs had strongly suggested staying out of the West Bank area and the Gaza Strip. Avoiding the second area would be easy because they had no desire to go to the Gaza Strip, but they *had* to travel through the West Bank if they were to reach Galilee, one of their main destinations.

———•—•———

"We were unsure about what travel would be like," Michael says, "or anything at all about this city, or whether we would be kidnapped off the street. I can't say we really had fear of it all, but it was just questionable because of the heightening of security and things going on."

It was overcast that day. A misty fog hung in the air as an eerie light broke through the clouds. Michael and John set out with their backpacks toward the old city, only a few hundred feet away. As they went through the gate, it was like entering another world. The buildings and walls of the city were made of centuries-old stone, and the streets were paved with cobblestones. It was very quiet. The streets were deserted at this early hour and most of the shops had not opened yet. Before the city came to life, it was easy to imagine what it must have been like, walking those streets over two thousand years ago.

The first place they wandered was the National Park, a place they felt they had frequented many times before. As they walked through the park and up to the old Jaffa Gate,[67] they could smell the aroma of freshly baked bread wafting through the air. They spotted a shop selling flat bread. Each of them bought a piece, still steaming hot. "It was probably much like the bread that was made two thousand years ago," Michael surmises. John agrees and adds, "So then we sort of walked around while we ate our 'ancient flatbread for breakfast.' We felt like we were back in the day. It was interesting because you walk through the city, and without anybody else there, it has a much more historical feel. Once the people started showing up, with their modern attire, and the kids start running the streets, riding their bicycles and things like that, you kind of lose that ancient feel."

They had taken maps with them, but decided not to follow a prescribed route, as they intended to cover pretty much all of the city anyway. They wandered off toward the left and ended up, quite by chance, at the Church of the Holy Sepulcher[68] only minutes later. It was not even six-thirty in the morning, and the place was packed with people from all walks of life and religious orientations. "It was hell at high mass times fifty," Michael explains. "Every ethnic and religious group you can think of from Japanese to Greek Orthodox to Catholics. Everybody is gathered in this area and there's . . . some [type of] celebration going on and it's a literal zoo in there. We hung around and felt the energy for a short while, and it just wasn't our cup of tea."

John concurs with Michael. "I have a hard time believing that [the Church of the Holy Sepulcher] would be the place [Jesus] was crucified because I had no reaction. I figured that I would have some sort of reaction to the place [considering] that I [as John the Apostle] was the one standing there, [at the foot of the cross during the time of the crucifixion] watching it happen. But I had no reaction to that place at all."

Michael and John had discussed in advance of the trip that they weren't interested in visiting any structures built in the Byzantine period [around the fifth century] or later. They knew a lot of the buildings and sites purported to be the original places where special events in the life of Jesus had taken place were probably not the original sites. Michael states: "We really did our homework and knew that the odds of anything being the exact spot [where something significant took place] were pretty slim." Their mission for this trip was simply to experience the energies of the city and whatever remembrances they could get in touch with.

As they left the church and continued to explore the city on foot, they got to see and experience firsthand how separate all the different religious and ethnic groups were from one another. As they gazed up at a hill between the Muslim and Jewish quarters, they saw a huge gold dome that looked like a Muslim place of worship. Being drawn to it, they began to walk up an alleyway in that direction. Suddenly, a Christian man appeared from around the corner and stopped them. "That is where our neighbors pray," the man told them. "You can't go there right now." Apparently, it was the Muslims' prayer time and off limits to outsiders.

"That is an interesting expression," John thought to himself.

So, they turned around and headed back down the hill, veering toward the right. As they did so, they stumbled on the Wailing Wall, so named because of the people who pray and cry at the wall every day. The Wailing Wall is all that remains of the massive King Solomon Temple built in ancient times.[69] It was interesting for John and Michael to see the separation between the sexes in Judaism even today.

John noted that "the women [were] way over on the right side, [and] behind a wall the men [were] all over on the left side." Michael and John worked their way through the crowd to the wall, so they could place their hands on it and meditate. There were small pieces of paper rolled up and stuck in nooks and crannies all over the place. These slips of paper had prayers written on them. People placed them there in hopes that God would answer their prayers. "We tried to meditate for a while, but it didn't really do too much for us there," says John.

The base of the temple which stood where the current Wailing Wall is now located had been the main temple during the time of Christ. This is where He would speak and teach in the courtyard. His followers believed that Jesus would destroy the temple and rebuild it again in three days. According to theologians, this was actually a metaphor for the death and resurrection of Jesus Christ Himself. There has been much speculation as to what the temple looked like. No one knows for sure, but the Jews still lament over its loss today. It's hard to imagine that this ritual of praying and crying at the wall has been taking place for centuries. Michael sums it up: "Not much has changed in two thousand years."

Above the Wailing Wall lies the Al-Aqsa Mosque, built in the seventh century by the Muslims after the death of their prophet Mohammed,[70] and the Dome of the Rock[71], with its enormous gold dome dominating the horizon. The Dome of the Rock, or Masjid Qubbat As-Sakhrah as the Muslims call it, is a prayer house capable of accommodating five thousand people at a time. This entire area is known as the Temple Mount to Christians and Jews because it was originally all part of the King Solomon Temple. The lower level, where the Wailing Wall is located, is zoned off from the upper level, where the mosque and Dome of the Rock are located. The Israelis have military checkpoints stationed around the wall, carefully screening visitors, much like the security at the airport. It is not easy to get in there. Arabs are not allowed in the Jewish sector and the Jews are not allowed into the Arab sector, at all.

Michael estimates that there were between three hundred and four hundred people at the wall early that morning. It was supposed to be a place of prayer and worship, yet it was not a quiet place. After a few minutes, John and Michael discovered that it was very difficult to meditate because of all the activity and noise going on around them, so they decided to move on.

"The streets really wander and you get lost . . . you go to dead ends and you have to turn around," Michael recounts. "We just wandered and took it all in."

As John and Michael rounded a corner and started walking down another lane, they were stopped by the United Nations police. Several UN cars and vans were jammed-packed into this narrow street. "They're searching for a bomb," someone told John and Michael. An all-too-frequent occurrence in Israel, the UN police had the bomb threat drill down pat. After detaining the small crowd for a few minutes while the police made sure the area was safe to pass, John and Michael were allowed to continue. They walked down a little further and made a couple of more turns until they ended up on a street where people were carrying crosses on their backs.[72] Unknowingly, they had come across the famous Via Dolorosa route, which is believed to be the route Jesus took when he carried his own cross piece through the streets of Jerusalem.

They stumbled onto the fourth or fifth station of the route and backtracked to the first station, reading about the different phases of the cross at each station. Today pilgrims reenact this scene every Friday by carrying a cross along the same path Jesus took. It starts at the eastern Jericho gate and meanders through the city streets and ends at the Church of the Holy Sepulcher, which many believe to be the spot where Jesus was crucified.

John and Michael watched this with incredulous fascination as person after person each carried a cross in procession along this route. "It was too much ritual for us," Michael states, "and both of us grew up in the Catholic Church. But we understood it was what these people needed for their spiritual growth."

<hr />

Leaving the Via Dolorosa re-enactment, John and Michael continued to roam the narrow streets of Jerusalem. They lost their bearings again and again because the streets are not well labeled. As they rounded a corner, they saw someone go up a set of steps into a building. John said, "Hey, let's go up these steps and see what's there." So they followed the gentleman up and, by default, found themselves in the room called the "The Upper Room." This is supposedly the site of the Last Supper[73], but Michael didn't buy it for one minute. "It no more was the room than my house," he said. "In the thirteenth or fourteenth century someone said 'This is the room' and they put up all these great arches. We ended up wandering around in there. We would never have found it otherwise."

They continued to walk around the city, taking in as much as they could. Finally, they exited out of the old Jericho Gate on the east side and walked to the Garden Tomb and nearby Skull Hill. I asked Michael and John if they felt a familiarity with the place. John described the area of the tomb as a very peaceful place. Michael said that they both had their doubts that the "tomb" presented was the actual place where Jesus' body was laid after his death. However, as they walked to the adjacent hill known as Skull Hill,[74] they both perceived, very strongly, that this was the real Golgotha, or the place where Jesus was crucified. It was truly a remarkable experience for both of them.

As soon as they reached the hill, John immediately had a strong visceral and emotional reaction. "So, [the hill near the Garden Tomb] is where I had my big reaction," John recounts. "And I realized this must be where He was crucified, which is what the British Society says. It says that when they did all the research, they discovered . . . the research and the Bible and everything says that it's between two roads that go to a single gate up from Jerusalem, so that it's an area between two roads. It was an area known for corporal punishment, which this place was, and Golgotha,[75] means 'skull hill.' There is this gigantic hill there that looks like a skull, so it makes perfect sense for that to fit all the descriptions. Standing there, I knew that was the spot, and so did Michael. Michael got the same feeling. We weren't necessarily too sure about the tomb, whether the tomb itself was correct, but it was the most accurate tomb representation that I could imagine. It was pretty amazing being there."

What follows is part of an interview I did with John as he describes what it was like for him return to Golgotha after two thousand years.

Sharon: So the Garden Tomb and Skull Hill . . . that's where you had a strong reaction. Was it more of an intuitive feeling? Emotional feeling? Or did you have a visual remembrance when you got there? Did you have any flashbacks?

John: I had no flashbacks. What I did have was . . . when I got there I immediately started to weep, started to cry. My eyes were just draining like crazy . . . like [tears] pouring out. The other thing that happened was that I got nauseous, really sick to my stomach. I was like . . . it gave me an intense emotional reaction.

Sharon: Do you think, perhaps, that was the way that John of Old was reacting? Did he throw up when he was standing there?

John: Oh, I am sure of that. I am positive that John of Old threw up during the whole thing because there's no . . . the emotions that I experienced in that regression and everything, there was no composure. You lost everything. It was such a physical reaction. You would have lost your lunch. You probably would have [relieved yourself all over] yourself. There was nothing [you could do about it] . . . the world had just collapsed. That's the only way I can say that. I will say Carol Berman, in the regression, stopped me before I got completely into the emotion of it.

Sharon: It was so intense.

John: It was so intense [that] she stopped me before I got further into it. I have no doubt in my mind, had she let me continue, it would have gotten far worse than what you hear in the [recording of the] regression.

Sharon: Did you have any flashbacks at all when you were standing there? Or was it more just a physical . . .

John: It was a total, emotional response. There were no visuals whatsoever. Now, I do know, like I said, the nauseous feeling that I had [had been] very powerful. I turned [and] I looked at Michael, and said, 'This is it.' And he said, in his very Michael way, he kept his face very straight and said, 'You know, I think you are right.' (John laughs.) Michael is the most composed person in the world at the most powerful moments. He is very dry when the spiritual [stuff] is hitting the fan. Michael is the most composed person you will ever meet in your life. (John laughs again.)

<hr />

After this powerful experience, they both concluded that this must have been the place where Jesus had been crucified, not at the Church of the Holy Sepulcher as presumed by many. If so, this hill would have been where John had stood, so many centuries before, at the foot of Jesus' cross, looking up at Him as He hung there—the only apostle who stayed to the very end. Only a few months before this, during the depth of his despair over the breakup of his marriage, John had had a flashback of his standing at the foot of the cross, sobbing, with one hand wrapped around the base of the cross and the other hand, stretched up, holding onto the foot of Jesus. This visual reminded me of the reading I had done for John at Cape Henlopen on September 14, 1999, when I saw the image of Jesus looking down at John from the cross, transferring His energy to John, from His eyes to John's.[76] My guides must have been showing me how Jesus had imprinted His energy signature upon John, the same John who is now the beacon for Jesus' return in the physical plane (i.e., His Second Coming).[77] This energy transfer was later confirmed in his past life regression in the fall of 2000.

After the intensity of their visit, they took a much-needed break and had lunch at a nearby café. When they were finished, they hired a cab driver to take them up to the Garden of Gethsemane[78] and the Mount of

Olives. This was a place that Michael particularly wanted to visit.

"So the driver took us to the Garden of Gethsemane," John recalls, "which is more like the courtyard of Gethsemane now. They have these gigantic olive trees that [look] a couple of thousand years old. That was interesting . . . seeing those trees, but [the place] didn't really do anything for me, other than that."

Because of a light rain that fell that day, the roads up the hill were slick and the cab had trouble getting up the hill. Finally, the car wouldn't go any further. It was only able to get about two-thirds the way up. Its wheels spun out every time the driver gave it more gas even with John and Michael both sitting in the back, giving the car more traction.

"Eventually it got to the point that the driver got so nervous about us being in the car, as he spun out, [that] he asked us to get out while he tried to drive up the hill," John describes. "So we stood on the side of the road while he [tried to go] up the hill. He and another car just sat there and spun tires, trying to get up this hill. They never got [any further] up the hill, so we ended up saying to our driver, 'This is good. This will work.' So we spent our time on the hillside [right] there."

"There were two reasons we wanted to go up [to the Mount of Olives]," Michael explains. "There was the classic view of Jerusalem as it looks from the hillside. The other reason was we knew this is where the encampment [of Jesus' followers] was set up all the time. Everyone would pitch their tents there rather than stay in the city. It was the large, sloping hillside coming from Jericho, coming from Jordan, coming from Galilee. Everyone would pitch a tent. They did not want to go into the city until they were ready for it. It was the free place, where the 'hippies' hung out. I knew I had to [see it]. More than any place in the city, I knew that this hillside felt like where we would spend time [as Jesus' disciples]. Back then, you would go into the city for the day [and] do whatever, but you always ended up back at this hillside. That felt like an old home, much more than the city did."

John felt the same feeling of having been there with Jesus. "Being on that hillside . . . There was definitely a familiarity about the view, about seeing the city on the other side of that little ravine," conveys John. "That . . . feeling of familiarity . . . I definitely got that. It was an interesting familiarity because . . . it was kind of like . . . Woodstock, or something like that. The stage is so far away [from] the crowds and everything. It kind of felt like that, like we were standing . . . so far away but we were looking over where the 'stage' is, which is the city. It was interesting to me in that way."

John and Michael took some pictures of the view from the Mount of Olives before leaving. Although they didn't reach the summit, they felt they had gone as far as they needed to have made a connection to the energy of the place and their past-life association with it.

After a few minutes, they had the cab driver take them back down the hill and drop them off on the east side of the city. Their goal was to find the place where Michael, as Philip, had died in that past life. History tells us of how he was crucified, upside down, just outside the old West Gate [near the Jaffa Gate] which is now closed off. Back in the day, this gate was a major entry point into the city and a prime place for making an example of any "trouble makers" to passersby who entered through the gate. To get there, they took a sidewalk that went around the outer perimeter of the city wall, and then they passed through a large green field until they came to where the old gate had been located.

"If you stand back from the city and you look at the way the rocks were laid out and everything, you can see where there used to be ramps . . . going up to where this gate was," John explains. "It made perfect sense where this gate would have been. And what is interesting is you would expect the ramp to come straight out a doorway or straight out a gate . . . you can tell by the way it was laid out [that one would have] come out that gate onto, almost like, a balcony, and the ramps went down left and right there. And so, they say that [this] gate was closed off in the Middle Ages for defensive reasons. Yeah, we were able to walk right up to it. I got a picture of Michael right in front of that gate, too."

It was necessary for Michael to go there in order to release his experience with the past. Upon arriving, he did a short meditation. I asked him how it felt being there, if he had felt anxiety when he first got there. "None whatsoever," he responded. "For me, it wasn't [about the] releasing of fear or anxiety, it was releasing a connection to it and saying, 'Okay, at this point in my life, I've taken in everything that I need to [take in] for that lifetime. I don't need to do a past life regression on it. I don't need to find more [answers to] questions about it. I've gathered all the energy and strength that I need from that lifetime.' That was a closing point for me on Jerusalem and Israel and that lifetime. It was a wind-down. I knew I was done with it. I'd taken everything I needed from that."

Michael's calm reaction surprised John a little. "He actually got to that moment, and he got very quiet. He felt the experience, and then he was over it real quick. He was done. 'Okay, let's go,' he said, which is [typical of] Michael," John chuckles.

That evening, John and Michael ate at a nice restaurant and reflected on their day. I asked them both to share their impressions of Jerusalem. The following are their responses:

Michael: My impression was it was ungodly exciting to go there, planning on going there, the anticipation of going there . . . but it was awfully nice to leave the city. And my feeling is that it was the exact same thing in the old days, two thousand years ago. There was a lot of excitement always built on traveling to Jerusalem, but when we got there, it was always fantastic to get . . . out of there. The energy and the tension of the city [are] ungodly now, [and] it felt the same way back then, be it with the Romans or the Jewish control, of the High Priests and the Sanhedrin—of their control of what went on back then. So it was a great anticipation of going there now, but I felt relieved to get out of the city.

It just told me . . . I could picture myself and all of us [apostles] walking up the hill, leaving the city and turning around and looking at it and saying, "You know what? We're good for six months or a year [before returning here]. I'm glad to shake the dirt from my shoes." It hasn't changed. There is so much energy tension [there]. You can feel it in the arrogance of the people that live there. You can feel it in the hatred of the suppressed that live there, also the Arabs. It's no different then than it is now. There's always a tension and an energy in that city. There was nothing we could do energy-wise to change that.

In the evening, I tried to do a little energy work. We did not try anything together, but I think, as we walked around the city, we tried to spread it as much as we could. Each site we'd go to I would try to instill a calming energy in those areas and try to do a grounding, but wholeheartedly knowing this tension is not going to change simply by us being there. There's too much else that has to be done. We can't do much to change that. John knows that, too. The rubber band [tension] is the tightest in the world, right at that point. There's no doubt, that's where it's all at.

John: Well, my experience is when we first went into the city, it was very serene and calm because nobody was out. But as all the individual egos started coming into play, as more and more people came in, we ended up having a big experience of definitely [sensing] tension between the different religions and cultures. Because it's just like putting all these cultures into this . . . contained area, and they all have to coexist. You can tell that it is not necessarily the happiest of situations.

As far as being in the city and feeling the tension, I think as long as those particular sects of different religions are working in such a separate and opposing way, there is always going to be tension in that city. It's when we can rend that veil and we can all say, 'Hey look, we are actually all talking about the same God,' that that city can actually be a point of real change for the world. But until those groups start to work together and realize that Allah is God, and [that] Mohammed and Jesus and Buddha [are] all prophets [and] examples [for us] to live by, we can't . . . I think it is always going to be tense.

As far as being in the city and feeling the tension . . . absolutely. Walking through the city you feel the tension. You look around. You see an old ascetic

Jewish man walking beside a Muslim man, and you see the physical movement of their bodies apart, as they walk by each other.

So it is a very tense city. And just like Michael said, it felt really good to leave that city. It was interesting [in that] we went in, we walked through it, we saw it, we did what we wanted to do, but it was time to leave, so [we said] 'Let's get out of here.' And then the next time we went in . . . it was funny because we went back into Jerusalem again, and I almost didn't want to go back in. It was like, 'Okay, kind of been there and done that. Don't necessarily need to see that again.' John Davis is not a city person. I don't like cities in general. I like the country, and I like being out away from the cities. Maybe that's a tie-over to that lifetime, where I really didn't like to hang out in the city. (John chuckles.)

———•◦•———

After their visit to Jerusalem, John and Michael spent the next two days in Jordan, a place they had both frequented in a past life, according to Michael's reader, Rena. John and Michael hired a cab driver to take them to the gate at the border crossing into Jordan, where they went through the Jewish passport checkpoint. They were loaded onto a bus and were taken three or four miles to the Allen B Gate, at the Jordanian border. When they got to the other side, they had to go through the Jordanian passport control, which took no time at all.

Michael had hired a driver, in advance, to take them to the ancient city of Petra. John remembers the driver, who was wearing a red sweater and collared shirt, was waiting for them when they arrived at the Allen B Gate. He was a very happy fellow—always smiling, with a gap in his front teeth. He followed them through customs. When they had finished with customs, he loaded their luggage into his car and headed out. Along the way, John made jokes about *McHale's Navy* to Michael because their driver looked so much like Ernest Borgnine.

Once on the highway, it was more like a high-speed chase than a sightseeing tour. Because Michael's schedule was so tight trying to get to Petra and to see it all in one day, they didn't have the time to take the more scenic route through the mountains as most tourists do. They drove and drove, at a fevered pitch, until they finally reached Petra. The driver drove them right up to the entrance of the ruins. From there, they decided to hire a guide for the first part of their visit, in order to get a proper introduction.

Upon approaching Petra, one must first cross over a crevice, or gorge, between two mountains to gain entrance into Petra. This approach was made famous by the movie, *Indiana Jones and The Last Crusade*, when Indiana Jones and his companions entered Petra on horseback. Now riding a horse toward the entrance is "the" tourist thing to do, especially since the movie has come out. So Michael and John rented two horses for the one hundred-yard ride to the canyon walkway. "So, Michael, of course, rides horses," explains John. "I don't ride horses, so the guide held my reins and walked me. Michael was actually riding. I was actually holding on for dear life," John chuckles.

They dismounted their horses and walked the rest of the way down. As they descended, their guide explained to them how the channels that one sees along the walls of Petra actually served as a basic plumbing system. It was designed to keep water moving through the city, with fresh running water on one side of the road and sewage water on the other.

As they passed statues and other artifacts, they were given a history of the Nabataeans and how they built Petra. The Nabataeans believed in reincarnation. Their symbol, a circle wheel within a spiral, can be found on a lot of their buildings.

John and Michael continued to wander down until they got to the opening of the gorge. As they rounded the corner, as if on cue, they heard the theme song to *Indiana Jones* echoing off the walls. "What happened was, some other tourist had brought the theme music from *Indiana Jones* with him on a boom box and was playing it inside the Treasury . . . the building you see in the movie, where Indiana Jones finds the Holy Grail. He thought it would be cool. [It was called] the Treasury because somewhere back in history they thought it was a treasury instead of the tomb that it actually is," John clarifies. "The people inside the building were all having a great time because they're inside of this thing, hearing this song. It was far cooler for us because we came walking out of that valley that you see in the movie, when you suddenly see Petra. We saw Petra and heard the *Indiana Jones* theme at the same time, which was really cool."

They wandered into the Treasury, took some pictures, and then went further back to explore the rest of the city on their own. "Come to find out, Petra is gigantic. It is an amazingly vast town. It is literally a city of tombs and buildings. There's a coliseum there. We walked down through the rest of it and saw the coliseum. One cliff face looked like a city block of buildings. It was just incredible," John elucidated.

As they walked down to the back of the city, adolescent boys hawking camel rides, horse rides, and donkey rides kept trying to get them to buy a ride. Michael found this amusing and started joking around with them. Soon, however, he found himself surrounded by all these kids who would not leave him alone. They were trying to get him to buy a donkey ride.

When John and Michael reached the end of the trail, just out of curiosity, John went up to see the donkey they had been talking about that was tied to the branch of a tree. The poor, tired little animal took one look at John, and assuming he was about to get mounted, let out a huge growl. 'Urrrraaaarrrgggghhhh!" the donkey bellowed, as if to say, "I don't think so!" Not wishing to antagonize the little fellow any further, John turned and walked away, but it made him chuckle inside.

By the time they had reached the back of the complex, it was already time to turn around and make their way back to the entrance. Having arrived around three in the afternoon, it had taken the better part of the day for them just to get there, which left only two hours to see everything. It was now five in the afternoon and they had thirty minutes to get back to the entrance. Unfortunately, they did not have time to enter the largest structure, which was the furthest from the entrance and the one that Michael had most wanted to see.

They began the long climb up and out. As they were trekking out, they came upon a group of Jordanian soldiers who had been visiting Petra, who were also leaving. John and Michael were behind them, following them out. It felt a little unnerving being around these soldiers because they were wearing their uniforms and carrying pistols and machine guns. As John rounded a corner, he encountered a soldier who turned around, and quickly brought something out of his pocket and held it up in front of John. At first John thought the soldier had been carrying a concealed weapon, which he was now pointing right in front of John's face. This startled him a little bit, until he realized that it was just a cell phone that the soldier was aiming backward in order to take a picture. John let out a sigh of relief and laughed to himself.

When they reached the top part, where the exit is located, they saw the gift shop. "Of course they have the *Indiana Jones* gift shop there because, you know, that's their claim to fame now," jokes John. "Their claim to fame is not the thousands-of-years-old ancient buildings. No, their claim to fame is a movie that was made in the eighties."

They also had Titanic souvenirs in the gift shop. Something John finds interesting is that most of the Arabic cultures he has encountered, especially while touring with the USO, are fascinated with the movie *Titanic*. "They have amazing amounts of Titanic stuff all over the place. And perfumes [like] 'Manly Man on the Titanic' and 'Titanic Adorable Lady.' These are perfumes sold overseas," John says.

They went up to meet their driver, who was going to arrange an Arabic meal for them, but Michael really wanted pizza. John would have preferred the Arabic food, but being a good sport, he went along with

Michael. Sitting down at the restaurant, they looked out the window at the mountains in the horizon. "It was a beautiful sunset," John recalls. "We sat and had the worst pizza I ever had in my life—absolutely horrendous!"

Afterward, they had their driver take them to their hotel. This was unlike any hotel they had ever been to before. For one thing, it was a walled-in, guarded complex. This was a little unnerving. They checked in and went up to their room, which had a huge balcony. John describes it:

> We ended up going to this hotel that Michael had arranged which had this balcony. You looked out over this balcony and you had a one-hundred-eighty degree panorama of the sun setting on these mountains all the way around. It was stunning, absolutely stunning. It was interesting because [when] we got in there . . . [when] we got into our room . . . they shut the gate behind us, and then the guards came out with the machine guns to watch the gates, so that nobody would come in and mess with the tourists. I thought that was kind of drastic.

The next morning they had to get up very, very early to meet their driver. "He met us for the drive back. Of course, he had to wait outside the gate," reflects John. "On our way back, he gave a sampling of the other road. There are two ways from Petra through the Allen B Gate. One of them is what they call the King's Trail, and the King's Trail has—it's through the mountains and you get to see all these historical ruins like old Arabian castles. Because of our having to get there so fast, we [took] the freeway on the way up there, [but on the way back we went on a] portion of the King's Trail, so we got to see some of that. We stopped at [a] Byzantine church that had amazing mosaics on the floor. It had . . . the [entire] map of the biblical area, so you could see things from the Bible all over this floor, but like from way, way back. If I was to go back again, I would make sure I gave myself enough time to go to the King's Trail because it was a very cool ride."

Arriving back at the Allen B Gate, they bid farewell to their driver and located the bus they were to take back into Israel. They boarded the bus but soon disembarked because it was just too hot to wait on the bus. Finding a seat on a nearby bench, next to the bus driver, who was also waiting for departure time, John and Michael struck up a conversation with a Danish couple. As they were conversing, a very old Arab man came walking up, very slowly. As he passed by the bus driver, he greeted him with "Allah mi'kh." The bus driver responded in kind. Curious, John leaned over to the bus driver and asked, "What does Allah mi'kh mean?" The bus driver responded, "It means 'God be with you.'"

Previous to the trip, Rena had told Michael that they would be running into an old friend—an older gentleman—with whom they had shared a past life, and that the recognition of such would be instantaneous. When it came time for everyone to board the bus, the old Arab man got on and sat across from John.

"I look over at this guy, and this guy is looking at me, and he seems very familiar," John recalls. "So, we started talking. He asks, 'Are you going to Jerusalem?' And I said, 'Yes, we're going to Jerusalem.' And he says, 'I am as well.' I suggested we share a ride. 'There's plenty of room,' I said, 'Why not? That way we can save some of the expense of a cab.' He thought it was a great idea [because otherwise] he was going to have to ride the bus. According to him, [the bus] takes a long time, and it's a real tough ride. So I said, 'Great.'"

"We ended up talking the whole way there. His name was Amam. He was born in Morocco, but now he lived in London as a British National. He came over to visit friends and family and was on his way to Jerusalem to pray in the mosque at Temple Mount," John recalls.

"After a little while, I started to realize that this was the man that Michael [had been] looking for over there," recalls John. So I said to Michael, 'Michael, this is the guy.' Michael was like, 'Well.' He kind of checked in on it to see if he felt the same way, and after a while Michael did believe that this was the guy."

The bus arrived at the Israeli border and let its passengers off at the checkpoint station.

"We joked. They were real friendly with us and let us go through," John says. John and Michael got out and walked up to the glass booth where four "fresh-out-of-high-school Jewish girls" were checking passports. They reminded John of a high school clique. They processed John's passport quickly.

One of the young women turned to Michael and said, "Baumann. Are you Jewish? You sound Jewish."

"Or German," Michael offered. "Ooh, maybe I shouldn't say German." He thought aloud. "It was really kind of funny," John remembers.

The girls were very funny, joking around with John and Michael. They asked them questions about where they had been and where they were going. They were definitely checking them out, but their U.S. passports held a lot of weight, and so they were processed quickly through, but it was not so easy for their companion, Amam.

John recounts his favorite story of the entire trip:

And then Amam comes up to do his paperwork. Amam was almost blind. His eyes were very bad. He was having a hard time reading the paperwork, so Michael actually helped Amam fill out all his paperwork. [He walked up to the window] and the questions started. The [passport agent] basically had to question Amam. Well, of course, because Amam was an Arab. They detained him for like thirty minutes at that gate. He got through one section [then] went through another section, where they screened his luggage, and they detained him there.

We went on through with no issues. Got all the way to the other side and we were waiting for him. We were waiting and waiting and waiting. At one point, we thought they were going to hold him all day. When we were just [about] to have to leave, we started to talk to these Danish people about riding with them.

Finally, Amam comes out. It took him forty-five or fifty minutes to get through the gate that took us two minutes to go through. He said, 'Thank you for waiting. Thank you for waiting.

'No problem,' I say. 'I'll get us a cab.' So I go off and find a taxi driver. [The driver] was a very big, Jewish man. He says, 'Where are you going?' We say, 'King Solomon Hotel in Jerusalem.' He says, 'Okay, I will drive you.'

So, he goes and gets his car and brings it up. [He is wearing a yamika, a prayer shawl, and has the Orthodox curls hanging from each sideburn.] Everything about him was very Hebrew. He's very nice. [But] he didn't realize we were bringing Amam.

He pops the trunk open. He comes over. He grabs my luggage and puts it into the car. [He] takes Michael's luggage, puts it in the car. Amam goes to hand him [his] luggage and the guy says, 'No, no, no, no, no! He can't come!' He didn't want Amam in his car—with his luggage in his car. He's trying to shoo Amam away.

I turned to the guy and said, 'Oh, no, no. He's coming with us.' And the guy looked at us. He gave me a look and turned and he looked at Michael. It's like Dad had just said no, so he better look to Mom. Right? So, he turned to Michael and Michael said, 'Oh, yeah. He's coming with us.'

We loaded [Amam's luggage] and got him in the car. The drive from the Jordanian border to Jerusalem was torture because this [cab driver] was [upset] that [Amam] was even in his car. The tension was thick. Just having Amam in the car really had the guy angry for the rest of the day. On our drive there, the guy would not speak. Every so often Amam would speak to him, and I was not sure whether he was speaking Arabic or Hebrew or what, but he would ask him a question and the guy would answer back. You could tell he was answering him back very negatively.

The driver was being very rude, and . . . . I didn't know what he was saying, so I turned to Amam and said, 'Is he going to take you to where you need to go?' Amam—who was in his seventies or eighties, a very old

man—said, 'I'm not sure. I may have to walk from your hotel.'
[The place Amam wanted to go was at least a couple of miles away from
the hotel.] He had all this luggage and stuff. There's no way this old man
was going to be able to do that. One way or another, I was going to get
him to where he had to go, even if I had to carry his luggage for him. I
said, 'Oh, no. He's going to take you to where you want to go.'

So I turned to the driver and said, 'We want to drop him off
first.' And the guy said, 'No. We're going to King Solomon.' I said,
'But no, he needs to go where he needs to go.' [The driver ignores
John's request.]

He was an old guy. I mean he was very old. and [the driver] was
going to make him carry his luggage. It's like saying, 'Here, carry all of
your luggage you seventy-nine, eighty-year-old man, and five miles up
the hill, through a city.' It was just disgusting.

So, Michael and I hatched a plan. [John chuckles at the memory
of it.] Basically, the deal with Amam is that we would split our fare
[three ways]. He would pay a third. So, the guy drives us to the King
Solomon Hotel, and we get out of the car. The guy gives us a number
[for the fare]. So we gave him two-thirds of his number. He says,
'Whoa! Where's the money?' We say, 'You'll get the rest of your
money when he gets to his gate.' [John laughs loudly at this.] And
you could tell that the driver was defeated. His shoulders slumped.
'Oh, all right.'

So, as I am turning to leave, I hear 'John! John!' I look back.
Amam is yelling out of the car window and starts to come out [of the
car]. I come over. He puts out his hand and shakes my hand. 'John.
Thank you so much, my friend! Thank you so much!' I said, 'Allah
Mi'kh, my friend.' [I loved being able to] help someone against racial
prejudice. This is my capper on the whole thing. I love that! [John
chuckles.]

I asked John how this had impacted him. Obviously, Amam's experience had touched him deeply. John reflects about this:

Being in that car was interesting because it kind of tells you
where we are in the world. These two guys in this car, though they
didn't look alike, they could have easily been brothers. They were both
basically white men. There was no real reason for them to hate each
other than their religions. What is interesting is, we are all praying to
the same God, so it really kind of shows where we are as humanity
right now, in our place in spirituality. There's so much division and
separation that if we were to just let go of the hatreds of the dogma of
all this and tap into the fact that we are all one. We're all dealing with
the same God/Universal Consciousness. That hatred in that car never
would have happened. Instead, what would have happened is that
that driver would have gladly driven him anywhere he wanted to go.

Then what probably, eventually, would have happened, the people in the world who are fundamentalists and blowing things up would no longer be blowing things up because of the fact that we are all one. It's the dogmatism . . . the dogma of religion [that] has created this huge separation, from not only God, but from each other. Because once we realize that we are all one, that's it.

John and Michael were glad to do what they could to help spread love and understanding, but they also knew their limitations in the face of so much conflict and hatred. They had taken in the flavor of the place and had done what energy work they could and now were glad to move on to the next part of their journey.

Michael had hired, in advance, a private guide to take them to Galilee and other stops in between. The next day, at six o'clock in the morning, their guide came to pick them up from the hotel. Mark Deckelbaum was a fifty-two-year old Canadian-born Jew, who had come to Jerusalem when he was in his early twenties, and had been giving guided tours to both Christians and Jews for about thirty years. He was an excellent guide and very knowledgeable about the region, having studied quite a bit of Biblical history, which was fortunate for John and Michael.

As Michael explains it:

> We told our guide right up front 'We want to go to true sites, as best as known back then. We don't care about churches nowadays, built in the twelve hundreds. We want to go to true sites and here is where we want to go, but we want to do it fast.' [At the end of the day] he said, 'All of what we did that day, traditionally, would be about a three-day tour. We did it from six o'clock in the morning to six o'clock at night.'

Their first stop was Qumran, home of the Essenes and where the Dead Sea Scrolls were discovered. Qumran is located in the desert. This is where Jesus was said to have received some of his spiritual training. They got there so early that the gates were still closed. The guide said, "We are not going to wait. We're going to pay our fee later on, when they [the docents] show up at seven o'clock in the morning."

It was going to be a very hot day. Even at half-past six in the morning, the sun was already beating down on them. As they walked among the ruins, Michael and John felt strongly that they had visited this place a number of times before. They went into the Essene cabin up on a hill, a place near where archeologists found the Dead Sea Scrolls. From their vantage point high up, they had a clear view of the Dead Sea, two miles off in the distance. However, because of the tensions between Israel and Jordan, the areas around the sea were zoned off, making it impossible for them to do the traditional floating in the salty water that visitors like to do.

The Essenes had certain rituals, one of which was cleansing themselves in baths before each meal. According to the literature and film provided [at the site], John the Baptist received training here for six months, and this is where he got the idea of baptizing people with water. According to their records, John left on his own while Jesus was away, studying in the Orient and Egypt. When Jesus came back, John was already performing baptisms.

Michael describes the Essenes and explains his feeling of kinship with the place:

> I know, in my heart, that John and I both probably spent some time there, at least visits before or after we started following [Jesus]. I don't know . . . I guess it was probably afterwards. Of course, [the Essenes] were the New Agers of the time. [They] didn't want to be related to the city. [Qumran] is at least fifteen to twenty miles south of the city.

John confirmed that he also felt a great connection to this place:

> We definitely had been there before. I had a sense that I had had many baths in that area. [John chuckles]. [The Essenes] very much believed in bathing, and they had ritual bathing pools and things. I definitely felt I had been there before. And actually, I felt I might have had a part in actually helping write some scrolls there but more along the lines of copying them as opposed to creating them. I kind of felt I had been a part of that process.
>
> And what's interesting about that is it would have made perfect sense because from the top of Qumran you can look over and you can see the area where John the Baptist did [the] baptizing. John and James and all those guys were familiar with John the Baptist. And so it would make perfect sense if Qumran were right there [that] the place of John's baptizing was right there. It would have made perfect sense for us to be in that area. That was way south . . . pretty far away from where Galilee was. We ended up having to drive a pretty good distance to get up to the Sea of Galilee.

When they finished with their visit at Qumran, they made their way to the Sea of Galilee. Their driver guide had to shepherd them through the West Bank first, where security was extremely tight. In fact, this was one of the areas the United States State Department had strongly advised against traveling through. The area was fenced off and was heavily guarded. As they got to the security checkpoint, Israeli men dressed in military fatigues and carrying rifles made them stop. "Where are your passports?" they wanted to know. John and Michael provided them with the requested documents. "Why are you traveling through the West Bank?" they wanted to know. "To visit the Sea of Galilee," Michael responded.

John and Michael watched from the car windows as the Israeli soldiers segregated the Arabs passing through the West Bank into their own little area. They wondered what would happen to them. After a tense delay, and some negotiating on the part of their guide, they were allowed to pass through. On the way up towards Galilee, the driver took John and Michael to a certain place on the Jordan River. John sets the scene:

> We drove past the Jordan River. We drove past the official site—the believed site—of where John the Baptist [performed his baptisms]. But you couldn't get to it because the Jordanian [soldiers were guarding] it and would shoot [any trespassers.] And then we ended up stopping at this tourist place up near the Sea of Galilee, still near the River Jordan that has been built for baptizing. And it is a total tourist stop, which is very much set up like a theme park in that you exit and enter through the gift shop. There are ramps [that go] down to the water.

Michael describes their visit:

> We went up to the classic spot where the Jordan River begins to where the Jordan baptismal is [located. They have it set up] like a regular tourist attraction, with concession stands, a trinket/gift shop, and all of that. We didn't want to spend money. John and I did not buy the traditional robe to go wading in the water. We literally ripped through the gift shop as fast as we could to get to the water [and] down the steps. We walked down to the water. It was pretty quiet. There was a small group near there doing their baptism. We dropped our shoes and rolled up our pants. We're standing in the water for about one minute. Not a place for meditation. We both picked that up. We looked at each other and [said], 'Well, it's a river, and that's about it. There's nothing special about it.'

The traditionally accepted spot where Jesus was baptized is located somewhere north of the Red Sea but south of the Jordan border crossing. Michael found the whole experience to be ineffectual:

> You can't visit [the actual spot where Jesus was baptized] because

they have it zoned off. The river at that point is a creek compared to up where [we were, which] is right at where the Jordan River is created out of the Sea of Galilee. It was one minute in the water—and [we're thinking] this is ridiculous; it's going through the motions. It meant nothing whatsoever to us to stand in that water because we weren't falling for the tourist trap.

After a few minutes of "been-there-so-what?" they continued on their way to Galilee, bypassing the fabled city of Jericho, well known in the Old Testament as the place where God, through the prophet Joshua, made the walls of the city fall down. They could not go there because, according to John, "it was too dangerous."[79]

From there they drove up north to Capernaum, the home of the Apostle Peter and where Jesus did most of his teaching. They saw the ruins of the old temple there and the remains of Peter's house. "We saw that the Catholic Church had built a church, which is suspended over top of the ruins of Peter's house, and it looks like a UFO that's hovering over top of this archeological site. It's terrible [looking]. And the only way you can see Peter's house was to go up into the church, walk to the center of the church and look down through a glass floor. The glass floor is all dusty so far underneath because of the desert and stuff. It was really [badly done]," John says.

Michael was hoping to find the original town of Bethsaida, which was the hometown of Philip. Archeologists are currently excavating in a spot where they think the old town may be located. Their guide took them there, but when they arrived, Michael intuitively knew that it wasn't the right spot. There was a location that Michael wanted to check out that he suspected might have been the actual spot, but he never got the opportunity to go there. There just wasn't enough time on their tight schedule.

As their cab sped along the highway, they passed by some trees growing on the side of the road. John and Michael could see water beyond them. Pointing toward the water, John asked the driver, "What is that?" He was hoping it was what he thought it was.

"That's the Sea of Galilee," their guide informed them.

John knew it. He had felt it in his heart. This is what he had been waiting for the entire trip. His pulse quickened as they got nearer. He and Michael peered through the trees from the car windows as they tried to look around the objects that were blocking their view. John was anxious to be back on those familiar shores again, the ones he had remembered in his regression. Would the visual image match the one he had seen in his mind's eye under hypnosis?

Sharon Prince

As anxious as they were to get to the beach, they would be making another stop first: Beatitude Hill, the place where Jesus gave his famous Sermon on the Mount. The visitor's center, run by the Catholic Church, was about to close, so they hurried to get there.

Upon arriving, they headed straight up to the top to look out over the Sea of Galilee, which is actually a huge lake. John recalls this magnificent sight:

> We basically went over and saw the hill. Went up on the top and understood why he [Jesus] would do a speech there. Because, if he were downhill, he would have had an amphitheatre, with a one-hundred-eighty degree panoramic view of the Sea of Galilee behind him, which is amazing. I absolutely believe that that was the spot where he did the Sermon on the Mount because . . . if I was going to do a speech in that time period, that's where I would have chosen. Your audience would be completely raked up and away from you. It's just a gorgeous backdrop. So you would have been able to basically sit there and talk to the crowd and thousands of people would have been able to see you in that situation. So, obviously, from an acoustics standpoint, [the situation would have called for] a banking wall behind him, but from a standpoint of being able to see you and possibly hear, it's a great spot for a speech.

After taking some pictures of this breathtaking view, Michael and John asked their guide to drive to the area which John and Philip would have traversed many times in those days: the beach at the Sea of Galilee. This was the one place that they had wanted to see more than any other. This would have been where they had first met Jesus, where they would have cast their nets as fishermen, where they would have set sail on many journeys to spread the gospel.

Their guide took them to a restaurant that served the traditional "St. Peter's Lunch," which was tilapia, deep-fried. Expecting a decent meal, John couldn't believe what they were served.

> We had the Apostle Lunch, which was the fish, which was the most disgusting thing I had ever seen or tasted in my life. They took a fish, basically, and they threw it in the deep fryer and [then] they threw it on a plate. It was disgusting. It was the most disgusting meal I had ever had in my life. That wasn't the fish I used to eat. I'm sorry. We had to eat it, of course, because we were there. [John chuckles.]

It was a full-sized fish, and as obnoxious as it was, John and Michael could not resist taking pictures of themselves holding it up, with the Sea of

Galilee in the background. After lunch, they walked onto the beach and put their feet in the water. They walked along the beach, like any tourist might, and collected rocks.

Michael: It was very exciting. [It was] our first glimpse of the Sea of Galilee. We know we spent many days out there on boats, fishing and traveling. We got to walk along that area.

John: When I was in Galilee, I could have sat there all day [and] just enjoyed the water. I felt very, very comfortable in Galilee.

The most dramatic moment of the entire trip for John was when they stopped walking along the shoreline and looked out across the lake. The surface of the water was completely flat, just like he remembered in his regression. On the other side was the same land John had seen, with its gentle, rolling hills. He knew that, even if this wasn't the exact spot where John had stood with his father, Zebedee, on the beach in that lifetime (though it certainly seemed so), that it was definitely the same view.

The only thing that did not make sense to him was the beach itself. They were walking on stones about two inches wide, like one might find on the beaches of Nice, France. It was not the coarse sand that John remembered walking upon or the sand that fell from his face as he lifted his head to look up at the face of Jesus.

> I was a little confused by all the rocks on the seashore because my regression remembered a coarse-sands sort of shore. Well, our driver informed us that the actual seashore of two thousand years ago would have been ten feet higher, and so what I was actually standing on would have been the sea bottom. The rocks I was standing on would have been sea bottom. But if you go up about ten feet, if you get up a little higher, you suddenly get into sandy soil. So, what I was remembering was the shoreline from way back when. What was there now is a rocky shoreline. It is interesting to me.

On their way out, they stopped at the Yigal Allon Center to view an exhibit called the "Jesus Boat." The boat was discovered in the mid-1980s, near the Valley of Ginnosar, on the Sea of Galilee, in a mud flat caused when the water from the Sea of Galilee was pumped out of the lake and into neighboring farms in an effort to save their crops from a drought. Carbon 14 dating places the age of the boat between 100 BC and 100 AD.[80]

In the old days, the Valley of Ginnosar was known as the "land of Gennesaret," where Jesus and his disciples landed after they crossed the Sea of Galilee. The boat is 26½' (length) by 7½' (width) by 4½' (height) and would have held up to fifteen people. The chances of it being the actual boat that Jesus rode in are slim, but it would represent what a large ship from that time would have looked like and could have easily held Jesus and all twelve of his disciples.

They continued on their way back to Jerusalem, going through the Plain of Megiddo. The hill beside this plan is called Armageddon. In fact, Armageddon means "Plain of Megiddo." According to John, "Historically, it is the one piece of ground that has had more battles on it than anywhere in the world." According to one interpretation of Revelations, it will be where the final battle will be fought before the Second Coming of Christ.

From there, they went to Nazareth, Jesus' hometown. They went to visit the small stone home of Mother Mary, which is enshrined inside a church. It has been visited by popes and pilgrims alike and is recognized by the Vatican as a place of worship. The Apostle John was given the sacred duty by Jesus while He was on the cross of caring for His mother until she died, which John faithfully did.[81]

John was interested in knowing what their guide thought of Jesus, being a Jew but also a biblical scholar. He recalls their discussion:

> [Our guide] was very, very knowledgeable about the Bible and he was an excellent guide. What I [found] most intriguing about him was he was very open about talking about his religion. At one point, I asked him a very interesting question. I said, "So, do Jews think of Jesus as a prophet?" And his response was, "I think of Jesus as a very good teacher, but I wouldn't call him a prophet. He had a lot of good things to say, but I don't call him a prophet." And I thought that was an interesting thing because the Muslims think of Jesus as a prophet. They think of Jesus in the end times, when Mohammed comes back, Jesus is going to return as well. They think Jesus is going to return from the dead and that he and Mohammed are going to work together, which I find really fascinating because Christians don't believe in anything [like that]. They've deified Jesus so that everybody else is wrong. I have to go back to what I love to say is that Jesus wasn't Christian. Christianity happened long after Jesus was dead. The Muslims are probably more open to the oneness of God because . . . they are able to establish that there are other prophets that are a part of other religions. What I find really fascinating is . . . and I'm not a proponent of any religion. I don't think organized religions [necessarily further our] enlightenment and spirituality. One of the things I find interesting about Islamic law is that [in one of their laws] Muslims are forbidden to deify Mohammed as Christians have deified Jesus, the son of Mary because Mohammed is not God. Mohammed

is the example of a perfect life. Allah is God. So, God is actually above. Basically Mohammed lived his higher self. That's what I believe [of] all of the religious messiahs and prophets—Buddha, Krishna, Jesus or Jeshua, and Mohammed. I believe that they all were able to come to a place of enlightenment in an enlightened way. Now they each had their own cultural differences they had to live within . . . confines. But they were each deified because they were the ones who were closest to God. It's a matter of . . . Christians have had crusades and all of these things because. . . they have decided that Jesus is the end-all-be-all. He is the Messiah. He is the one and everybody else is wrong. Well, when you hear someone like the Dali Lama say, "My religion is simple. My religion is kindness," I hate to say it but I don't think the man is going to hell. [John laughs.]

Finally, John and Michael returned to Jerusalem. After thanking their guide for a great tour, they headed to a restaurant for dinner and to unwind. It had been a long, but eventful day. They had returned to their roots of so long ago. Feeling satisfied, they went to their hotel for a few hours of sleep.

Very early the next morning they took a flight back to Athens. Upon arriving, they rented a car and drove to Delphi, the home of the oracle in ancient times. Incidentally, this was one of the places that I felt spiritually connected to when I had visited the temple in 1993. The city is located nearby in a beautiful mountainous setting, with quaint villages and ancient columns appearing here and there throughout the mist-covered hillsides along the way.

When they got to the town, they went in search of food. Most of the shops had not opened yet. They discovered a very nice restaurant, built on stilts off the side of a mountain, where they decided to have lunch. The restaurant opened early for them, probably because their customers had dwindled since the beginning of the off-season. John and Michael were the only customers and were given special service. They sat on the deck outside, looking out at the splendid view.

"John was very quiet," Michael remembers. "It was the day before the last day of the trip, and I wondered if he was thinking about what awaited him at home." John had ten wonderful days alone with his dear friend and companion, Michael. He had been many miles and centuries away from the reality of his impending divorce. Also, they had been traveling hard for several days at an exhausting speed, and John was worn out. He looked up at the mountain they were about to climb, to get to the ruins, and let out a sigh. "Oh my," he said to himself. "I am not looking forward to that big climb!"

After lunch, they walked up to the top of the mountain and had an excellent day exploring the ruins. They drove back to the Athens' airport later that day and checked into a hotel there.

The next day they took a flight to the beautiful, hilly island of Mykonos, with its white buildings and brightly colored flower window boxes. They rented a car and spent the whole day touring the island. They both liked the island very much. Michael definitely felt a connection to this place.

John muses about his experience at Mykonos:

> Yeah, I felt very comfortable there. In many ways it reminded me of Rehoboth, being on the seashore and a lot of Greek people [John laughs. His best friend, Tim, and his family are Greek and live in Rehoboth, Delaware.] Yeah, so we had breakfast in this little café and it was interesting to me because I was surrounded by all these guys who looked like Tevye from Fiddler on the Roof. [John chuckles.] They all have the little hats on and the gray wool stuff on and they really just looked that part. When I came home [it was] about a year or so later, [and I ate] at an American diner. I looked around the room, and I realized I was in a room full of people who looked like Tevye. So, it kind of reminded me that we are all pretty much the same wherever we go.

They spent the night at a hotel on the island, and the next morning they took a boat to the small, rocky island of Delos, a few miles southwest of Mykonos. Delos has twenty to thirty acres of intricate, decorative architecture from many centuries. Michael and John spent four or five hours exploring all the points of interest the island had to offer, which included many marble statues.

At the end of their excursion, they decided to drive to the very eastern edge of the island, where they stopped their car and got out. Through Michael's binoculars they looked out over the Aegean Sea at the islands in the distance. Using a map of the Greek Isles as a reference, they were able to pinpoint the direction of the island of Patmos. Michael could swear that he could just make it out in the distance.

In spite of their best efforts, they were not able to visit Patmos after all. Because it was off-season, the ferries were not making their regular runs. They finally had to give up. Michael describes the frustration of it:

> It had been the high season just a few weeks earlier. We could have gotten there in one morning, stayed there one night and left the next day. I tried over and over, and everything possible, to make it fit. We could not even rent a boat to get to that island fifty miles away. I can't tell you how many days I worked on this. The ferries would not give us confirmations. Finally, near the end of the month they said,

"Here's the schedule." Of course, it turned out to be just what we thought: one day there [on Patmos], [then] four or five days later to leave the island.

I wanted to go there because I thought this is the best I can do for John right now, but for whatever reasons, we can't get there. It wasn't meant to be. At that point, I think he [John] understood and accepted, too, that he wasn't supposed to be there at this point in time. Or, at least, everything he needed right now he had gotten from other places, and Patmos was to come later, if he needed to get there. That was as close as destiny would take him up to now.

John felt let down. He had held out hope, to that very day, that they could somehow manage to get there. Michael had already given up a day or two earlier. John shares his feelings and thoughts on Patmos:

I was kind of disappointed, of course. Sort of deflated [but] I'm a firm believer in that if it is supposed to happen, it will. And because it didn't, it wasn't supposed to have [happened] at that time. And now that I look back on it, I look at that and where I am in my life. It's sort of a representation of [my] life [back then]. Patmos [represented] end-times . . . the apocalypse and all those things. And I don't think we're there yet, and I don't think I am there yet. So, I don't think it is time for me to go back and touch that place yet. I do plan on going there some time in the future. But . . . it was just not meant to be. When the time comes for me . . . and I'm also kind of curious as to whether I need to go there by myself, be there alone. And, so, that may be a possibility.[82]

Resigning themselves to the situation, they bought passage on a high-speed ferry back to mainland Greece, to Athens. The boat trip back was really rough with rain and high waves spilling over the bow. It seemed to reflect the prevailing mood.

When they arrived in Athens, they hired a cab to get them to their hotel, in the heart of Athens, but for some reason the streets were blocked off. Something was going on, perhaps a festival, but they weren't sure. Unable to get them there, the cab driver dropped them off at the nearest underground train station so they could take the subway the rest of the way. The train let them off a few blocks from their hotel. They had to walk the rest of the way, with their suitcases in tow.

When they finally arrived at their hotel, John couldn't believe his eyes. "[It] was amazing," he remembers. "Michael had arranged for our last night there to be in this ultra swank hotel. When you walked out on the balcony of the hotel, you could look at the Acropolis. It was right there," he explains.

With a few hours left, they decided to spend the rest of their time wandering through the streets of Athens, visiting some of the shops and market places that are so prevalent in this large, bustling tourist center. They ended up at the Roman Market, which is actually a ruin, not a marketplace like they had expected. After a couple of hours, they headed back to the hotel and found a really fancy restaurant nearby where they would have one last nice dinner. They returned to their hotel and slept one last night in the lap of luxury. Early the next morning, they took a flight back to the States. Arriving in New York City, at JFK Airport, they embraced before parting ways.

What an adventure they had had! Their individual spiritual journeys, had led them to the place of their original spiritual journey with the Master, over two millennia ago. It must have been a tremendous feeling of completion and confirmation for both of them.

But our journey with John does not end here. It continues on, for his work has just begun. He is now speaking, traveling, and healing, very much as he did in his past life, but now the venues are contemporary. His audiences are modern, but the message is basically the same. He shares the knowledge, wisdom and energy imparted to him by the Master. Having witnessed Jesus teaching and healing others almost two thousand years ago, he now helps to carry His message forward into our modern world. He is helping all of us find Jesus' original message of love, a message that is timeless and not steeped in the religious dogma that has evolved over the centuries.

I believe John is preparing the way for the full return of the Christ Consciousness. He is the forerunner for Christ and he carries the Master's energy signature. When you are in his presence, you can feel the unconditional love of Jesus that surrounds him. When you look into his eyes, you sense the love and acceptance he has for everyone, which permeates from him. As a dear friend puts it:

> When you look into John's eyes, you instantly have one of two feelings: Either you want to pour out your inner heart and soul to him or you want to flee in order to hide the fear in your own heart from being discovered. You can only begin to imagine what it must have been like to look into the eyes of Jesus!

John is here to teach us to remember who we truly are: Children of God fully connected to the Divine and to one another. He is here to teach us to love one another, even as Jesus loves us, even as our Eternal Father/Mother in Heaven loves us, and to love ourselves.

CHAPTER SEVENTEEN

Stories of Healing

John returned from his trip to Israel and shared with me his fascinating journey. For him, it must have felt like a complete circle had been made. Now, more than ever, he was anxious to begin his spiritual mission. As 2006 came to a close, I made a commitment to myself to get back to work on the book. I contacted my friend, Vicki Warren, to see if she could refer me to someone who might help me get my book published. (Vicki is also a psychic reader, and has written a book called *Coffee, Donuts and God* a couple of years earlier.) She gave me the name and phone number of Rita Mills, the lady who had helped her publish her book. I e-mailed Rita in November 2006, but I was too busy with my job to follow up right then. Besides, I wanted to make one more pass over the manuscript before submitting it to her. So, after football season ended and my work load started to slow down a bit, I e-mailed her again to set up an appointment in February 2007.

We met at a French café and immediately hit it off. Rita is a tall, red-headed gal with a charming West Texas drawl. She had a twenty-year career at *The Houston Post*, a major metropolitan newspaper, which closed down about five years after she left. She can read people like a book and will tell you that she is good at "picking out a phony person." She quit the newspaper business in 1990 and went to the University of Houston as the managing editor of a publishing house there called Arte Publico Press where she stayed for four years. She left in 1997 and started her own book publishing consulting business called The Book Connection. Ten years after helping others publish their books, she started her own small publishing company called Blue Bonnet Boots and Books,[83] which specializes in books with a Texana theme. She started a children's picture book imprint, The ABC's, in 2006, that publishes the books that are the winners of The ABC's Children's Picture Book Competition.

I felt comfortable with Rita immediately and found myself pouring my heart out to her. As I told her the story about John, she listened with rapt attention. Did she believe me? Would she want to take on such a controversial topic? If I had to guess, taking into account her newspaper background, I would have said no.

However, she was fascinated by the subject. She wanted to give my manuscript to one of her best editors, Peggy Stautberg, to see if Peggy thought it was a viable project. She said she would get back to me in a couple of weeks, when Peggy had had time to read the manuscript and write a review. By our next meeting, Rita announced that not only did she believe me, but she wanted to take on my project because she felt that "this is what I have come here to do." I was dumbfounded! Rita and I have since become very good friends, and I owe her much more than I can ever repay.

When I first read Peggy's review of my manuscript and her editorial comments, I couldn't believe my eyes! The review was very favorable, and she said she couldn't wait to read more! She suggested that I add more material to the end of the book to catch the reader up to the present day, especially since the original draft had been completed seven years earlier, in May 2000. So, plans were made for me to write "the rest of the story." However, my personal life had plans of its own!

My new job had been a very good experience for me, but when my old boss left, things changed drastically. As the work environment became worse, I felt the Universe pulling me in a different direction. By June 2007, my situation with my new boss had become intolerable. I made a brave decision to suddenly change the entire direction of my life. I quit my job and went back out on the road with Randy that summer. It was the best decision I could have made. All the elements of my world were starting to come together. I would get to spend quality time with my husband again, travel around the country—which I loved to do—and get to see John more. I could also focus on my writing and spiritual work better without the stresses of work making it difficult to concentrate on writing.

In the spring of 2007, John really put himself out there with his speaking and healing work. I invited him to come to Texas in April. He flew into Austin and spoke at our new friend Anup's house. It was an amazing evening. John was really in his element. The living room at Anup's house was packed full of people curious to hear John's story. The next morning John and I did an early morning interview for the local TV station. When we finished, we went back to Anup's house to offer healings to those who wanted them. John and I worked together for the first time in giving healing sessions, and it was awesome! As John held each person's hands and sent him or her energy, he told them what their illnesses were related to. I sat in and added what I was getting from Spirit about how they could make the necessary changes in their lives that would sustain the healing they were receiving. We found that we worked well together, and it was very gratifying to be able to help others.

John has been facilitating healings for several years now and finds this work extremely fulfilling. He is amazed by what can take place through the power of God when people are willing to let go of their fears and be healed through faith. People often find it is very helpful to have someone, like John, facilitate a healing for them, so that they can step away from their egos long enough to let the healing take place within them. It is important for us to realize that healing is actually an *interactive* process which takes place between the healer, the person being healed, and God.

We have witnessed some significant healings taking place, especially in the last two or three years. The following are some truly amazing stories, told by the people who have experienced them.[84] The stories demonstrate what miracles can happen through the power of faith and love. I hope you enjoy these stories and realize that within each of us is the ability to heal ourselves through the power of God.

Diane's Story

[In] the summer of 2007, I was a cast member at the . . . Medieval Faire [in] Rock Creek, Ohio. John Davis was the director at that time. The week in between the first and second weekends of the faire, I was not feeling well. I was having headaches, blurred vision, [and] dizzy spells, and would black out for a brief period of time. I called the doctor, and he said he would call in medication for migraines for me.

Well, as the week went on it kept getting worse. The Friday before the second weekend a large lump developed on the base of my skull. It was about the size of a tennis ball and very hard. I knew right away that this is what [was] causing my problem. I was not near home as I live one-hundred-thirty-five miles away from the faire, so I called the doctor and he said to come and see him when I got back in town. Since I was not feeling well, I was certain I could not walk in the parade that weekend. So, I went to John before the morning [cast call] meeting and told him I was not feeling well, and [that I] was not going to walk in the parade.

I was happy just leaving it at that and going on with the day. John [asked me], "What is the problem?" I began to cry because I was very worried about what this large lump was and told him my story. Without hesitation, John grabbed my head, put his hand on the large lump, and pushed my face into his chest. All I could do was stand there and take it. He's not a small man—much stronger than I—so I stood there with my face in his chest and just cried for a few minutes. After John was done holding my head, he looked into my eyes and [asked,] "How do you feel now?" I told him I wasn't sure, that [I felt] kind of strange. I had stopped crying and was not hurting badly. I just felt different. John said. "Okay, you don't have to do parade. Go sit down for a bit."

After morning meeting, he asked me again how I was feeling. I told him I couldn't believe it, [that] I felt great and [the] lump was going away. John said to me, "You knew I would do that, didn't you?" I said to John, "No, if I was going to ask for your help with something it would be something major like my back since I have degenerative disc disease." He chuckled and said, "You don't need me for that; it's better." All of this took place before nine in the morning. By eleven I was feeling so great I couldn't even express it. The lump was gone [and] it felt like a little bruise was there, and that only lasted a day. My back is doing very [well]; it has stopped crumbling away and is getting stronger. This is only a sample of what John Davis has done for me. Physically, mentally, emotionally John has saved my life. I call him my "Wizard of Awes." He has taught me many life lessons and has done wonderful things for my entire family. John has also taught me how to not just help myself but to help others as well.

Diane Roberts, Ohio

Amber's Story as Told to John Davis by her Mother

It's Suzanne, Amber's mum. I was stunned when I saw your website, and all I will say is wow! Amber is the one that found it—figures. I really shouldn't be surprised at all and here's why. I'll start at the beginning because I don't know where else to start.

My mother died peacefully, at home, in January 2003. Amber and I lived with my parents at the time, and she was there when Mum passed. We had had hospice in [the home] for six months. They worked with my dad and Amber and [me] and they really did an outstanding job. Mum was really the only one who had a problem with the whole dying process.

Anyway, when she passed [away], the rector from the church was called in, and we sat around planning the service. Mum had been specific about certain things that she wanted, and she had written them down. Amber sat next to [the rector] and for comfort, we handed her Mum's Bible. She was just six [years old], about to turn seven in March. There needed to be a reading from the New Testament, and the chapter from John was chosen: the old stand-by, John 14:1-3, "Let not your heart be troubled . . ." [The] problem was we had nobody to read it. Everybody we asked thought they would get too emotional. Amber volunteered. [The] people in charge of the funeral services] rejected her because she was so young and didn't think she could learn the three verses in time. She insisted. Again, she was turned down. Somebody did finally read the verse, but after the service Mum's Bible disappeared. After searching high and low for it, I finally found it in Amber's bedroom with a bookmark in it in the book of John. Dad had a fit and took the Bible away from her, and she burst into tears and said, "But I was reading from John." I don't think he believed her. I was skeptical [myself] but went and got her my Bible and told her that she could use mine instead. (She didn't have a real Bible, just a children's version that was presented to her when she was baptized at the age of three in 1999.) On Saturdays, I would get up, and instead of finding her watching cartoons, I would find her curled up in the recliner reading from John.

I noticed that it was during faire season 2005 that she really began to be drawn to you, and of course in 2006, if I wanted my kid, I just needed to look for her at [your stage]. Amber is not drawn to people lightly, and there really is some sort of pull there. I [had] no clue what it is, but felt for a while that it went beyond the "funny, comedy, swordplay" stuff because honestly she's seen that all her life. I've done living history since she was born. If she doesn't like a person, there is a whole list of logical reasons, and the same [applies] if she likes someone. She's hung out with [other stage acts at faire] since she was six months old. That's because I hung out with them. She sought you out on her own or was drawn [to you].

In March 2005, I received a phone call that no parent wants to get. My daughter had gone with my father to her cousin's birthday party [in] Hanover, Pennsylvania. I had attended a memorial service for my godmother and was meeting them. They never made it. On my way up the road, I received a phone call from Hershey Medical Center, informing me that my daughter was in their trauma bay. There had been an accident. They wouldn't even tell me how badly she was injured—simply that she was still alive. After making several phone calls while driving up the road (Hershey is almost two hours from where I live), I was able to ascertain the nature of the accident and the extent of her injuries. It had been a fifty-mile-per-hour, head-on collision, which resulted in the death of the driver of the other car, and left my father horribly mangled and pinned in his burning car. According- ing to witnesses, flames were three to four feet high and passersby and folks from the area formed a bucket brigade to knock back the blaze until the volunteer fire department could arrive. Another gentleman knocked a hole in the rear window of the car and pulled Amber free. The car had filled with smoke, fire was blowing back through the dashboard and because the locks and windows were electronic and her arm was badly broken—she couldn't get out of the car. She had managed to unfasten her seatbelt and had jumped to the floor of the car—simply because that is what she had been taught: smoke rises. She got burned. The fire was following the gas line back to the gas tank, which rested under the rear seat of the car. Amber was effectively sitting on a time bomb.

The gentleman, whom I call "her angel," carried her over and handed her to his wife, who wrapped her in a blanket and held her until the paramedics arrived. They evalu- ated her and my father's girlfriend, who had also been pulled free of the car by several gentlemen, and called for choppers. Amber was airlifted to Hershey, my father's girlfriend to York Hospital. Dad remained pinned in the car until hydraulic equipment could be brought in to free him. Ultimately, he was taken to York Hospital as well for four orthope- dic surgeries and then flown to Hopkins Bayview, so they could treat his burns. He never came home from the hospital. Six months later, he succumbed to infection resulting from further injuries gotten while in a nursing home for rehabibilitation.

When I arrived at Hershey's trauma bay, I was just overwhelmed by how tiny and helpless Amber looked lying on the gurney, all tangled up in wires and tubes. She had taken a bad blow to the right side of her head, having gotten thrown against the door in the initial impact. She got thrown the other way as well, bumping her jaw against a set of antique wooden doll beds that were going as a present to her cousin. That bruised the other side of her face as well and left her with a loose tooth. Her right arm was broken, a one hundred percent displaced fracture that had to hurt like hell, considering that she is right-handed, and I was told that she removed her seat belt with it. It was a growth plate injury, meaning simply that if the plate was badly damaged—her arm would stop growing and she would eventually have to go through the very painful process of bone-lengthening surgery. She was still in a c-collar; they had not cleared her neck yet, meaning she could still have spinal cord damage. They had cleared her abdomen, but she would have the contusions from the seatbelt for two months. I had been told over the phone that her leg was broken, but when I arrived I discovered that it wasn't. However, it was badly lacerated from the broken window glass. When I talked to "her angel" on the phone about a month later, he apologized all over himself for her leg. But she was alive. I'd take her with stitches in her leg. It had happened trying to extricate her from the car. It turned out to be [a] bad laceration—almost into her kneecap— the glass severed muscle and nerves—leaving her with a permanently numb knee, and one that she would really have to work with in order to regain range of motion.

All these injuries were honestly not as much of a concern as her head injury. They hurt, I knew, but would heal. The head injury could be permanent. She drifted in and out of consciousness in the hospital and couldn't remember things that had happened the day before the accident. I was told by the pediatric neurologist that after six to eight weeks, what you see is what you get, with regards to what she would recover. I was told she had suffered Closed Head Trauma and that she had taken a bad blow to the head. My father and his girlfriend also had head injuries, but not as severe as Amber's. Airbags deployed for them. For some reason, she was thrown sideways into the door. There is no magic pill for recovery from a head injury. All you can do is learn to deal with the residual. I sat and cried, thinking of the struggle that she would have. I, too, have a permanent head injury, having suffered a massive stroke at the age of five. I didn't want my child to have to face some of the same things that I had faced growing up.

Her pediatrician wanted to wait to see how she went with regards to the head injury and noted that, additionally, she was showing symptoms of Post-Traumatic Stress Syndrome and thus, that was added to the diagnosis. [This was] expected, really, given everything she experienced and saw as a result of the accident. She saw the body of the driver of the other car removed and placed in a body bag right in front of her, and she saw my dad's unconscious girlfriend laid next to her in the field. She reached for Sandy but was held back by someone. She saw people climbing all over the Buick with buckets and fire extinguishers. She heard my dad screaming that his legs were on fire. Dad had hollered for her after the impact to see if she was okay, and she had answered him, but she said that he kept hollering for me and for Sandy. She knew that he was still in the car because she hadn't seen him lifted out, and of course, she knew the car was burning because she saw the smoke and flames. In fact the first question she asked me when I arrived at the trauma bay was, "Is Pop-pop dead?" She cussed out the chopper crew . . . because they had to cut away her clothes to assess her injuries, and, of course, they strapped her down to the backboard because she was thrashing around.

A counselor was recommended and she began with that, but her short-term memory was not what it was. She was also doing a great deal of stumbling. Dad died in September 2005, right after faire started in September. By [that time] she was really having a hard time and fourth grade was just not shaping up to be a good year. She was very close to her grandfather. His home was sold. We [had] lived with him, and we had to move out very quickly. There were a lot of things that were upsetting to me. I can't imagine how she felt between that and trying to cope with the memory issues. I felt like she was giving up on things in general. Frustrated, I went back to her pediatrician, who sent us to Kennedy Krieger Institute. He told me that all of the symptoms she was exhibiting were fairly typical of head injury. I knew that, of course. She was tested and found to have deficits relating to her head trauma. Coupled with her ADHD, that she had been diagnosed with [in] 2004, we were just not in a good place. Her IQ? 124. Her executive functioning? Low. I would give her two and three step directions like "Put your clothes in the laundry and take a shower." She'd stand in the bathroom and forget why she was there. I was [having to remind] her to actually EAT breakfast, instead of just fixing it. Bits and pieces of the accident were coming back to her but usually as nightmares. She'd run down the hall and launch herself into my bed at two in the morning and just cry and cry and cry. Her responses to things became very illogical, and she knew it and that angered her more because she didn't understand why this had happened. Her memory began to frustrate her as well and she would get very angry when she couldn't remember something and began giving up on a lot of things, including schoolwork. She lived in tears. The final straw came in September 2006.

Amber had returned to Irish Step dancing five weeks after the accident and finished out the semester—her arm still in a cast—simply for therapy, so that she could move the injured knee. Her doctor wasn't too wild about the impact with the floor and what further damage this might do to her knee [but] this was something that she had LOVED to do. She began dancing at the age of four, taking Highland dance and by age seven had switched to Irish [dance]. She was put in hard shoes within six months of starting lessons. She had simply loved to dance. She went back in 2005, but her heart wasn't in it. She stopped dancing at the faire, something that she would ALWAYS do, especially [during] the final pub show at the end of the night. I tried to encourage [her], but it became more like fussing. By 2006, I had given up. She went back to class and walked out declaring, "I don't want to do this anymore, Mummy. I want to quit." I asked why. [She said,] "I can't remember any of the steps to the dances I used to do." And she began to cry. I kept trying to encourage, but got frustrated myself and finally gave up. It broke my heart to see her just sitting at the final pub show, instead of dancing with everybody else.

In mid-October 2006, Sharon Wothke arrived at Maryland Renaissance Festival (MDRF) for her birthday. I've known Sharon for ten years and she used to travel with her husband's band, so I would see her every weekend for nine weekends. Lately she had not been at MDRF, but working instead and would pop in to see people around her birthday. Perfect timing. She is [a] talented Highland dancer, and I had no idea that she had other talents as well. I saw her and said hi, and she asked after Amber. She and other members of the band have known my child since she was six months old. I told her about the accident, and about Amber's injuries, and how frustrated we both were because there really didn't seem to be anything anybody could do expect simply deal with the residual symptoms. Kennedy Krieger had given me a plan for dealing with [Amber's] issues, but she was still sullen and wasn't smiling. She was irritable and frustrated because of the memory problems—very difficult to deal with, and we weren't off to such a good start with fifth grade, either. Remembering homework was a MAJOR issue even though she would write it down, and the teacher and I would double check her.

Faire was pretty much the something that she was looking forward to this year, and she told me that it was the only place where she had fun. I had noticed that she had attached herself yet again to the Hack and Slash show, and for the life of me, at the time, I had no clue why. She was in the audience in 2005, and I would hear bits of the "beer song" and stories of how she got wet from having "beer" spit in her direction by Hack (John's stage name). She thought this was all tremendous fun, so in 2006 when she returned to the Jury Rig stage, I really didn't bat an eye, just as long as I knew where she was. This was the time that she would crack a bit of a smile, and I figured if it made her happy, fine. Besides, you guys have been around FOREVER. It's not like I didn't know who you were.

In either case, in talking to Sharon, she took my hand and said with a smile, "I know someone who might be able to help you." I was expecting a doctor's name, or a therapist, or a clinic or something. She asked if I was open to anything. At this point, yes I was. I just wanted my child back. She smiled again and said, "A very good friend of mine is a healer. His name is John Davis." I was just stunned. "Hack?" [I asked.] She confirmed that it was and told me that I should talk to you (John). I agreed. Amber already had some sort of connection there and this would make her day. I told Sharon that Amber adored you. All I had heard for over a year was "Hack this…. and Hack that." The whole pull there was a bit odd to me because she had sought you out on her own and [it] kind of stuck. I still couldn't figure why. Of course now I know.

I remember pulling you aside and explaining part of my dilemma, and you told me to tell her to come and find you the following weekend. She still had no idea at this point, and I decided to have a discussion with her in the car on our way home from faire. "What if Mummy told you that there is somebody that might be able to help you with your memory issues?" "You mean I'd get my memory back and be able to remember things better?" "Maybe." I knew there were no guarantees here. "Would you be willing to talk to this person?" "I guess," [she replied.] "What if I told you that it was Hack?" Her eyes positively popped. "Oh thank you Mum!!!!" "Don't thank me; thank Ms. Sharon when you see her again. I told her about the accident and she told me about him. Neat, huh?" [I said.] "Yeah. Wow," [she responded.] She beamed, and of course ran off to find you the following weekend. The rest, as they say, is history. She doesn't talk about the healing experience itself too much. I think that is something she prefers to keep to herself. She told me a bit and you told me a bit, but I figure the rest is between the two of you.

I guess what I'm trying to say is that it all makes impossible, improbable, beautiful sense. You have helped her tremendously, not only with the memory issues [but] just with dealing with bumps in the road in general. She has decided that she wants to play the piano and is beginning to read music, something that requires a great deal of memory. I had difficulty with her [going to] Irish step dance classes in September and early October. She didn't want to go because she said that she couldn't remember the steps. Now she can't stand still and dances around the house. She is cooking and doing needlework and remembering her homework and SMILING!!!!!!! She has decided to re-join the children's choir at my parent's church and sings with about thirty other children once a month for [Sunday] services and for special services. She [is able to] memorize the music.

You have truly been a miracle in her life and in mine, really, because I have my child back. We still have [the] typical ten-year-old issues, but they're just that—typical ten-year-old issues (like the messy bedroom, and underwear behind my couch and under the bed, peanut butter on the bathroom floor, etc.) They say that things happen for a reason. I truly believe that. God bless.

Suzanne Devier, Virginia

The Mime's Healing Story

It was my first day in the new stilt-pants. They were a bit too long, so I had to keep hitching them up. The [mime] troupe stopped by a tree for some patrons to take pictures, and then we moved on. As I stepped away from the tree, I realized I had a problem. The second step convinced me that I wasn't going to recover from the problem. I didn't take a third step because I was on my way down. The bottom of my left stilt had gotten caught in the hem of my right stilt-pant leg and twisted around so badly that I landed wrong on the hill beside the chapel. I landed on my left elbow, and somehow managed to scuff my nose and my chin as well.

As is my habit when I fall in front of audience members, I sat up with what I hoped was an indignant expression, and brushed dirt and mulch from my costume, wondering exactly how bad the elbow was going to be. I looked around for large men to put my arms around so they could walk me back up. A medium large guy is near, and he comes. A little further off is a tall man, and I wave appealingly to him. He comes over wearing a wry grin, and I realize that I have waved down the man who signs my paychecks. How embarrassing. Well, the man I know and the man I don't know pop me back to my stilt-feet, and I wave to everyone and walk away cheerfully, brushing debris from my backside.

A little way off, I stop and face my partner with an enquiring expression, gesturing to my face. She frowns and points to two spots on my face, and mouths the word 'blood'. We head to Bruce's [face painting] booth, and I lean down with an urgent plea on my face, holding on to a gazebo post as he dabs white on me in an attempt at a hasty repair. "It's not great," he apologizes, showing me the mirror. But it's better than the bloody naked spots I saw when I looked at his mirror before.

When we finish our walkabout and get down, we're finished for the day. I realize that I had been babying the elbow [when] I try to remove my jacket. And it's bad. I know it's bad, because I had broken the right elbow last year, so I know what that feels like. I also know there's nothing to be done for it because if it is immobilized completely, I will lose full range of motion permanently.

I drive home right-handed, for once thankful for my automatic transmission, my left hand resting quietly in my lap. Once home, I fashion a sling from a bright scarf that is not only more attractive than hospital issue, but fits better and is more comfortable. I wear this on and off while I vacation with my family for four days at the beach, letting the three of them do the carrying and lifting [while] I supervise and organize.

I arrive at faire the next Saturday wearing the scarf sling and carefully insert my arm into the jacket sleeve, wondering how long this injury will plague me and how much it will affect my performance. I manage fairly well on all fronts, but [I] am glad of the scarf again by afternoon.

Sunday morning, the scarf is again in place, and as I wander towards sign-in, I see John, who asks what happened. I explain, and he hugs me sympathetically, holding the injured elbow. I relax and breathe against him, and my elbow begins to get hot. After a long hug, which nourishes me on many levels, John releases me. "Better?" he asks. "Yes," I respond, because of course I am better: warmer, safer, happier. Oh, and... my elbow feels... it feels... hmmm. I push the scarf aside and move my arm. It's better. No, it's a lot better. In fact, it may be ALL better. John chuckles. "'Kay?" he grins. "Mmmhmm," I respond, with a frown of puzzlement, still testing the elbow.

It doesn't hurt to put on my jacket. In fact, other than a slight soreness, my elbow functions normally. At day's end, I reach for the scarf and put my arm in, thinking to support it after several hours of use. The scarf doesn't make me feel any better. I take it off. I guess my elbow is healed. Whoa! So that's [my] story.

Anonymous, Maryland

Anup's Healing Story

Below is my story of experiencing Divine Love through John and Sharon, and of experiencing first hand, the remarkable power of faith healing. Up to this point in my life, as I continued to learn about religions, and as I began to experience 'religious' people and proselytizing (which sometimes is insulting to other faiths), I began to disrespect organized religion. I felt a need to unshackle free wills to experience life, but without any reduction in reverence and faith for the divine, or for the enlightened beings in whose names these powerful broker institutions had been created.

I have developed a kind of obsession [with] discussing religion, especially with the evangelicals, to churn people to think and not take the easy dictated path of rote routine and dogma, but to take the path of awareness, understanding, tolerance and un-conditional love— *without judgment for other peoples.* The gift of John's experience is to me an affirmation from God, of my beliefs, and of my critical approach to power-structured masculine desert religions.

I regularly tour Cincinnati, Ohio for work. On one such tour, I decided to visit Sally and Jason, wonderful friends that live in Toledo, Ohio, three hours from Cincinnati. During that visit Sally reported, "[The] husband of my colleague is a reincarnation of John the Apostle." As a Hindu, and growing up in India listening to firsthand stories of reincar-nation from several family members, I did not roll my eyes. I was curious, and got referred to John's website, and was also given a remarkable CD with a recording of John's past life hypnotic regression.

The background I come from did not make me roll my eyes, but it took more for me to just accept [the idea of] John-reincarnate. It was mostly what I heard in the regres-sion recording, and a few stories on John's website. [The] radical truths revealed therein that would not be familiar to one growing up as a Christian, were proof enough for me to believe in John's story, without a doubt.

After having met him, [and] knowing him—his Christ-like conduct of love, hu-mility, gentleness, humor—I wonder what basis one has to doubt their luck and fortune of knowing and meeting John the Beloved [and] shunning his story with intellectual bellicosity. People more readily believe a warmonger and his false pretexts to go to war than a man preach-ing love and [the] simplicity of pathways to the divine.

As soon as I returned from Ohio, I emailed John, asking him to consider a trip to Austin. To my surprise, he responded! I guess being in the early stages of 'coming out,' he was not yet being barraged by thousands of believers and seekers. Over the next six months, we exchanged emails discussing the similarities of Jesus' teachings, [as spoken of] in his regression, to Hindu/eastern beliefs. [We] discussed some stories, and in the course of these exchanges I also introduced to him a friend named Matt Bayuk.

Matt's voice had begun to fail in the last four years. He was unable to talk without his voice breaking [and was] not able to sing at all. His first passion is music. [He] has a budding career in singing with a band of his own, but was struck with an ailment that no professional or quack had been able to put a finger on. Matt had to hire a singer as a workaround. John was able to help Matt considerably through prayer, without ever [having met] him, a miracle indeed! This was very encouraging, and a story to help bring more people to my house for John's talk. *I recommend you read Matt's full story as well.* His band's website is www.playeronband.com

John e-introduced me to Sharon, a psychic who triggered John the Apostle within John Davis and has subsequently partnered with him to [assist him in] his mission. Sharon happens to live in Houston, Texas and coordinated John's trip to Texas, including [a speaking engagement in] Austin as well. I was thrilled and anxiously awaited [his arrival] while marketing his talk, [which] was to happen at my place, [by] sending out emails, putting out fliers, conversing with strangers, [and] leaving fliers at churches. (I knew it was mostly futile to leave fliers at church office mail boxes, but you never know when the seed planted in one allegedly hopeless indoctrinated mind may germinate and seek true light to grow further.)

In this process I met a woman—a monk—who had been to India/Nepal, and as soon as she held the flier in her hand and read a few lines, she said, "Whatever this is, must be true, as my head is tingling. It does that when something like this is true." I was happy to find a "non eye-roller." In this effort I also sent out emails to every yoga teacher in Austin, besides over one hundred twenty people in my e-vite address book. Stacy, my wife, was not happy about all this. This was all 'bull' to her. But she is sweet and relented very easily, for she will do almost anything for me.

Finally, at the destined hour, John arrived, I picked him up from the airport, brought him home, where he changed promptly to enjoy the warm Texas weather and sat outside and conversed with my neighbor while I went out to finish my errands. Then Sharon arrived a few hours later from Houston; I felt her festive energy instantly. She definitely had very unique eyes that had a penetrating attribute. We headed out to lunch with Matt and his buddy Charles at the famous Oasis overlooking Lake Travis. John could not wait to meet Matt, who [he] said had a special connection to Jesus.

It was a perfect day, [the] perfect atmosphere, and [the] company of wonderful people. The table was emotionally charged; I was sort of floating. Charles, who meditates daily, also felt the elation. John was telling his stories [and] Sharon was reading [for] Matt and Charles, [telling them about] their many past lives together. "You have been buddies for many lives, and you will notice [that] you end up in the same place, even after separating for a while," [she said]. I knew this to be true for them. She told [me] many things about my family and me that were all true; just amazing.

At one point, John felt the spirit go through him and he showed us how the hair on his hand stood straight up. This same thing I noticed [the] next day during his healing session with my neighbor's newborn baby, born with an extra chromosome—an ailment that causes death within two weeks of birth. (The baby is still alive, three months hence).

Anyway, we left the Oasis, I promptly got lost—because twice, I did not listen to the psychic (woman) sitting next to me. At least I was assured I was all male. We got back and prepared for the evening talk. One hundred Samosas (Indian stuffed potato pyramids)

came in on time, and I made Chai (Indian tea) for everyone. It was a wonderful group of people, about twenty-five, nowhere close to my expectations.

I did introductions, and then Sharon started with her portion of the talk, subsequently handing it over to John. The talk was amazing, and wonderful. All ears were glued to the sound stream from John. We ended with a quick relaxing meditation. I was touched by John's humility when immediately following the talk he asked me to critique his talk: "What did you think, what can I do better?" I was taken aback a bit. It was perfect—very down-to-earth, informal but spiced with mystery, suspense, humor, magic, and fascination, and yet realistic. Realistic because of just who John is. You see him smile and you feel instant relief.

I took pictures half way through the session in silent camera mode (photos online on http://picasaweb.google.com/semiprecious.com).

A friend of mine, Jenny Hoff, is an early morning news anchor for KXAN, local affiliate of NBC. She is an "eye-roller," but somehow she agreed to interview them both on live TV! It was a two-and-one-half minute slot, but this was just a start for John and Sharon, and they were very excited [for] this opportunity. Unfortunately, the day before the live interview, the channel asked us to not bring up any claims of who John is/was, so it was agreed to talk about faith healing, reincarnation etc. and then direct people to John's website. We had to wake up at six o'clock in the morning for the half-past seven interviews. It went very well.

Later on, interestingly, Jenny [told] me that her dad was very spiritual and had exposed her to reincarnation from the very beginning, even telling her about her past lives and her mission of this life: to be a spiritual leader! However, she still rolls her eyes.

Sharon and John stayed overnight at our place. [In the morning] I made my signature egg dish, using south Indian rasam powder as spice; John loved it, a perfect blessing for the deck that had been completed the night before. In the afternoon they did a faith healing . . . and then it was my turn. My feet needed a lot of help. This ailment has been with me for over a decade. It worsened this year to the point of [my] not being able to walk at all after an exhausting hike day or a dance night. Any night that followed reasonable effort by my feet, I had to crawl to the bathroom when nature called. I could not even stand up many times. I had even begun to use a walking stick for a day or two until the pain subsided. I had to wear shoes all the time so I could use arch supports. Arch supports were of help for some time, but at this point, even with their use I would have trouble. I used to have to put my feet down a certain way when walking, the shoe laces had to be pulled tight every hour so my feet felt supported, [and] I could feel bones rubbing at the ankle joint. I was losing the protective layer between joints, I think. A friend's wife [who is a] doctor once said it was arthritis. I never went to a doctor; [I] did not think they could do anything about it, and painkillers have their own side effects. Some nights I did break down and use painkillers to be able to sleep.

John and Sharon and I sat down for the healing session. John held both my legs above the ankle, kneeling on the floor. He closed his eyes and I followed. I heard Sharon say, "Your arches have fallen from the burden of [the] other people you help; help yourself first." Then John started to laugh, eyes closed. [He] saw a previous life of mine wherein I had abandoned my friends/family when [I was] forced [make a] long journey on foot, forced perhaps by a regime. I could not help the ones I loved, but I helped myself by continuing to walk, to save myself. Guilt from this made my feet ail. I was already in tears for no reason. I had been limping that day and after the session I was not; now I was not sure if I was limping before or not!

Next morning, for the first time, I had absolutely no pain, but it could have been just a passage of time cure. "My legs feel great," I said to Stacy. "I will believe it if you can walk after your brother's wedding night," she replied. The wedding was four days [after] John's talk at my place. We left for India. It was a 14-hour flight from Newark to India, direct. Horrible . . . flight, deliberately designed for third world travelers. I was so thrilled with my new legs that I walked around the plane a lot. When the outsourced Nigerian airhostesses expressed unhappiness, I . . . told them as to why I was enjoying being on my feet. I [convinced] one out of the three.

A few days later we got to the wedding venue, Lukhnow, by an overnight train from Delhi. I was up all day meeting and greeting long lost relatives at the resort, where the bride's family hosted everyone. The night arrived, the live 'band' arrived, the music started and I was the first one to start dancing. As the tradition is, the band and the groom's party walk and dance together to the welcome gate where the bride's family welcomes every member with garlands and hugs, and then onto the reception. This walk [and] dancing vigorously, and then being on my feet through the reception, with formal shoes that do not support my feet at all, was a certain disaster for the next day. [When I woke up the next morning I felt] somewhat afraid that the moment of truth was upon me, but I had to have faith. At least there was no pain during the night. Many times pain would surface only when I put my feet on the ground and put load on them. I put my feet down. I stood up! I was ABLE to stand up! And no pain!

"Stacy, look, I am walking, and no pain!"

She was very impressed. "Okay, okay. There is something to John, but this does not give you the excuse to abuse your feet. You should still go see a doctor."

I was in bliss, and I won't see a doctor. Since then, many days of exhaustive dancing has followed at worst a minor limp for the first minute of walking after getting up from bed. Using arch support actually causes pain. Now I walk around the house all day on my bare feet. I now only put on Indian slip-on-shoes (jooties) even to go out, and avoid the airtight shoes all together! I love it. I will continue to own the AustinDancer title www.myspace.com/austinDancer.

> Thank you, John, Sharon.
> Thank you, God. Thank You,
> Thank You, Thank You.
> Anup Pandey, Austin, Texas

———•·•———

Matt's Singing Story

I have been playing music and singing as long as I can remember. Learning to play instruments and writing music and words came very naturally to me. It was clear to me, at an early age, that this was my purpose in life, and I have worked hard to develop these skills with the hope that one day, I could help others by giving them something they can relate to both musically and lyrically.

I formed a group in college and we were met with great success. That which seemed to be destined for me came to pass without question. We recorded our third album in early 2001, and we were working hard to promote it. It was around this time that my voice began to deteriorate.

At first I thought nothing of it, but as time went on, it became more and more serious. I began seeing doctors who would perform painful endoscopies to simply tell me there was nothing wrong with me… but there obviously was. That was five years ago. Since then I have seen several doctors, several vocal coaches, hypno-therapists, and psychologists. Everyone had their theories, but no one could help me… and the problem eventually began affecting my ability to produce sound at all, even in my speaking voice.

It was a very difficult time for me. That which defined me for so long was being taken away, with no apparent reason or solution. I began to lose confidence in myself as well as hope. I was unable to write anything new.

I have always been a very spiritual person. I was brought up Catholic and found myself fascinated by other religions and spiritual beliefs as well. They were always a powerful inspiration in my writing. I had already explored healings such as kinesiology and had [had] several "balances" when a friend of mine told me about John. His story was fascinating, and I needed all the help I could get, so I sent [John] an email in November of 2006, asking him to pray for me. I didn't know what to expect, but I had received a response fairly quickly telling me he had felt a strong presence of Jesus when he read my email, and that I was in his prayers.

I was becoming very depressed at the time, and it was amazing to have heard back such a response. A few weeks went by, and I had another experience with my cousin who heals using alchemy, but although I was starting to feel better, my voice had not improved… but something felt different.

My family travels to Mexico once a year just before Christmas to spend time together, and I always bring my guitar so I can continue to play while I am on vacation. John sent me an email the first night I was in Mexico letting me know I was in his thoughts and offering a very wise insight into problems we face… in that "it's our thoughts that create us." For some reason, at that moment, it was exactly what I needed to hear. [For] the first days of the trip, my voice had come back to me, not one hundred percent, but I was speaking to people with ease. It was the first time in a very long time that I was able to speak this way. As the week went on, I began to regress, but not before I was able to partially sing for an entire audience of appreciative vacationers one random evening at a piano in the lobby bar.

We returned home, and things were back to the way they were… except again, something felt different. I said a prayer Christmas Eve asking God for my voice so that I may share it with the world. I caught a cold the second night back in the United States. One evening, stuffed up and tired, I sat in front of the piano. I had long loved the song "Hallelujah" by Jeff Buckley, and it had come to be my "theme" song over the past months, but I couldn't sing it… which hadn't kept me from trying. I sat down and began to play it. For one reason or another, this time, I was able to contort my muscles in a certain manner, and I could sing! I sang and sang, and although it didn't sound great, I was singing. I looked up above the piano and I was staring at a picture of the nativity scene. It was a rubbing of a famous piece of artwork that my family had made one trip to Italy. I broke down.

The memory of that night has not left me, and my voice continues to improve. They say healers don't do the healing themselves, but that they show people how to find the faith and power to heal themselves. I don't know why my voice left me in the first place or what it really took for me to begin to heal, but John has helped me find the power to heal, both physically and mentally, and for that, I will forever give thanks.

Matt Bayuk, Austin, Texas

Mary Jane's Story

Well, back in 1962 I was hit by a car that drove through a four-way stop. I was thrown through the windshield of the car and had many injuries from that accident; that is when my kidney started aching.

In 1971 I was hit by a train, pronounced dead twice and was determined I [would not die] because my oldest son was with me, and I needed to make certain he was all right. We both survived. As you can imagine, I had head injuries, many internal injuries, broken bones, and on and on and on from that wreck. One thing that stands out in my mind is my left arm. I cannot, have not, been able to lift it for years and years. Even after many years of physical therapy, I have difficulties.

Next, in 1981 I started choking when I would eat. I never knew why. The doctor stretched my throat two different times, and it would only help for a short period of time. Shortly after I started choking, I started having problems with my eyelids. They would just close for no apparent reason, and often times when I would blink they would not come back open without me physically taking my hand and opening [them]. Most of the time, [I was] just holding my eyes open until I was home, [like when] I was driving or [finished] doing whatever it was I was doing, [like] cooking, cleaning, [and] sewing.

I noticed some years later that I [would] have this twitching going on in my body. Not just a small twitch like you may get in your eye, but severe twitching and painful, also. This twitching would go throughout my entire body. After seven different doctors and lots of testing, I finally found someone who knew what my problem [was].

In 1994, I was diagnosed with a form of Muscular Dystrophy called Myasthenia Gravis (MG). This disease causes weak muscles throughout the entire body. Walking across the room or up steps is a [constant] challenge. Daily life was becoming harder and harder to live. [It was becoming] more and more difficult to do anything without being exhausted. I need to mention that during this time, in 1993 my youngest son died of cancer at age thirty-three. My father died a few years later and now, on top of that stress and my illness, I had to take care of my mother, who was not well at all.

Often times just to go up stairs to feed her or change her, I would have to stop halfway up and sit down on the steps to rest before I could finish going up. The doctors were very discouraging and said there was nothing they can do. They gave [me] many medications just to keep my eye muscles working, so I could keep my eyes open and told me "just learn to live with it. You will become weaker and eventually end up in a wheel chair." I was taking five pills a day just to keep my eyes open.

One day, my daughter told me about this amazing man she met, and he helped her and she was determined that I needed to meet him. I went to the festival one day, and she introduced me to John Davis. John, my husband, Bill, and I talked, and John held my hand, and it changed my life immediately. I was able to eat and walk and see and do things that I had not been able to do in years. Now I take one pill a month instead of five a day. My legs are stronger, and I can walk now. I am back to sewing, and doing things that I have not done in a very long time.

Words cannot explain the feeling that came over me that day. John held my hand, and he began to shake and tears were coming out of this man that I had just met. I was certain that whatever was going on was hurting him and that I drained his energy. That made me feel bad, really bad; I am still not really over that experience. But John said it took nothing away from him: he was able to go on and perform the rest of the day and still continue with his duties as the entertainment director of the festival. I went back and met with him another day to work on feelings that I needed to deal with and again he was an amazing help to me and my husband. There is not a day that goes by that sometime during the day one of us says, "Thank You, John."

Mary Jane Roberts, Ohio

Maria's Story

During the run of the Maryland faire in 2003, John would stay over during the week so he could work out at the local gym. During one of his workouts, he ran into a gym instructor named Richard, who was a big Hack and Slash fan. Richard struck up a conversation with John and, they became friends.

Richard was one of these fellows who fell in and out of love very quickly. John was used to seeing him bring a different woman to fair each weekend.

One weekend, Richard came to faire with a lovely young woman, whom he introduced to John as his new girlfriend, Maria. John thought she was a very nice person, but didn't really give her much thought.

The next weekend, Richard and Maria came back to the faire. Maria spoke with John and told him, "I've always wanted to read your tarot cards."

John said, "Oh, sure. I'd love to have that done." As soon as he said it he knew, intuitively, that she was sick and that there would be a purpose behind her reading for him. "I don't have my cards with me now, but I will come back next weekend and do the reading for you then."

So, the next weekend, she and Richard showed up again and met with John after one of his shows. "Are you ready for your reading?" Maria asked him.

"Yes," John replied. He took her and Richard back behind one of booths, near the stage, where there was a picnic table. They all sat down, and she began to set out her cards on the table.

With a secret, altruistic motive, he asked, "Do you mind if I hold your hand during this?"

"Oh, no, it'll be great," she responded.

As John reached out and took her hand, he had a very interesting experience. "It was the second time I had ever heard the higher self conversation,"[85] he explains. As he was sitting there holding her hand, he heard his higher self say to her higher self, "Are you ready to let this go?" Then he heard her higher self answer him back, "Yes, I am."

"Then pass that to me and I will pass it on," he told her. As soon as he said it, he could feel this energy coming from her that went through him and right out the top of his head. Right then, he felt this wave of energy come down into his body, which made his hands shake.

This surprised Maria. "Your hand is shaking," she said with concern.

John had to think quickly about how he could respond without giving himself away. "Yeah, it's because of the sword fighting. All the sword fighting that I do makes my hands shake after the show."

Accepting his answer, she continued on with the reading, which was actually quite good, according to John. She was able to peg some things going on in John's life at the time. After the reading, he stood up. "I've got to get ready for the next show," he said. "It was a pleasure talking to you. See you later." Then he left.

"I did not think anything more about it. My faith [told me] that it was done," John remembers.

The following week, as John was walking off the stage after his show, he looked up and saw Richard standing at the top of the hill, behind the seating area. He was talking on his cell phone as John approached him.

"Talk to her," he insisted as he handed to phone to John.

"Hello?" John said sheepishly.

It was Maria's voice, of course. "What did you do to me?" she confronted him.

Not wanting to put words in her mouth, he coyly responded, "Well, what do you think I did to you?" He could have told her outright, but he knew that her faith had already healed her. She just needed a confirmation now.

"Well, I think you healed me," she exclaimed.

"Well, that's what I did," John admitted. "So, what did you have?"

"I had terminal spider cancer. My doctors had given me six weeks to live. I had tumors from the base of my skull, running all the way down my spine to my tailbone, intertwined with my spinal column," she explained.

When she went back to the doctor, she no longer had any cancer in her body. The doctors were amazed and couldn't imagine what had happened. They declared it a medical miracle.

What is amazing to me about this story is that John had gotten Maria's permission to do the healing, through her higher self, even though her conscious mind had not actively participated in the healing. This type of exchange certainly eliminates the explanation that her mind had created the healing through the "placebo effect."[86] Since that time, John has spoken to Richard every year to find out how Maria was doing and he would say that she was doing fine.

John contacted Maria in 2007 to ask her if she would write her story and allow him to share it on his website. "You can use my story if you want, but I'm not going to write it," she told him. "There's no need for me to go back there. That's a part of my life that I don't want to talk about. That is no longer who I am or what I am about." Five years later, Maria is living a healthy, normal life. "I think it is wonderful that she has walked away from her disease and lives in the present moment without a second thought of ever having had an a ailment," John says.

There are more stories like these, some unwritten, but each unique. John and I are so very grateful to each person who has shared his or her story, whether in this book or not. We have had some incredible, extraordinary experiences over the years, and have met some wonderful people. We hope that you have enjoyed our story and have taken something to heart from it.

John of Old has returned as John of New, and he is sharing his message of Love with the world. He wants everyone to know that each of us can have God in our lives without the dogma of any given religion. We have God within us, and the Divine can touch our lives every day. Each of us can have a personal relationship with God, with Jesus (and with all the Masters), with our angels and guides. Miracles are happening everyday and the miracles are within you!

Bibliography

Epilogue

By John C. Davis

I truly do not believe it matters who I or anyone else was two thousand years ago. It is in this present moment that we are conscious. That being said, I have been blessed in my life to have been given a path that is so clearly defined, and I thank God for it every day. The memories of the life of John the Beloved have given me a clear vision of our own spiritual natures and, I believe, of the true message of my friend and teacher, Jeshua Ben Joseph. Since we are spiritual beings, He is here, now, in this present moment with us.

Jeshua came to empower us, to show us our potential. He came to exemplify the Way, the Truth, and the Life that we all are capable of achieving. He is a template as I believe all of the enlightened Avatars (Buddha, Krishna, and Mohammed) have been. We all are working with one divine source and, through our various cultural structures, have had enlightened beings that showed us the way. Jeshua was one such being. He understood the importance of our potential enlightenment, for it is through the enlightenment of the masses that the "Kingdom of Heaven" can be brought here to earth.

The danger of being an Avatar is that, in doing great works, people will deify the messenger. I believe that Jeshua would never have wanted to be deified. It would be at cross-purposes to his teachings. Jeshua said, "Greater works than I have done you shall do," "It is your faith that healed you," and "the Kingdom of God is within you." These statements are of empowerment. In deifying Avatars, people relinquish their power of enlightenment to some outside force.

He also said He was "the son of God," and "You are the children of God." It is the conscious awareness of our divinity that leads us to enlightenment. By saying He was, "the son of God" Jeshua accepted His divinity.

By saying that we are the children of God, He is telling us that we are divine—as divine as He.

People often ask me, "Where do you go from here?" or "What do you do with this information?" I am creating a nonprofit organization, the sole purpose of which is to gather together people of all faiths to share the common teachings of the Avatars, celebrate our cultural differences and, thus combined, do larger humanitarian works. And, in partnership, the organization will create a council and decide together which humanitarian works they wish to conquer.

My hope in bringing my story to the forefront is that it will reach the ears of those who are seeking enlightenment and assist them on their path. I thank you for the time you have taken in reading the story. I thank my truest and closest friend, Sharon, for chronicling our adventures; and I thank God for it all.

Reincarnation

by Judy Goodman

As John continues to merge "past life memories" into his
present life, what are some of the "truths" he has learned?

T he theory of reincarnation has been around much longer than our recorded history relates. Is it possible that we have lived before? Is it possible that we will live again? Some of the greatest minds of all times have contemplated the meaning and authenticity of this perception, and, in fact, to this day many case studies bring credibility to this idea.

What can be gained by finding answers to these, and other questions? Just knowing more about reincarnation might help ease our fear of death; or, having a better understanding of past life experiences might explain some of the complications we face in our lives today. Reincarnation does not appear to be dependent on a particular belief system, but it does apply to the universal question having to do with life after death.

Today, there are well-documented case studies of souls bringing a former knowledge into their current lifetime. When knowledge from the past travels into the present, is there something that we can learn? Yes, such events are happening today as part of the evidence of reincarnation. We are aware of multiple case studies that support the belief of many who feel they have lived before. More and more people are pursuing the path of understanding; sometimes this path begins as a way of finding answers to dreams, visions, and feelings of being someone other than ourselves. Whatever it is that drives us, we are clearly on a journey of achieving a higher knowledge; we are expanding on a universal truth that we are all the same; we are finding that nothing ever really dies.

Your physical DNA is the blueprint of your life here; it is an accumulation of genetics from your physical parents and your generational ancestors. This DNA helps to explain why you look the way you do, and it sometimes helps in the evaluation of medical, mental and social development. My own theory is that we are currently close to finding a missing part of the DNA structure that is a "constant" no matter who you may have been in an earlier life. This "missing piece" is what will help prove reincarnation. Another way of saying this: if in a past life you were Thomas Edison and if today there are samples of Edison's DNA, then you will have the missing DNA link that will match—therefore proving that a soul continues its journey even if it changes its race, sex and nationality. Your physical DNA will change from one lifetime to another, but your spiritual DNA never changes. Your spiritual DNA represents the genetics of your "soul," and has been the same since your beginning. This blueprint of your soul will simply be the lesser, or unknown, part of who you are in any given lifetime.

When is Earth incarnation no longer necessary? This could come at any time since the soul, in most cases, has always had the choice of whether or not to come back. Stepping back and getting outside of organized thinking, we will no longer need to incarnate when we have achieved our "oneness" with the Creator of our understanding. Consider that we each have a contract to grow spiritually; that same contract will be experienced as a race, a town, a state, a country or as a part of the Earth. The living Earth has its own agenda of growth and changes. With today's technology, we are more aware of the shifts that are underway. Many of the changes have been contributed to by humanity, but some are just the evolvement of the blue planet we call home.

There have never been more "notable souls" working on our behalf than at this time. Family clusters are reuniting to achieve goals that affect a greater number of people. This is evidenced by the fact that many members of the "Revolutionary Period" are returning to work together again. One by one, they are finding each other and remembering a past life together. This is particularly true of the "Masters" and "Teachers" that have walked the Earth before. As the process of remembering occurs, these souls are bringing knowledge from the past in order to work toward a better future.

Even so, each person will have to go through the process of their current lifetime, which may have its own challenges and disappointments. We are the total of all of the lives we have lived, but our allegiance must be to the lifetime we currently enjoy. Some have speculated that the process of reincarnation resulted from some sort of "fall" from grace. Not so! We reincarnate because we have the choice and the free will to do so. It is not a punishment, not a test!

How many times have you met someone who feels a strong pull to a memorable personality of history? How many Cleopatras, kings, queens, former presidents and disciples have you met? I want to give you a little bit more information that might help you understand why we hear of more than one person truly believing that they are the reincarnation of....shall we say, Thomas Jefferson. I want to discuss "fragmented souls" for just a moment.

Since my own birth I have walked in two worlds; one foot has been in the physical world and one has been in the spiritual realm. In other words, I have always been able to see "spirit" and communicate directly. Because of my connection and understanding of "spirit," one of the topics I have taught is "fragmented souls."

A few years back I made a visit to beautiful Monticello, home of Thomas Jefferson. It is not uncommon to see spirits when I visit especially old and historical properties. I was surprised, however, when I entered the Cabinet Room and saw the spirit of Jefferson. He was sitting in a chair that held candles on both arms; this provided the light that enabled him to read and do his writing. When the spirit of Jefferson realized that I could see him, and communicate with him, he wanted to talk. To make a long story short, I knew that there was a doctor living in California that was the reincarnation of Jefferson. Yet, sitting in front of me was the spirit of Jefferson. This is a classic example of how a soul can, and will, fragment and be in more than one place at the same time.

When the work ("soul contract") of a soul is very significant, they often choose to fragment and utilize several physical bodies to begin the reincarnation journey. There can be many explanations as to why numerous people will have the same memories of a past lifetime. In some cases, they may be carrying the fragment of the soul; in other incidents, they might have been a friend or part of that particular lifetime. What I am trying to say is you should not be overly concerned when you hear of more than one person claiming to be the reincarnation of the same former person.

In my work, I have found many fragmented souls, each one having the opportunity to fulfill the commitment to get a message out—each one will be carrying part of the "spiritual DNA." As an example, let us say that a soul has fragmented and will be in five different bodies. As each of the five lives out their life, they may have memories of being in a particular place in time. As they grow and mature, they will begin developing their belief systems; they will enter into work and family situations that will affect future choices.

If they are in a situation that *will not* allow them to embrace reincarnation and allow the memory to surface—the strength of that fragment will leave the physical body and move to the remaining four. This process may continue until just one person is making a choice to step out and embrace the memory. They will choose to live their life in such a way that the work and message will continue. Occasionally the message will be so important that the fragment will continue to work through more than one. When the message is universal in scope, this will often occur. This is not meant to complicate or further confuse you, but to let you know that you may sometimes hear of more than one person having the same memory or goal in life. Whatever it is that brings us to this point, the most important thing is how we honor the work of our soul.

The journey continues for 'John of New' . . . .

End Notes

[1] An aura is the invisible energy field that surrounds all living things. The aura around a person's body is the part of their spirit that extends outside of the physical body and may be observed by a person who is clairvoyant. With practice, many people are able to discern auras.

[2] A Renaissance Festival, also known as a faire, is a show where patrons are entertained by actors and musicians portraying characters from the Renaissance era.

[3] In the book *Journey of Souls* by Michael Newton, Ph.D., the author explains that souls enter their bodies at different times, but most souls enter after the first three months.

[4] John was remembering the first time he had seen the resurrected Jesus after His death. John had been so overcome upon seeing his friend again that he had fallen face down in the sand at the feet of Jesus.

[5] A channel is someone who is able to access information from the spirit realm using psychic abilities, such as clairaudience, and will often "speak" for a spiritual being, such as a spirit guide, angel, or Ascended Master. There are conscious channels, who allow a spiritual being to speak through them while they are awake, and there are full-body trance channels, who are unconscious while they allow an entity to use their bodies to fully communicate. In that case, the channel's voice or accent might change. A psychic reader who gives a normal reading will access information from the other side, and may even deliver messages, but does not usually allow a spiritual being to come inside of his or her body, or aura, to speak the exact words being conveyed by the spiritual entity.

[6] Kundalini is the spiritual energy in the body that rises up through the base of the spine to the crown of the head and outward, creating a euphoric, tingling feeling, connecting you with greater universal energy. This experience also provides the basis for out-of-body experiences and past-life travel, among other things.

[7] An out-of-body experience happens when a person's consciousness or spirit leaves the body and travels away from it, all the while still connected by a thin, etheric cord. The person can then travel wherever he wants and is able to see with his spirit "eyes" the way he would with his physical eyes.

[8] The astral body is a subtle etheric, spiritual body made of energy that looks exactly like one's physical body. When one travels out of body, one travels in his or her astral body.

[9] The griffin is a mythological beast that has the head and forequarters of an eagle and the body and hindquarters of a lion. It has been called the guardian of spiritual wisdom.

[10] During hypnoregression, a person is regressed, or taken back to an earlier time (either

in this life, or a previous one), using hypnosis, which is a trancelike state. The person being regressed is able to remember past events that his or her conscious mind has either forgotten or has not had access to.

[11] John was to discover soon after this that Jesus, before He died, had given John the Apostle the responsibility of caring for His mother, Mary, for the rest of her life.

[12] Reiki (pronounced "ray-kee") is the process by which a trained practitioner aligns the body's energy field with that of the universal life force. The purpose is to clear energy blockages and smooth the energy flow.

[13] Soul families consist of spirit beings who were created at the same time and who often reincarnate together in the same lifetimes. Often, they have a common goal or purpose, as John and I do.

[14] In Dolores Cannon's book *They Walked with Jesus,* Anna, who in her past-life was Naomi, Jesus' niece, remembered that "his eyes are blue…I never thought that blue eyes were kind and loving, but his are." In another Dolores Cannon book called *Jesus and the Essenes,* Katie, who remembers being Saudi, Jesus' teacher from the Essene community of Qumran, said of Jesus' crucifixion that He "is very calm. He has secluded himself away from a lot of the pain…there is not *total* suffering." In the same book, Ms. Cannon quotes the *The Archko Volume,* by Drs. McIntoch and Twyman (1887), which gives a Roman's firsthand account of seeing Jesus. This written report, which was sent back to Rome, describes Jesus, whose eyes "are large and a soft blue."

[15] Edgar Cayce, a famous channel known as "the Sleeping Prophet," would answer questions concerning health and spirituality while in a deep trance state.

[16] There are those who believe that John the Divine was John the Apostle, though he would have been very old when he died. John said that he believed that the man who wrote Revelations was John the Beloved. He felt compelled to go to Patmos someday and visit the cave where John wrote Revelations.

[17] Nick had received a prayer from Spirit whose purpose was to help people make a stronger connection to God, Jesus, and our angels. It was intended to send a wave of peace and love throughout the world.

[18] The coincidence of this was that I had sent Janet a copy of Nick's April 4 Prayer at the same time Janet was actually reading *The Messengers.* She had been ordering art history books from a bargain books order form when she came across the title *The Messengers.* Her eyes kept going back to the title, so she ordered it not knowing anything about it. She was just about to share it with me when she received my e-mail about the April 4th Prayer!

[19] In 1991, I was prompted to join a group of people on a trip to Sedona, Arizona, led by a spiritual leader whom I had only spoken to twice. Although it was scary going with a bunch of people that I didn't know, it turned out to be the best decision I could have made at the time. It brought me together with people who had spiritual gifts like me, and for the first time I felt like my spiritual gifts were understood and accepted.

[20] In the book *The Messengers,* Nick and his friends keep getting the sign of 444, either on signs, license plates, or being woken up at 4:44 a.m. When Nick asked one of his readers for clarification, she told him that it was a sign from the angels that meant that "the power of God's love" was intervening in his life.

[21] Many people around the world have had the phenomena of repeatedly seeing the number sequence of 11:11, or four ones. It has also been called the Doorway into the One, where the duality of our existence will fall away and we will see that

everyone and everything is connected. On key days, the earth receives the 11:11 energy, which has to do with an increased influx of light energy being sent to the earth to help awaken people to their true spiritual natures. I later figured out that I had sent my first letter to Nick on a day that had numerically represented four ones or 11:11.

[22] Jacquelyne Ellis' website is www.sacreddialogues.net.

[23] Atira's website is www. angelscribe.com/atira.html.

[24] What a powerful message! I found this when re-editing the book and it has more meaning for me now than it did then. It's been almost eight years, and it's still relevant for me.

[25] Excerpts from "They Walked with Jesus" © 2001 by Dolores Cannon. Used with permission of the author.

[26] John once pointed out that Rehoboth Beach had been established as a place for Christian gatherings in the early days.

[27] It occurred to me much later, that this profound message from the Master, which happened on August 11, 1999, had taken place on a significant astrological and spiritual day associated with 11:11, known as the Antarion Doorway. On this day, which coincided with a solar eclipse at 11:11 am, GMT, a shift was to have occurred in the consciousness of mankind. The Antarion Doorway is part of a greater period of spiritual transition for the earth known as the Antarion Conversion. The Antarion Conversion is believed to have started on January 11, 1992, when the earth received a huge influx of awakening energy and a significant change took place in the earth's spiritual vibration, and will culminate on December 31, 2011, when eleven gateways of spiritual consciousness will have been opened. (For more information, go to: http://www.v-j-enterprises.com/antarion.html.) Since that day, I have referred to the manifestation of 11:11's as the Christ Gateway, or an influx of Christed Energy moving into our collective consciousness.

[28] When John was very young, he contracted a very high fever and nearly died. He had no memory of this until he was later reminded of it by his older brother.

[29] Judy Goodman explains the concept of reincarnation and soul fracturing in an essay, on page 309.

[30] John's brother told him that while he was lying on the bed, John had said things like "I'm on the ceiling. I'm taller than you now. I'm up here," which seems to imply an out-of-body experience.

[31] This is not a misprint of the word "attunement." Though I realize that the reader will not find this word in a standard dictionary, this is the word that I received. To understand what the Master might have meant by using this term, I looked up the prefix, root, and suffix of "en-tune-ment." The meaning of the prefix "en-" means "in; into; used to intensify verbs." The word "tune" means "to adjust to a proper pitch or frequency; bring or come into harmony." The suffix "-ment" means "the act, fact, or result of doing (the root word)." So, to the best of my knowledge, the meaning of entunement, is "taking into one's self a higher spiritual frequency which brings one into harmony with God."

[32] Although Carol Berman did not direct John to go to this particular lifetime as John the Apostle versus other past lives, John has been told that people go where they need to go when being regressed.

[33] Some years later John would find a passage in a book about Edgar Cayce in which he had channeled information about the Sons of Belial and the Law of One.

[34] I got the distinct impression that the Master was referring to all the reincarnated

apostles who each hold a vibration, a "key" or a certain frequency that would connect with all the other "keys" to help hold or balance some type of spiritual energy connected to the Master Himself. I was given the image of a circle with evenly spaced points or markers, like the hour marks around a clock, which represented each of the apostles standing in a circle, each holding a piece of the puzzle that concerned ushering in Christ's Second Coming.

[35] Even though I knew how to spell Michael's last name (with two "n's"), and despite the fact that his guides had warned me not to misspell it, I accidently typed his last name with one "n" on the acknowledgments page in the original draft of the manuscript for this book. His guides had been right!

[36] Ironically, healers and readers seek the help of other healers and readers because often it is much easier to heal or read for others than to do those things for oneself.

[37] James Twyman's website is www.emissaryoflight.com.

[38] The Shekinah is held by many to represent the feminine attributes of the presence of God, *shekhinah* being a feminine word in Hebrew.

[39] Julia Hanson's and Cindy Shelton's joint website is www.hanson-shelton.com. Cindy Shelton's individual website: www.cynthialeeshelton.com.

[40] Eventually, I would have the privilege of meeting Judy in Houston in January of 2001 along with another person who had memories of being the Apostle Matthew. I would end up doing a reading for him that spring,

[41] Sacred Geometry—Ancient civilizations used sacred geometry to express spirituality through the use of certain mathematical patterns which allow the individual to achieve greater harmony and attunement to higher principles. Sacred Geometry allows the individual to understand nature and the universe through archetypal, geometric patterns. It is a way of touching the divine through understanding the basic building blocks of life and creation. Since God is the originator of the number patterns and sequences that we see in our physical world, studying these underlying principles may lead to basic truths and awareness of self within the greater context of all creation. Numbers are more than just symbols used to count or measure things, they are the building blocks—the very essence—of all that exists.

The following explanation is from website: www.spiraloflight.com/ ls_sacred.html

Printed by permission of LightSOURCE Arts, www.sacred-geometry.com

Sacred Geometry is the blueprint of Creation and the genesis of all form. It is an ancient science that explores and explains the energy patterns that create and unify all things and reveals the precise way that the energy of Creation organizes itself. On every scale, every natural pattern of growth or movement conforms inevitably to one or more geometric shapes.

As you enter the world of Sacred Geometry you begin to see as never before the wonderfully patterned beauty of Creation. The molecules of our DNA, the cornea of our eye, snowflakes, pine cones, flower petals, diamond crystals, the branching of trees, a nautilus shell, the star we spin around, the galaxy we spiral within, the air we breathe, and all life forms as we know them emerge out of timeless geometric codes. Viewing and contemplating these codes allow us to gaze directly at the lines on the face of deep wisdom and offers up a glimpse into the inner workings of the Universal Mind and the Universe itself.

The Golden Mean was used in the design of sacred buildings in ancient architecture to produce spiritual energy that facilitated connectivity with spiritual realms through prayer. Our reality is very structured, and indeed Life is even more structured. This is reflected though Nature in the form of geometry. Geometry is the very basis of our reality, and hence we live in a coherent world governed by unseen laws. These are always manifested in our world. The Golden Mean governs the proportion of our world and it can be found even in the most seemingly proportion-less (active) living forms.

Clear examples of Sacred Geometry (and Golden Mean geometry) in Nature and matter: All types of crystals, natural and cultured; the hexagonal geometry of snowflakes; creatures exhibiting logarithmic spiral patterns: e.g. snails and various shell fish; birds and flying insects, exhibiting clear Golden Mean proportions in bodies and wings; the way in which lightning forms branches; the way in which rivers branch; the geometric molecular and atomic patterns that all solid metals exhibit; and the way in which a tree spans out so that all its branches receive sunlight. Another, perhaps less obvious but most significant example of this special ratio can be found in Deoxyribonucleic Acid (DNA)—the foundation and guiding mechanism of all living organisms.

[42] A Star of David looks like this: ✡ The Star of David is an ancient symbol created by two triangles superimposed over one another, which forms a six-sided star.

[43] The Hall of Records, according to the Edgar Cayce foundation's website is, a place which ". . . contains 'a record of Atlantis from the beginnings of those periods when the spirit took form or began the encasements in that land . . .' (378-16) They extend through the first destructions of that ancient civilization, the exodus of Atlanteans to other lands, and the final destruction of Atlantis. [It] contains a description of the building of the Great Pyramid, as well as a prophecy of "who, what, where, would come [to make] the opening of the records . . ." (378-16)

[44] John the Apostle, according to Paul Solomon, "will be called John. The last name is not by birth, Peniel, but that name adopted for its meaning, 'where I met him face to face." Excerpt from *The Prophetic Revelations of Paul Solomon*, by W. Alexander Wheeler, Weiser, 1994, p. 163.

[45] Atlantis refers to a prehistoric civilization, according to Edgar Cayce, that lived on earth over fifty thousand years ago, on a continent somewhere in the Atlantic Ocean. Legend has it that the whole continent of Atlantis fell into the ocean from a huge explosion caused by the misuse of a powerful energy source.

[46] You can locate a map of the Giza Plateau via the websites listed in the References section of this book.

[47] John now believes that this policeman's presence actually grounded him and kept him consciously aware of this dimension for as long as possible.

[48] In Egypt, tourism is the number one business. That is why the government is so vigilant in making sure that tourist sites, such as the Giza Plateau, are heavily guarded by police. It is understandable that they would want to protect their most precious resources and to ensure that the tourists are safe.

[49] When I went out of body during my Felix regression, it took me about twenty minutes to recover enough to drive. I could only imagine what John went through that it would take him the equivalent of two nights worth of sleep to recover!

[50] Michael is indicating the same spot I had pointed to on the Map of the Giza Plateau he presented during my reading with him in Florida in February 2000, when he had asked me to point to where the opening of the tunnels was located.

[51] Joyce went on to describe in detail the hidden room under the Giza Plateau, what

John and Michael will eventually find in there, and who will be able to give them access to it. I am reserving this information because of future work to be done in Egypt, which may yet appear in another book.

52 Judy Goodman's website is www.judygoodman.com.

53 Julia Ingram's website is www.juliaingram.com.

54 Atira is able to discern people who have walked with Jesus by a distinct light in their aura. She has been able to identify a few apostles this way, including John, who also has this same light around him.

55 Michael's inserted quotations from the Master have been removed because of their prior mention in this book.

56 Michael always records his readings and then transcribes them, which has been very helpful in the writing of this book. To see the reading he quotes in this letter, please refer to Chapter 13, page 179-200.

57 Someone in Nick's office transcribed the reading and then sent it to me.

58 In Matthew 19:24 Jesus is quoted as saying, "I tell you the truth, it is hard for a rich man to enter the kingdom of heaven. Again I tell you, it is easier for a camel to go through the eye of a needle than for a rich man to enter the kingdom of God."

59 Rehabbing is a term used for buying dilapidated real estate, fixing it up and reselling it for a profit.

60 The Shroud of Turin is a linen cloth, centuries old, that bears the image of a crucified man that millions believe is Jesus Christ. Many thousands of hours of detailed, scientific study have been done on the Shroud, but there is still controversy as to whether it is real or a hoax. For detailed analysis of the Shroud of Turin, visit this website: www.sindone.org/en/welcome.htm. For the latest news about the Shroud, visit online at www.shroud.com.

61 For a picture of Jesus' "face" in the mist, and Mike with the "angels" go to www.johnofnew.com/photos.htm.

62 I interpret "one soul" to be an expression that means from the same soul group, not that John and the Master share one soul between them.

63 According to *The Catholic Encyclopedia*, (Herbermann), the Lamb represents Jesus Christ, the Dove represents the Holy Spirit and Jesus was holding a Rod when he raised Lazarus from the dead. In the book *Roma Sotterranea: Or, An Account of the Roman Catacombs*, (De Rossi & Northcote), the Divine Rod symbolizes the Power of Christ. Also, in the book *An Introduction to Early Christian Symbolism: A Series of Compositions from Fresco-Paintings, Glasses, and Sculptured Sarchophagi* by (W. Palmer), Jesus is symbolized in art using "the rod of power" to multiply loaves of bread, and change water into wine, and to raise Lazarus from the dead. He is also depicted giving the rod to Peter. In *Recognition of Christian Work* (McConnell, Moody and Fitt), the rod in the Old Testament is a symbol of service.

64 A name was given of somebody that John and I believe may have been Judas in that lifetime.

65 To visit John's on-line gallery, go to: http://johndavis.boundlessgallery.com.

66 John's website is www.johnofnew.com.

67 The Jaffa Gate is also known as David's Gate, which is located on the west side of Jerusalem. It is one of the original eight gates in Jerusalem's Old City walls. It was named because of Jaffa Road—now a modern highway—which leads to the ancient port town of Jaffa on the Mediterranean Sea.

68 In the 4th century, the Roman emperor Constantine built the Church of the Holy Sepulcher which is thought to be the burial place of Jesus. Empress Helena, mother

of Constantine, is credited for discovering the tomb of Jesus and the cross, on this site, in 325 AD. There is a pile of rock inside the church that is believed to be the visible remains of the base of the cross. In the 1970's, while restoration work and excavations were going on inside the Church of the Holy Sepulcher, they discovered that the place they believed to be Golgotha had originally been the site of a white limestone quarry. This quarry could have looked like a skull while being viewed from a distance, from the city. In the 1980's they found a ring, almost 12 cm in diameter, that had been struck into the stone, which they presume could have held a wooden cross more than 2 meters in length. Some historians accept the church as the location of the tomb of Jesus and the little rock inside the church as the location of Golgotha (or Calvary).

[69] The Wailing Wall, or the Western Wall, is the most holy place to pray in Judaism. The original King Solomon Temple was built on this site in the 10th century BC, but was destroyed in 586 BC by the Babylonians. A second temple was built on the ruins of the first, in 516 BC, but was later destroyed in 70 CE by the Romans. A third temple was never built after the last destruction. The wall is all that remains of the second temple.

[70] Within ten years of Mohammad's death, in 632 AD, Islam had spread throughout the Arabian Peninsula and had begun to spread to other parts of the world.

[71] The Muslims believe that the rock in the center of the dome is where Mohammed ascended to Heaven in 621 AD. According to Islamic tradition, he was accompanied by the Angel Gabriel, met many of the prophets from the Bible, such as Abraham and Moses, and was given the Islamic prayers and the teachings of the Qu'uran. It is considered the second most holy Muslim building. During the Crusades, the dome was conquered by the Knights Templar and was used as a royal palace by the Kings of Jerusalem.

[72] Via Dolorosa means "Way of Suffering" in Latin and is the name given to the path that Jesus walked on his way to his crucifixion. There are fourteen so-called Stations of the Cross, and the last five are inside the Church of the Holy Sepulcher.

[73] The Last Supper refers to the last supper that Jesus ate with his twelve apostles before His death.

[74] According the Garden Tomb Association in London, Skull Hill is Golgotha, where Jesus was crucified. A British general named Gordon visited the hill and garden in 1894 and had a strange, overwhelming feeling about the place. He had a dream that the Garden Tomb was where Jesus was buried and that the nearby hill, that resembles a skull in the right light, is where Jesus was crucified. Christians have believed for years that the Church of the Holy Sepulcher is the site for both Jesus' death and burial. Gordon was so convinced that he had found the actual place, that he raised money and founded the Garden Tomb Association in London, which bought the land and cares for it. They hold Sunday Church services here and visitors can explore the tomb, which many believe belonged to Joseph of Arimathea.

[75] Golgotha is an Aramaic word which means "skull." The English call it Calvary. Golgotha was the site where Jesus Christ was crucified. According to biblical scholars, the Romans took Jesus to a hill outside of Jerusalem to execute him. The hill was near an old quarry, and supposedly, if you looked at the hill from across the quarry you would see in the hillside what appeared to be the shape of a skull. Today, most biblical scholars agree that the exact location of Golgotha is unknown.

[76] Note my reading for John in Chapter 10, page 121-138.

[77] Note John's past life regression with Carol Berman, Chapter 11, page 139-154.

⁷⁸ The Garden of Gethsemane, which means "oil press," is located at the base of the Mount of Olives. This is where Jesus is said to have gone with some of his apostles after the Last Supper, to pray before his impending arrest. The garden today is comprised of a small stand of very old, twisted olive trees.

⁷⁹ The road leading to Jericho is a twisting, winding road, descending one thousand feet below sea level, with plenty of ravines and rocky outcrops where robbers can hide, waiting to ambush unsuspecting travelers. In Jesus' time it was known as the "Bloody Pass." In fact, Jesus used this road as the setting for his parable about the Good Samaritan, found in Luke 10:25-37. Most believe that Jesus used this to teach us that we should have compassion for all people, even those who are different from us. Others say that it also illustrates the importance of upholding the spirit of the Law as much as the letter of the Law.

⁸⁰ They estimate that the "Jesus Boat" was built in 40 BC and was used up until the first century AD. The boat would have been in use during Jesus' ministry. In 67 AD, there was a sea battle between Jewish rebels from Magdala, and the Roman Legions, who controlled the area. The Jewish rebels were defeated during this time, leaving many boat wrecks along the shoreline. Archeologists believe that the boat might have been sunk during this time.

⁸¹ According to a treatise that Pope Benedict XIV wrote in the mid-eighteenth century called The Feast of the Assumption, "John amply fulfilled Christ's order; in every way he forever cared for Mary with a sense of duty; he had her live with him while he remained in Palestine, and he took her with him when he departed for Ephesus, where the Blessed Mother at length proceeded from this life into heaven."

⁸² A psychic told Michael after the tour that John would probably return to Patmos someday, leading a small group of people himself.

⁸³ Since that time, she has added two new imprints to her publishing house: Against the Wind Books (books with passion and anti-establishment themes) and Shining Brightly Books (books leading the way in psychological, scientific and spiritual awareness).

⁸⁴ Each person has given us permission to use their real name with the exception of the "Mime," who preferred anonymity.

⁸⁵ Earlier, John had met an elderly woman, a friend of Michael's, who wanted to go with Michael and John to Egypt. She spoke fervently of how she was exercising to increase her strength and how she wasn't going to give up on the idea. But during a group conversation in her living room, her higher self told John's higher self that her body didn't have the strength to make the trip. John's higher self offered to carry her "energy" with him to Egypt, which her higher self accepted. As a confirmation that the exchange had been real, as Michael and John were leaving, she suddenly announced to them that she would not be going to Egypt with them after all.

⁸⁶ Placebo Effect—a sense of benefit felt by a patient that arises solely from the knowledge that treatment has been given.

References

Antarion Doorway: http://www.v-j-enterprises.com/antarion.html.

Appel, Rüdiger, Sacred Geometry: http://www.spiraloflight.com/ls_sacred.html.

Atira, intuitive: www. angelscribe.com/atira.html.

Ayto, John. *Brewer's Dictionary of Phrase and Fable, 16th Edition*. Revised by Adrian Room. 2000. New York: HarperCollins.

Bayuk, Matt, singer/songwriter: www.playeronband.com.

Bunick, Nick. *In God's Truth*. 1998. Charlottesville, VA: Hampton Roads Publishing Co.

_____, *Transitions of the Soul: True Stories from Everyday People*. 2001. Charlottesville, VA: Hampton Roads Publishing Co.

Cannon, Dolores. *Jesus and the Essenes*. 2000. Huntsville, AR: Ozark Mountain Publishing Co.

_____. *They Walked with Jesus: Past Life Experiences with Christ*. 2001. Huntsville, AR: Ozark Mountain Publishing Co.

Davis, John C.: www.johnofnew.com; see also www.johndavis.boundlessgallery.com.

Edgar Cayce Library, Virginia Beach, VA: www.caycelibrary.com; see also www.edgarcayce.org.

Ellis, Jacquelyne, intuitive: www.sacreddialogues.net.

The Epic of Gilgamesh. ed., N. K. Sandars. 1977. New York: Penguin Books.

Giza Plateau: Maps of the Giza Plateau can be found at these and other sites:

> www.cheops-pyramide.ch/image/map-Karte/giza-plateau.gif
> www.cheops-pyramide.ch/khufu-pyramid/great-pyramid/giza-plateau-
> alignments.GIF
> www.pbs.org/wgbh/nova/pyramid/resources/images/mapgiza.gif
> www.cairotourist.com/Map27.gif
> www.wayfaring.info/2006/10/24/pyramids-of-egypt-travel-wonder-at-giza/
> www.odeion.org/atlantis/giza-map2.jpg
> www.ask-aladdin.com/images/Giza_Plateau.gif
> www.aiwaz.net/uploads/gallery/432.gif
> www.andrewcollins.com/pics/Perring 1837 with Cygnus resized.jpg
> www.mercuryrapids.co.uk/giza1.jpg
> ebtx.com/theory/sahara2.gif
> www.opencheops.org/images/layoutofgizaWEB.jpg
> www.archaeology.org/0009/abstracts/thumbnails/osiris.gif

http://pymd.com/giza-map-names-prisse.jpg

Goodman, Judy, intuitive: www.judygoodman.com.

Hanson, Julia, and Cindy Shelton: www.hanson-shelton.com.

Hartmann, Kelly. *Enlightened through Darkness*. 2001. Aurora, CO: Shining Light Press.

Herbermann, Charles G. *The Catholic Encyclopedia, Volume 10*. 1913. NY: Encyclopedia Press, Inc.

Indiana Jones and the Last Crusade. George Lukas and Phillip Kaufman. Dir.,Steven Spielberg. 1989.

Ingram, Julia. *The Lost Sisterhood*. 2004. Ft. Collins, CO: Dream Speaker Creations.

_____, see also: www.juliaingram.com.

_____ and G.W. Hardin. *The Messengers: A True Story of Angelic Presence and the Return to the Age of Miracles*. 1997. NY: Pocket Star Books, A Division of Simon and Schuster, Inc.

McConnell, Alexander, William Revell Moody, and Arthur Percy Fritt, eds. *Record of Christian Work*. 1881. Chicago and NY: Fleming Revell Company.

Newton, Michael. *Journey of Souls*: *Case Studies of Life between Lives*. 1994. St. Paul, MN: Llewellyn.

Northcote, Rev. J. Spencer, and William R. Brownlow. *Roma Sotterranea: Or, an Account of the Roman Catacombs*. 1879. London: Longmans, Green and Co.

Palmer, W. Ed. J. Spencer Northcote. *An Introduction to Early Christian Symbolism: A Series of Compositions from Fresco-Paintings, Glasses, and Sculptured Sarcophagi*. Reprinted 2007. Whitefish, MT: Kessinger Publishing, LLC.

Prince, Sharon, author, intuitive: www.sharonprince.net.

Redfield, James. *The Celestine Prophecy: An Adventure*. 1995. NY: Warner Books, Inc.

Shroud of Turin: www.sindone.org/en/welcome.htm; see also www.shroud.com.

Stearn, Jess. *Edgar Cayce on the Millennium*. 1998. NY: Warner Books, Inc.

Twyman, James. *The Secret of the Beloved Disciple*. 2000. Scotland: Findhorn Press.

_____, see also www.emissaryoflight.com.

Virtue, Doreen. *Divine Guidance: How to Have a Dialogue with God and Your Guardian Angels*. 1999. Carlsbad, CA: Hay House, Inc.

Walsh, Neal Donald. *Conversations with God, Part 1*. 1995 (First Hardcover Edition, 1996). NY: G.P. Putnam's Sons.

Warren, Vicki. *Coffee, Doughnuts and God*.1995. Houston, TX: Inspired Choices Press. The book is available through www.vickiwarren.com.

Weiss, Brian, Hypnoregressionist: www.brianweiss.com.

Wheeler, W. Alexander. *The Prophetic Revelations of Paul Solomon: Earthward Toward a Heavenly Light*. 1994. York Beach, Maine: Samuel Weiser, Inc.

Who's Who in the Bible, ed. Paul D. Gardner. 1995. Grand Rapids, MI: Zondervan.

About Sharon Prince

Sharon Prince has been doing professional spiritual intuitive readings since 1992. She was born with a gift of awareness, which, through the years she has learned to develop. By the time Sharon reached college, her gift had become more apparent. In her early twenties, she started getting information about future events through insights and visions. But it wasn't until her early thirties that she realized that she was what people call a "reader." People started asking her for readings and recommended her to their friends.

Her most significant work has been with her good friend, John Davis, whom she met in the summer of 1997. She gave a reading to John in which she was told that John had "walked with Jesus." A follow up reading two weeks later confirmed this, when Sharon suddenly started channeling the powerful love energy of Master Jesus, in which John Davis was told he had been *John the Beloved Apostle*. She has read for him many times over the years, and they both have shared some incredible spiritual experiences together.

Formerly an elementary education teacher, Sharon has a B.A. in Psychology and a M.Ed. in Science Education.

www.SharonPrince.net

About John C. Davis

For over twenty years, John C. Davis has been entertaining and delighting audiences all over the country, and more recently the world, with his humor and swordsmanship in a professional comedy show called "Hack and Slash." Since the attacks of 9/11, John has spent several months every year traveling abroad, entertaining the troops. To date he has performed in fifteen countries at over eighty military bases.

John's spiritual awakening began fourteen years ago with some extraordinary experiences. A past life regression awakened him to his spiritual purpose and he is now devoted to bringing forth messages of love and healing from Master Jesus. Not only is John a captivating and motivational speaker, people have remarked that they feel the healing and love energy of the Master coming through John.

Experiencing John's stories and lessons he's learned in his own words and expressions is the best way to fully understand the message he brings.

God is within each of us. We can all
experience the connection everyday.

www.JohnofNew.com

About Judy Goodman

Internationally recognized speaker and teacher, Judy Goodman, may be without peer in her ability to access and teach knowledge from *the other side*. Judy is also highly acclaimed for her work in the corporate field and easily translates her skills into workable topics and language for each environment. She has been featured on radio and television! Her work is the subject of an award-winning book and she was recently featured on the Sci-Fi channel's *In Search Of.*

In my business career, I have had the benefit of hearing some truly charismatic speakers, such as Zig Ziglar, Brian Tracy, Tony Robbins, etc. And then, I heard Judy Goodman speak. Not only did she speak without a single note for three days' classes and seminars, she never lost the attention of the audience. We were all captivated by her message and her intuitive ability to zero in on each of our 'needy spots.' I rank Judy among the very finest seminar leaders and speakers in the country today, and her message is always enlightening and on target!

—**S. Burden**, *Business Executive, Atlanta, GA*

JudyKGoodman@aol.com

www.judygoodman.com
www.AskJudyGoodman.com

www.JohnofNew.com

www.SharonPrince.net